C000026618

1 MONTH OF FREE READING

at

www.ForgottenBooks.com

By purchasing this book you are eligible for one month membership to ForgottenBooks.com, giving you unlimited access to our entire collection of over 1,000,000 titles via our web site and mobile apps.

To claim your free month visit:

www.forgottenbooks.com/free186930

ISBN 978-0-266-19003-5
PIBN 10186930

This book is a reproduction of an important historical work. Forgotten Books uses
state-of-the-art technology to digitally reconstruct the work, preserving the original format
whilst repairing imperfections present in the aged copy. In rare cases, an imperfection in
the original, such as a blemish or missing page, may be replicated in our edition. We do,
however, repair the vast majority of imperfections successfully; any imperfections that
remain are intentionally left to preserve the state of such historical works.

UNIVERSITY OF CALIFORNIA PUBLICATIONS

IN

MODERN PHILOLOGY

VOLUME 5

CHARLES M. GAYLEY
H. K. SCHILLING
RUDOLPH SCHEVILL

EDITORS

BERKELEY
UNIVERSITY OF CALIFORNIA
1917

EDMUND SPENSER

A Critical Study

BY

HERBERT ELLSWORTH CORY

UNIVERSITY OF CALIFORNIA PRESS

BERKELEY

1917

TO MY FATHER AND MOTHER

364394

PREFACE

In such days as these, literary criticism seems trivially remote. But I have been compelled to be loyal to this task by my belief that the two unequivocally reconstructive forces in the world today are the labor movement and those sciences of human society which are just beginning to organize after a fashion similar to that achieved by the once bickering sciences of biology which were at last reconciled and made to move in concert by Darwin. Literature at present has but a tenuous relation with either reconstructive force. But to make an effort, however groping, to merge it organically in both is to obey a categorical imperative.

If literary criticism is to exonerate itself from parasitism, from triviality and pedantry in the community of new sciences of man like psychology and ethnology, it must assume a task which is epical in its requirements. First of all it must examine its philosophical implications, particularly those limitations and emancipations revealed by an examination of the problem of consciousness, the problem of knowledge, and logic. And it must make its results as far as possible the coherent fruition of the best that has been thought and said on the topic under consideration by all the critics of previous ages. Today, although we all recognize the perils of impressionism in literature and long for some sort of restoration of judicial balance, there are nowhere apparent any *a priori* esthetic canons or even "necessities" of thought as distinct from the general necessities of the pure reason and the practical reason long ago established by Kant. But these provide us with nothing like those "eternal principles" of taste in which the critics of the renaissance and the eighteenth century believed unless we choose to pervert Kant with an admixture of dogma as do some of his professed followers in the realm of metaphysics. As literary men, in an age when all kinds of traditions are on trial, we can avoid irresponsible impressionism only by what has been termed "collective criticism." In consequence I have felt obliged to make my book empirical in the sense that it is an attempt to come to certain conclusions about Spenser only on the basis of a vast number of experiences of other readers of Spenser in every decade from 1579 to 1917. These conclusions of mine may at first sight appear to be iconoclastic; but I think that careful consideration will show them to have grown with a logical and almost biological continuity from many earlier interpretations of Spenser.

Secondly, literary criticism, to become a vital member of the new community, must examine constantly its scientific fellows, general biological evolution, paleontology, ethnology, heredity, general psychology, comparative psychology, psychopathology, economics, history, the empirical study of ethical values, and the empirical study of esthetic values in the other arts, for hints of method, for facts, and for relevant interpretations. Most so-called scientific study of literature today professes to renounce interpretation. In so doing it only proves its ignorance of the most elementary principles of scientific methodology. It endeavors to limit itself to a logically and psychologically meaningless career of pure observation. By contrast, my method may seem like a mad endeavor to emulate the adolescent aspiration of Francis Bacon. But one does not need to become a supernatural encyclopedist to learn to make some modest and intelligent use of the sciences listed above.

Finally, an old master cannot be studied to any purpose in the twentieth century in utter isolation from twentieth century nationalism, imperialism, feminism, and that socialistic-syndicalistic controversy which is to be the twentieth century version of the old struggle between those who emphasize the social contract and those who emphasize the rights of the individual and of minorities. That time has passed which has allowed the literary men of the academy or of Grub Street to emulate Marie Antoinette and her courtiers in their game of pseudo-pastoralism. Already the academic student of literatures ancient and modern is the object of the gentle contempt of his more robust colleagues. And to answer them with the complaint that twentieth century tastes are "utilitarian" and ephemeral is to answer with an *argumentatum ad homines* which is not only a logical impropriety but a libellous misinterpretation of some profoundly significant facts. Meanwhile, outside the university, arises a new society which will some day ask the professor of literature what he has been doing during his long and comfortable seclusion. The labor theory of values may or may not be as illuminating as the marginal utility theory in the field of general economics but it will be the basis of certain questions asked the professor of literature with perfect justice by voices not so crude as some belletristic triflers suppose.

CONTENTS

Out upon him, with his vaunting preface, he speaks against my old friend, Edmund Spenser.

—Archbishop USHER, according to Aubrey.

THE SHEPHEARDS CALENDER

Newer historical perspective has taught us that we have sentimentalized too much about the renaissance, that it was infinitely more conservative and uncreative than the period which followed (the period of Descartes and Hobbes and Locke). But if we consider the renaissance from the restricted point of view of mere artistic achievement, there still remains much truth in Carducci's superb prose elegy on Italy, mother of the most impressive movements of that day.

A spectacle which others may call shameful but which to me seems to command sacred pity in full measure, the spectacle of a people of philosophers, of poets, of artists, who, in the midst of the foreign soldiers rushing in from every side, continue sadly and surely their work of civilization. Under the artilleries of all the nations crash down the very walls which saw so many flights of barbarians: the flame quivers around the monuments of antiquity, and the paternal houses are given up to pillage; the solitude of the fields laid waste is full of corpses; and yet the canvasses and the walls never were radiant with more awe-inspiring imaginings and forms more pure, never did more joyous forests of columns arise to shelter hours of leisure and diversions and meditations which were now failing; and the song of the poets dominates the sad blast of the foreign trumpets, and the printing-presses of Venice, of Florence, of Rome creak in the work of illuminating the world. It is not cowardice, for where there was the stock of the common people there was still resistance and glorious fighting. Nor is it careless preoccupation. Oh how much sadness in the sweet face of Raphael, what a wrathful frown in that of Buonarroti, and how much pain in the lineaments of Machiavelli and of Guicciardini! Ariosto smiles, but how sadly! Even Berni grows angry. Why insult those great intellects of the sixteenth century? Do we not all see the mysterious sorrow, the fatal anxiety which assaults them from every side? Ever great is sacrifice; but if it be a nation that sacrifices herself it is a divine thing; and Italy sacrificed herself to the future of the other peoples. Dear and holy native land! She recreated the intellectual world of the ancients, she gave the form of art to the tumultuous and savage world of the Middle Ages, she opened to men's minds a superior world of freedom and of reason; and of all she made a gift to Europe: then, wrapt in her mantle, she endured the blows of Europe with the dignity of Iphigeneia. So ended Italy.[1]

---

[1] From a translation made by Professor J. A. Child and the present writer for a volume of selections from Carducci and De Sanctis.

It was not only the torrents of ruthless invaders, however, that distracted Italy; it was also the blinding splendor of her new emotion.   When we think of Ariosto's poetry, a beautiful, mocking *Fata Morgana* of chivalry, and when we think of Tasso's madness, we must feel that it was well for England that the renaissance came to her slowly through her tough old humanists, rather than triumphant through her poets.   It was well, too, that, even in the early years of Elizabeth's reign, there were stubborn souls like Roger Ascham who represented the sturdy English capacity for being shocked.   Thus it was, at a momentous and critical period, that England was saved from the dangers that beset all great nations and intellects which are forced to cherish art for art's sake.   Roger Ascham's belief in the age of chivalry was no greater than Ariosto's.   But he did believe in the age of archery.   England's yeoman faiths made her so sluggish in her acceptance of modernity that she was not made mad by the heady wine of the renaissance.   Thus it was that when her dramatists read the brilliant non-moral *novelle* of Italy they were appalled, and introduced into these stories the moral Nemesis that elevated them into plays often crude but generally throbbing with tragic seriousness.   Thus it happened that, because the renaissance came to Spenser under the frown of those tough old humanists and because Spenser (like most "creeping Saxons") developed late, he remained, as Lowell calls him, the Don Quixote of poets and wrought heroically to make of England a Utopia.

The meager records of Spenser's boyhood give scant promise of the graceful pastoral achievement of the young poet who, in the April of his life, rather abruptly, from our point of view, began to pipe smooth ditties on the delightful miseries of calf-love.   Some fluent translations of Du Bellay and of Marot's paraphrases from Petrarch, sold for a pittance perhaps by a poor but clever schoolboy to an enterprising and eccentric Dutch refugee who assumed their authorship,[2] then a long silence,

---

[2] There seems to be no necessity for doubting that these translations are Spenser's. Dr. Emil Koeppel (*Englische Studien*, XV, 53 sq., and XXVII,

apparently, then suddenly an elaborate pastoral in which the author, though he assumes from his rough predecessor, Skelton, the homely and humble name of Colin Clout and speaks modestly at times of his oaten stops, is evidently aflame with a realization of genius that is being heartily encouraged by distinguished friends[3]—these are the only materials found in the search for the young poet's magic in its early process of distillation. If we may take literally the poet's own allusion to the year of his birth,[4] he was twenty-seven when, in 1579, he ventured to publish this first ambitious poem, a poem on which, we may safely conjecture, he had been at work since 1573, while he was at college. The unwary reader of today who, with some first-hand

100 sq.), has denied them to the poet with some plausible argument. But see Professor J. B. Fletcher, *Modern Language Notes*, October, 1898; Professor R. E. Neil Dodge, *Cambridge Edition of Spenser* (Boston and New York, 1908), Appendix I, and Mr. Lois Sigmund Friedland, "Spenser's Earliest Translations," *Journal of English and Germanic Philology*, XII, 434 sq., for a tempered examination and a refutation of Dr. Koeppel's conclusions. See also Professor Jefferson B. Fletcher, "Spenser's Earliest Translations," *Journal of English and Germanic Philology*, XIII (1914), 305 sq., for the most recent utterances in support of Mr. Friedland.

[3] Two years after the appearance of *The Shepheards Calender*, Peele introduced the lovelorn Colin Clout as a character into his play, *The Arraignment of Paris*. Gabriel Harvey's letters, of which more later, are full of praise. William Webbe (*Discourse of English Poetrie*, 1586), though depreciating English poetry in general, judged Spenser not inferior to Theocritus and Virgil.

"But nowe yet at the last hath England hatched uppe one Poet of this sorte, in my conscience comparable with the best in any respect; even Master *Spenser*." So Puttenham, or the author of *The Art of English Poesie* (1589), who mentions "that other Gentleman who wrate the late Shepheardes Callender" among the English poets to be commended. So also Francis Meres, *Palladis Tamia*, 1598, who ranked Spenser with Theocritus, Virgil, Mantuan, and Sannazaro but also, with his characteristically Elizabethan worship of all English poets, with a motley company of his countrymen. Sir Philip Sidney's famous praise in the *Apology for Poesie* is all the more precious for its careful reserve and for its attitude of grave scepticism towards practically all English poetry. These criticisms have been so often cited that it is hardly necessary to give explicit references here. A few attempts have been made to explode the truism that Spenser's fame was great and almost instantaneous. Such attempts, along with careful examination of the criticisms noted here and many more, will be found treated sensibly by Mr. C. R. Baskerville ("The Early Fame of The Shepheards Calender," *Publications of the Modern Language Association of America*, XXVIII, 291 sq.). Mr. Baskerville has, I hope, silenced permanently those few who are inclined to believe that Spenser remained obscure long after the publication of his pastoral.

[4] See *Amoretti*, LX.

or second-hand knowledge of *The Faërie Queene,* turns to the first pages of *The Shepheards Calender,* thinks of Keats (who died at twenty-six after writing "Lamia," "Isabella," "The Eve of Saint Agnes," "Hyperion"), and on that day he reads no farther. Nothing could be more justifiable. Even a young poet and a great poet may recollect his love emotions in a tranquillity most unpoetic. It is useless for Spenser's friend and commentator, "E. K.,"[5] to recommend to our attention "a prety Epanorthosis . . . and withal a Paronomasia" when he lauds such lines as

> I love thilke lasse, (alas! why doe I love?)
> And am forlorne, (alas! why am I lorne?).

Compared with such fustian the "Ode on Solitude," which Pope claimed to have lisped, and the "Genevieve," which Coleridge wrote at fourteen, are white-hot with genius. It is equally useless for us to inform the unwary reader of today that, after the faint promise of Wyatt, Surrey, and their immediate successors, the ease and grace of "Januarie" are wonderful. The average reader, the scorner of the historical point of view, must not be scorned by the student of literature. He must be shown patiently how the historical student learns first that *The Shepheards Calender* marks the large beginnings of modern English poetry and learns soon afterward that it still glows with some of the divinity that made it Scripture to the poets of Elizabeth's day. As Mr. Chambers says,

It is easy enough, in the light of literary history to understand this ill repute of Arcadia. The eighteenth century made the pastoral ridiculous. Ridiculous, when Corydon, in ruffles and knee-breeches, piped it to a Phyllis with patched cheeks and a ribbon on her crook; worse than ridiculous, when

---

[5] Some writers have been crass enough to suppose "E. K." to be Spenser himself. The best discussion of E. K.'s identity is to be found in Dr. James Jackson Higginson's *Spenser's Shepherd's Calender in Relation to Contemporary Affairs,* New York, 1912, pp. 165 sq., where the reader will find a very full account of the various theories of other commentators. Professor Fletcher and Dr. Higginson both argue plausibly that the poet may have looked over some of E. K.'s notes and made suggestions, leaving, however, no little of it to E. K.'s own discretion.

Marie Antoinette played the shepherdess in the gardens of the Trianon, while the real peasants were dying upon their nettle-broth outside.[6]

We must remember, however, that the Elizabethan Arcadia, a strange discordant Arcadia, was very real to Spenser.

Readers of Spenserian criticism are often led somewhat astray by the extreme views of two groups of critics who now discuss *The Shepheards Calender*. One group takes too seriously Spenser's own professed scheme with its underlying love-motive and correspondence of month and mood. Now since the love poetry is the least interesting part of Spenser's eclogues and since the harmony of month and mood is not only very capriciously worked out but is shot through and through with the tinsel of the pathetic fallacy, it seems to follow that *The Shepheards Calender* is hopelessly flimsy in structure and too often insipid in substance. This, however, is shown to be not the case by the other group of critics, who have done great good in turning from the epicure criticism of Spenser which began with the eighteenth century romanticists and reached such extremes in the nineteenth century in its almost complete disregard of Spenser's political and ecclesiastical allegory that it degrades the value of his poetry to something like that of a very choice, exotic, and luxurious confection. The critics of the second group, then, have done ingenious and stimulating work in disclosing the meaning of the guarded allusions and fables in the more polemical eclogues. Their researches have disclosed a young poet of such brave convictions that the most romantic reader can but be grateful for a richer vision of Spenser the artist. Though I am forbidden by my critical method to join any school in this estimate of Spenser, it is towards this second group that I must needs lean since their work is as yet but barely begun. Neither of these groups, however, has given sufficient emphasis to Spenser's most positive contribution to pastoral technique and to the enjoyment of his later-day readers

---

[6] *English Pastorals* (London and New York, 1895). The introduction has an admirable analysis of the moods of the old pastoral and some stimulating comments on Spenser in particular.

—an enchanting light touch that he learned in part from Chaucer and in part from Marot, a quality which, had it been caught up by the right poets, might have saved the pastoral from becoming what Professor Trent calls "a closed *genre.*"

Spenser, for all his interest in the jangling disputes of prelates and politicians, really longed to live for a while in Arcadia. But that had grown more and more difficult since the days of Theocritus. Spenser's state of mind was much like Milton's when he tried to sing the death of Lycidas but could not refrain from bitter questionings as to the rewards of poetry and noble living, as to the future of his church and his country. In the renaissance and long after, it was impossible to keep the eager and fiercely debated questions out of Arcadia. People lived too intensely. In the eighteenth century, the silly royal shepherds of France kept these questions out because these shepherds were supremely selfish.

From the days of Alexander Pope, at least, critics have either regretfully admitted or carped at the defective unity of *The Shepheards Calender.*[7] No one has given due praise to Spenser

---

[7] Pope was a very profound and lifelong admirer of Spenser. But unfortunately his only sustained discussion of the faërie poet is a rather unrepresentative treatment of *The Shepheards Calender* alone, which he prefixed, in the form of a "Discourse on Pastoral Poetry" to the 1717 edition of his *Pastorals.* Though these comments were obviously influenced by Dryden's preface to his translation of Virgil's eclogues, they were the best and fullest consideration of Spenser's youthful poem that had, up to that time, appeared. Pope showed an Augustan tendency, which few critics seem to have understood, a perfectly characteristic Augustan tendency to praise Spenser by easily reconciling him with the "Ancients."

"Among the moderns, their success has been greatest who have endeavored to make these ancients [Theocritus and Virgil] their pattern. The most considerable genius appears in the famous Tasso and our Spenser."

Pope criticises Spenser for his limitation of Mantuan's satirical eclogues and for his introduction of varied stanza-forms in the poem. Spenser should have used the everlasting couplet, of course. Spenser should not, it seems, have imitated the Doric of Theocritus by the use of "old English and country phrases." Yet Pope writes with discernment when he adds:

"As there is a difference betwixt simplicity and rusticity, so the expression of simple thoughts should be plain, but not clownish."

Pope was the first to give Spenser credit for the device of a "calendar." And he was the first to point out that Spenser's nature descriptions are not always closely appropriate to the month and that his general structure is not firm. Flat as all this may seem, Pope's comments are rather remarkable when we examine the vague praise and vague blame that had been meted out before.

for his lofty purpose of rearing a very complex structure—
Arcadia and love, poetry and ambition, politics and religion.
Nobody has praised Spenser for his earliest instance of that
superb scheming which, though it always outreached his
architectonic powers, was always heaven-storming. Only his
immediate followers in the sixteenth and seventeenth centuries,
Drayton, Browne, John Davies of Hereford, the School of the
Fletchers, were truly fired by the magnitude of his plans and
sought with crude enthusiasm to carry them out on an even
more stupendous scale. Spenser's elaborate and tottering struc-
tures are characteristic of the Phaeton-like genius of the English
Renaissance. Contrast Ariosto's easy mastery of unity in com-
plexity with Spenser's more daring complexity and confused
unity. The one is the product of Italian scepticism with neat
and definite boundaries; the other is the product of Elizabethan
faith ill-defined, like an enormous cloud luminous under the
fierce light of the sun.

The elaborate confusion of pastoral material was of course
in part the result of a long procession of "makers" who, lured
by the indolent laughing sunshine of Theocritus, tuned their
song imperfectly to his in troublous seasons with more and more
variation, especially when the savagery and intensity of the
Middle Ages brought convictions so grim that the gentle pagan-
ism of the old singer of Sicily has remained elusive, not quite
comprehensible to this day. The graver, mellow notes of Virgil,
with their tinge of mystery, with their uneasy persuasion to
pastoral felicity, and their troubled refinement, the homely
touches and quarrelsome moralising of Mantuan, the fairy grace
of Clement Marot with its delicate and wistful gaiety, the scran-
nel pipes of Barclay and Googe and Turberville in England—all
these forced the new singer into a rich confusion.[8]

---

[8] Discussions of the sources of *The Shepheards Calender* are legion.
For special commendation one should note the careful investigations of
O. Reissert ("Bemerkungen über Spenser's Shepheards Calender und die
frühere bukolik," *Anglia*, IX, 205–224) and F. Kluge ("Spenser's Shep-
herd's Calender und Mantuan's Eclogen," *Anglia*, III, 266–274), which
have been the starting point for many. W. W. Greg's *Pastoral Poetry and*

All this confusion the young poet set out to harmonize through his design of a calendar of months appropriate to his various moods, a design the mere name of which he took from that strange medley, the *Kalendrier des Bergiers*. In "Januarie" Colin bewails the winter of his woe, the cruelty of Rosalind. In "April," as Professor Herford says finely, "a glowing and rapturous song of praise," Colin's Song to Eliza or Queen Elizabeth, "breaks like sunshine upon the tearful shepherds, ...a song in which the high Elizabethan chivalry for the first time rings out clear." In the full summer glory of "June" comes the climax, this time a contrast with the mood of the month; for Rosalind has flouted Colin for Menalcas. In "December" the young poet compares himself to the dying year in his numb despair. But this innovation, like those others which we shall note presently, Colin is too capricious, or, rather, too absorbed in more intense meditations to work out with perfect symmetry.

There was a far greater force than such graceful, artificial conceits to mould the lineaments of the poem. For beneath the parti-colored vestures of the pastoralists, the warm, quiet golds of Theocritus, the majestic purple and silver of Virgil, the coarse russet of Mantuan, the gay iridescent hues of Marot, there beat the great heart of England which gave a new personality to Spenser's eclogues. Professor Greenlaw has clearly shown the vital forces at the base of *The Shepheards Calender*. The first great national force was the spirit of Chaucer,

> That old Dan Geffrey (in whose gentle spright
> The pure well head of poesie did dwell).

Pastoral Drama, London, 1906, is rich with well-marshalled learning, delicate sympathy, and acute judgments. Professor C. H. Herford's edition of *The Shepheards Calender* (London, ed. 3, 1907), is very stimulating, especially the notes, which make some incisive comparisons. Those of Spenser and Bion, Spenser and Marot, and Spenser and Mantuan are particularly commendable. Professor Courthope in his chapter on Spenser in *The Cambridge History of English Literature* says some noteworthy things about Spenser and Mantuan. Professor Henry Morley's *Clement Marot, and Other Studies* (London, 1871) makes a detailed study of Spenser's great debt to the French poet. Professor W. R. Mustard's *The Eclogues of Baptista Mantuanus* (Baltimore, 1911), is not only a readily available edition of the original but also contains some useful comparative editorial material on Mantuan's followers.

More mighty yet in their moulding of the "new poet" were the momentous political issues that were then swaying England with mingled exaltation and fear.[9] Chaucer, with his blithe realism and his stout championship of the humble parson as contrasted with the luxurious monk and the ribald friar, and England's danger from an alliance with France through the contemplated marriage of Queen Elizabeth and Alençon, her danger from Queen Mary, Spain, the Pope, as well as the growing sense of her magnificent possibilities as a world power, a Shepherdess of the vast Seas—these chiefly impelled Spenser to sing in a style of amazing richness. For, with his compound of easy Elizabethan colloquialism (to which Chaucer's engaging naturalness encouraged him in defiance of such Italianate mummers as Gascoigne), of the revived magic of Chaucer's own tongue, of certain rough, bracing dialects, and of some quaint coinages of his own, Spenser was one of the greatest builders of a new and varied literary language for the radiant throng of intensely national poets who were already impatient to give Elizabeth's England a supreme place in the world's poetry. And with his scorn of corruption, with his earnest questionings he has blown soul-animating strains for even the remote reader of today.

But this remote reader of today, who has turned contemptuously from "Januarie," is, perhaps, still unconvinced. In truth even one with the inspired antiquarianism of Charles Lamb could but measure the lines of this first eclogue with a dull eye. Yet there is no reason to doubt the existence of the

[9] From Professor Edwin A. Greenlaw's penetrating articles I shall quote some shrewd suggestions to which I shall occasionally make additional comments which should not be fathered on him. With his study of "The Shepheards Calender" (*Publications of the Modern Language Association,* September, 1911) should be read his "The Influence of Machiavelli on Spenser" (*Modern Philology,* October, 1909), "Spenser and the Earl of Leicester" (*Publications of the Modern Language Association,* September, 1910), "Spenser and British Imperialism" (*Modern Philology,* January, 1912), and "The Shepheards Calender. II" (*Studies in Philology,* XI, University of North Carolina). Genuine difficulties with some of Professor Greenlaw's interpretations have been raised by Dr. Percy W. Long ("Spenser and the Bishop of Rochester," *Publications of the Modern Language Association,* December, 1916, pp. 713 sq). But none of them seems to me sufficiently conclusive to affect my discussion here or elsewhere.

cruel Rosalind.[10]   There is no reason to doubt that Spenser
during his sojourn in the "North" burned with a youthful ardor
so true that years afterward its memory inspired some of the
most courtly and winning lines in *Colin Clouts Come Home
Again.*   From his friend Gabriel Harvey we get an alluring
glimpse of the lovers when he praises Spenser for "the loftinesse
of his conceit whom gentle Mistresse Rosalinde, once reported to
have all the Intelligences at commandment, and another time,
Christened her Signior Pegaso." From this Professor Herford
has gracefully fancied "a pleasant picture of high-bred and
cultured love-making, ... the young Cambridge graduate 'read-
ing the Tuscan poets on the lawn' of some gray Lancashire
manor-house for the disport of a Rosalind who, like Shake-
spere's, was evidently prone to a pleasant jest, but was assuredly
not, like her, 'many fathoms deep in love.'"   The languid,
affected verses of "Januarie" may suggest that the young
poet was no more in love than his sprightly mistress. His melan-
choly seems decorously studied.   The Elizabethans doubtless
lauded such lines as

> Ye gods of love, that pitie lovers payne,
> (If any gods the paine of lovers pitie,)

where the toying with mere words was in the most approved
amorous manner of the day.   But these do not appeal to the
modern reader as precisely a cry of anguish.   Yet the critic who
would deny a poet sincerity in love because he writes insincere
verses is surely purblind from having looked long at books

---

[10] See Dr. Percy W. Long's "Spenser's Rosalind," *Anglia*, XXXI,
1906, for a brief history of the various attempts to solve the identity of
the poet's early lover and for some clever and plausible arguments suggest-
ing the name of Elizabeth North, a daughter of the famous translator of
Plutarch's *Lives.*   A careful later account may be found in Dr. Higgin-
son's *Spenser's Shepherd's Calender.*   Dr. Higginson carefully recounts
once more the history of the theories and regretfully differs from Dr.
Long's final suggestion against which he urges some difficulties real but
not (I think) final.   Dr. Higginson's own constructive suggestions of a
"platonic" affection for a Mary Sidney or an Elizabeth Carey are not
over-urged; nor are they at all convincing.   I shall often have occasion
to insist (especially in my chapter on the *Amoretti*) that the later-day
concerted attempt to refine away most of the reality from Elizabethan love-
affairs has been very badly overdone; it has become a scholastic fad.

and little at life. Twelve years after *The Shepheards Calender* appeared, Colin defended the love of his youth chivalrously in answer to those shepherds who railed at her "despite."

> For she is not like as the other crew
> Of shepheards daughters which emongst you bee,
> But of divine regard and heavenly hew,
> Excelling all that even ye did see.
> Not then to her, that scorned thing so base,
> But to my selfe the blame, that lookt so hie:
> So hie her thoughts as she herself have place,
> And loath each lowly thing with loftie eie.

If the reader turns to "Februarie" his first impression will be that Colin's pipes, which he broke in dejection at the end of "Januarie," were of a certainty poorly mended. From the graceful if conventional music of the first eclogue he turns to a dissonant jigging tune that seems at first to be raw vigor and no more.[11] The rhythm is roughly iambic and anapaestic. And the archaisms are more frequent and more barbaric. But short acquaintance should bring admiration of the quaint richness, the extraordinary vigor and vividness of the lines in which old Thenot rebukes a querulous youth for his insulting comparison of winter and age.

> The soveraigne of seas he blames in vaine,
> That, once seabeate, will to sea againe.
> So loytring live you little heardgroomes,
> Keeping your beastes in the budded broomes:
> And when the shining sunne laugheth once,
> You deemen the spring is come attonce.
> Tho gynne you, fond flyes, the cold to scorne,
> And, crowing in pypes made of green corne,
> You thinken to be lords of the yeare.
> But eft, when ye count you freed from feare,
> Comes the breme winter with chamfred browes,
> Full of wrinckles and frostie furrowes,
> Drerily shooting his stormy darte,
> Which cruddles the blood, and pricks the harte.

---

11 Such, I think, is a fair first impression in spite of the fact that the measure has its affinities, as Professor Saintsbury has pointed out in his *History of English Prosody*, with the measure which Coleridge used in *Christabel* to conquer a new audience in the Renaissance of Wonder.

Truly and refreshingly rustic are the lines in which Cuddie joys arrogantly in his youth and love.

> Seest howe brag yond bullocke beares,
> So smirke, so smoothe, his pricked eares?
> His hornes bene as broade as rainebowe bent,
> His dewelap as lythe as lasse of Kent.
> See howe he venteth into the wynd,
> Weenest of loves not his mynd?
> Seemeth thy flocke thy counsell can,
> So lustlesse bene they, so weake, so wan,
> Clothed with cold, and hoary wyth frost.
> Thy flocks father his corage hath lost.

Most notable is the slight infusion of humor, an element almost foreign to the pastoral, except for a few touches in Theocritus, and too seldom present, alas, in Spenser. To assert that Spenser had little or no sense of humor is, however, too sweeping. Spenser was evidently tempted by Chaucer to enliven the too serious bucolic poetry with realistic humorous touches. It remained for Drayton, in an elaborate imitation of *The Shepheards Calender* to carry out with more elaborateness what Spenser, perhaps from his absorption in the political and religious crises of the day, meditated but shortly forgot. There are glimmers of rough humor in Cuddie's defiant abuse.

> Ah, foolish old man! I scorne thy skill,
> That wouldest my springing youngth to spil.
> I deeme thy braine emperished bee
> Through rusty elde, that hath rotted thee:
> Or sicker thy head veray tottie is,
> So on thy corbe shoulder it leanes amisse.
> Now thy selfe hast lost both lopp and topp,
> Als my budding braunch thou wouldest cropp:
> But were thy yeares greene, as now bene myne,
> To other delights they would encline.
> Tho wouldest thou pype of Phyllis prayse:
> But Phyllis is myne for many dayes:
> I wonne her with a gyrdle of gelt,
> Embost with buegle about the belt:
> Such an one shepeheards woulde make full faine,
> Such an one would make thee younge againe.

And after Thenot's long homily there is a coarse retort that
reminds one of Chaucer's host or, more closely, perhaps, of the
authentic note of the real English shepherd, the rough humor
of the immortal Mak of the miracle play. .

> THENOT
> Such was thend of this ambitious Brere,
> For scorning eld—
>
> CUDDIE
> Now I pray thee, shepheard, tel it not forth:
> Here is a long tale and little worth.
> So longe have I listened to thy speche,
> That graffed to the ground is my breche.

Though the humorous touches are forced and few, Spenser must
have realized, through the study of Chaucer's tales, that the
infusion of some vivacity might do much to save the languid
pastoral from perdition. This suggestion was caught up more
definitely by Drayton, Browne, and other followers of Spenser
in poems often playful and sometimes professedly humorous;
and, finally, Milton, more remotely, in "L'Allegro," consum-
mated this tradition which, if it had been carried on more en-
thusiastically by other great and discerning poets, would have
delayed the slow degeneration of the pastoral.

But the most fruitful trace of Chaucer's influence in "Feb-
ruarie" is the fable which exasperated the incorrigible Cuddie,
a fable which, says Thenot,

> ....I cond of Tityrus in my youth,
> Keeping his sheepe on the hils of Kent.

Tityrus is the name which Spenser transferred from Virgil to
Chaucer. And although the fable is not to be found in the works
of the master, this will not disappoint anybody but echo-hunters.
In the spirit of Chaucer and under the shadow of his name
Spenser utters, as Professor Greenlaw has shown, those religious
ideals on the fulfilment of which, so he believed, hung the pro-
tection of England. There grew an Oak on the green, once
strong and benignant,

> But now the gray mosse marred his rine,
> His bared boughes were beaten with stormes,
> His toppe was bald, and wasted with wormes,
> His honor decayed, his braunches sere.

At his feet grew a bragging Briar from which the shepherd girls gathered flowers and which harbored the nightingale. Emboldened by these gracious attentions the Briar cried out against his old comrade.

> "Why standst there," quoth he, "thou brutish blocke?
> Nor for fruict nor for shadowe serves thy stocke.
> Seest how fresh my flowers bene spredde,
> Dyed in lilly white and cremsin redde,
> With leaves engrained in lusty greene,
> Colours meete to clothe a mayden queene?
> Thy wast bignes but combers the grownd,
> And dirks the beauty of my blossomes round.
> The mouldie mosse, which thee accloieth,
> My sinamon smell too much annoieth.
> Wherefore soone, I rede thee, hence remove,
> Lest thou the price of my displeasure prove."
> So spake this bold Brere with great disdaine:
> Little him answered the Oake againe,
> But yielded, with shame and greefe adawed,
> That of a weede he was overcrawed.

So it chanced that one day when the Husbandman passed, the Briar complained with much persuasive spite.

> "Ah, my soveraigne, lord of creatures all,
> Thou placer of plants both humble and tall,
> Was not I planted of thine own hand,
> To be the primrose of all thy land,
> With flowring blossomes to furnish the prime,
> And scarlot berries in sommer time?
> How falls it then that this faded Oake,
> Whose bodie is sere, whose braunches broke,
> Whose naked armes stretch unto the fyre,
> Unto such tyrannie doth aspire;
> Hindering with his shade my lovely light,
> And robbing me of the swete sonnes sight?
> So beate his old boughes my tender side,
> That oft the bloud springeth from wounds wyde:
> Untimely my flowres forced to fall,
> That bene the honor of your coronall.

> And oft he lets his cancker wormes light
> Upon my braunches, to worke me more spight:
> And oft his hoarie locks downe doth cast,
> Where with my fresh flowretts bene defast.''

Little availed it for the Oak to reply. Furious, the Husband-man sought his axe and, though the cold steel itself seemed to turn from the grim task, the venerable tree fell groaning. Yet brief was the vain joy of the Briar; for the barbarous winter found him unsheltered, pierced him with frost, burdened him with snow, and left him drooping to be trodden into the mire by the cattle. The uninitiated reader is at once captivated by the fine energy and picturesqueness of the tale and somewhat puzzled by its apparently shifting point of view. Spenser's sympathies are seemingly elusive. Surely, one thinks, surely in a naïve and simple fable the hero and the heavy villain should be more clearly distinguished. Moreover, the comments of the industrious E. K. are in no way illuminating. There is, then, an uncomfortable bewilderment that attends the reading of this tale in a mood too literal. But now, at last, we gather from the observations of Professor Greenlaw, an interpretation which makes the story luminous. The key is found in the hitherto rather mysterious lines that tell how the ''senceless yron'' seemed loth to do its deadly work.

> For it had bene an auncient tree,
> Sacred with many a mysteree,
> And often crost with priestes crewe,
> And often halowed with holy water dewe,
> But sike fancies weren foolerie,
> And broughten this Oake to this miserye.

Professor Greenlaw proceeds:

The Oak stands for the ancient religion, once good and great, but brought by superstition to ruin, ''pitied of none.'' The Briar, cause of the Oak's downfall, was planted by the Husbandman, who represents the English People.... This Briar, ''puffed up with pryde and vaine pleasaunce,'' is the proud Anglican church, and also comes to ruin when deprived of the support afforded by the sturdy elements in the old religion, elements which taken away leave nothing but the pride and ambition that lead to destruction. Thus the allegory of this most interesting poem is threefold: on the surface, concealing the deeper meaning of the poem, is the comparison between youth and age; then there is the comparison between the ill-considered, violent love characteristic of youth and the more sober view characteristic of maturity; all this leads to the main purpose, to represent the way in which, despite worthy elements, the old religion, degraded by superstition, meets a well-deserved ruin and is supplanted by the Anglican form, which in turn deserves destruction for its emptiness and overweaning.... No one who is familiar with the conditions in church and politics in the year 1579 will fail to see that in the application of the fable to the Anglican church lies the point of the satire; it is small wonder, then, that E. K. innocently passes over any explanation that might bring the author into an uncomfortable situation. From a literary point of view, the splendid quality of this eclogue proceeds from the masterly way in which the three elements are blended: Spenser is already master of a complex allegory.[12]

Spenser's satirical manner in *The Shepheards Calender* is, then, thoroughly Parthian. Invariably he hurries us away from those unpastoral altercations which sound so like echoes from the world of his contemporaries into some more remote, tranquil part of Arcadia where the dissonant notes of reality sound but faintly. Perhaps it is partly his desire to make us forget for a time, lest we resent, those sombre warnings of his; perhaps

---

[12] Dr. Higginson (*Spenser's Shepherd's Calender*) has disagreed here with Professor Greenlaw very radically. Dr. Higginson has contributed a mass of ingenious speculations, much of it really proved, to our later-day discussion of Spenser's political and ecclesiastical allegories and satires. But here and elsewhere, when he takes issue with Professor Greenlaw, he is certainly unconvincing. I am no partisan. The views of both men are sufficiently harmonious with my own discoveries and convictions to make possible a triple alliance with few dangers of a schism of long duration. But, in all but one of the cases where they cross swords I find myself shoulder to shoulder with Professor Greenlaw. According to Dr. Higginson, the fable of the Oak and the Briar relates to the fall and execution of the Duke of Norfolk (see pp. 45 sq.). But his arguments are very uneven and often sophistical or fantastic. Here he makes the Husbandman symbolize Elizabeth, a device that seems awkward enough and doubly unconvincing when we study Spenser's allegorical use of the Husbandman in "Mother Hubberds Tale." For this identification Higginson claims "probability" and adds: "For the remainder of my theory I have no absolute proof." If his "probability" is his foundation it is certainly built on shifting sand. And the upper structure is most airy. See also the sustained attack on Professor Greenlaw in Appendix A, pp. 338–346, "Mr. Greenlaw's Theory," which very seriously misstates, at times, Professor Greenlaw's ideas and phrasing (compare, especially, pp. 341–342 with the essay attacked), and which advances very flimsy positive arguments. Dr. Higginson seems to have no conception of what I shall describe throughout my book as Spenser's *Parthian* manner.

it is partly a genuine and wistful desire to find a serene Arcadia that prompts the poet to give us in "March" a light *scherzo.* Blue sky and swallow and hawthorne dainty with buds shyly appear as "breme Winter with chamfred browes" turn sullenly away. Yet even this dialogue between two youthful shepherds, Willye and Thomalin, concerning the boy Love, adapted from a playful idyl or epigram of Bion in a metre partly reminiscent of the English ballad but perhaps recalling more directly the pert tail-rhymed stanzas in which Chaucer wrote whimsically of Sir Thopas, is tinged at the close with a vague foreshadowing of that melancholy so characteristic of all lofty spirited youth, a melancholy which is never long absent from *The Shepheards Calender.* In Bion's brief poem, an old husbandman smiles to hear from the child Ixeutas how he shot his little arrows at Eros, thinking him a bird.

"Pursue this chase no longer, and go not after this bird. Nay, flee far from him. 'Tis an evil creature. Thou wilt be happy, so long as thou dost not catch him, but if thou comest to the measure of manhood, this bird that flees thee now, and hops away, will come uncalled, and of a sudden, and settle on thy head."[13]

In Spenser's poem the pangs of love are more gravely foreseen. Willye is already familiar with the tiny god with wings spotted like the peacock and with silver bow. Love shoots at Thomalin from an "Yvie todde" and wounds him in the heel. Despite, then, the gay meter and a touch or two of sprightly realism (the pumice stones which Thomalin, after exhausting his quiver, hurls at the naked god and the fowling net in which, we are told, Willye's father once caught Love), the prevailing mood is melancholy in premonition of an unrequited love to come.

"Aprill" needs little comment. It is here that Hobbinoll sings for Thenot, Colin's "laye of fayre Elisa," Queen Elizabeth, that sensuous ode which marked "the highest reach of the English lyric" when it appeared. In this song, "tuned ... unto the Waters fall," the "varying anapaestic and iambic move-

---

[13] Andrew Lang's translation: *Theocritus, Bion, and Moschus* (London and New York, 1901).

ments have," as Professor Herford says, "a wayward and wanton buoyancy in accord with rapturous tone of the whole; while the more sedate four-footed verse brings the revelry of each stanza to a dignified close." The young poet is no servile courtier; he is aflame with the growing splendor of England's state and with the unimaginable glory of her future.

Ye dayntye Nymphs, that in this blessed brooke
    Doe bathe your brest,
Forsake your watry bowres, and hether looke,
    At my request.
And eke you Virgins that on Parnasse dwell,
Whence floweth Helicon, the learned well,
        Helpe me to blaze
        Her worthy praise
Which in her sexe doth all excell.

Of fayre Elisa be your silver song,
    That blessed wight,
The flowre of virgins, mav shee flourish long
    In princely plight.
For shee is Syrinx daughter without spotte,
Which Pan, the shepheards god, of her begot:
        So sprong her grace
        Of heavenly race,
No mortal blemishe may her blotte.

See, where she sits upon the grassie greene,
    (O seemely sight!)
Yclad in scarlot, like a mayden queene,
    And ermines white.
Upon her head a cremosin coronet,
With damaske roses and daffadillies set:
        Bayleaves betweene,
        And primroses greene,
Embellish the sweete violet.

Tell me, have ye seene her angelick face,
    Like Phoebe fayre?
Her heavenly haveour, her princely grace,
    Can you well compare?
The redde rose medled with the white yfere,
In either cheeke depeincten lively chere.
        Her modest eye,
        Her majestie,
Where have you seene the like, but there?

Pan may be proud, that ever he begot
    Such a bellibone,
And Syrinx rejoyse, that ever was her lot
    To beare such an one.
Soone as my younglings cryen for the dam,
To her will I offer a milkwhite lamb:
    She is my goddesse plaine,
    And I her shepherds swayne,
Albee forswonck and forswatt I am.

I see Calliope speede her to the place,
    Where my goddesse shines,
And after her the other Muses trace,
    With their violines.
Bene they not bay braunches which they doe beare,
All for Elisa in her hand to weare?
    So sweetely they play,
    And sing all the way,
That it a heaven is to heare.
   . . . .

And whither rennes this bevie of ladies bright,
    Raunged in a rowe?
They bene all Ladyes of the Lake behight.
    That unto her goe.
Chloris, that is the chiefest nymph of al,
Of olive braunches beares a coronall:
    Olives bene for peace,
    When wars doe surcease:
Such for a princesse bene principall.
   . . . .

Bring hether the pincke and purple cullambine,
    With gelliflowres;
Bring coronations, and sops in wine,
    Worne of paramoures;
Strowe me the ground with daffadowndillies,
And cowslips, and kingcups, and loved lillies:
    The pretie pawnce,
    And the chevisaunce,
Shall match with the fayre flowre delice.

Now ryse up, Elisa, decked as thou art
    In royall aray;
And now ye daintie damsells may depart
    Echeone her way.
I feare I have troubled your troupes to longe:
Let Dame Eliza thank you for her song: .

> And if you come hether
> When damsines I gether,
> I will part them all you among.

Then, once more, in "Maye," the intensity of the young
singer who would guard with such high devotion his church and
state, burns through the filmy vesture of the purely Arcadian
pastoral. Palinode begins blithely enough:

> Is not thilke the mery moneth of May,
> When love lads masken in fresh aray?
> How falles it then, we no merrier bene,
> Ylike as others, girt in gawdy greene?
> Our bloncket liveryes bene all to sadde
> For thilke same season, when all is ycladd
> With pleasaunce: the grownd with grasse, the wods
> With greene leaves, the bushes with bloosming buds.
> Yougthes folke now flocken in every where,
> To gather may buskets and smelling brere:
> And home they hasten the postes to dight,
> And all the kirke pillours eare day light,
> With hawthorne buds, and swete eglantine,
> And girlonds of roses, and sopps in wine.
> Such merimake holy saints doth queme,
> But we here sytten as drownd in a dreme.

Palinode, however, is soon put out of countenance by the frown-
ing Piers. Palinode, according to E. K., represents the Catholic
pastor. But it is easy to see that Spenser's commentator is only
veiling cautiously but not too closely what is in fact an onslaught
upon the sybaritic Anglican prelates.

"In all the writings of the Puritans of this period," explains Dr.
Higginson, "it is necessary to emphasize two features which are of the
greatest importance in order to understand rightly Spenser's ecclesiastical
satire. The first is that Cartwright and the Puritans not only affirmed
that the Anglican Church differed little or not at all from the Catholic
in many points, but that they constantly spoke of the Anglicans as if
they were Catholics. Parker became the 'Pope of Lambeth,' and the
bishops 'that viperous brood' of prelates...'smelling too much of Anti-
christ's stench,'...the regiment of the Church they called 'Antichristian
and develish,' and they said they might 'as safely subscribe to allow the
dominion of the Pope'; the Book of Common Prayer they compared to
the 'Popish dung-hill, the mass-book, full of all abominations.' "[14]

---

[14] Dr. Higginson cites much more evidence, pp. 25 sq.

It becomes easy for us, after learning this, to appreciate the fervor and the power in savage denunciation by Piers.

> "Those faytours little regarden their charge,
> While they, letting their sheepe runne at large,
> Passen their time, that should be sparely spent,
> In lustihede and wanton meryment.
> Thilke same bene shepeheardes for the Devils stedde,
> That playen while their flockes be unfedde.
> Well is it seene, theyr sheepe bene not their owne,
> That letten them runne at randon alone.
> But they bene hyred for little pay
> Of other, that caren as little as they
> What fallen the flocke, so they han the fleece,
> And get all the gayne, paying but a peece.
> I muse, what account both these will make,
> The one for the hire which he doth take,
> And thother for leaving his lords taske,
> When great Pan account of shepherdes shall aske."[15]

Under the thin disguise of "Algrind" Spenser boldly praises Bishop Grindal, whose refusal to crush the reforming Puritans cast him out of court favor.[16] Here we have an instance of the iron in Spenser which is too little regarded by his critics intent as they are on their assertions that he bowed his head low in fulsome eulogy of the crown.[17] On the contrary, if one begins in charity to think of Spenser's championship of those in their adversity which might well include over-loyal friends like himself, one ends by contemplating with profound admiration the persistence with which the Don Quixote of poets leaped to the rescue at the gravest danger of public and powerful displeasure. The transparency of the allusions in "Maye" is more notable than the caution. Remember too that the whole poem appeared

---

[15] Professor Greenlaw compares these lines with Chaucer's about the parson ("Prologue," ll. 477 sq.), and Palinode's attitude (ll. 63 sq.) with Chaucer's description of the monk.

[16] For a good brief account of Grindal's quarrel with the queen over the "prophesyings," his bold letter, and his subsequent submission, see Dr. Higginson, pp. 28–29.

[17] I agree with Dr. Higginson's theory that Spenser was probably working on *The Shepheards Calender* from about 1573 to 1579 and that "the cautious manner in which Spenser and E. K. refer to Grindal makes it probable that the eclogue was completed soon after the Archbishop's disgrace [1577], when the Queen's anger was greatest" (pp. 99–100).

with a dedication to Sidney at a time when he was in disgrace; that "October" contains a bold hint advocating Leicester's marriage with the queen when (as Spenser probably then living at Leicester House must have known well) that lord was in a most precarious situation. We should wander too far to dilate here on the poet's sublime exaltation of the dead, disgraced Lord Grey of Wilton as Justice incarnate, the splendid Sir Artegall. It is enough now to recall the illustrious sonnet which, in 1586, the poet addressed to his old comrade, Gabriel Harvey. Harvey was then riddled by the irresistible shafts of the brilliant young university wits whose eulogies Spenser might well have preferred to encourage by drawing away from their victim, the unfortunate scholar, once a self-erected dictator of letters in his little circle, now too sorry a figure to be even a tragic failure. Yet Spenser writes, with courageous steadfastness:

> Harvey, the happy above happiest men
> I read: that, sitting like a looker-on
> Of this worldes stage, doest note with critique pen
> The sharpe dislikes of each condition:
> And, as one careless of suspition,
> Ne fawnest for the favour of the great;
> Ne fearest foolish reprehension
> Of faulty men, which daunger to thee threat;
> But freely doest of what thee list entreat,
> Like a great lord of peerelesse liberty;
> Lifting the good up to high Honours seat,
> And the evill damning evermore to dy.
> For life and death is in thy doomeful writing:
> So thy renowme lives ever by endighting.

But though, as we shall see, Spenser's loyalty to some friends in distress brought him undeserved troubles, this particular bestriding of an old brother-in-arms brought him no harm and Harvey no good. For Tom Nashe, Harvey's inveterate foe, was none the less ready to combine his riotous worship of Spenser with his equally riotous billingsgate against the native of Saffron Walden. Nashe suggests that the sonnet, which Harvey published with his characteristic complacency, was a forgery though he added that Spenser's "name is able to sanctifie any thing, though falsely ascribed to it." I must not curtail one choice sample of Nashe's journalism.

Immortall *Spencer*, no frailtie hath thy fame, but the imputation of this Idiot's friendship: upon an unspotted *Pegasus* should thy gorgeous attired *Fayrie Queene* ride triumphant through all reports dominions, but that this mud-born bubble, this bile on the browe of the Universitie, this bladder of pride newe blowne, challengeth some interest in her prosperitie.'"[18]

But we must return to "Maye." As in "Februarie" we find, according to Professor Greenlaw, an opening discussion which develops two points of view, complex allegory alluding to the dangers that lower at the Puritans, an apparently innocent gloss by E. K., and a fable at the close. In the Chaucerian fable of the Fox and the Kid, which Piers tells, Spenser warns both parties in the Anglican church to beware of the plots of Catholicism, the Fox. So thinks Professor Greenlaw. Dr. Higginson is of another mind.

Spenser, the member of a University whose academic calm was constantly disturbed by active resistance of authority, by bitter denunciations and tumultuous expulsions, has taken up the cudgels in behalf of his party, and has treated the Anglican to a thinly disguised attack in this, the most Puritan of his eclogues.

I incline, in this instance, toward the theory of Dr. Higginson. I find his detailed explanation of the allegory over-ingenious at times and at times fantastic. But his arguments to show that the fable is a warning to young Essex against Burghley (the Fox as in "Mother Hubberds Tale"), are very plausible.[19]

The fable of the Fox and the Kid is not without some slight touches of the master's elvish humor with which Spenser, as I have already insisted, would most certainly have enlivened the

---

[18] See *Works* (ed. McKerrow, London, 1904), I, 281, and 326–327.

[19] I regret that Dr. Higginson, whose theories are often perilous tight-rope walking, finds it necessary to be so cavalier in his attitude toward Professor Greenlaw. After all, the most striking point, for the purposes of a large interpretation of Spenser, lies in the fact that Professor Greenlaw, Dr. Higginson, Professor Padelford, and the present author, working for some years quite independently of each other, should agree on so many new and significant hypotheses which challenge such a radical revision of the current attitude toward Spenser, the courtier.

pastoral more frequently had he been concerned only with art for art's sake. The Fox, pleading admittance into the Kid's abode, edges his wiles with a slightly sinister humor that his victim little comprehends: he claims kindred on the basis of the fact, artfully disguised, that an ancestor of the Kid made an excellent meal for a hungry grandsire of his. To the Kid, who inquires too tenderly after his state of health, the Fox replies:

> "Sicke, sicke, alas! and little lack of dead,
> But I be relieved by your beastlyhead.
> I am a poore sheepe, albe my coloure donne:
> For with long traveile I am brent in the sonne.
> And if that my grandsire me sayd be true,
> Sicker, I am very sybbe to you:
> So be your goodlihead doe not disdayne
> The base kinred of so simple swaine.
> Of mercye and favour, then, I you pray,
> With your ayd to forstall my neere decay."

Cruder, but not without their lighter satirical relish, are the comments of Palinode in which he flouts the fable, but immediately and inconsistently begs it of Piers to give to his illiterate colleague to misapply in his next sermon.

> "Truly, Piers, thou art beside thy wit,
> Furthest fro the marke, weening it to hit.
> Now I pray thee, lette me thy tale borrowe
> For our Sir John, to say to morrowe
> At the kerke, when it is holliday:
> For well he meanes, but little can say."

But the young enthusiast is too serious, too austere in his bold attack on the ecclesiastical policy of Elizabeth and Burghley to emulate with any abandon the humor of that nun's priest's tale which gladdened the journey to Canterbury.

With "June" the little love-drama of Colin reaches a climax in part unreal, in part real. In an unique and exacting stanza (*a b a b b a b a*), Hobbinol and Colin Clout discourse melodiously of Rosalind's perfidy and Colin's consequent poetic silence. Hobbinol exhorts his friend to go southward to the country of happy shepherds where lodge no night-ravens,

But frendly Faeries, met with many Graces,
And lightfoote Nymphes, can chace the lingring night
With heydeguyes, and trimly trodden traces,
Whilst systers nyne, which dwell on Parnasse hight,
Doe make them musick for their more delight;
And Pan himselfe, to kisse their chrištall faces,
Will pype and daunce when Phoebe shineth bright:
Such pierlesse pleasures have we in these places.

Colin laments, as a very young man loves to do, over his lost youth.

Tho couth I sing of love, and tune my pype
Unto my plaintive pleas in verses made;
Tho would I seeke for queene apples unrype,
To give my Rosalind, and in sommer shade
Dight gaudy girlonds was my common trade,
To crowne her golden locks; but yecres more rype,
And losse of her, whose love as lyfe I wayd,
Those weary wanton toyes away dyd wype.

In vain good Hobbinol recalls his young friend's high inspiration.

I sawe Calliope wyth Muses moe,
Soone as thy oaten pype began to sound,
Theyr yvory luyts and tamburins forgoe,
And from the fountaine, where they sat around,
Renne after hastely thy silver sound.
But when they came where thou thy skill didst showe,
They drewe abacke, as halfe with shame confound,
Shepheard to see, them in theyr art outgoe.

Colin replies with a humility which may well exasperate some readers but which, for those who remember Milton's sonnet on arriving at the age of twenty-three, will have its delicate note of true pathos. Here indeed, rather than in the love-motive, lies the intimate appeal of the subdued music of "June," at least for all who have known the sorrow of silence or even the fear of silence for the young poet. The wistfulness of the young singer, hesitant at the threshold of his career, is divinely real. To one who cannot escape from his century the pastoral tone lends a vagueness that misleads.

"Hope exhausted" is the "Embleme" of "June." And of a certainty "Julye," in rough, vigorous septenaries, is unpoetic enough to augur a surcease of inspiration. It is a dialogue in which proud Morrell on a hill and humble Thomalin on a plain discourse of shepherds' duties.[20] It has the same quaint pre-Raphaelite disregard of perspective which one finds in the famous dragon fight in the first book of *The Faërie Queene*. Morrell from a tiny pasteboard hill talks easily with Thomalin on the plain and tries to allure him from where mere Christian lowliness prevails to the summits where luxurious pastors dwell. The symbolism is a curious inversion of Mantuan's pastoral allegory in which the austere and soaring mountain ranges connote true majesty and nobility of ideals. There is little doubt that Morrell is Bishop Aylmer of London, a foe to the simple religion which Spenser championed.[21] At the close a terse, grotesque fable, apparently adapted from the strange myth of the death of Aeschylus, tells how an eagle (Elizabeth), soaring high, thought Algrind's bared head was chalk and dropped a shellfish (the Puritan Party) to crush it upon the head of the aged shepherd to his dire hurt so that he now lies in lingering pain.[22] Thus vaguely but daringly Spenser, who worshipped "Elisa," but worshipped her this side idolatry, allegorizes his queen's attempt to overwhelm the Puritans through the agency of Archbishop Grindal who, turning from the ugly commission, was the only one injured. Though the story is accompanied by no hint from E. K. its bold criticism should not have been too obscure for Spenser's contemporaries if they chose to interpret its hidden message.

Once more the satirist makes a Parthian retreat and directs our attention from the discords of life to a joyous singing-contest

---

[20] Dr. Higginson (pp. 181–203) has worked out what seems to me to be very judicious and plausible identifications of these two characters. We have not the space for his results here, but no student of Spenser should neglect to examine them.

[21] The best research adds confirmation upon confirmation. Dr. Higginson's account of Aylmer and of the "charges which Thomalin brings against the Anglican hierarchy" are capital (see pp. 100–101).

[22] See Herford's edition of *The Shepheards Calender*, pp. 151–152.

in Arcadia. This species of poetry, made immortal by Theocritus, had a more continuous history than any other type of bucolic verse. For even in the Dark Ages, its gay zest appealed to austere churchmen and had much to do with the popular *débat*. But Spenser's eclogue, except for the banter of the two contestants and their customary pledges or prizes, especially the "mazer ywrought of maple" wondrously carved with warring bears and tigers and "wanton yvie-twine," does not descend quite directly from this venerable lineage. Rather, the heart of the poem, the incomparable rollicking duet, which plays so deftly on the verge of Mother Goose doggerel yet remains true song, springs up freshly from popular more than literary ancestry, from the *pastourelle* and Robert Henryson's fresh *Robin and Makyne*. I find it impossible to understand Professor Herford, usually so sure in his appreciation, in his rather left-handed praise of this eclogue. He does, however, accurately point out that the simpler dramatic vivacity of Spenser's song-contest, light, and free from the more literary charm of Virgil and of even Theocritus, free from alternate utterances each a finished epigram, is to be expected since "in English hands—even those of Spenser—the literary contest should divest itself of its luxuriant poetic apparel and become a test chiefly of a ready tongue." Perhaps Professor Herford's faint praise is due to the uneven quality of the eclogue as a whole. Certainly nothing could be more dull than the close, a despairful quasi-sestina of Colin's, interesting only as a further proof of Spenser's metrical virtuosity. No adverse comment could be more cogent than the fact that William Smith, one of the most wretched of Elizabethan poetasters, made this sestina the prey of one of the crudest plagiarisms in the history of literature.[23] But the cheapest fustian ought not to keep us from reverting to the roundelay of Willie and Perigot, with its adroit suggestion of popular improvisation.

---

[23] *Chloris*, 1596, Sonnet XX.

PER. It fell upon a holly eve,
WIL.   Hey ho, hollidaye!
PER. When holly fathers wont to shrieve:
WIL.   Now gynneth this roundelay.
PER. Sitting upon a hill so hye,
WIL.   Hey ho, the high hyll!
PER. The while my flocke did feede thereby,
WIL.   The while the shepheard selfe did spill;
PER. I saw the bouncing Bellibone,
WIL.   Hey ho, bonibell!
PER. Tripping over the dale alone;
WIL.   She can trippe it very well:
PER. Well decked in a frocke of gray,
WIL.   Hey ho, gray is greete!
PER. And in a kirtle of greene saye;
WIL.   The greene is for maydens meete.
PER. A chapelet on her head she wore,
WIL.   Hey ho, chapelet!
PER. Of sweete violets therein was store,
WIL.   She sweeter then the violet.

    . . . .

PER. As the bonilasse passed bye,
WIL.   Hey ho, bonilasse!
PER. She rovde at me with glauncing eye,
WIL.   As cleare as the christall glasse:
PER. All as the sunnye beame so bright,
WIL.   Hey ho, the sunne beame!
PER. Glaunceth from Phoebes face forthright,
WIL.   So love into thy hart did streame:

    . . . .

PER. Therewith my soule was sharply gryde:
WIL.   Such woundes soone wexen wider.
PER. Hasting to raunch the arrow out,
WIL.   Hey ho, Perigot!
PER. I left the head in my hart roote:
WIL.   It was a desperate shot.

    . . . .

PER. But whether in paynefull love I pyne,
WIL.   Hey ho, pinching payne!
PER. Or thrive in welth, she shalbe mine,
WIL.   But if thou can her obteine.
PER. And if for gracelesse greefe I dye,
WIL.   Hey ho, gracelesse griefe!
PER. Witnesse, shee slewe me with her eye:
WIL.   Let thy follye be the priefe.

PER. And you, that sawe it, simple shepe,
WIL.   Hey ho, the fayre flocke!
PER. For priefe thereof, my death shall weepe,
WIL.   And mone with many a mocke.
PER. So learnd I love on a holye eve,
WIL.   Hey ho, holidaye!
PER. That ever since my hart did greve.
WIL.   Now endeth our roundelay.

It is the new life of the pastoral, the gaiety of Chaucer, the fairy grace of Clement Marot, the buoyancy of Theocritus, but, above all, the artless felicity of simple folk, long lost in bucolic poetry, now divined, strangely enough, by an aristocratic poet.

After this, understanding Spenser's method as we now do, we are not surprised to find a reaction in "September," the harsh climax of the satirical eclogues. The thronging, crabbed archaisms, with which the rude and fiery verse stumbles and grows half inarticulate provoked the contempt of Samuel Johnson.[24] It is not to be expected, however, that the great dictator, disgusted with the anemic, purposeless pastorals of his own day, should understand the reality of the anger that burns so fiercely in this the most audacious part of *The Shepheards Calender*. Spenser here follows Mantuan more closely than in "Julye." But there is no doubt whatsoever that the setting, despite some deliberate mystification, is English. The alien lands, whence Diggon Davy, the wanderer, returns bitter and poverty-stricken, mean London. Diggon Davy, so we are told by E. K., is a "very freend to the author hereof" and "had bene long in forraine countryes, and there seene many disorders." To Hobbinol, who

---

[24] In *The Rambler* for July 24, 1750, the doctor scored the pastoral, quite rightly, as a special blight in Augustan poetry. He was plainly infuriated by the languid eclogues of his day and was hardly in the mood to sing the praises of the masters who were indirectly responsible for their existence. Johnson gives some praise to Virgil but has more to blame. His only reference to *The Shepheards Calender* is an attack on the archaisms of "September." The doctor's general animadversions on the pastoral as a decadent influence in Augustan poetry were perfectly sound. And inasmuch as no one, since the days of Spenser himself, has interpreted "September" until within the last few years, it is no discredit to the doctor to note that he was blind to its fervor in the midst of his ursine growls at the inconsistency between the homely dialect and the learned thought that many pastorals affect.

has remained peacefully in their native shire, Diggon Davy relates the shipwreck of his spirit in the land of feuds and corruption. Hobbinol is stirred alternately with pity and with a haunting fear at the audacity of Diggon Davy's charges against unscrupulous pastors and against predatory courtiers who fatten their purses with church property. The shepherds seem to speak hoarsely—in sorrow and terror—as though half-hidden from each other in mist and grim darkness. The uncouth accents of the wanderer certainly voice Spenser's own beliefs. Wolves are lurking once more in England while the shepherds quarrel among themselves or glut their greed to deck their mistresses. A fable, the usual climax of the eclogues of this type, about Roffy and his dog, drives home the warning: while the petty bickering rages within the walls of the Anglican church, while the courtiers bury their talons in church spoils, the Catholics lie in wait to smite. Certainly this eclogue lent savagery to Milton's grim words in *Lycidas*.[25]

[25] There has been considerable controversy over the exact meaning of this fable. Dr. Grosart identified Roffy with Young, Bishop of Rochester. Dr. Higginson considered this view untenable but he seems to have been unaware of the discovery which Dr. Israel Gollancz brought before the British Academy (November 27, 1907), in which he practically established Dr. Grosart's hypothesis on the basis of a book with Harvey's handwriting on the title page as follows: ''Ex Dono Edmundi Spenseri Roffensis Secretarij, 1578,'' which proves Spenser's relations with Young to have been such as to make the Bishop a likely object of his hero-worship. See also Professor Greenlaw's comments on this eclogue in ''The Shepheards Calender,'' pp. 432 sq. Professor Frederic Morgan Padelford, in ''Spenser and the Puritan Propaganda'' (*Modern Philology*, XI, July, 1913, 85–106) has some valuable suggestions for the student of Spenser's political and ecclesiastical satire, particularly his interpretation of the fable of Roffy. I am not, however, convinced by his arguments suggesting that so many of the eclogues were written during the brief period of his episcopal secretaryship for Young.

Professor Padelford's introduction makes an important point about Puritanism in general in the time of Spenser: ''The confusion that attends the use of the terms 'Puritan' and 'Puritanism' as applied to sixteenth-century England can best be appreciated through the analogous use of the words 'socialist' and 'socialism' today. The 'stand-patter' calls every effort at economic reform 'socialistic,' and the arch-conservative lavishes the title 'socialist' upon professors of political science, social workers, municipal reformers, labor leaders, and utopians and anarchists of various stripes, with generous indiscrimination.

'' 'Puritan' and 'Puritanism' are employed with corresponding looseness, and consequently such diverse personalities as Archbishop Grindal, Bishop Cox, the Earl of Leicester, Sir Philip Sidney, and Thomas Cart-

But the next eclogue, "October," though still restive with burning questionings, leads us into clearer, more spacious air. Its appeal must far surpass that of any other part of *The Shepheards Calender*. For here, through the dialogue of Piers and Cuddie concerning the vulgar contempt of poetry and its lofty mission, we catch a glimpse of Colin in the background without his shepherd's pipes but fingering delightedly the pistons of a new instrument, his bright trumpet for *The Faërie Queene*. "October" glows with the great question that assails, at times, the most courageous of poets and seers. Is it worth while to cry out the high truths in the wilderness? It is significant that Colin himself does not appear in the discussion. What must have been the dual faith and doubt with which his own spirit was wavering is here parted in his portraiture of Cuddie, a brilliant young poet who inveighs against the decadent present, who longs wistfully for the fancied golden age of Maecenas and Augustus, and the portraiture of Piers, the apostle of hope, whose music is full of high, exultant promise of *The Faërie Queene*.

> Abandon then the base and viler clowne:
> Lyft up thy selfe out of the lowly dust,
> And sing of bloody Mars, of wars, of giusts:
> Turne thee to those that weld the awful crowne,
> To doubted knights, whose woundlesse armour rusts,
> And helmes unbruzed wexen dayly browne.

---

wright are all denominated Puritans, or credited with Puritan sympathies. Yet Grindal regarded Cartwright as a dangerous fellow who was poisoning the minds of the young men of Cambridge; Bishop Cox did not hesitate to class the Puritans with the Papists as very anti-Christ; and, to borrow a suggestion from Matthew Arnold, fancy the distress of Sidney or of Leicester if he had found himself confined for three months to the 'Mayflower,' with only the Pilgrim Fathers for a solace! Like 'socialism' today, 'puritanism' in the sixteenth century was a relative matter.''

See also Dr. Percy W. Long's ''Spenser and the Bishop of Rochester,'' *Publications of the Modern Language Association of America*, XXXI, (December. 1916), 713 sq. Dr. Long raises timely warnings against the kind of interpretation of the meager facts of Spenser's life in which Professor Greenlaw and I indulge. I fear that I am even more open to suspicion than is Professor Greenlaw and I heartily recommend Dr. Long's ingenious speculations as an antidote to my own. But I feel that my position is, at present, as tenable as his while I feel at the same time greatly indebted to him for investigations which must put us all on our guard against an alluring theory.

> There may thy Muse display her fluttrying wing,
> And stretch her selfe at large from east to west:·
> Whither thou list in fayre Elisa rest,
> Or if thee please in bigger notes to sing,
> Advaunce the worthy whome shee loveth best,
> That first the white beare to the stake did bring.

The allusion to the arms of Leicester and to the love of Eliza-
beth for the brilliant erratic lord is, as I have said before, no
truckling but a daring piece of hero-worship especially when
one considers the situation of Leicester at the time when it
appeared. Even more like the etherealized Spenser seems Piers
when he shows Cuddie how Colin's memory of unrequited love
will be only as a clarion calling him to endless questing.

> ... For love does teach him climbe so hie,
> And lyftes him up out of the loathsome myre:
> Such immortal mirrhor as he doth admire,
> Would rayse ones mynd above the starry skie,
> And cause a caytive corage to aspire;
> For lofty love doth loath a lowly eye.

And the drooping Cuddie, fired by these words, chants Spenser's
own theory of ἐνθουσιασμός, the celestial inspiration of poetry,[26]
in Dionysiac verses that stirred even the sullen approbation of
Ben Jonson, though doubtless to a somewhat more hedonistic
interpretation than Spenser intended! For Drummond re-
corded of Ben that "he hath by heart some verses of Spenser's
Calender about wyne, between Coline and Percye." But Cud-
die's words were of higher import than this suggests.

---

[26] Of ἐνθουσιασμός Spenser, according to E. K., "discourseth in his
booke called *The English Poete*, which booke being lately come to my
hands, I mynde also by Gods grace, upon further advisement, to publish."
But *The English Poete* is lost. Did some of it creep into Sidney's *Defense
of Poesie?* Were Spenser, Sidney, Dyer, Kerke, Drant, Leicester, Harvey,
Greville, and others part of an English society which, under the name of
"Areopagus," emulated the Pléiade? For arguments pro and con, see Pro-
fessor J. B. Fletcher's "Areopagus and Pléiade," *Journal of Germanic
Philology,* XX; Dr. A. H. Upham's *The French Influence on English
Literature* (New York, 1908); Dr. Howard Maynadier's "The Areopagus
of Sidney and Spenser," *Modern Language Review,* IV, 289–301; and
Dr. Higginson's *Spenser's Shepherd's Calender,* pp. 257–286.

Thou kenst not, Percie, howe the ryme should rage.
O if my temples were distaind with wine,
And girt in girlonds of wild yvie twine,
How I could reare the Muse on stately stage,
And teach her tread aloft in buskin fine,
With queint Bellona in her equipage!

"Reading these words today," says Mr. Greg, "they may well seem to us the charter of the new age of England's song; and the effect is rendered all the more striking by the rhythm of the last line with its prophecy of Marlowe and mighty music to come.... And throughout this high discourse the homely names of Piers and Cuddie seem somehow more appropriate, or at least touch us more nearly than Mantuan's Sylvanus and Candidus, as if, in spite of all Spenser owes to foreign models, he were yet conscious of a latent power of simple naïve inspiration, capable, when once fully awakened, of standing up naked and unashamed in the presence of Italy and Greece."

And this eclogue, more than any other of Spenser's, inspired his follower, Wither, to sing the lark-song even in prison and kindled Milton to the outburst that we never tire of quoting:

Alas! what boots it with uncessant care
To tend the homely, slighted, Shepherd's trade,
And strictly meditate the thankless Muse?
Were it not better done, as others use,
To sport with Amaryllis in the shade,
Or with the tangles of Neæra's hair?
Fame is the spur that the clear spirit doth raise
(That last infirmity of noble mind)
To scorn delights and live laborious days;
But the fair guerdon when we hope to find,
And think to burst out into sudden blaze,
Comes the blind Fury with abhorrèd shears,
And slits the thin-spun life. "But not the praise,"
Phœbus replied, and touched my trembling ears:
"Fame is no plant that grows on mortal soil,
Nor in the glistering foil
Set off to the world, nor in broad rumor lies,
But lives and spreads aloft by those pure eyes
And perfet witness of all-judging Jove;
As he pronounces lastly on each deed,
Of so much fame in heaven expect thy meed."

"November" is the most courtly of the eclogues. Perhaps it was for that reason that E. K. felt it to be the greatest in the series and far superior to its model by Marot, whom he considered an indifferent poet. But, as Professor Herford neatly phrases it, "Marot excels in the familiar, Spenser in the lofty." That the somewhat ponderous E. K. was not so much the unjust partisan that he has been dubbed but rather a well-meaning critic impervious to the appeal of intimate verse is attested further by his slurring passing reference to Horace's *Odes* in a note on "December," where he asserts that they are "full of great wit and learning yet of no great weight and importaunce." Nor are we able to share unreservedly the commentator's great admiration for Spenser's poem, despite the lament for Dido which, with all its languorous beauty, pales beside the great pastoral elegies which have enriched the centuries of song. The jangling of polemical shepherds and the gay pastimes of innocent Arcadians are silenced while Spenser celebrates with melodious artificiality a bereavement in the family of Leicester.[27] We must not think this, to be sure, merely the servile tribute of a fortune hunter. The brilliant Leicester, long the queen's favorite and one of her most likely suitors, achieving within the narrow boundaries of England diplomatic victories as dramatic as Drake's exploits on the seas of the West, must have appealed to the utopian poet not as the selfish schemer that he was, but really as the magnanimous Arthur, God-anointed for the throne of England and for Gloriana, as he is drawn resplendent in *The Faërie Queene.* So ardent was the support of the young dreamer, even when Leicester was hard-pressed by his French rival, and so bold were its shadowings in the early poems, that the unpleasant secretaryship in Ireland may almost certainly be interpreted as a kind of dismissal from the court center.[28]

---

[27] On the puzzling but really important problem of the identification of Dido see Dr. Higginson, pp. 234–242. If the theory that Dr. Higginson rather favors is sound it is important evidence for the belief that "Spenser enjoyed the confidence of Leicester to a strong degree, or perhaps that he thought he did." Dr. Higginson adds that this "furnishes an interesting parallel to *Virgil's Gnat,*" which, as we shall see in my chapter on the *Complaints,* reveals a very dramatic situation in Spenser's life.

[28] See Professor Greenlaw's "The Shepheards Calender," and "Spenser and the Earl of Leicester." This matter is taken up in detail in my discussion of the *Complaints.*

Let the reader remember these things before his lip curls at the elaborate formalities of "November." Thenot importunes his comrade for a pleasant song, but Colin replies that this is a time for grief. Dido, daughter of the great shepherd, is drowned. After a pharisaical apology for his "rimes ... rugged and unkempt," he sings an elegy of remarkable technical grace if no more. For the first time he experiments with the alexandrine with which he perfected the Spenserian stanza. Here he uses it as the beginning of an even more complicated structure which has been best described by Professor Dodge as "opening sonorously with an alexandrine, sinking through melodious decasyllables to the plaintive shorter verses, and rising at the close into another decasyllable, to fall away in a brief refrain." Once, at least, in an echo direct from Marot and thence from Moschus, the poem rises to exquisite perfection.

> Whence is it that the flouret of the field doth fade,
>   And lyeth buryed long in winters bale:
> Yet soone as spring his mantle hath displayde,
>   It floureth fresh, as it should never fayle?
> But thing on earth that is of most availe,
>   As vertues braunch and beauties budde,
>   Reliven not for any good.
>   O heavie herse!
> The braunch once dead, the budde eke needes must quaile:
>   O carefull verse!

There is real splendor in the Christian hope toward the close.

> Why wayle we then? why weary we the gods with playnts,
>   As if some evill were to her betight?
> She raignes a goddesse now emong the saintes,
>   That whilome was the saynt of shepheards light:
> And is enstalled nowe in heavens hight.
>   I see thee, blessed soule, I see
>   Walke in Elisian fieldes so free.
>   O happy herse!
> Might I once come to thee! O that I might!
>   O joyfull verse!

But this turn, here carefully led up to by two stanzas which contrast the medieval doctrine of the shallowness of earthly

existence and the medieval comfort in the life eternal, sounds
perfunctory, as it generally does in the pastoral elegies of the
renaissance.   It has none of the pagan audacity with which
Menalcas sings the apotheosis of Daphnis in the eclogue of
Virgil, who originated this turn of the pastoral lament into a
song of rejoicing, a pagan dream in which the elysian wan-
derer never loses sight of his tender Mother Earth and his old
comrades.   That half-doubting Christian rhapsodist aspires to-
ward a dead girl who is hopelessly distant.   This half-believing
pagan philosopher feels subtly in the forest about him the
beneficent touch of Daphnis who has strayed back to him from
the stars.   .

MENALCAS.

Yet will I sing in turn, in my poor way,
My song, and raise thy Daphnis to the stars—
Raise Daphnis 'o the stars. He loved me too.

MOPSUS.

Could aught in my eyes such a boon outweigh?
Song-worthy was thy theme: and Stimichon
Told me long since of that same lay of thine.

MENALCAS.

Heaven's unfamiliar floor, and clouds and stars,
Fair. Daphnis, wondering, sees beneath his feet.
Therefore gay revelries fill wood and field,
Pan, and the shepherds, and the Dryad maids.
Wolves plot no harm to sheep, nor nets to deer;
Because kind Daphnis makes it holiday.
The unshorn mountains fling their jubilant voice
Up to the stars: the crags and copses shout
Aloud, "A god, Melancas, lo! a god."
Oh! be thou kind and good unto thine own!
Behold four altars, Daphnis: two for thee,
Two piled for Phoebus. Thereupon I'll place
Two cups, with new milk foaming, year by year;
Two goblets filled with richest olive-oil:
And, first with wine making glad the feast—
At the fireside in snowtime, 'neath the trees
In harvest—pour, rare nectar, from the can
The wines of Chios. Lyctian Aegon then
Shall sing no songs, and to Damoetas' pipe
Alpheseboeus dance his Satyr-dance.

And this shalt thou lack never: when we pay
The nymphs our vows, and when we cleanse the fields,
While boars haunt mountain-heights, and fishes streams,
Bees feed on thyme, and grasshoppers on dew,
Thy name, thy needs, thy glory shall abide.
As Bacchus and as Ceres, so shalt thou
Year after year the shepherd's vows receive;
So bind him to the letter of his vow.

MOPSUS.
What can I give thee, what, for such a song?
Less sweet to me the coming South-wind's sigh,
The sea-wave breaking on the shore, the noise
Of rivers, rushing through the stony vales.[29]

Nor can the elegy for Dido stir us like the pantheism (with its inconsistent but exalting gropings towards a faith in the survival of personality) of Shelley, "a phantom among men," with face "like Cain's or Christ's," dreaming of the dead Keats in an age of proud intellectual adventure.

Peace, peace! he is not dead, he doth not sleep—
He hath awakened from the dream of life—
'Tis we, who lost in stormy visions, keep
With phantoms an unprofitable strife,
And in mad trance strike with our spirit's knife
Invulnerable nothings—*We* decay
Like corpses in a charnel; fear and grief
Convulse us and consume us day by day,
And cold hopes swarm like worms within our living clay.

He has outsoared the shadow of our night;
Envy and calumny and hate and pain,
And that unrest which men miscall delight,
Can touch him not and torture not again;
From the contagion of the world's slow stain
He is secure, and now can never mourn
A heart grown cold, a head grown gray in vain;
Nor, when the spirit's self has ceased to burn,
With sparkless ashes load an unlamented urn.

He lives, he wakes—'tis Death is dead, not he;
Mourn not for Adonais.—Thou young Dawn,
Turn all thy dew to splendor, for from thee
The spirit thou lamentest is not gone;

---

[29] Charles Stuart Calverley's translation (London, 1908).

Ye caverns and ye forests, cease to moan!
Cease, ye faint flowers and fountains, and thou Air,
Which like a mourning veil thy scarf hadst thrown
O'er the abandoned Earth, now leave it bare
Even to the joyous stars which smile on its despair!

He is made one with Nature: there is heard
His voice in all her music, from the moan
Of thunder to the song of night's sweet bird;
He is a presence to be felt and known
In darkness and in light, from herb and stone,
Spreading itself where'er that Power may move
Which has withdrawn his being to its own;
Which wields the world with never-wearied love,
Sustains it from beneath, and kindles it above.

He is a portion of the loveliness
Which once he made more lovely; he doth bear
His part, while the one Spirit's plastic stress
Sweeps through the dull dense world, compelling there,
All new successions to the forms they wear;
Torturing th' unwilling dross that checks its flight
To its own likeness, as each mass may bear,
And bursting in its beauty and its might
From trees and beasts and men into the Heaven's light.

The splendors of the firmament of time
May be eclipsed, but are extinguished not;
Like stars to their appointed height they climb,
And death is a low mist which cannot blot
The brightness it may veil. When lofty thought
Lifts a young heart above its mortal lair,
And love and life contend in it for what
Shall be its earthly doom, the dead live there
And move like winds of light on dark and stormy air.

Here, truly, the poet faces eternity with haggard face but with blazing eyes.

In "December," the close, as in "January," the opening, Colin stands before us alone. The pastoral year, with its seasons of gladness and sorrow, is reviewed in a minor key, so that "it broadens into a kind of tragic allegory of life which closes the round of months with philosophic dignity.[30] Like "Janu-

---

[30] Professor R. S. Neil Dodge, *The Cambridge Edition* of Spenser (Boston and New York, 1908).

arie'' it is very unreal, especially when we remind ourselves that this lament of old age comes from a young man. Spenser's last eclogue is superior, however, to ''Januarie'' in fresh details. Colin tells us with much charm how he learned the lore of the woods,

> Where I was wont to seeke the honey bee,
> Working her formall rowmes in wexen frame,
> The grieslie todestoole growne there mought I se,
> And loathed paddocks lording on the same:
> And where the chaunting birds luld me a sleepe,
> The ghastlie owle her grievous ynne doth keepe.
>
> . . . .
>
> To make fine cages for the nightingale,
> And baskets of bulrushes, was my wont:
> Who to entrappe the fish in winding sale
> Was better seene, or hurtful beastes to hont?
> I learned als the signes of heaven to ken,
> How Phoebe fayles, where Venus sittes and when.

But these fresh details appear because the poem derives from Marot's quaint and gracious *Eclogue au Roy* written by the old poet to Francis I, and closing, be it noted, in a tone of cheerful hope far different from the last lines of Spenser's poem of imagined old age. We must certainly reverse, for these poems, E. K.'s judgment of the two poets. Nevertheless we must remember always, or we shall carp too testily at Colin's insincerity, that from youth in premonitory moods we have received many of our most precious songs of the winter of life. Indeed the great poets, when they reach old age, are often serene and talk little of the snows. Colin will hang his pipe on a tree and await imminent death. Marot tranquilly awaits help from his king and plans to take down his pipe, long silent, to sing in mid-winter the music of summer.

In that weariness of the last lines of Spenser's pastoral the most hearty apologist can but see a foreshadowing of the slow decay of bucolic poetry. Mr. Greg epitomizes with such sweep and precision the picturesque history of formal shepherd-poetry from the days of Theocritus to the days of its death in the eighteenth century, that his paragraph will serve to give us perspective as we turn to recall the qualities of *The Shepheards Calender.*

When the kind first makes its appearance in a world already old, it arises purely as a solace and relief from the fervid life of actuality, and comes as a fresh and cooling draught to lips burning with the fever of the city. In passing from Alexandria to Rome it lost much of its limpid purity; the clear crystal of the drink was mixed with flavours and perfumes to fit the palate of a patron or an emperor. The example of adulteration being once set, the implied contrast of civilization and rusticity was replaced by direct satire on the former, and later by the discussion under the pastoral mask of questions of religious and political controversy. Proving itself but a left-handed weapon in such debate, it became a court plaything, in which princes and great ladies, poets and wits, loved to see themselves figured and complimented, and the practice of assuming pastoral names becoming almost universal in polite circles, the convention, which had passed from the eclogue on to the stage, passed from the stage into actual existence, and court life became one continual pageant of pastoral conceit. From the court it passed into the circles of learning, and grave jurists and administrators, poets and scholars, set about the refining of language and literature decked out in all the fopperies of the fashionable craze. One is tempted to wonder whether anything more serious than light loves and fantastic amours can have flourished amid eighteenth-century pastoralism. When the ladies of the court began to talk dairy-farming with the scholars and statesmen of the day, the pretence of pastoral simplicity could hardly be long kept up. Nor was there any attempt to do so. In the introduction to his famous romance d'Urfé wrote in answer to his objectors: ''Responds leur, ma Bergere, que pour peu qu'ils ayent connoissance de toy, ils sçauront que tu n'es pas, ny celles aussi qui te suivent, de ces Bergeres necessiteuses, qui pour gaigner leur vie conduisent les trompeaux aux pasturages; mais que vous n'avez toutes pris cette condition que pour vivre plus doucement et sans contrainte.'' No wonder that to Fontenelle Theocritus' shepherds ''sentent trop la campagne.'' But the hour of pastoralism had come, and while the ladies and gallants of the court were playing the parts of Watteau swains and shepherdesses amid the trim hedges and smooth lawns of Versailles, the gates were already bursting before the flood, which was to sweep in devastation over the land, and to purge the old order of social life.[31]

Such, then, is Spenser's first considerable poem, coming on the crest of a wave of national fervor and splendid with England's hope, yet, by a strange antinomy, couched in a form already doomed. Yet it served Elizabeth's epic laureate well.

---

[31] Walter W. Greg, *Pastoral Poetry and Pastoral Drama* (London, 1906), 7 sq.

We have gone far enough to begin reflection upon the two great problems in the study of Spenser which have made controversy for more than three centuries, problems which will be more effectively considered in connection with *The Faërie Queene,* but which should be approached here as we look back over *The Shepheards Calender.* I refer to Spenser's defective control of unity and his allegorizing impulse. No one has stated the significance of Spenser's architectonic failings more broadly and justly than Professor Courthope. He pays high tribute to the comprehensiveness of the poet's genius.[32]

His imagination received an impulse from every one of the great sources of thought which in the sixteenth century were agitating the mind of Europe. Catholicism, Mediaeval Romance, the Philosophy of the Renaissance, the Morality of the Reformation, all contributed elements to the formation of his poetical conceptions. He wanted no quality required to place him in the same class with Homer, Virgil, Dante, Shakespeare, Milton, and, perhaps, I may add Chaucer, but that supreme gift of insight and invention which enables the poet to blend conflicting ideas into an organic form.' It must be added that to produce such a form out of the materials at his disposal was probably impossible, so that—apart from a certain defect of judgment implied in the selection of subject—the lack of unity that characterizes Spenser's creations is the result not so much of his own incapacity as of the circumstances of the times.

I prefer to survey the very bases of Professor Courthope's judgment from another mood, a mood of wonder at the audacity of those Spenserian minsters of song with their unresolved harmonies of exotic minarets and dizzy soaring spires. I have already remarked that Spenser's tottering structures are characteristic of the Phaeton-like genius of the English renaissance. None of the supreme poets, except Dante and Goethe, have essayed anything so immense. Of these two, Dante alone compassed his visions, although Goethe's final poise and reach was far greater than Spenser's.

The first interesting disapproval of that other questionable quality of Spenser's, his allegorizing and moralistic habit, came from the *Mythomestes* of Henry Reynolds in 1633. Reynolds

---

[32] *A History of English Poetry* (London and New York, 1897), II, 234.

found Spenser among the very few English singers who would endure; but he found reason for mildly urging a grievance.

> Next, I must approve the learned *Spencer*, in the rest of his Poëms no lesse then his *Fairy Queene*, an exact body of the *Ethicke* doctrine; though some good judgments have wisht, and perhaps not without cause, that he had therein beene a little freer of his fiction, and not so close rivetted to his Morall.[33]

It is a pity that our romantic hedonists do not express their conceptions with the tempered simplicity of this mystic of the seventeenth century. From his day there have seldom been wanting writers, as distinguished as Sir William Temple[34] at least, who for various reasons have repudiated the allegory. In the eighteenth century, however, the Augustans were almost unanimously in favor of it. Addison, in his maturity, said some charming and discerning things about it. It won from Samuel Johnson, intent on crushing the *poetae minimi* who were writing Spenserian bagatelles, a somewhat grudging appreciation of their master. It remained for Hurd and other early romanticists to show that first impatience against Spenser's shadowed didacticism which culminated in the beautiful but somewhat spineless appreciations of such literary epicures as Leigh Hunt and which colored with its too garish hues the superb essay of Lowell. Lowell's clever Luciferian utterances have often been quoted.

> The true use of Spenser is as a gallery of pictures which we visit as the mood takes us, and where we spend an hour or two at a time, long enough to sweeten our perceptions, not so long as to cloy them.... When-

---

[33] *Mythomestes wherein a short survay is taken of the nature and value of true Poësie, and depth of the Ancients above our Modern Poëts.* See J. E. Spingarn's *Critical Essays of the Seventeenth Century,* I, 144 sp.

[34] See the essay *Of Poetry* (1685), reprinted in Professor Spingarn's *Sir William Temple's Essays on Ancient & Modern Learning and on Poetry* (Oxford, 1909). "*Spenser* endeavoured to Supply this with Morality, to make Instruction instead of Story, the Subject of an Epick Poem. His Execution was Excellent, and his Flights of Fancy very Noble and High, but his Design was Poor, and his Moral lay so bare that it lost its effect: 'tis true, the Pill was Gilded, but so thin that the Colour and the Taste were too easily discovered." Nevertheless, Temple selected Spenser along with Ariosto and Tasso as the three supreme modern heroic poets to name with the Ancients and added: "After these three I know none of the Moderns that have made any Atchievements in *Heroick* poetry worth Recording."

ever, in the ''Faery Queen'' you come suddenly on the moral, it gives you a shock of unpleasant surprise, a kind of grit as when one's teeth close on a bit of gravel in a dish of strawberries and cream.

But Milton had referred to his master as ''Our sage and serious Spenser, whom I dare to name a better teacher than Scotus or Aquinas.'' And in the greatest essay ever written on Spenser, an essay which reacts against the romantic hedonists with an eloquence that surpasses them in their own music, Professor Edward Dowden uses the words of Milton like a solemn refrain.

In England of the age of Elizabeth what place is filled by the poetry of Spenser? What blank would be made by its disappearance? In what, for each of us who love that poetry, resides its special virtue? Shall we say in answer to these questions that Spenser is the weaver of spells, the creator of illusions, the enchanter of the Elizabethan age; and that his name is to us a word of magic by which we conjure away the pain of actual life, and obtain entrance into a world of faery? Was Spenser, as a poet of our own time names himself, ''the idle singer'' of his day— that day not indeed ''an empty day,'' but one filled with heroic daring and achievement? While Raleigh was exploring strange streams of the New World, while Drake was chasing the Spaniard, while Bacon was seeking for the principles of a philosophy which should enrich man's life, while Hooker, with the care of a master-builder, was laying the foundation of polity in the National Church, where was Spenser? Was he forgetful of England, forgetful of earth, lulled and lying in some bower of fantasy, or moving in a dream among imaginary champions of chivalry, distressed damsels, giants and dragons and satyrs and savage men, or shepherds who pipe and shepherdesses who dance forever in a serene Arcady?

Assuredly it was not thus that a great Englishman of a later age thought of Spenser. When Milton entered upon his manhood, he entered upon a warfare; the peaceful Horton days, days of happy ingathering of varied culture, days of sweet repose amid rural beauty, were past and gone; and he stood with loins girt, prepared for battle in behalf of liberty. And then, in London, when London was a vast arsenal in which weapons were forging for the defence of truth and freedom, Milton in his moment of highest and most masculine ardour, as he wrote his speech on behalf of unlicensed printing, thought of Spenser. It was not as a dreamer that Milton thought of him. Spenser had been a power with himself in youth, when he, ''the lady of his college,'' but such a lady as we read of in ''Comus,'' grew in virginal beauty and virginal strength. He had listened to Spenser's ''sage and solemn tunes,''

"Of turneys and of trophies hung;
Of forests and inchantments drear,
Where more is meant than meets the ear."

And now, in his manhood, when all of life had grown for him so grave, so glorious with heroic effort, Milton looks back and remembers his master, and he remembers him not as an idle singer, not as a dreamer of dreams, but as "our sage and serious Spenser, whom I dare to name a better teacher than Scotus or Aquinas."[35]

There have been also critics who would serve neither under the gonfalon of James Russell Lowell nor under the oriflamme of Edward Dowden. There have been those who would mediate. From this point of view Professor Courthope has some very discriminating things to say.

It seems to me impossible to hold with Mr. Lowell that the moral of Spenser's poem counts for nothing; the sense, no less than the form of his allegory is essential and is a characteristic part of his work. But I dissent still more decidedly from those who consider that he is to be primarily regarded as a moral teacher. Spenser does not allegorize like Dante, because he believes all sensible objects to be mirrors of hidden truths; nor like Langland, because this method of writing is useful for the moral instruction he wishes to convey. Allegory is to him mainly interesting in so far as it serves the purpose of poetry. From the first glimpse we obtain of him, in his correspondence with Gabriel Harvey, down to his last experiences at Court, recorded in "Colin Clouts Come Home Again," the requirements of his art are always in his mind; and the motive of every one of his greater compositions when detached from the cloudy words with which he chooses to cover it, is found to be primarily poetical.

It is true that Spenser is not to be regarded primarily as a moral teacher. But I hope to show in the following chapters that if Spenser did devote much thought to the requirements of his art, he was thinking of an art much more spacious than that

[35] "Spenser, The Poet and Teacher." This essay first appeared in Dr. Grosart's edition of Spenser. Dowden reprinted it in *Transcripts and Studies.* That most brilliant and affable French historian of our literature, M. J. J. Jusserand, takes issue very courteously with Professor Dowden's thesis. See *A Literary History of the English People* (London, 1906), II, 499. It is not easy to avoid wavering before the learning and the eloquence of this distinguished critic, but here, at least, I must persist in casting my allegiance with Edward Dowden. For an admirable detailed account of the ethical influence of Spenser on Milton see Professor Edwin Greenlaw's "A Better Teacher Than Aquinas," University of North Carolina *Studies in Philology,* XIV (April, 1917), 196 sq.

mere technique of which too many hypercultivated people of
our own generation are forever prating. I hope to prove that
Spenser was, without inconsistency or discord, both practical
man and dreamer. I shall give you a synthesis of the vital
elements in the works of those critics who, according to the
different idiosyncrasies, passions, and revelations of their cen-
turies and according to their own personalities, have registered
various judgments and impressions of the faërie poet which
irresistibly and inevitably shape themselves into a collective
estimate much like that in "Spenser, the Poet and Teacher."
I shall analyze the works of Spenser more elaborately than they
have ever been analyzed before and the portrait which I shall
draw should establish the essential truth of the essay by Edward
Dowden. The word "artist" which Professor Courthope uses
too often connotes, with men of letters, the mere stylist. Spen-
ser's utterances on the subject of "art" to Gabriel Harvey prove
on rereading to be casual, after all, and unorganized and incon-
sistent.[36] For his profoundest and most abiding convictions on
art, an art reverently wedded to the life of the day and the
life of eternity, let us recall those two ardent stanzas in
"October."

> Abandon then the base and viler clowne;
> Lyft up thy selfe out of the lowly dust,
> And sing of bloody Mars, of wars, of giusts:
> Turne thee to those that weld the awful crowne,
> To doubted knights, whose woundlesse armour rusts,
> And helmes unbruzed wexen dayly browne.
>
> There may thy Muse display her fluttryng wing,
> And stretch her selfe at large from east to west;
> Whither thou list in fayre Elisa rest,
> Or if thee please in bigger notes to sing,
> Advaunce the worthy whome shee loveth best.
> That first the white beare to the stake did bring.

---

[36] And if they are to be considered of special significance we may note,
with Professor Greenlaw, at least one passage in the letters, and a very
important passage, too, which makes light of the "primarily poetical
mood." See "Spenser and the Earl of Leicester."

This may be described as mere cunning allusion to Elizabeth and to Leicester's escutcheon; rhetorical grovelling for court favor, sincere only in its earnest attention to stylistic finish. But I have already called attention to its inopportuneness and its loyal audacity. Surely these fiery words of Piers to Cuddie reveal an interest in something more than we have come, since the days of Walter Pater, to talk of as "art." Lowell's unhappy reference to the gravel in the strawberries and cream, with its hedonistic implications, has placed him, in his attitude toward Spenser, among critics far less lofty-minded, certainly, than himself. On the other hand the word "teacher" seems perforce so bound up with pedant and preacher in the crudest sense, that it has been difficult (since the days when Childe Harold, Alastor, and Endymion wandered about the earth to minister deliciously and exclusively to their own immortal souls) to conceive of teaching as anything but impertinent prose. Thus it is that Professor Dowden's phrases, caught from Milton, may give pause to Professor Courthope. It may be possible thus to think of Professor Dowden as belittling Spenser as a ministrator of pleasure. Yet the very luxuriance of Dowden's phrases establish the sheer poetry of true teaching (so rare in our age and our universities) and prove triumphantly his appreciation of Spenser's luxuriance as well as Spenser's didacticism.

"A better teacher than Scotus or Aquinas." Yet we are told by the Dean of St. Paul's, that in giving himself credit for a direct purpose to instruct, Spenser "only conformed to the curiously utilitarian spirit which pervaded the literature of the time." It is the heresy of modern art that only useless things should be made beautiful. We want beauty only in play-things. In elder days the armour of a knight was as beautiful as sun-light, or as flowers. "In unaffected, unconscious, artistic excellence of invention," says one of our chief living painters, "approaching more nearly to the strange beauty of nature, especially in vegetation, mediaeval armour perhaps surpasses any other effort of human ingenuity." What if Spenser wrought armour for the soul, and, because it was precious and of finest temper, made it fair to look upon? That which gleams as bright as the waters of a sunlit lake is perhaps a breastplate to protect the heart; that which appears pliant as the blades of summer grass may prove at our need to be a sword of steel.

If the reader will recapture, then, the authentic note of *The Shepheards Calender,* as of all the poetry of Spenser, he will recover more than the grace, the music, the pretty silvery vignettes of Arcadian scenery, the extraordinary range of metrical resources, the sensuousness of the set-pieces. He will even pass beyond, while delighting in them, that captivating freshness, the faint touches of humor, the blithe if not quite confident realism, the vigorous fable technique, the frolic and buoyancy of the roundelay of Willie and Perigot, the note of Chaucer, which have hitherto been hardly appraised at all. He will discern, beneath the love-plaints of ''June,'' the hesitant poet, eager with his hope, melancholy with youth's quaint self-questionings. In the veins of Spenser's ecclesiastical and political satire, though the issues thereof may seem almost dead now, will be revealed something flowing light and bright like quicksilver. The discerning reader, observing that to Spenser the practical and the visionary melt together in a large harmony, will be fired by the championship of Leicester and the arguments for Puritanism, be he conservative or radical, Protestant, Catholic, or Agnostic, not because he cares for Leicester or for Puritanism, but because here lurks something quintessential, something deeper than polemics.

CHAPTER II

THE FAËRIE QUEENE. BOOKS I–III

"He who, at forty, reads 'The Faërie Queene' with as much delight as at twenty, is pretty sure to be a wise and a happy man." Thus writes Hillard, the first American editor of Spenser. No poet has ever had a more choice and a more continuously loyal audience than Spenser. Yet no other supreme poet, not even Dante, has been so imperfectly understood by such an army of acute and eloquent critics. No single age has as yet begun to comprehend the innumerable facets, the myriad flashes of history, and philosophy, poetry and prophecy, in *The Faërie Queene,* like the jewels of fabulous oriental lore splendid enough alone to light for sultans and genii a hall leagues long, like De Quincey's cathedral, with a glow here blinding, here mysterious, revealing here some silent god and here just touching the slumbering fires of some forgotten treasure. Professor Mackail has told us most succinctly and surely how to approach *The Faërie Queene:* "the child's vision must, if it were possible, be combined with the scholar's understanding. This is a hard saying, but the thing itself is hard. The course lies straight and narrow between the rock and the whirlpool. Appreciation only comes of study; study too often dims and sophisticates appreciation." No critic, no poet, no age has yet fully appreciated *The Faërie Queene.* And our own age, now confused with both the wholesome and the pathological onslaughts of realism, with the stern prophecies of an austere neo-classicism, yet remaining still audacious with the questing fire of romanticism, the Renaissance of Wonder—our own age misunderstands Spenser with that romantic wilfulness which began with Hurd and which developed into the exquisite but treacherous epicure-worship of Leigh Hunt, of Lowell, of William Butler Yeats. Like Hurd and Lowell, Yeats attributes Spenser's use of allegory to an unworthy truckling to the British Philistine.

[Spenser] was, I think, by nature altogether a man of that old Catholic feudal nation, but, like Sidney, he wanted to justify himself to his new masters. He wrote of knights and ladies, wild creatures imagined by the aristocratic poets of the twelfth century, and perhaps chiefly by English poets who had still the French tongue; but he fastened them with allegorical nails to a big barn door of common sense, of merely practical virtue. Allegory itself had risen into general importance with the rise of the merchant class in the thirteenth and fourteenth centuries; and it was natural when that class was about for the first time to shape an age in its image, that the last epic poet of the old order should mix its art with his own long-descended, irresponsible, happy art.

Then Mr. Yeats goes on to say some of the best things that have ever been said about allegory, but he goes on also to misapply his dicta in a winning but fallacious censure of *The Faërie Queene.*

Allegory and, to a much greater degree, symbolism, are a natural language by which the soul when entranced, or even in ordinary sleep, communes with God and with angels. They can speak things which cannot be spoken of in any other language, but one will always, I think, feel some sense of unreality when they are used to describe things which can be described as well in ordinary words. Dante used allegory to describe visionary things, and the first maker of *The Romance of the Rose*, for all his lighter spirits, pretends that his adventures came to him in a vision one May morning; while Bunyan, by his preoccupation with heaven and the soul, gives his simple story visionary strangeness and intensity: he believes so little in the world, that he takes us away from all ordinary standards of probability and makes us believe even in allegory for a while. Spenser, on the other hand, to whom allegory was not, as I think, natural at all, makes us feel again and again that it disappoints and interrupts our preoccupation with the beautiful and sensuous life he has called up before our eyes. It interrupts us most when he copies Langland, and writes in what he believes to be a mood of edification, and the least when he is not quite serious, when he sets before us some procession like a court pageant made to celebrate a wedding or a crowning. One cannot think that he should have occupied himself with moral and religious questions at all. He should have been content to be, as Emerson thought Shakespeare was, a Master of the Revels to mankind. I am certain that he never gets that visionary air which can alone make allegory real, except when he writes out of a feeling for glory and passion. He had no deep moral or religious life. He has never a line like Dante's ''Thy Will is our Peace,'' or like Thomas à Kempis's ''the Holy Spirit has liberated me from a multitude of opinions,'' or even like Hamlet's objection to the bare bodkin. He had been made a poet by what he had almost learnt to call his sins. If he had not felt it necessary to justify his art to some serious friend, or perhaps even to ''that rugged forehead,'' he would have written all his life long, one thinks, of the loves of shepherdesses and shepherds, among whom there would have been perhaps the morals of the dovecot. One is persuaded that his morality is official and impersonal—a system of life which it was his duty to support—and it is perhaps a half understanding of this that has made so many generations believe that he was the first poet laureate, the first salaried moralist among the poets. His processions of deadly sins, and his houses, where the very cornices are arbitrary images of virtue, are an unconscious hypocrisy, an undelighted obedience to the ''rugged forehead,'' for all the while he is thinking of nothing but lovers whose bodies are quivering with the memory or the hope of long embraces. When they are not together, he will indeed embroider emblems and images much as those great ladies of the courts of love embroidered them in their castles; and when these are imagined out of a thirst for magnificence and not thought out in a mood of edification, they are beautiful enough; but they are always tapestries for corridors that lead to lovers' meetings or for the walls of marriage chambers. He was not passionate, for the passionate feed their flame in wanderings and absences, when the whole being of the beloved, every little charm of body and of soul, is always present to the mind, filling it with heroical subtleties of desire. He is a poet of the delighted senses, and his song becomes most beautiful when he writes of those islands of Phaedria and Acrasia, which angered ''that rugged forehead,'' as it seems, but gave to Keats his *Belle Dame sans Merci* and his ''perilous seas in faery lands forlorn,'' and to William Morris his ''waters of the wondrous Isle.''

It is strange that any one, a poet above all, who had read the sublime cantos on Mammon and on Mutabilitie should deny to Spenser a right to occupy himself with universal matters moral and religious. Against Yeats we may pit a sound, clean-cut passage from one of the surest of recent Spenserian scholars. Miss Lillian Winstanley has summed up perfectly the balance of qualities in Spenser.

Spenser's Puritanism saved him from seizing upon those pagan and sensuous elements in classical literature which proved a pitfall to so many of his contemporaries; it made him blind to the more dangerous aspects of Platonism and helped to concentrate his attention on that which is noblest and most characteristic in Plato—his ethical genius; on the other hand Spenser's Platonism preserved him from the, artistically at any rate, no less dangerous pitfalls of Puritanism; it helped to preserve him from mental narrowness by showing him the best possible examples of freedom and flexibility of mind and taught him what, as a poet, it was most essential he should know—that beauty is not only consistent with moral earnestness, but may be made to contribute to it in the most powerful way.[1]

---

[1] *Edmund Spenser: The Fowre Hymnes* (Cambridge, England, 1907), p. xi.

Mr. Yeats, like most romantic poets, has divorced dreaming and doing and it is not strange that he cannot understand an age when Cellini turned from his delicate hammering on the soft curves of some golden urn to fire the cannon-shot which (so he boasted) struck down the haughty Bourbon; when Michelangelo, the most Platonic of mystical lovers and sonneteers, dreamer of statues as he contemplated the huge, inert masses of stone, could rear the material dome of St. Peters; when Leonardo da Vinci turned from his mysterious portraits of holy women to attract around him a group of scurvy rogues and move them with his jests to ribald laughter that he might watch their gross lineaments cunningly, when he turned further to his pioneering in the realms of mechanics, hydraulics, military and civil engineering; when Sidney was at once outrider for English novelists and international diplomat, sonneteer, knight-errant, and soldier; when Spenser was, as we have already seen, pastoralist and shrewd critic of university, church, and state, planning as inseparable parts of the same noble life-work a useful, brilliant career as a statesman and a vast epic of unfathomable national faith.

As we first approached Spenser the pastoralist we glanced at the renaissance through the prose threnody that Carducci wrote for his fatherland. Let us once more widen our vision, this time with a memorable passage from Professor Mackail's essay on Spenser.

Throughout the whole sphere of life, in its crimes and virtues, in its attempts and achievements, that age was possessed by a spirit of excess, an intoxication of greatness. It set itself deliberately to outdo all that had hitherto been done. It built and voyaged and discovered and conquered colossally. In our own National Gallery, where it is one of the splendours of the great Venetian Room, is a portrait by the Brescian painter Moretto, of Count Martinengo-Cesaresco, killed young in the French wars of religion. He is richly dressed in silk and furs, a gilded sword-hilt showing from under the heavy cloak. On a table by him are an antique lamp and some coins. His elbow rests on a pile of silken cushions, and his head leans, with a sort of intensity of languor, on his open palm. The face is that of one in the full prime of life and of great physical strength; very handsome, heavy and yet tremulously sensitive, the large eyes gazing at something unseen, and seeming to dream of vastness. On his bonnet is a golden plaque, with three words of Greek inscribed on it, ιοὺ λίαν τοθῶ ''Oh, I desire too much.'' Who the Giulia was whom he desired is among the things that have gone to oblivion; but the longing which the portrait has immortalized is not for one woman, were she like Beatrice or Helen, but for the whole world. These ambiguous words are a cloudy symbol; and that picture is a portrait of the Renaissance.

In such an age of excess, but with a certain Anglo-Saxon sobriety, Spenser set himself, as he told Harvey, to "overgo" Ariosto, that is, even the Italian renaissance itself, and indeed Tasso and Virgil and Homer as well.[2] How was this to be done? How was the universally praised "new poete" to write a new epic? All the masters of heroic verse had aggrandized some great action in their country's past. Spenser, like all singers of the renaissance, was aglow with visions of the past. But while Ariosto, amid the sufferings of Italy the "Iphigeneia" of modern Europe, could do little more than yield to the mere intoxication of chivalry and romance, Spenser did not forget that high seriousness which is the charge of the Muse of epic poetry. To the staid Augustan of the eighteenth century Spenser seemed a great poet debauched by Ariosto. To many romanticists Spenser is too sober. They luxuriate over him with desultory, hedonistic indolence but they turn with greater admiration to the enchanting smile of Ariosto. The smile of Ariosto is as mysterious as that of Mona Lisa. But while Leonardo caught for us forever that strange, eternal smile of secret wisdom, the smile of Ariosto eludes us. Now it steals in barely perceptible after the clarion-call of chivalry. *O gran bontà de' cavallieri antiqui!* Great is chivalry—but a child's dream. The smile is gay and sad. The poet is trying to heal the sick world with visions of a splendid past, but he more than half doubts that past. Again comes the joyous smile of a child who gives his fancy free rein and builds the castle of his own truth, so airy, so fragile! The singer tosses his fragile dreams about like light iridescent balls. Then, in a flash, as we pore owl-faced over the wild tale, fascinated by the marvel of it and spell-

---

[2] See Harvey's letter in *Works* (ed. Grosart, Huth Library, 1884), I, 94–96.

bound by the vividness of it, we are caught by the smile of mockery at our own credulity. Then the poet's lips curl with the cynic's smile. Most winning of all is Ariosto's serene smile through his tears. He turns from his page to look at the world; he peers from his refuge and sees Italy but a herding-ground of Goth and Frank. His anger lightens from his eyes; his lips murmur bitter things inaudible; but he turns again to his dream, his art. Here, at least, says he with a smile still sad, is peace. But in Spenser the intoxication of the renaissance was blended with that sturdy Anglo-Saxonism which glowed alike in the ferocity and generosity and loyalty of Beowulf and in the gloomy and fanatical but sublime faith of Cromwell's Ironsides. How was the "new poete" to "overgo" the classical makers who exalted a narrow but stately past and Ariosto, that Mr. Worldly Wiseman of poetry who played with a gorgeous but largely fantastic past? To Spenser came a vision so audacious that even his warmest admirers have not yet comprehended it: a vision to write an epic which would *make* history through the great light of a cloudy allegory fairly incandescent with prophetic convictions, an epic not of the past but of the future. England was threatened by foes as widespread and sinister as those who rioted through Italy. But Spenser had an Anglo-Saxon faith in his queen.

To The Most High
Mighty And Magnificent Empresse
Renowmed For Pietie, Vertue,
And All Gratious Government
ELIZABETH
By The Grace Of God Queene Of
England Fraunce And Ireland
And Of Virginia,
Defendour Of The Faith, &C.
Her Most Humble Servaunt
EDMUND SPENSER
Doth In All Humilitie
Dedicate, Present And Consecrate
These His Labours
To Live With The Eternitie
Of Her Fame.

She was his heroine, his Faërie Queene, Gloriana, glory incarnate. Splendid but outrageous flattery, say the text-book men. On the contrary Spenser was a shrewd and bold critic of Elizabeth, as *The Shepheards Calender* has already shown us, as his other works will show even more vividly. We must needs, then, believe that, in one who could criticize so acutely and fearlessly, an admiration so lofty as that shown in the dedication was pure, sincere faith. Professor Greenlaw has been one of the first to see the thing steadily and see it whole.

> Taken as a whole, these writings of Spenser's present an interpretation of Elizabethan political idealism without parallel elsewhere. To regard him as a "functionary" of Leicester, of Essex, or of any other man, or to regard him as a morose and disappointed applicant for the favors of the great, is wholly unjust. Those who find in him the master of a sweetly flowing verse that has made him the "Warwick of poets" shall have their reward. But he was more than this. Dreamer of dreams, Galahad of the quest for Beauty, he was also of good right a member of that little group of men who saw beyond the welter of court intrigue and petty politics the glorious vision of an imperial England. He had his limitations, it is true; at first sight he seems to fail to realize the idea of the nation in the larger sense; one does not find in him the passionate love of native land that quivers through the lines attributed by Shakespere to the dying John of Gaunt. His loyalty is personal; he conceives the State as Machiavelli conceived it; to him the Prince is the State. Yet on the whole, the two great poets who were the glory of Elizabethan England are of one accord. The splendid lines of Faulconbridge defying a conqueror to set foot on British soil breathe the spirit that animates all Spenser's work, and the England of Gaunt's adoration was to the poet of allegory his sovereign lady queen.[3]

I shall have occasion to show later that Spenser had a larger loyalty to his country than Professor Greenlaw readily allows. But it is enough here to emphasize nothing more than Spenser's warm loyalty to Elizabeth, purified as it was by his courageous public recognition of her faults. To Spenser it was enough to be the queen's unbowing, clear-eyed, but reverent thurifer and

---

[3] "Spenser and British Imperialism," *Modern Philology* (1912), IX, 370. See also Dr. Grosart's edition, I, 168–171, for a characteristic, exaggerated, but spirited, loyal defense of Elizabeth and of Spenser's admiration well worth pondering in these days when it is conventional to jeer at the great queen.

from his golden swinging censer would steal transporting mists and odors.

Just here we may confront Mr. Yeats with his own beautiful description of allegory and symbolism, "a natural language by which the soul when entranced ... communes with God and with angels" and speaks "of things which cannot be spoken of in any other language." If Mr. Yeats had understood that Spenser, despite many incidental allusions to past events, was creating what was essentially a new epic type, an heroic poem whose main themes set forth the great national achievements of the future, he would not have denied to Spenser allegory, the tongue which "Dante used ... to describe visionary things." Spenser himself gives us the *clou* in his characteristic Parthian way, in his letter to Raleigh. "The general end" of this "darke conceit" is "to fashion a gentleman or noble person in vertuous and gentle discipline." Since this was to be made "plausible and pleasing" by "being coloured with an historicall fiction" the poet chose for his hero the name of Arthur, a name to conjure with in all centuries in England. But Arthur was not to be the Arthur of the known legends. He was to be the accepted lover of Gloriana, the Faërie Queene. "In that Faery Queene I meane glory in my generall intention, but in my particular I conceive the most excellent and glorious person of our soveraine the Queene, and her kingdome in Faery Land." Who then was Arthur? He was "magnificence," says the poet. That is, he symbolized the moral quality praised by Aristotle and his followers that we may best understand today by blending the modern meanings of magnanimity and magnificence.[4] But who was Arthur? What was the political allegory? We turn to the poet; but he has made a Parthian retreat. He had expressly declared a double allegory for the whole poem, but it remains only partly explained. Since the days of Upton's edition of

---

[4] M. Jusserand points out that Spenser's virtues were not, as the poet asserted, drawn entirely and consistently from Aristotle but from Piccolomini and other "moderns." See *Modern Philology*, III, 373–383, "Spenser's 'Twelve Private Morall Vertues As Aristotle Hath Devised.'"

The Faërie Queene, however, many have accepted the suggestion
that Arthur was Leicester, the sinister but brilliant patron of
the poet, the reputed champion of Puritanism, the favorite of
the queen, a lord who, for all the dark stories that still cling about
his name, might easily be worshipped by a poet who could by
training and conviction hold with him fervently in so many
of his professed ideals. No wonder the poet put forward his
suggestion of the marriage of Gloriana and Arthur, audacious,
for all the encouragement of thronging rumors, with Parthian
reticence. No wonder his prefatory sonnets again and again
implore the various lords at the court to protect his vaguely
interpreted but boldly insinuating poem against misreading and
calumny. "If I finde ['these first twelve bookes'] to be well
accepted, I may be perhaps encouraged to frame the other
part of polliticke vertues in his person, after that hee came to
be king." In the full ecstasy of his faith, then, the poet dreamed
of writing an *Odyssey* to his *Iliad.* He was to make history for
Elizabeth and Leicester in his first twelve books. He was, if
these books were "well accepted," and if Gloriana and Arthur
were married, to write an epic sequel celebrating the deeds of
Leicester as king-consort or, perhaps, boldly prophesying for
Leicester and Elizabeth the ways that they should follow to be
illustrious. A new epic type that turns from the old mode of
remembering and exalting the past to foreshadowing the
future! Could we accept my theory would it not be a final
and triumphant justification of Spenser's "darke conceit,"
his moral and political allegory? Would it not reveal depths
in *The Faërie Queene* sufficient to allure even the most casual
readers? To be sure he tells in his letter to Raleigh of "Xeno-
phon preferred before Plato, for that the one, in the exquisite
depth of his judgement, formed a commune welth such as it
should be, but the other in the person of Cyrus and the Per-
sians fashioned a governement, such as might best be: so much
more profitable and gratious is doctrine by ensample, then by
rule." But this does not mean that in order to be concrete one

must dwell with the past. It means merely that narrative seemed better to the poet than philosophy for all its divinity. And Spenser's Utopia was to him so near that nothing could be more concrete, dared he utter himself to the full. In Chaucer the "new poete" had learned of England how

> In th' olde dayes of the king Arthour,
> Of which that Britons speken great honour,
> Al was this land fulfild of fayerye.
> The elf-queen, with hir joly companye,
> Daunced ful ofte in many a grene mede;
> This was the olde opinion, as I rede.
> I speke of manye hundred yeres ago;
> But now can no man see none elves mo.[5]

Chaucer, in one of his rare wistful turnings from the parti-colored life of his time, was dreaming of a golden age long gone. In a trice he would return to everyday with a sly hit at the "holy freres" who had driven such glamoury away. So, too, Spenser had at times recalled wistfully Arcadia, a pastoral golden age. But we may well imagine young Spenser, in the days after Elizabeth had put out the baleful fires of religious persecution kindled by Mary at Smithfield near his home, dwelling delightedly over these opening lines of the "Wife of Bath's Tale" and seldom caring to read on. For, as the confidence and love of all merry England welled toward the new queen, it must have seemed to Chaucer's young follower that these fairies (not the tiny creatures of folk-lore as Hughes stupidly suggested) had returned as English men and women. And would not Arthur return as the Celtic bards had dreamed? Would he not return in a year, tomorrow, to a country so splendid with promise to "a noble and puissant nation rousing herself like a strong man after sleep, and shaking her invincible locks . . . like an eagle muing her mighty youth, and kindling her undazzled eyes at the full midday beam?" What false tradition had married Arthur to Guenever? Surely he was destined for Gloriana. And when the poet came under the spell of Leicester

---

[5] See Dr. Howard Maynadier's suggestions in *The Arthur of the English Poets* (Boston and New York, 1907), 262 sq.

what more natural than to dream of him as Arthur reincarnate?
Stories of a projected marriage of Elizabeth and Leicester
swarmed thick ''as motes in the sonne-beem.'' What poet in
the days of Elizabeth could plan an epic on the past when the
present was so much greater and when the imminent future was
rushing in with chariot-speed to transcend all? Mr. Yeats and
innumerable other critics do Spenser great wrong in describing
him as ''by nature altogether a man of that old Catholic feudal
nation'' rearing sadly in *The Faërie Queene* a mausoleum for
the old irrecoverable age of chivalry. One of Mr. Yeats' best
critics, Mr. John Bailey, objects to good purpose against this
conception of our poet as a mere ''dreamer of dreams born out
of his due time.''

Spenser knew better. He was too wise to deny himself the great pos-
sibilities opened out to him by the new learning. He could look back
wistfully on the heroic side of feudalism, and keep it alive, so far as
might be, in his great poem; he could cling longingly to the old language
that was passing away; but the old ignorance, the old childishness, had no
friend in him. He rejoiced through all his being in the ordered splendours
of the new art. In his delighted hands they attained at once to all but
their highest height.[6]

England, then, was Faërie Land becoming rapidly a Utopia far
more wonderful than that described by More in the first dawn
with such lofty desire, but with such sly qualifications. Spenser
would write history before it was made in fact. This is the
secret of Spenser's immense and cloudy scheme with its superb
arrogation of omniscience.

It is not surprising that a poem outlined on such a mighty
scheme should prove imperfect in structure since Spenser, like
all true Elizabethans, attempted the superhuman. Nowadays we
are careful not to rear those Babels of song. But I am not sure
that our gain in poise is a gain in positive self-knowledge; and
I am certain that something has failed the modern artist which

---

[6] The strongest presentation of Spenser as ''the poet of a dying race''
is to be found in George Edward Woodberry, *The Torch* (New York,
1905), 115 sq. Mr. Woodberry does well to stress the importance of
the past for *The Faërie Queene* but, like Mr. Yeats, he overemphasizes it.

must be recaptured if he would reach the highest rank. It is better to have failed with Spenser than to achieve a finished work with, let us say, even such a perfect artist as Rossetti. However, it will take a hardy eulogist to assert that Spenser did not fail definitely as far as structure is concerned.

Dryden was the first to make a sure and detailed criticism of the structure of *The Faërie Queene.*

There is no uniformity in the design of Spenser: he aims at the accomplishment of no one action; he raises up a hero for every one of his adventures; and endows each of them with some particular moral virtue, which renders them all equal, without subordination, or preference. Every one is most valiant in his own legend: only we must do him that justice to observe, that magnanimity, which is the character of Prince Arthur, shines throughout the whole poem; and succours the rest, when they are in distress. The original of every knight was then living in the court of Queen Elizabeth; and he attributed to each of them that virtue which he thought most conspicuous in them; an ingenious piece of flattery, though it turned not much to his account. Had he lived to finish the poem, in the six remaining legends, it had certainly been more of a piece; but could not have been perfect, because the model was not true. But Prince Arthur, or his chief patron, Sir Philip Sidney, whom he intended to make happy by the marriage of his Gloriana, dying before him, deprived the poet both of the means and spirit to accomplish his design.[7]

It is a significant evidence of Dryden's genius as a critic that he was the first and last writer to note the most subtle cause of Spenser's failure. While the most obvious cause was undoubtedly the magnitude of the scheme, a magnitude so stupendous that no one but a supreme poet could have even conceived it, yet the fact that Spenser's hero (Leicester, not Sidney) died, probably before Spenser had completed his third book, must have been to a hero-worshipper so sincere, the most deadly of destructive influences. The third book shows many signs of confusion. The fourth book is chaos. The fifth book, as an isolated poem, is better, but its strands are not well woven into the poem as a whole. The sixth book is almost completely disjointed and closes with a bitter anticlimax.

---

[7] *A Discourse concerning the Original and Progress of Satire* (1693). *Essays of John Dryden* (ed. Ker, Oxford, 1900), p. 28.

John Hughes, a typical eighteenth century classicist and a great lover of Spenser, followed Dryden's attack on the unity of *The Faërie Queene* with even greater severity.

> The several Books appear rather like so many several Poems, than one entire Fable: Each of them has its peculiar Knight, and is independent of the rest; and tho some of the Persons make their Appearance in different Books, yet this has very little Effect in connecting them. Prince *Arthur* is indeed the principal Person, and has therefore a share given him in every Legend; but his Part is not considerable enough in any one of them: He appears and vanishes again like a Spirit; and we lose sight of him too soon, to consider him as the Hero of the Poem.

But Hughes suggested, somewhat diffidently, a mode of defense that had a long life.

> But as it is plain the Author never designed it by those Rules, I think it ought to be consider'd as a Poem of a particular kind, describing in a series of Allegorical Adventures or Episodes, the most noted Virtues and Vices: to compare it therefore with the Models of Antiquity, would be like drawing a Parallel between the *Roman* and the *Gothick* Architecture. In the first there is, doubtless, a more natural Grandeur and Simplicity: in the latter, we find great Mixtures of Beauty and Barbarism, yet assisted by the Invention of a Variety of inferior Ornaments; and tho the former is more majestick in the whole, the latter may be very surprising and agreeable in its Parts.[8]

It will be observed that this is not a defense of its unity, but rather a mildly sympathetic explanation of its romantic lack of organization. Thomas Warton, the greatest critic of Spenser in the eighteenth century, had practically nothing new to say on this matter.[9] It remained for the first important romantic critic of Spenser, Bishop Hurd, to carry the war into the camp of the enemy.

Meanwhile John Upton strove zealously but somewhat speciously to defend the unity of *The Faërie Queene* on purely classical grounds. "How readily," he cries, "has every one acquiesced in Dryden's opinion? *That the action of this Poem is not one.*"[10] Critics, we are told, attacked Homer once in the

---

[8] *The Works of Spenser* (London, 1715), I, xliii–xliv.

[9] *Observations on the Faërie Queene.* See Chapter VII of this book for a detailed analysis of Warton.

[10] *Spenser's Faërie Queene* (London, 1758), I, xx sq.

same way.   Spenser's action centers around Arthur as Homer's around Achilles. "Nor can it be fairly objected to the unity of the Iliad, that when Achilles is removed from the scene of action, you scarcely hear him mentioned in several books." Agamemnon, Diomed, Hector, become the heroes of successive books.

For his extensive plan required his different heroes to be shown in their different characters and attitudes. What therefore you allow to the old Grecian, be not so ungracious as to deny your own countryman.

Again 'tis observable that Homer's poem, though he sings the anger of Achilles, is not called the Achilleid, but the Iliad; because the action was at Troy. So Spenser does not call his poem by the name of his chief hero; but because his chief hero sought for the Fairy Queen in Fairy Land, and therein performed his various adventures, therefore he entitled his poem The Fairy Queen.

Homer's device of keeping Achilles away from the field until he outshines all is compared with the purposed holding-off of Arthur till the end where he was to accomplish all that the other knights had failed to do.

Upton's unique attempt in so stoutly maintaining Spenser's absolute agreement with Homer was, of course, doomed to failure. It was not until Hurd worked out the suggestion of Hughes with romantic bravado that there began a mode of defense destined to at least a capricious permanence. His remarks on the "Plan and Conduct" of *The Faërie Queene* open with a fine romantic swagger.

Spenser, though he had long been nourished with the spirit and substance of Homer and Virgil, chose the times of Chivalry for his theme, and Fairy Land for the scene of his fictions. He could have planned, no doubt, an heroick design on the exact classic model: or, he might have trimmed between the *Gothic* and the classic, as his contemporary Tasso did. But the charms of *fairy* prevailed. And if any think he was seduced by Ariosto into his choice, they should consider that it could be only for the sake of his subject; for the genius and character of these poets was widely different.

Under this idea then of a *Gothic*, not classical, Poem, the *Fairy Queen* is to be read and criticized. And on these principles, it would not be difficult to unfold its merit in another way than has been hitherto attempted.

Hurd draws the usual parallel between classical and Gothic architecture, which had some vogue since Hughes ventured upon it as throwing some light on Spenser, and adds:

> The question is not, which of the two is conducted in the simplest and the truest taste: but whether there be not sense and design in both, when scrutinized by the laws on which each is projected. . . . It was as requisite for the *Fairy Queen* to consist of the adventures of twelve Knights, as for the *Odyssey* to be confined to the adventures of one Hero: justice had otherwise not been done to his subject.
>
> If you ask then, what is this *Unity* of Spenser's Poem? I say, it consists in the relation of its several adventures to one common *original*, the appointment of the *Fairy Queen;* and to one common *end*, the completion of the *Fairy Queen's* injunctions.

This is not urged as classical unity, but unity of another sort. Hurd thinks that the introduction of Arthur was a mere afterthought, an expedient from classical models which narrated only one action. "The truth was, the violence of classic prejudices forced the poet to affect this appearance of unity, though in contradiction to his *Gothic* system." Spenser, according to Hurd, never should have attempted to ally the Gothic and the classical unities. The critic turns to an entirely different defense based on a new attitude towards its allegorical character, an attitude at first coldly explanatory which later develops into that hostility towards the "darke conceit" that has warped most later appreciations

> His twelve knights are to exemplify as many virtues, out of which one illustrious character is to be composed. And in this view the part of Prince Arthur in each book becomes *essential*, not *principal;* exactly, as the poet has contrived it.

Hurd thinks the objection to Prince Arthur and the unity of the poem is unanswerable on any other grounds.

> But how faulty soever this conduct be in the literal story, it is perfectly right in the *moral:* and that for an obvious reason, though his critics seem not to have been aware of it. His chief hero was not to have the twelve virtues in the *degree* in which the knights had each of them their own (such a character would be a monster;) but he was to have as much of each as were requisite to form his superior character. Each virtue, in its

perfection, is exemplified in its own knight; they are all, in a due degree, concentered on Prince Arthur.

The conclusion is, that, as an *allegorical poem* the method of the *Fairy Queen* is governed by the justness of the *moral: as a narrative poem*, it is conducted on the ideas and usages of *Chivalry.* In either view, if taken by itself, the plan is defensible. But from the union of the two designs there arises a perplexity, and confusion, which is the proper, and only considerable, defect of this extraordinary poem.

It is unfortunate that Hurd felt constrained to go further and to point the way to the complete repudiation of the allegory for a long line of brilliant romantic essays including even those of Lowell and Yeats. On the better side, it is not too far afield to trace this same current, not without a marked flow of independent thinking, in a recent gallant defense by an American critic. Professor Trent, which is truly suggestive and points in an important direction.

Some critics, ... especially those who rely on formulas, are disposed to question Spenser's high rank as an artist, particularly on account of the lack of unity they discover in "The Faerie Queene." Unity is a very indefinite word, and formulas are often misleading. There is probably little unity of action in the poem, save such as is really factitious; and such unity of substance and motive as it seems to possess might not stand the test of a searching analysis. We may admit that in order to be a great work of sustained art a poem must exhibit some sort of unity, but to demand of a product of the Renaissance the kind of unity we find in the masterpieces of classical times seems to be a procedure that is both unnecessary and unfair. Why is it that we ask for unity? It is not for the sake of certain feeling of satisfaction it produces in us? If so, and if "The Faërie Queene" leaves upon some readers no sense of dissatisfaction, is it not rational to believe that it possesses unity of some sort for those readers? What sort of unity can that be? Surely a unity of tone, of atmosphere, pervades it and renders it a harmonious whole to those who love it; and since we are the wealthier in proportion as our sources of enjoyment increase, it seems wise to stretch our critical formulas until they allow us to include "The Faerie Queene" among the world's great poems.[11]

Professor Trent does well to call upon us for a severe revision of our canons of unity. No one should deny the absolute im-

---

[11] Introduction to an edition of Spenser (N. Y., Crowell, 1903). Reprinted in *Longfellow and Other Essays* (N. Y., 1910).

portance of unity. But we are very slow to realize the unifying
principles of a new work of art just as we are very slow to
recognize a strongly individualistic poem as belonging to an
old and imperishable *genre*. It is of the first importance to
remember not only the grandeur of Spenser's scheme but also
to remember that, although its unifying strands were astonish-
ingly new, they were not necessarily impossible of fulfilment.
If the letter to Raleigh had survived without a single stanza
of *The Faërie Queene* it is probable that most critics would have
accepted its scheme for unity as fairly plausible. It is Spenser's
failure that has lead the critics to go too far and repudiate the
scheme itself, a scheme, which, to be sure, required a poet far
greater than any who had yet lived but which, for a child of the
English renaissance bent on "overgoing" all predecessors with
perhaps the most exalting conviction that ever flamed out in an
epic poet, is understandable. But while I maintain the scheme
to have been as plausible as it was audacious I find myself, after
a survey of all the critics of the unity of *The Faërie Queene*,
always returning to Dryden's remark on the death of Spenser's
hero. Reality refused to pour itself into Spenser's mighty
mould for an epic of the future. The break-up of the vast struc-
ture of the poem itself, the increase of the casual and the
episodical, the inflow of chaos, the cry of despair in the last
stanzas of the sixth book were inevitable.

Just here we may consider the charge of tediousness so fre-
quently brought against *The Faërie Queene*. Many suppose this
due to the allegory. But, as we have seen, a refusal to accept
the allegory means that the reader must deny himself an appre-
ciation of qualities that make the poem intensely human in its
great convictions and dramatic disillusion. To condemn the
imperfections of structure without a profound admiration for
the daring of the design is to engender a false sense of tedious-
ness. Readers who uncritically abuse both allegory and struc-
ture are left with little more than Spenser's pictorial luxuriance
and sensuous music, two gifts of great richness yet cloying when

isolated from their essential concomitants. Professor Dodge has, more acutely than any other critic I recall, laid his finger on the only tenable cause for complaint of this kind.

> This peculiarity of organization...is hardly the cause that so many have found the *Fairy Queen* tedious. They might complain, rather, that the poem is not grounded in action, that in those simple human energies which alone could sustain an epic or a romance at such length it is sadly wanting. And they would complain with some reason. Spenser's knights pass from chivalric feat to chivalric feat with due enterprise, but the eye of their creator is less often upon the doing than the deed. Scene follows scene in the narrative, less often an encounter of active forces than a picture of spiritual conditions. Spenser, indeed, had not that delight in the realities of living action, that native sense for the situations that lurk in the conflict of living energies, which were the gift of the poet he particularly emulated. The combats of his knights, for example, how often they seem to be repetitions of a set ceremony! To Ariosto each combat is a new and quite peculiar act of life; it is the outbreak of forces that meet in a fresh combination or under fresh conditions; simple or intricate, it has a spirit and growth of its own. That unending recurrence of encounters, therefore, which is the special infirmity of romance, becomes in his poem a manifestation of exuberant vitality. In the *Faery Queen*, on the other hand, spirited as some few of the combats are, particularly those in the second book, one recognizes only too clearly that Spenser's heart is not in this eager work. Nor is it in that active conflict of will with will, of purpose with circumstance, which is the life of the poetry of action. Even in those scenes which are most truly dynamic, not merely picturesque or expository, scenes like the meeting of the Red Cross Knight with Despair, the action, the power, is mainly embodied in one personage; there is little interplay of forces. For situations his sense is at times curiously fallible; as when Britomart at the close of her combat with Arthegall, and during and after the negotiations for truce, is left standing, like an image, with her sword uplifted to strike.

After passing on to a suggestive (but not sufficiently uncompromising) defense of the allegory, Professor Dodge concludes irrefutably: "Surely, had the *Faery Queen* been pure romance, it would have been a much less exquisite creation.[12] Then he goes on:

> For, in fine, the world of the *Faery Queen* is not altogether the world of romance; it is, if possible, more remote, more strange, more diverse.

---

[12] One should not forget, in this connection, Mr. Woodberry's praise of Spenser's general allegory and its universality. See *The Torch*, pp. 121 sq.

By its forest fountains meet Venus and Diana, almost within the ken of Christian knights and ladies, and in its castles or upon its open hillsides and heaths, among gentry and retainers and shepherds and very rabble, side by side with giants and monsters, move sheer incarnations of the immaterial. It is a world of jarring elements gathered from antiquity and the Middle Ages and the Renaissance, and harmonized by the serenest of poetic imaginations. In such a world as this, if we can breathe its atmosphere, we shall not crave the vigor and sparkle of movement that are at such full tide in the *Orlando Furioso*, nor even the graver human energies of the great epics: it has a life to which these are not essential. For, externally a poem of action, meant to rival Ariosto's, the *Faery Queen* is at heart but the vision of a contemplative mind to which the main realities of life are beauty and the law of the spirit. If it quickens at rare intervals into action full and vigorous, the quickening is but for a moment, and when it subsides we are not regretful. Faint in passion, faint even in pathos, the poem appeals most intimately to that "inward eye" which can read forms and hues of beauty, and feature and bearing as they reveal the spirit, and to the mind that can read the spirit in speech. And this world that Spenser has created can never be to us a mere Kubla Khan paradise of romance. Amid its throng of ideal creatures, though we may not feel the force of the express moral doctrine they enact, we shall feel the force of the poet's own bent. His temper of grave and sweet spirituality, always human, that tone of the mind which is ever the chief spring of moral influence, this will be unescapable, and, in the end, it will be as much as the pure magic of his imagination that will seem to impart to the poem its peculiar and imperturbable atmosphere.

I must, however, take exception to two points. *The Faërie Queene* is neither passionless nor essentially serene. It is not so passionate over "fierce warres and faithfull loves" (though over even these it is more passionate than Professor Dodge allows us to believe) as it is passionate over its empire-building, its nation-worship. In our days of intense subjectivity, before the dread month of August, 1914, it was hard to understand that the triumph of a nation and the fall of a nation can draw from great souls an outcry as passionate as Romeo's at the sight of Juliet. Herein lies the reason why Taine thought falsely that De Musset, who sang of the grisette and of his own aberrations, was more passionate than Tennyson, who suffered agony over the mystery and the fall of civilizations such as that symbolized by Arthur's realm. That Spenser is not essentially serene can be shown clearly as we follow the growth of the great disillusion that bursts its floodgates at the close of *The Faërie Queene*. I shall attempt to show, however, that he ultimately conquered himself and was, at the last, in his swan-songs, divinely serene. But it is ungracious to linger over differences with a critic who has brought us within sight of a truth of the utmost importance for the appreciation of Spenser and most momentous for modern literature. After Professor Dodge had rightly hit upon Spenser's indifference to action as the only reasonable cause for the complaint of tediousness, after he had gone on most happily to justify even Spenser's indifference to action, I marvel that he did not take a third step and point out how in this very subordination of *simple* action Spenser points out the way for the modern epic. As we contemplate the growth of the modern novel and as we grope towards international peace we are inclined to think regretfully of the epic as a dead *genre*. But the epic is too mighty and perfect a form, in its ability to enclose within itself the ideals of a nation and the wisdom of an epoch and a courage that includes mere swordplay as but an incident or an ephemeral mode, to give way to a new *genre*. Only, as wars grow dim, as contemplation takes its proper place in relation to doing, action of such an elementary order as that of war must grow less absorbing. It is interesting to note how the poets of *Paradise Lost* and *The Idylls of the King* followed Spenser in this. Of the three poets Milton, the greatest, alone definitely flings down the gage in his master-epic where he declares himself

> Not sedulous by nature to indite
> Wars, hitherto the only argument
> Heroic deemed, chief maistrie to dissect
> With long and tedious havoc fabled knights,
> In battles feigned (the better fortitude
> Of patience and heroic martyrdom unsung).

But the interesting paradox of the decline of war in the English Epic I hope to develop in detail more properly in another book For our purposes it is of importance only to note that in precisely this respect Spenser may be held to be greater than Ariosto

however the Italian poet may have outdistanced the Elizabethan
in other matters. Ariosto felt that elementary action must dom-
inate in the epic. So, in an age that dreamed of greater things,
he played half cynically with an infinitely varied, a vivid, but
an unreal chivalric and martial life. In this same age Spenser,
less disturbed by the futile turbulence of invaders, apprehended
vaguely a more forward-looking way of writing epic with a full
recognition of the growing importance of the life of contempla-
tion to modernity. And if Spenser went too far and subordi-
nated *all* action, he at least blazed the trail for the epic that
must come with the vision of Janus and sing of those heroic
actions which William James sketches in his "Moral Equivalent
of War."[13]

There remains but one more point to consider as we approach
The Faërie Queene: Spenser's stanza and its incomparable
music. "One of the best tests in the world of what a poet really
means," says Mr. Chesterton, "is his metre. He may be a hypo-
crite in his metaphysics, but he cannot be a hypocrite in his
prosody." Spenser's stanza, also, has been attacked as tedious.
To those who consider it wedded as it is to Spenser's great con-
victions it can never be tedious. Nor do I believe that it could
be tedious even to the upholders of art for art's sake if they felt
to the full its infinite richness. As we consider the form let us
fill our ears with its music.

> Into the inmost temple thus I came,
> Which fuming all with frankensence I found,
> And odours rising from the altars flame.
> Upon an hundred marble pillors round
> The roofe up high was reared from the ground,
> All deckt with crownes, and chaynes, and girlands gay,
> And thousand pretious gifts worth many a pound,
> The which sad lovers for their vowes did pay;
> And all the ground was strow'd with flowres, as fresh as May.

Some overtrained modern readers will object to what they con-
sider the banality of the seventh line. Some lovers of Spenser

---

[13] Mr. Woodberry is the only critic of Spenser that I know who has
even approached this momentous point which ought to have been obvious
centuries ago. He hints at it in *The Torch,* p. 131.

will wish that I had chosen another stanza with a more obvious music. So I will recall some enchanting echoes familiar to the most cursory reader of *The Faërie Queene.*

> And more, to lulle him in his slumber soft,
> A trickling streame from high rock tumbling downe,
> And ever drizling raine upon the loft,
> Mixt with a murmuring winde, much like the sowne
> Of swarming bees, did cast him in a swowne:
> No other noyse, nor peoples troublous cryes,
> As still are wont t' annoy the walled towne,
> Might there be heard: but carelesse Quiet lyes,
> Wrapt in eternall silence farre from enimyes.

Last I will quote the rhetorical but justly famous stanza on the dragon's fall that inspired Milton's vision of the awful encounter between Satan and St. Michael.

> So downe he fell, and forth his life did breath,
> That vanisht into smoke and cloudes swift;
> So downe he fell, that th' earth him underneath
> Did grone as feeble so great load to lift;
> So downe he fell, as an huge rocky clift,
> Whose false foundacion waves have washt away,
> With dreadfull poyse is from the mayneland rift,
> And, rolling downe, great Neptune doth dismay;
> So downe he fell, and like an heaped mountaine lay.

How anybody who ever read three such examples of the stanza —and these give but little conception of its range in *The Faërie Queene*—could pronounce the form tedious I am at a loss to understand. Among the throngs of good things that Professor Saintsbury has said about Spenser there is none better than his retort to the milder charge of monotony often brought against the Spenserian stanza: "As for monotony, it is just as monotonous as flowing water." Saintsbury's impetuous idiom reminds us of James Thomson's somewhat artificial but none the less lovely phrasing in *The Seasons* when he remembers

> The gentle Spenser, Fancy's pleasing son,
> Who, like a copious river, pour'd his song
> O'er all the mazes of enchanted ground.

Yet the charge of tediousness or monotony along with other objections have been brought against the Spenserian stanza for centuries. And, although English criticism reveals a long line of admiring comments it was not until the second half of the eighteenth century that the stanza was eulogized in any significant detail. It is strange that it remained for Beattie, the gentle poetaster who was once lionized for his *Minstrel,* to write the first elaborate and thoroughly appreciative comments. A letter to Dr. Blacklock (September 22, 1766) reveals the placid Beattie in the process of composition.

Not long ago I began a poem in the style and stanza of Spenser, in which I propose to give full scope to my inclination, and to be either droll or pathetic, descriptive or sentimental, tender or satirical, as the humour strikes me; for, if I mistake not, the manner which I have adopted admits equally of all these kinds of composition. I have written one hundred and fifty lines, and am surprised to find the structure of that complicated stanza so little troublesome. I was always fond of it for I think it the most harmonious that ever was contrived. It admits of more variety of pauses than either the couplet or the alternate rhyme; and it concludes with a pomp and majesty of sound, which, to my ear, is wonderfully delightful. It seems also very well adapted to the genius of our language, which, from its irregularity of inflexion and number of monosyllables, abounds in diversified terminations, and consequently renders our poetry susceptible of an endless variety of legitimate rhymes.

Of special significance is Beattie's point that the English language is infinitely rich for the stanza. To be sure Spenser took many odd liberties with structure and spelling. And there are always some to accuse him of having been too free with his archaisms. His vandalisms on orthography and grammar are, at worst, venial sins. His archaisms have bred a long and living controversy. In the seventeenth century Sir William Davenant said crassly that "the unlucky choice of his stanza hath by repetition of Rime brought him to the necessity of many exploded words."[14] Shrewd old Thomas Fuller was at the other extreme, but nearer the truth when he observed that "though some blame [Spenser's] ... Writings for the many Chaucerisms used by him yet to the learned they are known not to be blem-

---

[14] See Chapter VII for a more detailed account of Davenant.

ishes, but rather beauties to his Book.'' It is hardly too para-
doxical to say that Spenser has been condemned by modern
readers in some of the very words which he rescued from
oblivion. Yet the old language does cause some obscurities that
would have probably puzzled Spenser himself, and many obscur-
ities that drive away the faint-hearted modern who would run
and read. This is the only serious charge against the archaisms
and it should never be filed except in the graceful and gracious
words of Campbell who says of Spenser's language that ''it is
beautiful in its antiquity, and like the moss and ivy on some
majestic building, covers the fabric of his language with roman-
tic and venerable associations.'' We must go back to Dryden
(as all critics are bound to do very frequently) to find the last
words on the subject.

[Milton's] antiquated words were his choise, not his necessity; for
therein he imitated Spenser as Spenser imitated Chaucer. And though,
perhaps, the love of their master may have transported both too far,
in the frequent use of them; yet, in my opinion words may then be laud-
ably revived, when either they are more sounding, or more significant, than
those in practice; and, when their obscurity is taken away, by joining
other words to them which clear the sense; according to the rule of Horace,
for the admission of new words. But in both cases a moderation is to be
observed in the use of them. For unnecessary coinage, as well as unneces-
sary revival runs into affectation; a fault to be avoided on either hand.

Spenser and Beattie may be further vindicated against Davenant
and his crew by a characteristic passage from the swaggering
and irrepressible ''Christopher North,'' who has been too soon
forgotten for his sins.

The only proof of the pudding is the eating of it. The Faery Queen
proves that in choosing, that in inventing his stanza, Spenser did sufficiently
consult the genius of the English language, which is in all things superior
to any other language now spoken by men. It makes one sick to hear such
a man as Warton talk ''of the frequent repetition of the same termination
being a circumstance natural to the Italian, which deals largely in identical
cadences.'' The English language deals far more largely in every thing
that is good either for sense or sound, and we will thank you to shew us
seventy-four cantos, of a good many hundred lines each, forming half a
poem, so rich in rhymes, without monotony, repetition, or imperfection, as
Spenser's seventy-four, which, had he lived, he could with equal ease, grace,

and power, have made a hundred and fifty. Warton, after the fashion of
Spence, classes "the most striking and obvious of the absurdities which the
constraint of his stanza led our author into"; but the list, with all his
familiarity with the Faery Queen, is very meagre indeed, and proves the
very reverse of what he rashly adventured to shew—the immeasurable merits
of the stanza, and Spenser's miraculous power in wielding it at will in
every mood and in adaptation to every subject. Finally, Tom himself con-
fesses, that ";it is indeed surprising, upon the whole, that Spenser should
execute a poem of uncommon length [forty thousand lines?] with so much
spirit and ease, laden as he was with so many shackles, and embarrassed
with so complicated a bondage of rhyming. Nor can I recollect, that he
has been so careless as to suffer the same word to be repeated as a rhyme
to itself, in more than four or five instances; a fault, which if he had more
frequently committed, his manifold beauties of versification would have
obliged us to overlook. Why, then, all that palaver about the genius of
the English language not permitting that to be done which Spenser did
like winking, and which so many English poets, good, bad, and indifferent,
have done since, without turning a hair? "Laden with shackles!" What
does that mean? If you take it literally, have we not seen Londoners
dance hornpipes in chains and breeches, as well as the most active High-
lander in Lochaber, in kilts without drawers? "Complicated bondage of
rhyme!" Poo—poo—poo. Is the Jew's harp of our day a pleasanter
and more powerful instrument than that on which King David played?
Some simple musical instruments sound sweetly enough, but the more the
number of stops or strings, the more sweetly they bear sway over the
souls of Gods and men; and 'tis not less absurd to speak of a great poet
"embarrassed with the complicated bondage of rhyme," than of a great
musician complaining to St. Cecilia, and beseeching her to pardon him
for the imperfections of his voluntaries, on account of the perfections of
his instrument. One word more and we have done: a language like the
Italian, so open that you cannot speak it without rhyming, is the very
worst of all—for rhymes should not come till they are sought—if they
do, they give no pleasurable touch—"no gentle shock of mild surprise"—
but, like intrusive fools, keep jingling their cap and bells in your ears,
if not to your indifference, to your great disgust—and you wish they were
all dead. Not so with the fine, bold, stern, muscular, masculine, firm-knit
and heroic language of England. Let no poet dare to complain of the
poverty of its words in what Warton calls "identical cadences." The
music of their endings is magnificent, and it is infinite. And we conclude
with flinging in the teeth of the sciolist, who is prating perhaps of the
superiority of the German, a copy, bound in calf-skin, of Walker's Rhym-
ing Dictionary, for the shade of Spenser might frown while it smiled, were
we to knock the blockhead down with our vellum volume of the Faery
Queene.[15]

---

[15] *Blackwood's Magazine*, XXXIV, XXXVI, and XXXVII, Edinburgh,
1833–35. This garrulous and enthusiastic essay, for the most part a

We must remember too, with Professor Dodge, that when Spenser invented his stanza, "it was, in part, a necessity."[16] Blank verse needed the long development in the mighty forge of the Elizabethan dramatists. The couplet was degraded by the unmetrical fifteenth century and the prevailing ignorance of Chaucer's technique, and, in any case, it was not large enough for epic poetry. The rhyme royal (ababbcc) was a lovely form, but too delicate and, as Professor Dodge well says, "the arrangement of the rhymes at the close restricted free movement." Spenser had learned from the Italians the use of *ottava rima* (abababcc). It is a marvellously fluent but not a stately stanza and its smart pistol-shot at the close would have caused many a discord in *The Faërie Queene*. It is strange how persistent is the notion that the poet, by a laborious and most artificial transposition in the lines of the *ottava rima*, remoulded it to his own purpose. Phillips[17] suggested this in the seventeenth century; it satisfied even the fine intuition of Lowell; and, in spite of accurate accounts by many later critics, it has appeared in the last edition of the *Encyclopaedia Britannica*. As a matter of fact Spenser found already shaped to his purpose "a fine old sonorous stanza" (ababbcbc), though a bit heavy and pedantic, which Chaucer and other English poets had adapted from the French, and which, with the addition of the six-foot line, the alexandrine, now lingering, now flowing swiftly and

summary of the first book, is full of shrewd comments and contagious eulogy. John Wilson, "Christopher North," a slovenly giant of a man, was one of the few romanticists who admitted any taste for Spenser's moral allegory. Unfortunately, eighteenth century sentimentalism (which the romanticists made the mistake of catching up while they were revolting quite rightly against many serious but less mortal defects) inhibited for North any real and deep appreciation of the allegory of *The Faërie Queene*, for all his protestations.

16 *Cambridge Edition*, p. 135. The reader should turn to this admirable detailed appreciation from which I quote a few phrases in this paragraph.

17 Edward Phillips in his *Theatrum Poetarum Anglicanorum* (1675) thus phrases the old notion: "How much more stately and majestic in epic poems, especially of heroic argument, Spenser's stanza (which I take to be but an improvement upon Tasso's Ottava Rima, or the Ottava Rima itself, used by many of our once-esteemed poets) is the above the way, either of couplet, or alteration of four verses only, I am persuaded were it revived, would soon be acknowledged."

sinuously, Spenser moulded into the greatest simple stanzaic creation in any language.[18]

He who makes light of the wonderful intuition which added a line and lengthened it by a foot can be but a writer of most pedestrian prose. In our own day Swinburne fashioned his intoxicating stanza for "Dolores" simply by striking off the last foot of the last line of a familiar and often banal lyric stanza. He made a majestic and apparently complicated strophe for some of his odes by joining to eight simple pentameter lines, rhymed alternately, the abrupt, rushing, and fiery stanza of Milton's "On the Morning of Christ's Nativity." Such creations come only from a wizard's light but final and momentous touch. As to variety, its possibilities in the stanza of *The Faërie Queene* are considerable. Some critics have, indeed, attempted to circumscribe its resources with absurd canons. In 1625 William L'isle noted that the alexandrine should invariably have a strong caesura after the third foot.[19] And in the next century, even Thomas Warton adhered to the same superstition. As a matter of fact, just as the alexandrine may be either lingering or smoothly rapid in its flow, so its beauty in Spenser is largely due to cunning variety in the placing sometimes of one pause, sometimes two, sometimes three, or in occasionally allowing it to slide on without pause to its close. How markedly the rhythm of the entire stanza admits of variation is to a certain extent indicated in Mr. Yeats' happy contrast of the stanza as used by Shelley in *Laon and Cyntha* and by its inventor. Commenting on a stanza from Shelley's poem, Yeats says:

The rhythm is varied and troubled, and the lines, which are in Spenser like bars of gold thrown ringing one upon another, are broken capriciously.

---

[18] See Professor E. P. Morton, "The Spenserian Stanza Before 1700," *Modern Philology*, IV, 639 sq., for some interesting theories with regard to the origin of the Spenserian alexandrine.

[19] "The Bartasian verse [i.e., the alexandrine] (not unlike herein to the Latin Pentameter) hath ever this propertie, to part in the mids betwixt two wordes: so much doe French prints signifie with a stroke interposed.... The neglect of this hath caused many a brave stanza of the Faerie Queene to end but harshly, which might have been prevented at the first; but now the fault may be sooner found than amended."

Nor is the meaning the less an aspiration of the indolent muses, for it wanders hither and thither at the beckoning of fancy. It is now busy with a meteor and now with throbbing blood that is fire, and with a mist that is a swoon and a sleep that is life. It is bound together by the vaguest suggestion, while Spenser's verse is always rushing on to some preordained thought.

But though the movement of *The Faërie Queene* is never febrile it is not always quite so arrowy as Mr. Yeats suggests. It may have a kind of rapidity that no one has appreciated so gracefully and judiciously as Matthew Arnold. In contrasting Homer's rapidity and Spenser's and in disclaiming the Spenserian stanza for purposes of translating the Greek epics, Arnold goes on to say:

Yet I will say, at the same time, that the verse of Spenser is more fluid, slips more easily and quickly along, than the verse of almost any other English poet.

> ''By this the northern wagoner had set
> His seven-fold team behind the steadfast star
> That was in ocean waves yet never wet,
> But firm is fixt, and sendeth light from far
> To all that in the wide deep wandering are.''

One cannot but feel that English verse has not often moved with the fluidity and sweet ease of these lines. It is possible that it may have been this quality of Spenser's poetry which made Dr. Maginn think that the stanza of *The Faery Queen* must be a good measure for rendering Homer. This it is not: Spenser's verse is fluid and rapid, no doubt, but there are more ways than one of being fluid and rapid, and Homer is fluid and rapid in quite another way than Spenser. Spenser's manner is no more Homeric than is the manner of the one modern inheritor of Spenser's beautiful gift —the poet, who evidently caught from Spenser his sweet and easy-slipping movement, and who has exquisitely employed it; a Spenserian genius, nay, a genius by natural endowment richer probably than even Spenser; that light which shines so unexpected and without fellow in our century, an Elizabethan born too late, the early lost and admirably gifted Keats.

Then, as in the stanza on the abode of Morpheus, in some of its richest, most suave harmonies, it is like honey and wine poured slowly from the lovely curving lips of an old amphora. It can croon tenderly. It can chuckle like a brook. It can flame out.

Again, as in the stanza on the dragon's fall, it moves ponderously with an iron ring.

The first book of *The Faërie Queene* shows the sense of architecture, of "mind in style," that remained triumphant in the poet as long as history promised to fashion itself in accordance with his dreams. If the Red Cross Knight symbolizes the spirit of England, as I believe he does, there will occur, to some readers, a difficulty in admitting the appropriateness and coherence of an allegory that shadows a nation as Faërie Land and its spirit as this single one of Gloriana's many knights. Yet Spenser speaks often of Britain, the country from which Prince Arthur comes to seek Gloriana in Faërie Land though he tells us explicitly in the opening stanzas of the second book that Faëric Land is England. Again he points out in his letter to Raleigh that Elizabeth is celebrated not only as Gloriana but as Belphoebe. But these turnings should disturb no one; for the allegory of Spenser is often the more beautiful for being a crystal maze in which the astonished and delighted reader who surrenders himself wholly to its mysterious adumbrations and vivid flashes will see reflections of familiar figures sometimes as clear as day yet bewildering in their strange doublings and turnings. The Red Cross Knight has been interpreted by Professor Frederick Morgan Padelford, one of the most brilliant of Spenser's American critics, as a portrait of Henry VIII.[20] But among

---

[20] Beginning with some fruitful suggestions by Upton and by Mr. J. Ernest Whitney (*Transactions of the American Philological Association,* XIX), Professor Padelford (*The Political and Ecclesiastical Allegory of the First Book of The Faërie Queene,* Boston, 1911), undertakes an elaborate exposition which, whether right or wrong, is rich in suggestions. Though I am at variance with him at the outset I have found much that I could agree with and much more that is most suggestive. I have already spoken of a new school of critics, mostly American, among whom Professor Greenlaw is the most distinguished and successful and Professor Padelford, Professor Philo Buck, and Dr. Percy Long are members of growing reputation, who have focused on Spenser's political allegory to such good effect that they have greatly enriched our appreciation of Spenser and made possible a conception of the poet which, while retaining much of the old, may be called strikingly new. Most critics have preferred to leave Spenser's political allegory pleasantly and vaguely alone. It is indeed most difficult and undoubtedly casual and capricious. In the later books it certainly changes character and grows more episodical.

the many difficulties that this theory offers, looms the fact that
the hero, whom Professor Padelford considers to be the his-
torical father of Gloriana, appears in *The Faërie Queene* as "a
tall clownish younge man" whom the great queen reluctantly
knights in accordance with a boon which she had rashly granted
before knowing its purport. This fact seems to me far more
formidable than the slight difficulty in the way of my interpre-
tation. Moreover, the fact that Spenser calls this knight Saint
George would indicate that the poet chose to shadow forth the
British spirit under a most felicitous name. It was, too, most
appropriate to conceive of Saint George as originally "a tall
clownish younge man" leaping in one bound from the character
of lout to knight. "Merrie" England had always cherished the
"male Cinderella" as the most popular hero of epic and romance
because of the English love of democracy. Beowulf, the first
great national hero, Havelok, and many more were "male Cin-
derellas" because, however much talk there was of birth and
divine right in hall and bower, the blood of England has always
been more like the blood of her first mighty popular poet, Lang-
land, than like that of the feudal baron. Gareth, the hero of
those books in Malory which are, more than any others, drenched

---

For, if my theory of Spenser's gradual disillusion is true, it follows that
the political allegory would fade slowly as the poem progressed, giving
place more and more to pure and irresponsible romance which would come
to the poet as something of a solace. This is probably the scarcely known
reason why critics have shrunk from the difficult task of following out
the revelations in the letter to Raleigh, so Parthian in its avowed eagerness
to avoid some "gealous opinions and misconstructions." In 1758 Upton
published some very valuable suggestions. But his following was so slight
that half a century afterward Scott, in an article on Todd's edition (*Edin-
burgh Review*, VII (1805), 214), lamented that "although every thing
belonging to the reign of the Virgin Queen carries with it a secret charm
to Englishmen, no commentator of the Faery Queen has taken the trouble
to go very deep into those annals, for the purpose of illustrating the
secret, and, as it were, esoteric allusions of Spenser's poem." The curious
reader may also find some interest in Isaac D'Israeli's "Allegory" (*Ameni-
ties of Literature*, II (ed. London, 1842), 408–431). The moral alle-
gory of the first book was given an interesting and enthusiastic exposi-
tion by John Ruskin in a well known passage and, somewhat differently
and more elaborately, by Professor H. M. Percival (*The Faerie Queene,
Book I*, xiv-xxi (London, 1893). For the moral allegory of Book I see
also Professor Padelford's "Spenser and the Theology of Calvin," *Modern
Philology* (May, 1914), 9 sq.

in May, appeared, we remember, at Arthur's court as a "male Cinderella." And Gareth was probably one of Spenser's chief models for the Red Cross Knight. And England loved to tell stories of this sort about her most popular kings and their essential democracy. Shakespeare's great trilogy traces the growth of Prince Hal from the "Male Cinderella" who idled away his gay youth among cut-purses and tapsters to the brilliant warrior and imperial monarch who, for all his splendor, did not forget on the field of Agincourt that he was like the common sentinel begotten not of the purple but of the same "Merrie" England which produced knights and yeomen as brothers. Professor Padelford would trace in the adventures of the Red Cross Knight the history of the English Reformation. But though there may be brief allusions to past events in this book and though there are certainly clear and more frequent allusions to well known historical events in the later and more confused portions of the poem, I believe, calling *The Faërie Queene* as I do an epic of the future which sought to prophesy history, that Spenser intended merely to voice a personal and a popular English fear of the danger of leaving Una (Truth) to be the paramour of Duessa (Falsehood, Mary Queen of Scots), who would lead St. George to be the prey of Orgoglio (the Catholic Church). For it was only Truth who would lead the British spirit against our common and ancient foe the Dragon (the Devil). Spenser saw England tempted by the tinsel splendor and the luxurious corruption of the House of Pride. I do not think that he was violently opposed to the religious principles of the Church of Rome as many critics (unfortunately but quite naturally many of them Roman Catholics) have supposed; though every one who reads the history of England and of English convictions in the days of Elizabeth can realize how persistent and how sincere and, for all the fanaticism and bigotry, how far from groundless was the widespread fear of the Church of Rome as a political power. Spenser's House of Pride, however, was in his own English Church, as his early poems show, quite as much as in the Catholic countries. But we have seen how in "September," certainly not long before he began *The Faërie Queene*, Spenser had uttered a sinister warning against Rome much like that given long afterwards with equal fervor by Milton in his *Lycidas*. To give way even momentarily to Rome would, Spenser thought, bring St. George to the cave of Despair whence only Truth with great difficulty might rescue him. In other words, England would lose her national integrity, become false to herself, and mourn her own death in life. Though there are a few incidents in this book that might be considered to have something of the character of the formal episode undiscerningly imitated from classical epic poetry it is, in the light of my interpretation, a most skilful piece of structure, elaborate but sound, firm and, in its essentials, clear.

This fervor, for all its fanaticism a most noble fervor, should appeal alike to Catholic, Protestant, Agnostic, and Positivist (for its fervor is a part of its universality and Duessa is not so much a temporary and localized evil as Falsehood, who threatens us for all time)—this fervor turns us again to a contrast with Spenser's chief epic master, Ariosto, whom I have called the Mr. Worldly Wiseman of poetry. Professor Dodge traces the curious vicissitudes in Ariosto's reputation, almost as changeful and glittering as the poet's own genius, before the *Orlando Furioso* fell into the hands of Spenser.[21] Ariosto's fame, for all the controversy and pedantry that hissed about it, was ever splendid, but his irresponsibility and iridescent play of moods set his puzzled friends and foes, for decade after decade, agog in a strenuous game of classification which still allures keen disputants. Before the *Orlando Furioso* had appeared to dazzle the critics the poet himself was confronted with the great problem of the relations of heroic and romantic poetry.

---

[21] "Spenser's Imitations from Ariosto" (*Publications of the Modern Language Association of America*, 1897, XII, especially 157 sq.), and *The Cambridge Edition*, 131 sq. M. Jusserand (*A Literary History of the English People*, 1906, II, 503–504) is sceptical of Dodge's results but to little purpose. M. Jusserand goes on to greatly overrate the influence of Tasso.

And, though Ariosto left his advisor Bembo meditating on Aristotle to turn gaily down his own wayward and winding path, Trissino was already making phantom theories and writing an epic falsely classical as if some mad dweller in Laputa might have tried to recreate a giant by grafting a thin layer of flesh on the fossil remains of some prehistoric animal.

Finally Pigna, in 1554, found it necessary to claim for the *Orlando Furioso* supremacy as a *romanzo*, rather than as a *poema eroico*. And to this very day, in spite of Ariosto's immense constructive ingenuity, it is easier to claim for Spenser the credit of having at least begun his *Faërie Queene* on a more uncompromising epic pattern. The best that can be said for Ariosto's unity and general purpose has been vivaciously said by De Sanctis.[22]

As the unity of the world in its infinite variety is in its spirit or in its laws, so the unity of this vast poem is in the spirit or in the laws of the world of chivalry.

The centripetal force is very weak in this world of liberty and individual initiative; and it takes the angel Michael or the demon to drag the knight-errants to Paris where the fighting is. And they are there only a few times and barely for a day; for on the following day they run once more after the phantasms of their passions, drawn by love, by vengeance, by glory, and all eager for strange and marvellous adventures. The very emprise of Agramante is not a religious or political deed, but it also is a great adventure occasioned by the desire for vengeance. Paris is a fixed point where Charles and Agramante are with their armies on the offensive and defensive; but their paladins and knights, for the most part kings and lords, go wandering over the world and Paris is only a rendezvous at which the branches of narrative are united at times and rest, and of which the poet makes use to arrange and knot the threads in certain great intervals. For above this anarchy of chivalry there is a serene and harmonious mind who holds the threads in his hand and weaves them sapiently and knows how to prick the curiosity and not weary the attention, to avoid congestion and confusion in this great variety and spontaneity of movements, bring suddenly before you again characters and events which you thought he had forgotten, and in the greatest appearance of disorder gather the threads again, he alone calm and smiling in the midst of so many clashing elements. Paris is the principal knot of the woof; it is a sort of lighthouse which from time to time flashes and illumines everything around.

---

[22] From a translation made by Professor J. A. Child and the present writer for a volume of selections from Carducci and De Sanctis.

The scene opens at Paris just when the Christian peoples have suffered a great rout. And just when the need is greatest Rinaldo, Orlando, Brandimarte go away. Rinaldo runs after Bayardo; Orlando runs after Angelica; and Brandimarte runs after Orlando.... And while these characters run, Agramante sets fire to Paris and Rodomonte enters it alone and spreads terror in it. Paris is saved because a miraculous rain puts out the fire and Rinaldo, guided by the angel Michael, arrives just in time and defeats the Pagans. Agramante, who was laying siege, is besieged. The Pagan knights are also errant. Ferraù seeks out Orlando whose helmet he has sworn to take away. Gradasso seeks for Rinaldo from whom he wishes to take Bayardo; Sacripante seeks for Angelica. The poem begun at Paris closes at Paris with the marriage of Ruggiero and the death of Rodomonte.

It can be maintained, in spite of many accusations which have been periodically renewed from the days of Thomas Rymer to Aubrey De Vere, that the influence of this wayward poet over Spenser was mainly for good.[23] But it is also truer that, as soon as Spenser began to falter before his great disillusion, the Mr. Worldly Wiseman of poetry allured him into a maze of sheer romance, beautiful, yet leading sometimes far away from the

---

[23] Thomas Rymer, in an unsettled age, showed himself an uncompromising Augustan by naming Spenser with Virgil and by attacking the influence of Ariosto. In his preface to a translation of Rapin's *Reflections on Aristotle's Treatise of Poesie* (1674), he wrote: "*Spencer*, I think, may be reckon'd the first of our *Heroick Poets;* he had a large spirit, a sharp judgment, and a *Genius* for Heroic Poesie, perhaps above any that ever writ since *Virgil*. But our misfortune is, he wanted a true *Idea*, and lost himself by following an unfaithful guide. Though besides *Homer* and *Virgil*, he had read *Tasso*, yet he rather suffer'd himself to be misled by *Ariosto;* with whom blindly rambling on *marvellous* Adventures, he makes no Conscience of *Probability*. All is fanciful and chimerical, without any uniformity, without any foundation in truth; his Poem is perfect *Fairy-land*.

They who can love *Ariosto* will be ravish'd with *Spencer*, whilst men of juster thoughts lament that such great Wits have miscarried in their Travels for want of direction to set them in the right way. But the truth is, in *Spencer's* time, *Italy* it self was not well satisfied with *Tasso;* and few amongst them would then allow that he had excell'd their *divine Ariosto*. And it was the vice of those Times to affect superstitiously the *Allegory;* and nothing would then be currant without a mystical meaning. We must blame the *Italians* for debauching great *Spencer's* judgment; and they cast him on the unlucky choice of the *stanza* which in no wise is proper for our Language."

At the other end of the centuries we find Aubrey De Vere writing of "Ariosto whom ... [Spenser] too often imitated, but from whom he derived little save harm." One could write a valuable thesis on the attitudes of critics towards the influence of Ariosto on Spenser alone. Since, however, I shall have occasion to refer to this subject in other places I will close

scheme propounded in the letter to Raleigh. Nevertheless, if
either poem really needs defense, Spenser's Phaeton-like poem
is more defensible as epic. Today there are two widely current
attitudes towards the epic. One denies the title to such poems
as the *Orlando Furioso* and *The Faërie Queene*. Another, headed
perhaps by Croce, denies the reality of *genre* altogether. The
second point of view may be briefly dismissed as denying to
criticism a most luminous method of classification. It is only
less important to study the relations of two masterpieces by
different authors under a similar heading than to note the rela-
tions of two works by the same poet. As a protest against the
purism of the first attitude, the anarchistic criticism of Croce
is full of suggestion. Let us not, however, deny the reality of
genre; let us rather avoid the old error of certain renaissance
critics and use neither Homer nor Virgil as a Procrustean mould.
Let us broaden our definitions gradually, reasonably, but freely.
If we do this we shall, as I have already intimated, gain courage
against a third point of view that the epic is a dead *genre* belong-
ing to a splendid and irrecoverable ideal of the past. We shall
see Ariosto and Spenser groping in modern times toward epic
forms that will be possible even after international peace.
Ariosto's poem is an epic in its wonderful synthesis of all the
emotions and wisdom of the greatest epoch of Italy. It is full
of stirring if extravagant martial splendor and movement. But
it is lacking in national fervor and high-seriousness. Spenser
regained high-seriousness by the only method possible for an
epic of his times: by subordinating but not banishing warlike
action. In just this way, perhaps, warlike action will be sublim-

---

here with a curious quotation from Mrs. Browning's *A Vision of Poets*
(1844), which is worth noticing as a saccharine libel on Spenser and a
very undiscerning appreciation of Ariosto.

> And Spenser drooped his dreaming head
> (With languid sleep-smile you had said
> From his own verse engenderèd)
> On Ariosto's, till they ran
> Their curls in one: the Italian
> Shot nimbler heat of bolder man
> From his fine lids.

ated into a life of deeds less crude and irrational but no less heroic in an age when contemplation takes its place in proper relation to action.

Doubtless Spenser gave too much emphasis to the significance of the deed rather than to the doing. But that is a pardonable excess for a savior of the epic.[24] And Ariosto retained his vivacious action only at the cost of chilling scepticism, his sneer at chivalry. On the other hand Spenser frankly tells us that his Red Cross Knight was to represent Holiness, a quality in whose reality he devoutly believed. Some have been troubled by the inconsistency of Holiness, an abstract perfection led astray by hypocrisy, falsehood, pride, and despair. This is to utterly misunderstand Spenser. He meant to show how the Red Cross Knight, St. George, the Spirit of England, might attain to perfect holiness by avoiding certain sinister influences. And in this fervid prophecy we see beating the great heart of England as national conviction never glowed in Ariosto. Just here Spenser does in truth ''overgo'' his great master as an epic poet. Spenser's critics have overemphasized the shadowy nature of his beings. When we consider the full meaning of St. George and Una, Archimago and Duessa, Sansloy, Orgoglio, Satyrane, Prince Arthur, we realize that they are Spenser's profoundest hopes and fears for England masquerading as knights and ladies. These rainbow riches of Spenser's idealism, at first scarcely distinguishable in outline, become tangible. The disguise of masquerade, the element of unreality drops down as the folds of drapery over the flanks of the Venus de Milo and all grows as tangible as sculpture, pale, to be sure, because these knights and ladies died long ago, as the color has fled from old

---

24 Compare Professor George Saintsbury (*History of English Literature: Elizabethan*, London and New York, 1887): ''I am inclined to think that the presence of these undermeanings [i.e., allegory] with the interest which they give to a moderately instructed and intelligent person who, without too desperate a determination to see into milestones, understands 'words to the wise,' is a great addition to the hold of the poem over the attention and saves it from the charge of mere desultoriness, which some, at least, of the other greatest poems of the kind (notably its immediate exemplar, the *Orlando Furioso*), must undergo.''

statues, but universal, the firm full curves discernible from every side.

All critics have hitherto found something irreconcilable be-tween epic and romance. But let us reconsider. Epic is history, exalted to be sure, but in certain deep essentials more true than history. Romance chooses no time instead of the definite past of epic; romance is irresponsibly and delightedly unreal. But is it not possible that romance is material for a new kind of epic as ballads have been material for the old? At first there were genuine medieval epics. But pure romance material seemed to elude the larger form. And the richest romance of all, the Arthurian romance, even in the long metrical forms and the gigantic prose redactions, even in the great compilation of Malory, refused to assume perfect epic lineaments. Yet, I re-peat, is it entirely impossible that romance is material for a new kind of epic as ballads have been for the old? The Middle Ages seems to have faded out just as it was on the point of making its supreme heroic poem by harmonizing an infinite chaos of Arthurian tales into cosmos. For in the Middle Ages the Arthurian romances increased and grew up like a confused cathedral reared heavenward by more than four different cen-turies and by more than four different races each alien time and spirit adding a small serene chapel or a quaint little garden or remodeling the front that faced the dawn with bolder, firmer lines or sending up a new audacious spire. The Middle Ages faded. But Ariosto dared to plunder freely the riches of romance and he produced a work which falls short of the greatest epic only in national conviction and high-seriousness. Fortunately for Spenser some of the Italian and English advo-cates of Ariosto strove to defend his poem by adding to its real allegorical episodes many profoundly absurd and fantastic allegorical interpretations of its most wayward cantos. To an Anglo-Saxon this union of allegory and romance became plaus-ible precedent. And so Spenser lost somewhat in vividness but regained the patriotic fervor and the lofty purport through allegory. Nor did Spenser forget national ballads and history for his minor episodes at least. But for the main strands of an epic of the future, an epic intended to *make* history, what could be more appropriate inspiration than romance? Stories about no time, romances interpreted by allegory, were his proper sources for a prophetic account of the long quest by which St. George, the spirit of England, might attain holiness and conquer the dragon of evil.

One feels the unfaltering conviction of the first book not only in the coherence of the main strands of allegory, but in the swiftness of its movement. We are given a brief but vivid picture of the hero, stately with his silver shield, on his great charger. We get but a glimpse of Una, whose radiant face we shall not see until the poet, with a master-stroke of dramatic fitness, allows her to be seen without her dark veil when alone and in anguish she rests from her wanderings under a paternal tree where her beauty makes "a sunshine in the shady place," and again when Sansloy (Lawlessness) tears off her veil and is stirred to wild lust by the loveliness of Truth. With the characters briefly outlined, Spenser pours out his adventures with extraordinary ease and copious directness. In a moment we are in the mazeful wood. In another moment the Red Cross Knight faces the monster Errour in her darksome cave. The description of the fight is given with a graphic freshness that often failed the poet later. The mingled fear and rancor of the monster and her desperate leap upon the knight's shield at the climax have uncanny reality. The loathesome details, enhanced by the fine simile of the Nile, are strangely, almost perversely touched by a sublimity that strongly appealed to Edmund Burke. In another moment the victor and his lady are out of the wood and meet the wizard Archimago who, in the guise of a hermit, leads them to a harborage which Spenser describes in an exquisite stanza with something like a child's ignorance or forgetfulness of evil, in subtle dramatic harmony here, with the psychological situation of his hero and heroine.

> A little lowly hermitage it was,
> Downe in a dale, hard by a forests side,
> Far from resort of people, that did pas
> In traveill to and froe: a litle wyde
> There was an holy chappell edifyde,
> Wherein the hermite dewly wont to say
> His holy thinges each morne and even-tyde:
> Thereby a christall streame did gently play,
> Which from a sacred fountaine welled forth alway.

Then comes the false dream in the form of Una, at Archimago's conjuration, to tempt the sleeping knight to sensual abandon. All these incidents, with copious but never tumultous swiftness, in one little canto.

The second canto is equally swift and equally coherent. We pass from the false hermitage to the wonderful cave of Morpheus and back again. We fly from Una with the Red Cross Knight half believing with him that we have seen the lady in the embrace of a wanton squire, despite the poet's assurance that we are gazing at the creatures of the enchanter. We are swept on to the sudden duel of the Red Cross Knight and Sansfoy (Faithlessness); the winning of the fair witch Duessa. We are startled by the tree that bleeds and by the story that it is Fradubio (Doubt), enchanted by that same treacherous witch. We get a vague, sinister, and horrible glimpse of Duessa in her own true guise, a little naked hag with her deformities half hidden in the water. And if we remember our Virgil and our Ariosto we feel that these incidents are none the less Spenser's, from whom they flow with such marvelous swiftness and richer appropriateness. Here, truly, one feels the intoxication and the truth of Taine's transport.

A character appears, ... then an action, then a landscape, then a succession of actions. characters, landscapes, producing, completing, arranging themselves by instinctive development, as when in a dream we behold a train of figures which, without any outward compulsion, display and group themselves before our eyes. This fount of living and changing forms is inexhaustible in Spenser; he is always imaging; it is his specialty. He has but to close his eyes, and apparitions arise; they abound in him, crowd, overflow; in vain he pours them forth; they continually float up, more copious and more dense. Many times, following the inexhaustible stream, I have thought of the vapors which rise incessantly from the sea, ascend, sparkle, commingle their golden and snowy scrolls, while underneath them new mists arise, and others again beneath, and the splendid procession never grows dim or ceases.

Then the story turns to Una. Only here do we first come to know her in a series of tender stanzas which are unmatched for their plenilune loveliness.

> Nought is there under heav'ns wide hollownesse,
> That moves more deare compassion of mind,
> Then beautie brought t'unworthie wretchednesse.

Let us listen to a poet on "the poet's poet." Says Francis Thompson:

The mournful sweetness of those lines is insurpassable; and they are quintessential Spenser.... Wherein lies their power? The language is so utterly plain that an uninspired poet would have fallen upon baldness. Yet Spenser is a mine of diction (as was remarked to us by a poet who had worked in that mine). But here he had no need for his gorgeous opulence of diction: a few commonest words, and the spell was worked. It is all a matter of relation: the words take life from each other, and become an organism, as with Coleridge. And it is a matter of music; an integral element in the magic of the passage is its sound. In this necromancy, by which the most elementary words, entering into a secret relation of sense and sound, acquire occult property, Spenser is a master.[25]

Spenser's women, especially Una, have inspired some of the most eloquent passages in English criticism. It is most epical and most appropriate that a lion should be the comrade of Una. Her chief beauty lies in the perfect solution of the strength and the tenderness in her. As Professor Dowden has it:

Throughout Spenser's poem, although Una is so young, so tender, so mild, while the knight is stout and bold, there is a certain protectiveness on her part towards him; yet this is united in such a way with gentle, fervid loyalty and trust that it seems to imply no consciousness of superiority.

---

[25] *Works* (New York, 1913), III, "The Poet's Poet." I have taken some liberties with this fine passage by suppressing its interesting but untenable thesis that Spenser was primarily a lyric poet. Thompson's essay is very choice, but disappointing for a production by Thompson.

No wonder that Wordsworth did not hesitate to compare Una even with Desdemona.

> Two will I mention, dearer than the rest—
> The gentle Lady married to the Moor;
> And heavenly Una with her milk-white lamb.

Never does Spenser strike a more poignant note than in the final scene of this canto where Sansloy slays the lion and bears off the maiden with ferocious ecstasy.

The fourth canto contains one of those famous set-pieces in *The Faërie Queene* that have been thrown into unjust prominence: unjust because, though they are quite as wonderful as their admirers have claimed, though they are easily detachable, yet they are thought by the superficial reader to stand out like an unusually bold and perfect section of relief in a frieze which for the most part has been worn by the storms and the centuries to a venerable but confused and monotonous ruin. The adventures of the Red Cross Knight at the House of Pride are incomparable in their way and perfect when extracted. But they are also absolutely organic and they cast no shadow over most of the surrounding episodes. Kent, the illustrator of Birch's edition of *The Faërie Queene* (1751), crowded the great pageant of the Seven Deadly Sins into a small picture which is a libel on Spenser's description, giving it an appearance of faults that it does not have. One feels that Aubrey de Vere must have had some such picture as Kent's before his eyes or in his mind when he so uncritically attacked the procession. "Christopher North" may set us right with his shrewd and enthusiastic defense.

The Set-out would seem somewhat grotesque on the road from London to Brighton, and would sorely puzzle the tollmen. Even on canvass 'twould look not a little queer. Painting, perhaps, should have little or nothing to do with such subjects "for her power is limited," and so is her canvass. But poetry may do what she will—for her works, in words, are for the imagination—the senses are soon reconciled to whatever she orders them to see—for it all seems, whether near or afar off, to have an existence in nature. Or if the *esse* be too much for our faith, it is satisfied with the *posse*, of which these strangenesses are supposed the shadow. We hardly know how it is with us on conceiving this procession of Pride moving along the royal road of Spenser's stanzas. Sometimes we seem to see all the animals, distinguishable each by his proper attributes, and as distinguishable the riders—Car and Queen. Oftener not—but at one moment Slowth, perhaps, on his ass—at another Wrath on his lion— then Satan sole sitting on the beam—now a confusion of images—monstrous but full of meaning—at once beasts absolute and emblematical— and sometimes we suspect we have but abstract Ideas of Qualities and Vices. By such visionary alternations of thought and its objects, the whole moral mind is moved along with the image, and there is no end to the feelings of the one—to the other's flight.

If I venture to compare the effect of the pageant of the Seven Deadly Sins to that of a circus-parade as seen by a child many will think me perverse or dully prosaic. Yet I believe that on such an analogy we may best appreciate this procession unparalleled as it is in all literature for barbaric opulence. To a child's vision a circus-parade is at once gorgeous and delightfully tawdry, terrific and grotesque. So assuredly is the chariot of Lady Pride drawn by those outlandish beasts lurching along in anarchical company.

> But this was drawne of six unequall beasts,
> On which her six sage counsellours did ryde,
> Taught to obay their bestiall beheasts,
> With like conditions to their kindes applyde:
> Of which the first, that al the rest did guyde,
> Was sluggish Idlenesse, the nourse of sin;
> Upon a slouthfull asse he chose to ryde,
> Arayd in habit blacke, and amis thin,
> Like to an holy monck, the service to begin.
>
> And in his hand his portesse still he bare,
> That much was worne, but therein little redd;
> For of devotion he had little care,
> Still drownd in sleepe, and most of his daies dedd:
> Scarse could he once uphold his heavie hedd,
> To looken whether it were night or day:
> May seeme the wayne was very evill ledd,
> When such an one had guiding of the way,
> That knew not whether right he went, or else astray.
>
> From wordly cares himselfe he did esloyne,
> And greatly shunned manly exercise;
> From everie worke he chalenged essoyne,
> For contemplation sake: yet otherwise

His life he led in lawlesse riotise;
By which he gnew to grievous malady;
For in his lustlesse limbs, through evill guise,
A shaking fever raigned continually.
Such one was Idlenesse, first of this company.

And by his side rode loathsome Gluttony,
Deformed creature, on a filthie swyne:
His belly was upblowne with luxury,
And eke with fatnesse swollen were his eyne;
And like a crane his necke was long and fyne,
With which he swallowed up excessive feast,
For want whereof poore people oft did pyne:
And all the way most like a brutish beast,
He spued up his gorge, that all did him deteast.

In greene vine leaves he was right fitly clad;
For other clothes he would not weare for heat;
And on his head an yvie girland had,
From under which fast trickled downe the sweat:
Still as he rode, he somewhat still did eat,
And in his hand did beare a bouzing can,
Of which he supt so oft, that on his seat
His dronken corse he scarse upholden can:
In shape and life more like a monster than a man.

. . . .

And next to him rode lustfull Lechery
Upon a bearded gote, whose rugged heare,
And whally eies (the signe of gelosy,)
Was like the person selfe, whom he did beare:
Who rough, and blacke, and filthy, did appeare,
Unseemely man to please fair ladies eye;
Yet he of ladies oft was loved deare,
When fairer faces were bid standen by:
O who does know the bent of womens fantasy?

. . . .

And greedy Avarice by him did ride,
Uppon a camell loaden all with gold:
Two iron coffers hong on either side,
With precious metall full as they might hold,
And in his lap an heap of coine he told;
For of his wicked pelfe his god he made,
And unto hell him selfe for money sold:
Accursed usury was all his trade;
And right and wrong ylike in equall ballaunce waide.

And next to him malitious Envy rode
Upon a ravenous wolfe, and still did chaw
Betweene his cankred teeth a venemous tode,
That all the poison ran about his chaw;
But inwardly he chawed his owne maw
At neibors welth, that made him ever sad;
For death it was, when any good he saw;
And wept, that cause of weeping none he had;
But when he heard of harme, he wexed wondrous glad.

. . . .

And him beside rides fierce revenging Wrath,
Upon a lion, loth for to be led;
And in his hand a burning brond he hath,
The which he brandisheth about his hed:
His eies did hurle forth sparcles fiery red,
And stared sterne on all that him beheld:
As ashes pale of hew, and seeming ded;
And on his dagger still his hand he held,
Trembling through hasty rage, when choler in him sweld.

His ruffin raiment all was staind with blood,
Which he had spilt, and all to rags yrent,
Through unadvized rashnes woxen wood;
For of his hands he had no governement,
Ne car'd for blood in his avengement:
But when the furious fitt was overpast,
His cruell facts he often would repent;
Yet, wilfull man, he never would forecast,
How many mischieves should ensue his heedlesse hast.

. . . .

And after all, upon the wagon beame,
Rode Sathan, with a smarting whip in hand,
With which he forward lasht the laesy teme,
So oft as Slowth still in the mire did stand.
Huge routs of people did about them band,
Showting for joy; and still before their way
A foggy mist had covered all the land;
And underneath their feet, all scattered lay
Dead sculls and bones of men, whose life had gone astray.[26]

---

[26] The symbolism of animals and sins has been traced back to Jerome
and other theologians.   But an examination of bestiaries and sermons, of
the mounted sins in Lydgate's *Assembly of Gods*, of the marked similarities
in Gower's *Mirrour de l'Homme*, and of even the homely realism of Lang-
land and the horrid grotesqueness and ferocity of Dunbar only lends
new impressiveness to Spenser's picture.   It is noteworthy that the two
Spenserians who followed this episode most elaborately fell back imme-
diately to the inferiority of Spenser's predecessors.   Dr. Joseph Beaumont

There is a fine sweep in the last stanza that brings the whole chaotic picture plunging before the reader's vision. Such is the grim warning which Spenser gave to England of the danger of comradeship with corruption and falsehood. One sees how absolutely inseparable is the allegory from all the other poetical elements.

The combat between the Red Cross Knight and Sansjoy, Duessa's rescue of the conquered Saracen, her journey to the awful abode of Night where we find ourselves so close to the forces that are working silently with fearful power to destroy Faëry Land, her journey to hell to seek cure for Sansjoy—all these episodes are less absorbing than what has gone before. One feels a slight loosening in the architectonic grasp of the poet. When we recall the sixth book of the *Aeneid*, that journey of Aeneas through Hades which gives significance and unity to Virgil's huge scheme, we realize that Spenser's imitation, though often vivid and grand, is a mere intercalation.

But in the sixth and seventh cantos the poet recovers his control. He brings the abandoned Una and the Red Cross Knight to the turning point. Una, unveiled, is saved from the assault of Sansloy by the fauns and satyrs and is at last lead away by their kinsman, Sir Satyrane, "Plaine, faithfull, true, and enimy of shame." Doubtless we may assume with Professor Padelford that these grotesque, naïve wood-creatures represent the common people who, in their crude way, worship truth. I think that Sir Satyrane, a satyr's son, is intended to be a knight who rose from lowly origins to distinction, a type always dear to the England that always worshipped the bow and the clothyard shaft. Whether or not Spenser dared to shadow forth the birth and training of some definite knight in a story which, for all its laudations, is a dubious compliment, does not matter. When we remember how frequently modern

---

had the temerity to essay a procession of mounted sins and lost himself in outrageous extravagance. Dr. Samuel Woodford gave up the animals and sank into tameness. The most careful examination of Spenser's sources which I know is by Professor J. L. Lowes, *Publications of the Modern Language Association of America* (September, 1914), XXIX, 388 sq.

readers have recoiled from what they consider to be Spenser's aristocratic intolerance we have here an episode to ponder over. Spenser does have a hard word for the "raskall many" in the last canto of this very book. What place is there for proletarians when the knights seldom eat? The critics recall Chaucer and praise what they choose to call his democracy. If they recalled Langland and his continuators it would be well. But Chaucer's democracy has been much over-emphasized. Spenser's words are no more bitter than the outcry in *The Clerk's Tale*. Moreover, we should remember that Spenser's aristocracy, because he was on the frontiers of thought in his time, is not so much a scorn of the people as a quest of an ideal so eager that he could not wait for the populace always so conservative. Whenever his anger blazes out it is not against the people but against the mob. Many a stout adherent of democracy is quite at one with him in this respect, particularly since social psychology has made its rapid strides and we have become familiar with such works as Summer's *Folk-Ways*, Wallas's *Human Nature in Politics*, and Trotter's *The Instincts of the Herd in Peace and War*. Such hatred as Spenser's is, at worst, nothing but the last infirmity of an idealist and a high-minded radical. Chaucer, on the other hand, was democratic because of his smiling tolerance of things as they are. Even the most uncompromising foe of any form of aristocracy will find something to praise in the allegory of the satyrs which is an expression of a certain faith in the people, elementary to be sure, but not so very far removed from Abraham Lincoln's. Truth, abandoned by the knight from Gloriana's court for Falsehood, is given harborage by the people who love naïvely, even stupidly, but instinctively and with a lovely reverence.[27]

Meanwhile what has happened to the Red Cross Knight who has left Una to be rescued by the Satyrs and Sir Satyrane?

---

[27] Perhaps the reader, when we come to *Mother Hubberds Tale*, will agree with me in finding there a certain tenderness in Spenser's treatment of the husbandman who is the allegorical representation of the common people.

What would have happened to England if Mary of Scotland had become queen? England would have returned to Catholicism. To Spenser it seemed that the Church of Rome would rule with such crushing despotism that England would lose her national strength and individuality. So we learn that, in company with Duessa, St. George wandered into the domains of the giant Orgoglio (Carnal Pride in temporal rule—the Church of Rome), who cast the knight into a dungeon to starve but took Duessa for his paramour.

> From that day forth Duessa was his deare,
> And highly honourd in his haughtie eye;
> He gave her gold and purple pall to weare,
> And triple crowne set on her head full hye,
> And her endowd with royall majestye:
> Then, for to make her dreaded more of men,
> And peoples hartes with awfull terror tye,
> A monstrous beast ybredd in filthy fen
> He chose, which he had kept long time in darksom den.

> Such one it was, as that renowmed snake
> Which great Alcides in Stremona slew,
> Long fostred in the filth of Lerna lake,
> Whose many heades out budding ever new
> Did breed him endlesse labor to subdew:
> But this same monster much more ugly was;
> For seven great heads out of his body grew,
> An yron brest, and backe of scaly bras,
> And all embrewd in blood, his eyes did shine as glas.

> His tayle was stretched out in wondrous length,
> That to the hous of hevenly gods it raught,
> And with extorted powre, and borrow'd strength,
> The everburning lamps from thence it braught,
> And prowdly threw to ground, as things of naught;
> And underneath his filthy feet did tread
> The sacred thinges, and holy heastes foretaught,
> Upon this dreadfull beast with sevenfold head
> He set the false Duessa, for more aw and dread.

Again we have the grim warning that Spenser had voiced in his youthful "September" and that Milton was to voice in his youthful *Lycidas*.

But Una, fleeing while Satyrane and Sansloy clashed in fierce combat, meets first the woeful dwarf with her lord's armor and, in another moment, Prince Arthur, Magnanimity, the poet's hero, Leicester. Spenser's moral zest is here so splendidly poetical that it puts allegory beyond the most obstinate cavil, strive we ever so misguidedly to read into the episode the familiar drone of the pulpit. Samuel Crothers has written happily in praise of this celebration of magnanimity of which he says:

This is a virtue that has often been overlooked by those who have the care of youth. They make much of prohibitions, and not enough of noble incitements. They do not picture the good life as a magnificent achievement calling into play all virile powers.[28]

> At last she chaunced by good hap to meet
> A goodly knight, faire marching by the way,
> Together with his squyre, arayed meet:
> His glitterand armour shined far away,
> Like glauncing light of Phoebus brightest ray;
> From top to toe no place appeared bare,
> That deadly dint of steele endanger may.
> Athwart his brest a bauldrick brave he ware
> That shind, like twinkling stars, with stones most pretious rare.
>
> And in the midst thereof, one pretious stone
> Of wondrous worth, and eke of wondrous mights,
> Shapt like a ladies head, exceeding shone,
> Like Hesperus emongst the lesser lights,
> And strove for to amaze the weaker sights:
> Thereby his mortall blade full comely hong
> In yvory sheath, ycarv'd with curious slights;
> Whose hilts were burnisht gold, and handle strong
> Of mother perle, and buckled with a golden tong.
>
> His haughtie helmet, horrid all with gold,
> Both glorious brightnesse and great terrour bredd;
> For all the crest a dragon did enfold
> With greedie pawes, and over all did spredd
> His golden winges: his dreadfull hideous hedd,
> Close couched on the bever, seemed to throw
> From flaming mouth bright sparckles fiery redd,
> That suddeine horrour to faint hartes did show;
> And scaly tayle was strecht adowne his back full low.

---

[28] "The Romance of Ethics, in *Among Friends* (Boston and New York, 1910), p. 238.

Upon the top of all his loftie crest,
A bounch of heares discoloured diversly,
With sprincled pearle and gold full richly drest,
Did shake, and seemd to daunce for jollity;
Like to an almond tree ymounted hye
On top of greene Selinis all alone,
With blossoms brave bedecked daintily;
Whose tender locks do tremble every one
At everie little breath, that under heaven is blowne.

In the ensuing combat, in which Prince Arthur and his squire
Timias engage Orgoglio and Duessa mounted on her terrible
beast, Spenser once more arrests the reader by the very out-
landishness of the situation.[29]   The battle closes in two of those
stanzas which I have described as moving ponderously with
an iron ring.

Whom when the Prince, to batteill new addrest
And threatning high his dreadfull stroke, did see,
His sparkling blade about his head he blest,
And smote off quite his right leg by the knee,
That downe he tombled; as an aged tree,
High growing on the top of rocky clift,
Whose hartstrings with keene steele nigh hewen be;
The mighty trunck halfe rent, with ragged rift
Doth roll adowne the rocks, and fall with fearefull drift.

Or as a castle, reared high and round,
By subtile engins and malitious slight
Is undermined from the lowest ground,
And her foundation forst, and feebled quight,
At last downe falles, and with her heaped hight
Her hastie ruine does more heavie make,
And yields it selfe unto the victours might;
Such was this gyaunts fall, that seemed to shake
The stedfast globe of earth, as it for feare did quake.

---

[29] Professor Padelford's interpretation becomes here very strained in
its attempt to explain every detail of the combat. When Duessa (who to
Professor Padelford is Mary I of England in spite of her identification
with Mary Queen of Scots in Book V) sprinkles poison from a golden cup
on the squire, we are told to consider this the restoration of the Mass.
When Arthur wounds one of the deformed beast's heads, it is an allegory
of the divine interposition when Mary died, since each of the beast's heads
represents a Catholic country. No man, not even the meditative Spenser,
ever described a battle as graphic as this on such a pattern.

It is difficult for some people to tolerate the following description of the unmasking of Duessa with its revolting filthiness. And certainly it is no wonder that King James sought revenge for this brutal scarification of his mother. But I must remind the reader that it is uncritical to accuse Spenser of a purely religious hatred. Professor Greenlaw shrewdly observes that Spenser's conception of Duessa is "more the plotter against the Queen than the representative of Antichrist." We must constantly keep in mind the fact that Spenser's Puritanism was many removes from that which was to close the theatres. Most of the latest investigation has gone to establish the fact that Spenser was not a dissenter but a low churchman and, we may safely add, a low churchman who would have found the simplicity of worship he sought by no means incompatible with much of the beautiful Catholic ritual. He was a low churchman only because he saw corruption in the high church of England. On the other hand, as Professor Greenlaw reminds us, "Spenser speaks with scorn of the Puritan predilection for plain and bare churches, and, in the *Faërie Queene*, is far from complimentary when he compares the sect to the Crab, who

> Backward yode, as bargemen wont to fare
> Bending their force contrary to their face,
> Like that ungracious crew which faines demurest grace.

Spenser's quarrel, then, with Catholicism was purely political and, as such, exaggerated but not without its justification or at least its inevitability. As to Spenser's brutality towards Mary Queen of Scots it is certainly impossible to offer any complete defense. But Duessa was Falsehood as well as Mary. And robust idealists are often brutal and Rabelaisian in their destructive criticism.

The ninth canto begins with a stanza which, as Professor Dodge points out, contrasts notably in its faith in chivalry with Ariosto's mock invocations.

> O goodly golden chayne! wherewith yfere
> That vertues linked are in lovely wize,

> And noble mindes of yore allyed were,
> In brave poursuitt of chevalrous emprize,
> That none did others safety despize,
> Nor aid envy to him, in need that stands,
> But friendly each did others praise devize
> How to advaunce with favourable hands,
> As this good Prince redeemd the Redcrosse Knight from bands.

Arthur tells his grateful friends of his early training and of his vision of Gloriana:

> "Forwearied with my sportes, I did alight
> From loftie steed; and downe to sleepe me layd;
> The verdant gras my couch did goodly dight,
> And pillow was my helmet fayre displayd:
> Whiles every sence the humour sweet embayd,
> And slombring soft my hart did steale away,
> Me seemed, by my side a royall mayd
> Her daintie limbes full softly down did lay:
> So fayre a creature yet saw never sunny day.

> "Most goodly glee and lovely blandishment
> She to me made, and badd me love her deare;
> For dearely sure her love was to me bent,
> As, when just time expired, should appeare.
> But whether dreames delude, or true it were,
> Was never hart so ravisht with delight,
> Ne living man like wordes did ever heare,
> As she to me delivered all that night;
> And at her parting said, she Queene of Faries hight.

> "When I awoke, and found her place devoyd,
> And nought but pressed gras where she had lyen,
> I sorrowed all so much as earst I joyd,
> And washed all her place with watry eyen.
> From that day forth I lov'd that face divyne;
> From that day forth I cast in carefull mynd,
> To seek her out with labor and long tyne,
> And never vow to rest, till her I fynd:
> Nyne monethes I seek in vain, yet n'ill that vow unbynd."

Arthur and St. George exchange tokens. The narrative had been moving slowly, almost at complete repose. Suddenly it leaps forward with a velocity most startling in *The Faërie Queene*.

So as they traveild lo! they gan espy
An armed knight towards them gallop fast,
That seemed from some feared foe to fly,
Or other griesly thing, that him aghast.
Still as he fledd, his eye was backward cast,
As if his feare stil followed him behynd;
Als flew his steed, as he his bandes had brast,
And with his winged heeles did tread the wynd,
As he had been a fole of Pegasus his kynd.

Nigh as he drew, they might perceive his head
To be unarmd, and curld uncombed heares
Upstaring stiffe, dismaid with uncouth dread;
Nor drop of blood in all his face appeares,
Nor life in limbe: and to increase his fcares,
In fowle reproch of knighthoodes fayre degree,
About his neck an hempen rope he weares,
That with his glistring armes does ill agree;
But he of rope, or armes, has now no memoree.

We may well agree with "Christopher North" and Upton, whom he quotes, "that such a picture of a desponding, terrified, poor creature, in the utmost agonies of fright and despair was never drawn so lively by any poet or painter." The abrupt and violent course of action is then as abruptly and violently dammed by a suspense as the Red Cross Knight questions Trevisan, who

... answerd nought at all, but adding new
Feare to his first amazement, staring wyde
With stony eyes and hartlesse hollow hew,
Astonisht stood, as one that had aspyde
Infernall furies, with their chaines untyde.
Him yett againe, and yett againe bespake
The gentle knight; who nought to him replyde,
But trembling every joynt, did inly quake,
And foltring tongue at last there words seemd forth to shake:

"For Gods deare love, sir knight, doe me not stay;
For loe! he comes, he comes fast after mee!"
Eft looking back, would faine have runne away;
But he him forst to stay, and tellen free
The secrete cause of his perplexitie:
Yet nathemore by his bold hartie speach
Could his blood frozen hart emboldened bee,
But through his boldnes rather feare did reach;
Yett, forst, at last he made through silence suddein breach.

What is the fearful apparition which has so unmanned him?
We listen eagerly as Trevisan tells the story of his meeting with
Despayre and of the suicide of Sir Terwin. Then the narrative
movement breaks through the obstruction and flows, not with its
first velocity, but with the easy rapidity of a swollen current that
makes the gazer dizzy.[30]

> Ere long they come, where that same wicked wight
> His dwelling has, low in an hollow cave,
> Far underneath a craggy clift ypight,
> Darke, dolefull, dreary, like a greedy grave,
> That still for carrion carcases doth crave:
> On top whereof ay dwelt the ghastly owle,
> Shricking his baleful note, which ever drave
> Far from that haunt all other chearefull fowle;
> And all about it wandring ghostes did wayle and howle.
>
> And all about old stockes and stubs of trees,
> Whereon nor fruite nor leafe was ever seene,
> Did hang upon the ragged rocky knees;
> On which had many wretches hanged beene,
> Whose carcases were scattered on the greene,
> And thrown about the cliffs. Arrived there,
> That bare-head knight, for dread and dolefull teene,
> Would faine have fled, ne durst approchen neare,
> But th'other forst him staye, and comforted him in feare.
>
> That darkesome cave they enter, where they find
> That cursed man, low sitting on the ground,
> Musing full sadly in his sullein mind:
> His griesie lockes, long growen and unbound,
> Disordred hong about his shoulders round,
> And hid his face; through which his hollow eyne
> Looked deadly dull, and stared as astound;
> His raw-bone cheekes, through penurie and pine,
> Were shronke into his jawes, as he did never dyne.
>
> His garment nought but many ragged clouts,
> With thornes together pind and patched was,
> The which his naked sides he wrapt abouts;
> And him beside there lay upon the gras

---

[30] "Christopher North" is the only critic who has even begun to accord
a real appreciation to the movement of this canto. He says: "The action
in the Faery Queen moves quick though we have seen it complained of as
moving slow. It moves fast or slow as the one pace or the other is re-
quired. Here it moves in double-quick time, and in a moment we are at
mouth of a cave."

A dreary corse, whose life away did pas,
All wallowd in his own yet luke-warme blood,
That from his wound yet welled fresh, alas!
In which a rusty knife fast fixed stood,
And made an open passage for the gushing flood.

Nothing could show better the poet's confident skill than the sequel in which he dares to transcribe the very words of this squalid and terrible Portent. Among the many imitators of this scene most of the Spenserians contented themselves, like Giles Fletcher, with following the description closely but discreetly avoiding the speech. Sir Joseph Beaumont, in his *Psyche,* is the only Spenserian I remember who attempted after the master to put words into the mouth of Despayre; and he failed hopelessly. Spenser's achievement is a masterpiece of sophistical argument. The Red Cross Knight leaps forward with furious denunciation. Despayre seems at first to shrink and mildly reproves the hero in a craftily general discourse on the futility of life. Gradually the demon turns to a praise of that "eternal rest" of which Spenser himself, from his youth to the days of his fragments on Mutabilitie, wrote with such eloquence. But Spenser did not believe in the coward's rest or a pale inaction after death as described with such cunning persuasion by Despayre alluding to Sir Terwin's state:

"He there does now enjoy eternall rest
And happy ease, which thou doest want and crave,
And further from it daily wanderest:
What if some little payne the passage have,
That makes frayle flesh to feare the bitter wave?
Is not short payne well borne, that bringes long ease;
And layes the soule to sleepe in quiet grave?
Sleepe after toyle, port after stormie seas,
Ease after toyle, death after life does greatly please."

To Spenser, as we shall see, the life after death was rather an eternal quest, within all-hail of peace, but ever restless in noble achievement and self-development. The Red Cross Knight, however, is half convinced and wonders at Despayre's "suddeine wit." Just at this point he loses himself. The fiend goes on with sinister subtlety to justify his own acts before God, to talk of the inevitability of death and the brevity and irony of life with a music that almost stills the heart-beat. Thus the cunning demon steals gradually from his defensive attitude until, with a sudden and appalling directness as though he had leaped from a cowering posture to full height, he denounces his own accuser:

> "Thou, wretched man, of death hast greatest need,
> If in true ballaunce thou wilt weigh thy state:
> For never knight, that dared warlike deed,
> More luckless dissaventures did amate:
> Witnes the dungeon deepe, wherein of late
> Thy life shutt up for death so oft did call;
> And though good lucke prolonged hath thy date,
> Yet death then would the like mishaps forestall,
> Into the which hereafter thou maist happen fall.

> "Why then doest thou, O man of sin, desire
> To draw thy dayes forth to their last degree?
> Is not the measure of thy sinfull hire
> High heaped up with huge iniquitee,
> Against the day of wrath, to burden thee?
> Is not enough, that to this lady mild
> Thou falsed hath thy faith with perjuree,
> And sold thy selfe to serve Duessa vild,
> With whom in al abuse thou hast thy selfe defild?"

As "Christopher North" says, "No Atheist he, indeed, but an orthodox divine." Only Una, strong and tender, saves the hero from the knife pressed into his trembling hand. Professor Percival observes:

Never once before has Una addressed the knight with such severity. His wronging of *her* had only drawn forth pity and forgiveness, but when he is about to harm *himself*, and wrong all the better part of his nature, then only is her indignation roused, and she calls him what he has long before deserved to be called. No where does Una shine so bright in the light of a heroine as she does here. How unselfish is Truth!

And Aubrey De Vere says of this allegory of Despayre:

It proves that narrative poetry may, in the hand of a great master, fully reach the intensity of the drama, and carry to the same height those emotions of pity and terror through which to purify the soul was, according to Aristotle, the main function of tragedy.

Just here Spenser rises above three of his austere muses—
Medieval Asceticism, Puritanism, Calvinism.   These, for all
their strength for the strong, are but the gospel of death to
a defeated man; and it is with a profound sense of congruity
that Spenser puts their convictions into the mouth of a fiend.
To some they might be like the thrilling trumpet-call to the
divine conqueror on the Judgment Day.   To the erring Red
Cross Knight their noble but treacherous other-worldliness
meant nothing but the call to self-destruction.

In the tenth canto the movement is leisurely; the allegory is
elaborate and almost mechanical.   But this account of the Red
Cross Knight in the House of Holinesse is of very great interest
if we remember the poet's fierce denunciations of the Anglican
Church in *The Shepheards Calender* and *Mother Hubberds Tale.*
For here, as the complement to his bold destructive criticism,
he builds the minster of an ideal faith which England should
espouse.[31]   Far different from the tawdry and crumbling House
of Pride and the gruesome castle of Orgoglio is the House of
Holinesse.

> There was an auncient house not far away,
> Renowmd throughout the world for sacred lore
> And pure unspotted life: so well they say,
> It governd was, and guided evermore,
> Through wisedome of a matrone grave and hore;
> Whose only joy was to relieve the needes
> Of wretched soules, and helpe the helpelesse pore:
> All night she spent in bidding of her bedes,
> And all the day in doing good and godly deedes.
>
> . . . .
>
> Arrived there, the dore they find fast lockt;
> For it was warely watched night and day,
> For feare of many foes: but when they knockt,
> The porter opened unto them streight way,
> He was an aged syre, all hory gray,
> With lookes full lowly cast, and gate full slow,
> Wont on a staffe his feeble steps to stay,
> Hight Humiltá.   They passe in, stouping low;
> For streight and narrow was the way which he did shew.

---

[31] Professor Padelford conceives this canto to shadow forth the growth
of the Church of England but finds no particular references.   Of course
not.   This is no gilded flattery to amend for his fierce satires.   This was
to be the church of En   and's future.

Each goodly thing is hardest to begin;
But enterd in, a spatious court they see,
Both plaine and pleasaunt to be walked in,
Where them does meete a francklin faire and free,
And entertaines with comely courteous glee:
His name was Zele, that him right well became;
For in his speaches and behaveour hee
Did labour lively to expresse the same,
And gladly did them guide, till to the hall they came.

There fayrely them receives a gentle squyre,
Of myld demeanure and rare courtesee,
Right cleanly clad in comely sad attyre;
In word and deede that shewd great modestee,
And knew his good to all of each degree;
Hight Reverence. He them with speaches meet
Does faire entreate; no courting nicetee,
But simple trew, and eke unfained sweet,
As might become a squyre so great persons to greet.

Far different, too, is this quiet cheerfulness from the acrid Puritanism which was growing fast when Spenser wrote this canto. The lovely ministrations of aged Dame Coelia and her daughters, Faith and Hope, are followed by the iron whip of bitter Penance. But from this grim punishment the knight is soon brought to one who (though the soul of Christianity) has been forgotten by all creeds more than any other spirit—Charity, who of late has been remembered faintly by some who do her profane honors that mock her because they arise from crude sentimentality, often casual, often insincere, often misguided. This lady, whom Spenser sometimes forgot himself, his Charissa, he has painted with a beauty that does much to absolve him of his forgetfulness.

She was a woman in her freshest age,
Of wondrous beauty, and of bounty rare,
With goodly grace and comely personage,
That was on earth not easie to compare;
Full of great love, but Cupids wanton snare
As hell she hated, chaste in worke and will;
Her necke and brests were ever open bare,
That ay thereof her babes might sucke their fill:
The rest was all in yellow robes arayed still.

> A multitude of babes about her hong,
> Playing their sportes, that joyd her to behold;
> Whom still she fed, whiles they were weak and young,
> But thrust them forth still, as they wexed old:
> And on her head she wore a tyre of gold,
> Adornd with gemmes and owches wondrous fayre,
> Whose passing price uneath was to be told;
> And by her syde there sate a gentle payre
> Of turtle doves, she sitting in an yvory chayre.

The last ministration symbolizes Spenser's most cherished ideal, an ideal born of a harmony of Christianity and Platonism, Heavenly Contemplation. Up a steep hill, along a narrow path, goes the Red Cross Knight led by Mercy to this old man who often saw God Himself. He was an old man

> With snowy lockes adowne his shoulders shed,
> As hoary frost with spangles doth attire
> The mossy braunches of an oke halfe ded.

We have here, perhaps, a faint hint of discord, a touch of medieval asceticism. But any excess of other-worldliness is firmly repudiated. The sage shows the knight a wonderful vision of the celestial city but bids him turn back to his work on earth, to carry his new exaltation into heroic action.

In the account of the combat of the Red Cross Knight with the Dragon (Evil) who has ravaged Eden, the kingdom of Una's father, Spenser falls short of a successful culmination. The whole conception of St. George or England wresting from the serpent Eden, man's heritage of peace, the land lost by the original sin for all the human race, is hyperbolical. It is evident that the poet, with his hope for England still immeasurable, was also planning a climax for his last book. He implores the muse to restrain her furious inspiration

> Till I of warres and bloody Mars doe sing,
> And Bryton fieldes with Sarazin blood bedyde,
> Twixt that great Faery Queene and Paynim King,
> That with their horror heven and earth did ring.

In the dragon fight he heaps extravagance upon extravagance until the whole episode sinks into the grotesque to rise only

with the stanza on the dragon's fall. As Dr. Maynadier once
pointed out to me, the whole setting is quaintly pre-Raphaelite.
The hills seem low and close together and made of pasteboard.
Or perhaps one thinks of Dürer. The description of the
dragon's approach is worthy of the German's grimmest art.

> By this the dreadfull beast drew nigh to hand,
> Halfe flying and halfe footing in his haste,
> That with his largenesse measured much land,
> And made wide shadow under his huge waste;
> As mountaine doth the valley overcaste.
> Approching nigh, he reared high afore
> His body monstrous, horrible, and vaste,
> Which to increase his wondrous greatnes more,
> Was swoln with wrath, and poyson, and with bloody gore.
>
> . . . .
>
> His flaggy winges, when forth he did display,
> Were like two sayles, in which the hollow wynd
> Is gathered full, and worketh speedy way:
> And eke the pennes that did his pineons bynd,
> Were like mayne-yardes, with flying canvas lynd,
> With which whenas him list the ayre to beat,
> And there by force unwonted passage fynd,
> The clowdes before him fledd for terror great,
> And all the hevens stood still, amazed with his threat.

We think of Dürer when we picture the dragon's huge bulk
crowded into the foreground and Una on a tiny peak only a
perilous inch away and, yet another inch in another direction,
the toy battlements of a city. In the sustained description of the
battle we feel the poet goading himself to mere rhetorical excess.
Professor Courthope avowed a preference for Orlando's battle
with the orc. But the episode in Ariosto is not material for
legitimate contrast. It is graphic. But Ariosto was abandoning
himself to the ludicrous as he conceived of Orlando calmly row-
ing his boat into the huge jaws of the sea-monster, propping
them apart with his anchor, and hewing out red ruin within.
Never does Ariosto rise here to the canorous grandeur that
almost saves the poet of *The Faërie Queene* when he celebrates
the monster's death.

> So downe he fell, and forth his life did breath,
> That vanisht into smoke and cloudes swift;
> So downe he fell, that th' earth him underneath
> Did grone, as feeble so great load to lift;
> So downe he fell, as an huge rocky clift,
> Whose false foundacion waves have washt away,
> With dreadfull poyse is from the mayneland rift,
> And, rolling downe, great Neptune doth dismay;
> So downe he fell, and like an heaped mountaine lay.

The excess of the culminating episode of the first book is partly atoned for also by a quiet denouement in which the poet wisely focuses on Una of whom Aubrey De Vere has said:

As long as Homer's Andromache and Nausicaa, Chaucer's Cecilia, Griselda, and Constance, the Imogen of Shakespeare, or the Beatrice of Dante, are remembered, so long will Una hold her place among them.

Here the poet essays a fuller description of her, as she comes to her wedding; but even here he wisely leaves much to suggestion.

> So faire and fresh, as freshest flowre in May;
> For she had layd her mournefull stole aside,
> And widow-like sad wimple throwne away,
> Wherewith her heavenly beautie she did hide,
> Whiles on her wearie journey she did ride;
> And on her now a garment she did weare
> All lilly white withouten spot or pride,
> That seemd like silk and silver woven neare,
> But neither silke nor silver therein did appeare.

A little flurry of excitement occasioned by a letter of false protestation from Duessa saves the narrative from tameness. Appropriately enough, it is Una who answers the witch's charges with finality. And with divine appropriateness, in the last stanza of the narrative proper, as the poet, with his characteristic Elizabethan restlessness, hastens his hero away to Faërie Land once more to serve Gloriana, Spenser gives us a brief glimpse of Una, last of all, as we have seen her nearly always—as Truth seems to be, nearly always, in the sight of our world—in sorrow, alone.

Dean Kitchin clearly points out the allegorical significance and sureness of the transition to Book Two.

In the First Book the Christian comes out firmly assured in his belief, and that, not as a mere effort of the imagination, or as a devotional sentiment, but as a severe intellectual enquiry and sifting of the truth, a "proving all things" in order to "hold fast that which is good." For this combination of reason with religion was deemed not only allowable but essential in the sixteenth century, and bore fruit in the appeals to men's judgment and personal reason as against authority, to common sense as against the iron rules and quibbles of the later Scholastics, to the personal study of the Bible as against a blind reliance on a traditional and sacerdotal system. In the Second Book we have the Christian working out, with many lets and slips, the moral ends of his existence, moderate and manly, the true "gentleman" in the right sense of the word. The Book expresses, in fact, the profound belief of the age in morality as the natural sequel of a true and enlightened faith. And Duessa and Archimago are introduced at the opening of the "pageant," as Spenser calls it, not merely as artistic links, binding Book with Book, but more especially to indicate this close connection of religion with morality. For falsehood and the false Church, said the age, fight against purity of life as well as against truth of doctrine, and the magician and the witch go on "deceiving and deceived" to the end.

It follows that Spenser, having risen to this high conception of the purpose of these Books, is obliged to break away from the plan he laid down for himself in his well-known Letter to Sir Walter Raleigh. To have worked out the twelve Books as representing "the twelve moral virtues," each with its own knight and its own adventures, would have demanded a far narrower treatment of these two opening Books. Instead of ranging over the whole extent of human life and interests as they do, pourtraying Holiness and Temperance, we should have had the adventures of the liberal soul struggling against extravagance or stinginess, or the brave man attacked by temptations of rashness and cowardice. The genius of the poet happily delivered him from his own bonds, and enabled him to deal with his subject with a dignity and completeness which makes each Book a work by itself, and a commentary on the whole breadth of human life."

It may have been that Spenser drank deep from Tasso's *Gerusalemme Liberata* for the first time when he was at work on his second book. The influence of Tasso, which is very strong here, seems to have been only intermittent and momentary as if the English poet who abandoned himself joyously to Ariosto's worldly glitter caught from the more serious Italian a sense of painful hesitation that awakened his own Puritan apprehensions and drew him hastily back from his luxurious perusals of the creator of the voluptuous and feverous Armida, while the gayer, harder Italian simply awakened his joy in a crowded and splendid life. Even Book Two is more prevailingly influenced by Ariosto, teeming as it does with grotesque but vivid situations. There are figures which loom up like some of the huge masculine figures of Rubens. Professor Dodge has taken issue with Campbell's and Hazlitt's oft-cited comparison of Spenser and Rubens. It is true that we never see in *The Faërie Queene* the Flemish painter's huge blondes. But some of the large and impetuously drawn figures of Book Two, Furor and Pyrochles for instance, are limned with something of the heavy strength which we see in that dead giant Christ whom Rubens has portrayed in the "Descent from the Cross" in Antwerp. These great figures move seriously but rapidly and with strange vividness in queer, complicated situations over which the wilful poet of the *Orlando Furioso* would have clapped his hands in delight. Under the influence of Tasso, on the other hand, Spenser had been led to fill the book with tropical flowers of passion with all the strange and alluring colors and perfumes but without that peculiar perfume that conquers like an opiate, flowers of passion that, unlike Tasso's, may be contemplated with a broad knowledge that is philosophic serenity.

That Sir Guyon or Temperance should be tempted by such passions has seemed to some to be bad allegory. But the answer I gave to the accusers of Holiness holds here. Guyon, though he preaches too much, is, in spite of some of Spenser's critics, a thoroughly human, though somewhat vaguely sketched hero who becomes Temperance incarnate through a series of trials over which, being a man, he naturally falters at times. Samuel Crothers has said the last word on this subject.

I should not regard any one as a fit teacher of youth who is not able to grasp Spenser's main intent and to sympathize with it. He represents Temperance not as a kind of weakness to be protected, but as a kind of strength to be exercised. This is a point of view which we sometimes miss. In our solicitude for the weak whom we shield from temptation, we forget the needs of those who are naturally strong, and in whom should be kindled an admiration for one of the manliest of the virtues.

Sir Guyon is no weakling. He appears "all armd in harnesse meete."
His way leads him by the Idle Lake, through the House of Mammon
and the Bower of Blisse....

Sir Guyon, being no paragon but only a knight-errant, sometimes for-
gets himself. But when he remembers what he is and whither he is bent,
he overcomes temptation. Temperance, it appears, is a form of personal
liberty. It is the determination of a strong man to be himself and to go
about his own business. The Bower of Blisse may have its attractions, but
they must not keep him from his quest....

It were well to have everybody taught to think of Temperance as some-
thing more than a series of prohibitions. It is the effort of a strong man
to master his might.[32]

The second book is, as we have seen, well linked with the
first; it is only in the later books that Spenser loses his grasp
of continuity. Here the familiar figures of Archimago and
Duessa bring on the first complication, the barely averted en-
counter of Sir Guyon and the Red Cross Knight. Then the
story takes its direct course. Never, for any long interval, are
we allowed to lose sight of Guyon's purpose—the destruction of
Acrasia's bower of sensual delight. His first real adventure is
with two of the victims of the voluptuous enchantress, with
Mordant and Amavia, two lovers brought to their death by the
man's weakness and infidelity. The picture of the dying Amavia
and her nursling is done in a vein of realism always within reach
of Spenser, when he desired it, and with a tenderness which
the poet of *The Faërie Queene* shares with Shakespeare.

> Als in her lap a lovely babe did play
> His cruell sport, in stead of sorrow dew;
> For in her streaming blood he did embay
> His litle hands, and tender joints embrew;
> Pitifull spectacle, as ever eie did vew.

And when Guyon has solemnly sworn revenge he takes up in his
mailed arms the babe

---

[32] It may be well to reinforce this shrewd defense with a passage by
Mr. Bailey.

"No one has ever read the *Faery Queen* without feeling that it was
a school of honour as well as a paradise of beautiful things and a forest
of strange adventures. No one reads it without being certain that its poet
was no mere languid dreamer of dreams of the senses. In spite of all the
strength he lavished on the bower of Acrasia, his poem as a whole remains
a trumpet-call to the praise of brave men and the honour of pure women."

> Who, with sweet pleasaunce and bold blandishment,
> Gan smyle on them, that rather ought to weepe,
> As carelesse of his woe, or innocent
> Of that was doen; that ruth emperced deepe
>   In that knightes hart....

In the second canto we are brought to the House of Medina (the Golden Mean) and her two sisters Elissa (Sullenness, Stinginess, or better, I think, Prurience combined with Hypocrisy), and Perissa (Prodigality and Lasciviousness). Here the poetry flags markedly and the characters become puppets moving stiffly as though on wires. But, like the canto on the House of Holinesse, this episode is of great value as a direct and very personal revelation of the poet's general ethical doctrines. He takes some liberties with the Aristotelian doctrine of the golden mean. One extreme, Elissa, who should represent defect, is clearly portrayed as the mistress of the extreme Puritan temperament, as the sullen lady of the savage and morose Sir Huddibras, the very knight, it will be remembered, who became the hero of Butler's satire on the Puritans of his day. The opposite extreme, Perissa, is the paramour of the Saracen Sansloy. No doctrine appears more persistently in Spenser's utterances than that of the golden mean; and, if he was not always consistent, no poet ever strove more nobly to give perpetual allegiance to it. But Medina, though hinted at as the lover of Guyon, never appears, as a person, again. In spite of the pallor and the mechanical quality of this episode, there emerges one chaotic incident with which the poet of the *Orlando Furioso* would have been delighted. Sansloy and Huddibras are always fighting, to the great enjoyment of their ladies. Guyon hears the tumult.

> The noyse thereof cald forth that straunger knight,
> To weet what dreadfull thing was there in hand;
> Where when as two brave knightes in bloody fight
> With deadly rancour he enraunged fond,
> His sunbroad shield about his wrest he bond,
> And shyning blade unsheathd, with which he ran
> Unto that stead, their strife to understond;
> ·And at his first arrivall, them began
>   With goodly means to pacifie, well as he can.

The two barbarians, however, promptly join forces against Guyon. Ariosto would have managed this strange "triple warre" with a rare blend of martial clashing and sly farce. Spenser, too, is not unaware of the grotesqueness of it all and showers paradoxes about it. But he is serious none the less and is inspired to celebrate Guyon with one of the most stately similes and daring stanzas in the whole poem. The wonderful meter, with its persistent introduction of a conflicting trochee in the middle of the lines, is full of the restless and confused swagger of the open sea.

> As a tall ship tossed in troublous seas,
> Whom raging windes, threatning to make the pray
> Of the rough rockes, doe diversely disease,
> Meetes two contrarie billowes by the way,
> That her on either side doe sore assay,
> And boast to swallow her in greedy grave;
> Shee, scorning both their spights, does make wide way,
> And with her brest breaking the fomy wave,
> Does ride on both their backs, and faire her selfe doth save.

The following episode is also strongly marked by the influence of Ariosto's taste for the grotesque. Braggadochio, the coward who steals Guyon's horse and spear is, as Professor Dodge pointed out, a partial counterpart of Ariosto's Martano, who steals the armor of Grifone.[33] The theory that Braggadochio, as boon comrade of the crafty old dotard Trompart, is Spenser's bold satire of Alençon, who, with the aid of Simier, sought the hand of Elizabeth to the apparent delight of the coquettish queen and the horror of Leicester's party and most of England, is probably sound.[34] If the reader considers this daring beyond possibility he must keep in mind the cumulative

---

[33] Although some of the characteristics of Braggadochio, such as his boasting that he prefers to fight without a sword, remind one of Mandricardo, I think it is misleading to call Spenser's coward, as Professor Dodge does, a combination of Martano and Mandricardo. For Mandricardo was a Tartar in fact and in colloquial metaphor whom Spenser would have taken very seriously as a hero. Pyrochles seems to me to be a copy of Mandricardo.

[34] I shall discuss Spenser's attitude towards this marriage more fully in my account of "Mother Hubberds Tale."

evidence of Spenser's audacity as I marshal it throughout my book. And the reader should note that this allegory is so cunningly devised in Spenser's Parthian manner that while it would irresistibly carry its undermeaning to many Elizabethan readers, it does not betray the poet red-handed. You know what he means but you cannot prove it. Any student of Elizabethan and Jacobean literature knows how constantly the poets of that era played with fire in this manner and how frequently they were persecuted for their temerity. No one of them quite paralleled Spenser in fierce vituperation; no one of them was more Parthian. And if the reader finds it hard to believe in the sincerity of the poet who wrote the dedication to the queen and who yet wrote satires with such a mortal aim, then the reader should remember John Stubbs who, when his right hand was cut off for his fierce pamphlet against the French marriage, removed his hat with his left and cried "God save the Queen!" the moment before he fainted in anguish. It is very probable that Spenser wrote or sketched this episode at the very time when the doubt and the excitement ran high, though it was not published until it had become past history. But Spenser did publish or boldly circulate his satire, "Mother Hubberds Tale," on the same subject, an act that, as we shall see, brought him into some sinister complications.

In the story of Braggadochio there is a certain hard humor that somewhat tempers the virulence. When one thinks of Shakespeare's fools, one sees Spenser's limitations, but the humor is there, especially in Braggadochio's amusing speeches and threats. And the satire is further relieved by that magical entrance of Belphoebe (Elizabeth in her private life).

> Eft through the thicke they heard one rudely rush;
> With noyse wherof he from his loftie steed
> Downe fell to ground, and crept into a bush,
> To hide his coward head from dying dreed.
> But Trompart stoutly stayd to taken heed
> Of what might hap. Eftsoone there stepped foorth
> A goodly ladie clad in hunters weed,
> That seemd to be a woman of great worth,
> And, by her stately portance, borne of heavenly birth.

Her face so faire as flesh it seemed not,
But hevenly pourtraict of bright angels hew,
Cleare as the skye, withouten blame or blot,
Through goodly mixture of complexions dew;
And in her cheekes the vermeill red did shew
Like roses in a bed of lillies shed,
The which ambrosiall odours from them threw,
And gazers sence with double pleasure fed,
Hable to heale the sicke, and to revive the ded.

In her faire eyes two living lamps did flame,
Kindled above at th' Hevenly Makers light,
And darted fyrie beames out of the same,
So passing persant, and so wondrous bright,
That quite bereav'd the rash beholders sight:
In them the blinded god his lustfull fyre
To kindle oft assayd, but had no might;
For with dredd majestie and awfull yre
She broke his wanton darts, and quenched bace desyre.

Her yvorie forhead, full of bountie brave,
Like a broad table did it selfe dispred,
For Love his loftie triumphes to engrave,
And write the battailes of his great godhed:
All good and honour might therein be red:
For there their dwelling was. And when she spake,
Sweete wordes, like dropping honny, she did shed,
And twixt the perles and rubins softly brake
A silver sound, that heavenly musicke seemd to make.

Upon her eyelids many Graces sate,
Under the shadow of her even browes,
Working belgardes and amorous retrate,
And everie one her with a grace endowes,
And everie one with meekenesse to her bowes.
So glorious mirrhour of celestiall grace,
And soveraine moniment of mortall vowes,
How shall frayle pen decrive her heavenly face,
For feare, through want of skill, her beauty to disgrace?

So faire, and thousand thousand times more faire,
She seemd, when she presented was to sight;
And was yclad, for heat of scorching aire,
Al in a silken camus lylly whight,
Purfled upon with many a folded plight,
Which al above besprinckled was throughout
With golden aygulets, that glistred bright,
Like twinckling starres, and all the skirt about
Was hemd with golden fringe.

Below her ham her weed did somewhat trayne,
And her streight legs most bravely were embayld
In gilden buskins of costly cordwayne,
All bard with golden bendes, which were entayld
With curious antickes, and full fayre aumayld:
Before, they fastned were under her knee
In a rich jewell, and therein entrayld
The ends of all their knots, that none might see
How they within their fouldings close enwrapped bee.

Like two faire marble pillours they were seene,
Which doe the temple of the gods support,
Whom all the people decke with girlands greene,
And honour in their festivall resort;
Those same with stately grace and princely port
She taught to tread, when she her selfe would grace,
But with the woody nymphes when she did sport,
Or when the flying libbard she did chace,
She could them nimbly move, and after fly apace.

And in her hand a sharpe bore-speare she held,
And at her backe a bow and quiver gay,
Stuft with steele-headed dartes, wherewith she queld
The salvage beastes in her victorious play,
Knit with a golden bauldricke, which forelay
Athwart her snowy brest, and did divide
Her daintie paps; which, like young fruit in May,
Now little gan to swell, and being tide,
Through her thin weed their places only signifide.

Her yellow lockes, crisped like golden wyre,
About her shoulders weren loosely shed,
And when the winde emongst them did inspyre,
They waved like a penon wyde dispred,
And low behinde her backe were scattered:
And whether art it were, or heedelesse hap,
As through the flouring forrest rash she fled,
In her rude heares sweet flowres themselves did lap,
And flourishing fresh leaves and blossomes did enwrap.

The satirical episode is given a hard and grotesque climax in Braggadochio's stupid and bestial interruption of Belphoebe's noble speech in praise of honor and against court idleness.

"Who so in pompe of prowd estate," quoth she,
"Does swim, and bathes him selfe in courtly blis,

> Does waste his dayes in darke obscuritee,
> And in oblivion ever buried is:
> Where ease abownds, yt's eath to doe amis:
> But who his limbs with labours, and his mynd
> Behaves with cares, cannot so easy mis.
> Abroad in armes, at home in studious kynd,
> Who seekes with painfull toile, shal Honor soonest fynd.
>
> "In woods, in waves, in warres she wonts to dwell,
> And wilbe found with perill and with paine;
> Ne can the man, that moulds in ydle cell,
> Unto her happy mansion attaine:
> Before her gate High God did sweate ordaine,
> And wakefull watches ever to abide:
> But easy is the way, and passage plaine
> To Pleasures pallace; it may soone be spide,
> And day and night her dores to all stand open wide."

This fine speech, which Milton remembered in his praise of Chastity in *Comus*, has an effect on Braggadochio that must have startled Elizabeth herself while it must have raised a shout of satisfaction from all angry Englishmen and must have caused all English partisans of Alençon to gnash their teeth years after the affair was closed.

> "In princes court—" The rest she would have sayd,
> But that the foolish man, fild with delight
> Of her sweete words, that all his sence dismayd,
> And with her wondrous beauty ravisht quight,
> Gan burne in filthy lust, and, leaping light,
> Thought in his bastard armes her to embrace.
> With that she, swarving backe, her javelin bright
> Against him bent, and fiercely did menace:
> So turned her about, and fled away apace.

Grotesqueness and graphic force continue in the next canto in which appears Furor, a huge and terrible figure, goaded on by the fierce hag Occasion, dragging a youth by the hair and beating him incessantly. The account of Guyon's combat with Furor would have delighted Ariosto. Like most of the combats in this book it is done with a martial fire that sets these battles apart from Spenser's less happy attempts and with a sturdy realism which, while remaining poetry, is always fearless of the proximity of prose. Furor attacks Guyon with no well directed force,

> But as a blindfold bull at randon fares,
> And where he hits, nought knowes, and whom he hurts, nought cares.

> His rude assault and rugged handeling
> Straunge seemed to the knight, that aye with foe
> In fayre defence and goodly menaging
> Of armes was wont to fight; yet nathemoe
> Was he abashed now, not fighting so,
> But, more enfierced through his currish play,
> Him sternly grypt, and, hailing to and fro,
> To overthrow him strongly did assay,
> But overthrew him selfe unwares, and lower lay.

> And being downe, the villein sore did beate
> And bruze with clownish fistes his manly face;
> And eke the hag, with many a bitter threat,
> Still cald upon to kill him in the place.
> With whose reproch and odious menace
> The knight emboyling in his haughtie hart,
> Knitt all his forces, and gan soone unbrace
> His grasping hold: so lightly did upstart,
> And drew his deadly weapon, to maintaine his part.

At the palmer's warning that this is one not to be slain with steel, Guyon throws aside his sword, grapples again with Furor, and binds him. The unhappy victim of Furor then tells an outlandish tale of how, deceived by a treacherous fiend into believing in his lady's infidelity, he slays first the unfortunate maiden then, learning of her innocence, murders his friend, and finally pursues the woman who had assisted in the deception, becoming thus the legitimate prey of Furor and Occasion. What follows is once more a scene that would have greatly diverted and strongly appealed to Ariosto. The youth tells how, as he leaped with drawn sword after the treacherous woman,

> "Feare gave her winges, and rage enforst my flight:
> Through woods and plaines so long I did her chace,
> Till this mad man, whom your victorious might
> Hath now fast bound, me met in middle space:
> As I her, so he me poursewd apace,

> And shortly overtooke: I, breathing yre,
> Sore chauffed at my stay in such a cace,
> And with my heat kindled his cruell fyre;
> Which kindled once, his mother did more rage inspyre.''

The usual brace of preachments from Guyon and the palmer is happily cut short by the entrance of Atin (Strife), who flashes in with a rapidity that once more gives the lie to those Macaulay-esque readers who are forever prating of Spenser's languor and tedium.

> Thus as he spake, lo! far away they spyde
> A varlet ronning towardes hastily,
> Whose flying feet so fast their way applyde,
> That round about a cloud of dust did fly.
> Which, mingled all with sweate, did dim his eye.
> He soone approached, panting, breathlesse, whot,
> And all so soyld, that none could him descry.
> His countenance was bold, and bashed not
> For Guyon's lookes, but scornefull eyglaunce at him shot.
>
> Behinde his backe he bore a brasen shield,
> On which was drawen faire in colours fit,
> A flaming fire in midst of bloody field,
> And round about the wreath this word was writ,
> *Burnt I doe burne.* Right well beseemed it
> To be the shield of some redoubted knight:
> And in his hand two dartes exceeding flit
> And deadly sharp he held, whose heads were dight
> In poyson and in blood of malice and despight.
>
> When he in presence came, to Guyon first
> He boldly spake: ''Sir knight, if knight thou bee,
> Abandon this forestalled place at erst,
> For feare of further harme, I counsell thee;
> Or bide the chaunce at thine owne jeopardee.''
> The knight at his great boldnesse wondered,
> And though he scornd his ydle vanitee,
> Yet mildly him to purpose answered;
> For not to grow of nought he it conjectured.

The allegory, always most ingenious and generally very vivid in this book, becomes almost an absurd pun when we learn that

Atin has been sent by his master, Pyrochles,[35] who is "all dis-
posd to bloody fight," to seek Occasion.   When Atin is shown
Occasion bound, he bids defiance to Guyon.   The canto closes
with admirable vivacity.

> With that, one of his thrillant darts he threw,
> Headed with yre and vengeable despight:
> The quivering steele his aymed end wel knew,
> And to his brest it selfe intended right:
> But he was wary, and, cre it empight
> In the meant marke, advaunst his shield atweene,
> On which it seizing, no way enter might,
> But backe rebownding left the forckhead keene:
> Eftsoones he fled away, and might no where be seene.

In the fifth canto, with the entrance of Pyrochles himself, the
narrative rushes on gaining speed and spirit all the time.

> After that varlets flight, it was not long,
> Ere on the plaine fast pricking Guyon spide
> One in bright armes embatteiled full strong.
> That as the sunny beames doe glaunce and glide
> Upon the trembling wave, so shined bright,
> And round about him threw forth sparkling fire,
> That seemd to him to enflame on every side:
> His steed was bloody red, and fomed yre,
> When with the maistring spur he did him roughly stire.
>
> Approching nigh, he never staid to greete,
> Ne chaffar words, prowd corage to provoke,
> But prickt so fiers, that underneath his feete
> The smouldring dust did rownd about him smoke,
> Both horse and man nigh able for to choke;
> And fairly couching his steeleheaded speare,
> Him first saluted with a sturdy stroke:
> It booted nought Sir Guyon, comming neare,
> To thincke such hideous puissance on foot to beare.

There is a steady crescendo which, though extravagant, is never
inartistic and which is at once allegorical and vivid.   There is

---

[35] "(πῦρ, fire, ὀχλέω, to move, disturb.)   One manifestation of the
irascible, contentious, or passionate element in the soul: the wrath that
burns without cause, that wilfully seeks 'occasions.'   Child of self-indul-
gence (Acrates) and malice (Despight): Acrates, son of Phlegethon (the
river of fire) and Jarre (discord)."   —Dodge.

also a touch of grim Anglo-Saxon humor, the "understate-
ment" in which the poet of *Beowulf* so delights, when Guyon
deals his adversary such a huge buffet that

> He made him stoup perforce unto his knee,
> And doe unwilling worship to the saint,
> That on his shield depainted he did see:
> Such homage till that instant never learned hee.

The impetuosity of the narrative is broken by Guyon's usual
sermon over his fallen foe. But in another moment we are
bewildered and amused by a new situation quite as grotesque
and quite as graphic as the strange medley that has preceded
it. Guyon permits the eager Pyrochles to unbind Furor, whom
Occasion promptly incites against his perverse liberator. She
brings her minion a flaming brand with which he smites the
pagan until the knight is fain to cry for help which Guyon, at
the palmer's stern admonishment, refuses.

Atin flees away in search of Cymochles,[36] the brother of
Pyrochles, who had of late withdrawn himself to the Bowre of
Blisse. Atin's discovery of Cymochles is described with no Puri-
tan reticence.

> There he him found all carelessly displaid,
> In secrete shadow from the sunny ray,
> On a sweet bed of lillies softly laid,
> Amidst a flock of damzelles fresh and gay,
> That rownd about him dissolute did play
> Their wanton follies and light meriment;
> Every of which did loosely disaray
> Her upper partes of meet habiliments,
> And shewd them naked, deckt with many ornaments.

> And every of them strove, with most delights
> Him to aggrate, and greatest pleasures shew:
> Some framd faire lookes, glancing like evening lights,
> Others sweet wordes, dropping like honny dew;
> Some bathed kisses, and did soft embrew
> The sugred licour through his melting lips:
> One boastes her beautie, and does yield to vew
> Her dainty limbes above her tender hips;
> Another her out boastes, and all for tryall strips.

---

[36] "Passion fierce and fickle as the sea waves (κῦμα), whence the name;
characterized by long fits of sensual indolence." —Dodge.

> He, like an adder lurking in the weedes,
> His wandring thought in deepe desire does steepe,
> And his frayle eye with spoyle of beauty feedes:
> Sometimes he falsely faines himselfe to sleepe,
> Whiles through their lids his wanton eies do peepe,
> To steale a snatch of amorous conceipt,
> Whereby close fire into his heart does creepe:
> So he them deceives, deceivd in his deceipt,
> Made dronke with drugs of deare voluptuous receipt.

The eighth line of the last stanza is in precisely the mode of Tasso when he hunts the word. And there is a quality of half fearful insinuation that is more like Tasso than Spenser. But with Spenser the recoil is always immediate and uncompromising. Atin's stirring words arouse both Cymochles and the reader.

> Attin, arriving there, when him he spyde
> Thus in still waves of deepe delight to wade,
> Fiercely approching, to him lowdly cryde,
> "Cymochles! oh! no, but Cymochles shade,
> In which that manly person late did fade!
> What is become of great Acrates sonne?
> Or where hath he hong up his mortall blade,
> That hath so many haughty conquests wonne?
> Is all his force forlorne, and all his glory donne?"
>
> Then pricking him with his sharp-pointed dart,
> He saide: "Up, up! thou womanish weake knight,
> That here in ladies lap entombed art,
> Unmindfull of thy praise and prowest might,
> And weetlesse eke of lately wrought despight,
> Whiles sad Pyrochles lies on sencelesse ground,
> And groneth out his utmost grudging spright,
> Through many a stroke, and many a streaming wound,
> Calling thy help in vaine, that here in joyes art dround."

This episode was undoubtedly suggested by the story of how Carlo and Ubaldo summoned Rinaldo from Armida's bower in the *Gerusalemme Liberata*. But as we turn from Tasso's half morbid luxuriance, half-delighted, half-troubled, to Spenser's all but unabashed description of the lascivious scene and to his quick and unperturbed cry of hearty scorn, we realize that

while in Tasso the febrile vision lingers to the end, in Spenser
it has vanished completely at the fierce shout of Atin. And
while Spenser's lovely witches are spurned, Tasso's Armida is
a heroine who returns at the close, with little transformation, to
fill Rinaldo and the poet's readers once more with her sultry
oriental languor.

Canto Six tells the story of Phaedria (Immodest Mirth) with
a frank delight that seems at first like the very innocence of a
young sinner. No sooner had Atin brought Cymochles from the
Bowre of Blisse before, coming to a river, they

> . . . Saw whereas did swim
> Along the shore, as swift as glaunce of eye,
> A litle gondelay, bedecked trim
> With boughes and arbours woven cunningly,
> That like a litle forrest seemed outwardly.
>
> And therein sate a lady fresh and fayre,
> Making sweete solace to herself alone;
> Sometimes she song, as lowd as larke in ayre,
> Sometimes she laught, that nigh her breth was gone,
> Yet was there not with her else any one,
> That might to her move cause of meriment:
> Matter of merth enough, though there were none,
> She could devise, and thousand waies invent,
> To feede her foolish humour and vaine jolliment.

The damsel, although she refused Atin, was ready enough to
take Cymochles into her shallop.

> Eftsoones her shallow ship away did slide,
> More swift then swallow sheres the liquid skye,
> Withouten oare or pilot it to guide,
> Or winged canves with the wind to fly:
> Onely she turnd a pin, and by and by
> It cut away upon the yielding wave;
> Ne cared she her course for to apply:
> For it was taught the way which she would have,
> And both from rocks and flats it selfe could wisely save.
>
> And all the way, the wanton damsell found
> New merth, her passenger to entertaine:
> For she in pleasaunt purpose did abound,
> And greatly joyed merry tales to faine,

Of which a store-house did with her remaine:
Yet seemed, nothing well they her became;
For all her wordes she drownd with laughter vaine,
And wanted grace in utt'ring of the same,
That turned all her pleasaunce to a scoffing game.

And other whiles vaine toyes she would devize,
As her fantasticke wit did most delight:
Sometimes her head she fondly would aguize
With gaudy girlonds, or fresh flowrets dight
About her necke, or rings of rushes plight;
Sometimes, to do him laugh, she would assay
To laugh at shaking of the leaves light,
Or to behold the water worke and play
About her little frigot therein making way.

Her light behaviour and loose dalliaunce
Gave wondrous great contentment to the knight,
That of his way he had no sovenaunce,
Nor care of vow'd revenge and cruell fight,
But to weake wench did yield his martiall might:
So easie was, to quench his flamed minde
With one sweete drop of sensuall delight;
So easie is, t'appease the stormy winde
Of malice in the calme of pleasaunt womankind.

Soon she brings the charmed Cymochles to her island.

It was a chosen plott of fertile land,
Emongst wide waves sett, like a litle nest,
As if it had by Natures cunning hand
Bene choycely picked out from all the rest,
And laid forth for ensample of the best:
No dainty flowre or herbe, that growes on grownd,
No arborett with painted blossomes drest,
And smelling sweete, but there it might be fownd
To bud out faire, and her swete smels throwe al arownd.

Here Phaedria lulls the wanton Saracen with a song which shows how warmly Spenser felt the temptation of that quietism which he put before in the mouth of Despayre—an attitude in which fanatical Puritan and voluptuary find common ground—and which the poet repudiated in what were probably the last stanzas he ever wrote. Here, in the song of Immodest Mirth, he paraphrases, with exquisite daring, one of the loveliest passages in the Bible.

> The lilly, lady of the flowring field,
> The flowre deluce, her lovely paramoure,
> Bid thee to them thy fruitlesse labors yield,
> And soone leave off this toylesome weary stoure:
> Loe, loe how brave she decks her bounteous boure,
> With silkin curtens and gold coverletts,
> Therein to shrowd her sumptuous belamoure!
> Yet nether spinnes nor cards, ne cares nor fretts,
> But to her mother Nature all her care she letts.

But in another moment we are told of the meeting of Phaedria (who leaves Cymochles asleep) and Guyon whom she finds awaiting passage. Guyon is, to be sure, led astray from his palmer by the damsel who fears equally the cursed Atin and the sober man of God. As they skim over the water Phaedria gaily sings in harmonious rivalry with the birds.

> And she, more sweete then any bird on bough,
> Would oftentimes emongst them beare a part,
> And strive to passe (as she could well enough)
> Their native musicke by her skilful art:
> So did she all, that might his constant hart
> Withdraw from thought of warlike enterprize,
> And drowne in dissolute delights apart,
> Where noise of armes, or vew of martiall guize,
> Might not revive desire of knightly exercize.

But Guyon, though courteous, is in no wise seduced by her loose ways. In a moment we feel the shock of his combat with the awakened Cymochles. And Phaedria is only too glad to ferry back her latest guest, so self-contained in his attitude towards her allurements and so fierce in his disruption of the shallow peace of her islet. Then, as Guyon turns away from the shore, mastering a gust of anger at the railing and threats of Atin, a sudden and disjointed climax gives a queer but most effective close to the canto.[37]

> Whylest there the varlet stood, he saw from farre
> An armed knight, that towardes him fast ran;
> He ran on foot, as if in lucklesse warre
> His forlorne steed from him the victour wan;

---

[37] Professor Dodge thinks that Bojardo had no influence on Spenser. But this striking scene bears some marked resemblances to one in the *Orlando Innamorato* where Mandricado, half-consumed by fire, leaps into a fountain. The curious may find other plausible traces of the Ferrarese poet in *The Faërie Queene*.

> He seemed breathlesse, heartlesse, faint, and wan,
> And all his armor sprinckled was with blood,
> And soyld with durtie gore, that no man can
> Discerne the hew therof. He never stood,
> But bent his hastie course towardes the ydle flood.

> The varlett saw, when to the flood he came,
> How without stop or stay he fiersly lept,
> And deepe him selfe beducked in the same,
> That in the lake his loftie crest was stept,
> Ne of his safetie seemed care he kept,
> But with his raging armes he rudely flasht
> The waves about, and all his armour swept,
> That all the blood and filth away was washt,
> Yet still he bet the water, and the billowes dasht.

It was Pyrochles tortured by the fire which Furor had dashed into his body. Atin leaps in after the unhappy knight to prevent him from drowning himself. The description of the two struggling so impetuously and so absurdly in the sluggish waves of this stream is equally stirring and laughable. Only the art of Archimago, who arrived at this moment, saved the fierce pagan from death in agony.

Guyon's next adventure is with Mammon.

> At last he came unto a gloomy glade,
> Cover'd with boughes and shrubs from heavens light,
> Whereas he sitting found in secret shade
> An uncouth, salvage and uncivile wight,
> Of griesly hew and fowle ill favour'd sight;
> His face with smoke was tand, and eies were bleard,
> His head and beard with sout were ill bedight,
> His cole-blacke hands did seeme to have ben seard
> In smythes fire-spitting forge, and nayles like clawes appeard.

> His yron cote, all overgrowne with rust,
> Was underneath enveloped with gold,
> Whose glistring glosse, darkned with filthy dust,
> Well yet appeared to have beene of old
> A worke of rich entayle and curious mould,
> Woven with antickes and wyld ymagery:
> And in his lap a masse of coyne he told,
> And turned upside downe, to feede his eye
> And covetous desire with his huge threasury.

> And round about him lay on every side
> Great heapes of gold, that never could be spent:
> Of which some were rude owre, not purifide
> Of Mulcibers devouring element;
> Some others were new driven, and distent
> Into great ingowes, and to wedges square;
> Some in round plates witouten moniment:
> But most were stampt, and in their metal bare
> The antique shapes of kings and kesars straunge and rare.

The dark creature seems not so much like a man as an immense grim statue, but a statue which the rare volatilizing imagination of the poet infuses with life and causes to move, terrible, heavy. To Charles Lamb's subtle mind the power of imagining this figure with his strange unreality and strange reality was a cardinal proof of the sanity of supreme genius.

In [Spenser] ... we have names which announce fiction; and we have absolutely no place at all, for the things and persons of the *Fairy Queen* prate not of their "whereabout." But in their inner nature, and the law of their speech and actions, we are at home, and upon acquainted ground. The one turns life into a dream; the other to the wildest dreams gives the sobrieties of everyday occurrences. By what subtle art of tracing the mental processes it is effected, we are not philosophers enough to explain, but in that wonderful episode of the cave of Mammon, in which the Money God appears first in the lowest form of a miser, is then a worker of metals, and becomes the god of all the treasures of the world; and has a daughter, Ambition, before whom all the world kneels for favours—with the Hesperian fruit, the waters of Tantalus, with Pilate washing his hands vainly, but not impertinently, in the same stream— that we should be at one moment in the cave of an old hoarder of treasures, at the next at the forge of the Cyclops, in a palace and yet in hell, all at once, with the shifting mutations of the most rambling dream, and our judgment yet all the time awake, and neither able nor willing to detect the fallacy—is a proof of that hidden sanity which still guides the poet in the wildest seeming-aberrations.

It is not enough to say that the whole episode is a copy of the mind's conceptions in sleep; it is, in some sort—but what a copy! Let the most romantic of us, that has been entertained all night with the spectacle of some wild and magnificent vision, recombine it in the morning, and try it by his waking judgment. That which appeared so shifting, and yet so coherent, while that faculty was passive, when it comes under cool examination shall appear so reasonless and so unlinked, that we are ashamed to have been so deluded; and to have taken, though but in sleep, a monster for a god. But the transitions in this episode are every whit as violent as in the most extravagant dream, and yet the waking judgment ratifies them.

Guyon restrains Mammon, who is turning to push back his hills of gold underground with the slow, heavy haste and fear of a reptile, and asks his name. Mammon, like a reptile at bay, gains courage with his enforced answer.

> Thereat, with staring eyes fixed askaunce,
> In great disdaine, he answerd: ''Hardy Elfe,
> That darest vew my direfull countenaunce,
> I read thee rash and heedlesse of thy selfe,
> To trouble my still seate, and heapes of pretious pelfe.

> ''God of the world and worldlings I me call,
> Great Mammon, greatest god below the skye,
> That of my plenty poure out unto all,
> And unto none my graces do envye:
> Riches, renowme, and principality,
> Honour, estate, and all this worldes good,
> For which men swinck and sweat incessantly,
> Fro me do flow into an ample flood,
> And in the hollow earth have their eternall brood.''

The argument between the two that follows is rich in persuasion both for the allurements of gold and for the higher splendor of renunciation; it moves stately like a harangue and is so full of sustained majesty that it is perfectly appropriate for an epic.

> ''All otherwise,'' said he, ''I riches read,
> And deeme them roote of all disquietnesse;
> First got with guile, and then preserv'd with dread,
> And after spent with pride and lavishnesse,
> Leaving behind them griefe and heavinesse.
> Infinite michiefes of them doe arize,
> Strife and debate, bloodshed and bitternesse,
> Outrageous wrong and hellish covetize,
> That noble heart, as great dishonour, doth despize.

> ''Ne thine be kingdomes, ne the scepters thine;
> But realmes and rulers thou doest both confound,
> And loyall truth to treason doest incline:
> Witnesse the guiltlesse blood pourd oft on ground,
> The crowned often slaine, the slayer cround,
> And sacred diademe in peeces rent,
> And purple robe gored with many a wound;
> Castles surprizd, great cities sackt and brent:
> So mak'st thou kings, and gaynest wrongfull government.

"Long were to tell the troublous stormes that tosse
The private state, and make the life unsweet:
Who swelling sayles in Caspian sea doth crosse,
And in frayle wood on Adrian gulf doth fleet,
Doth not, I weene, so many evils meet.''

At last the monster is constrained to prove his arguments by
leading Guyon to his domains near by hell's gates, where they
pass an army of portents. Many poets, since Virgil at least,
have tried their hands at similar descriptions, but none have
surpassed Spenser in the conquest of a huge crowded canvas
where every one of the closely massed figures, limned with a few
swift strokes, is palpitating with life.

Through that thick covert he him led, and fownd
A darkesome way, which no man could descry,
That deep descended through the hollow grownd,
And was with dread and horror compassed arownd.

At length they came into a larger space,
That stretcht it selfe into an ample playne,
Through which a beaten broad high way did trace,
That streight did lead to Plutoes griesly rayne:
By the wayes side there sate infernall Payne,
And fast beside him sat tumultous Strife:
The one in hand an yron whip did strayne,
The other brandished a bloody knife,
And both did gnash their teeth, and both did threten life.

On th' other side, in one consort, there sate
Cruell Revenge and rancorous Despight,
Disloyall Treason, and hart-burning Hate;
But gnawing Gealosy, out of their sight
Sitting alone, his bitter lips did bight;
And trembling Feare still to and fro did fly,
And found no place, wher safe he shroud him might;
Lamenting Sorrow did in darknes lye;
And Shame his ugly face did hide from living eye.

And over them sad Horror with grim hew
Did alwaies sore, beating his yron wings;
And after him owles and night-ravens flew,
The hatefull messengers of heavy things,

> Of death and dolor telling sad tidings;
> Whiles sad Celeno, sitting on a clifte,
> A song of bale and bitter sorrow sings,
> That hart of flint a sonder could have rifte:
> Which having ended, after him she flyeth swifte.

It was this passage that Milton, in his first sustained attempt at sublimity, chose to follow almost servilely.[38] Past these awful portals stole Mammon and Guyon to a door very close beside which opened at Mammon's approach to suck them in. Behind this door there lurked a fiend who is described with the suggestiveness of Milton at his highest control of pictorial vagueness and awe.

> Soone as he entred was, the dore streight way
> Did shutt, and from behind it forth there lept
> An ugly feend, more fowle than dismall day,
> The which with monstrous stalke behind him stept,
> And ever as he went, dew watch upon him kept.

> Well hoped hee, ere long that hardy guest,
> If ever covetous hand, or lustfull eye,
> Or lips he layd on thing that likte him best,
> Or ever sleepe his eiestrings did untye,
> Should be his pray. And therefore still on hye
> He over him did hold his cruell clawes,
> Threatening with greedy gripe to doe him dye,
> And rend in peeces with his ravenous pawes,
> If ever he transgrest the fatall Stygian lawes.

No one has praised the description of the cave itself better than Hazlitt, who writes of "the portentous massiness of the forms, the splendid chiaro-scuro and shadowy horror."

> That houses forme within was rude and strong,
> Lyke an huge cave, hewne out of rocky clifte,
> From whose rough vaut the ragged breaches hong,
> Embost with massy gold of glorious guifte,
> And with rich metal loaded every rifte,
> That heavy ruine they did seem to threatt;
> And over them Arachne high did lifte
> Her cunning web, and spred her subtile nett,
> Enwrapped in fowle smoke and clouds more black then jett.

---

[38] *In Quintum Novembris.* See the *Cambridge Edition* of Milton (Boston and New York, 1890), 351.

> Both roofe, and floore, and walls were all of gold,
> But overgrowne with dust and old decay,
> And hid in darkenes, that none could behold
> The hew thereof: for vew of cherefull day
> Did never in that house it selfe display,
> But a faint shadow of uncertein light;
> Such as a lamp, whose life does fade away;
> Or as the moone, cloathed with clowdy night,
> Does shew to him that walkes in feare and sad affright.

Guyon's answers here always transcend his usual sermons and rise into something like an austere ode. Scene succeeds scene with steadily accumulating impressiveness.

> Thence forward he him ledd, and shortly brought
> Unto another rowme, whose dore forthright
> To him did open, as it had been taught:
> Therein an hundred raunges weren pight,
> And hundred fournaces all burning bright:
> By every fournace many feendes did byde,
> Deformed creatures, horrible in sight;
> And every feend his busie paines applyde,
> To melt the golden metall, ready to be tryde.
>
> . . . .
>
> But when an earthly wight they present saw,
> Glistring in armes and battailous aray,
> From their whot work they did themselves withdraw
> To wonder at the sight: for, till that day,
> They never creature saw, that cam that way.
> Their staring eyes, sparckling with fervent fyre,
> And ugly shapes did nigh the man dismay.

One would have expected the advent of the nineteenth century, of our modern factories and monsters of the ocean before such a scene could have been possible to the poetic imagination. All these scenes and, above all, the following episode, a climax where it would seem that imagination had already made climax impossible, make the lover of Spenser protest when he remembers the long line of purblind critics who have denied to the creator of Mammon and of Philotime (Ambition) the possession of sublimity.[39]

---

[39] One of the most exasperating comments may be found in the opening paragraph of Swinburne's essay on Marlowe (reprinted in *The Age of Shakespeare*), in which Marlowe's erratic descendant denies to Spenser the quality of sublimity in order to make Marlowe the first English master of the power which he so justly worships.

He brought him through a darksom narrow strayt,
To a broad gate, all built of beaten gold:
The gate was open, but therein did wayt
A sturdie villein, stryding stiffe and bold,
As if that Highest God defy he would:
In his right hand an yron club he held,
But he himselfe was all of golden mould,
Yet had both life and sence, and well could weld
That cursed weapon, when his cruell foes he queld.

Disdayne he called was, and did disdayne
To be so cald, and who so did him call:
Sterne was his looke, and full of stomacke vayne,
His portaunce terrible, and stature tall,
Far passing th' hight of men terrestriall,
Like an huge gyant of the Titans race;
That made him scorne all creatures great and small,
And with his pride all others powre deface:
More fitt emongst black fiendes then men to have his place.

Soon as those glitterand armes he did espye,
That with their brightnesse made the darknes light,
His harmefull club he gan to hurtle hye,
And threaten batteill to the Faery knight;
Who likewise gan himselfe to batteill dight,
Till Mammon did his hasty hand withold,
And counseld him abstaine from perilous fight:
For nothing might abash the villein bold,
Ne mortall steele emperce his miscreated mould.

So having him with reason pacifyde,
And the fiers carle commaunding to forbeare,
He brought him in. The rowme was large and wyde,
As it some gyeld or solemne temple weare:
Many great golden pillours did upbeare
The massy roofe, and riches huge sustayne,
And every pillour decked was full deare
With crownes, and diademes, and titles vaine,
Which mortall princes wore, whiles they on earth did rayne.

A route of people there assembled were,
Of every sort and nation under skye,
Which with great uprore preaced to draw nere
To th' upper part, where was advaunced hye
A stately siege of soveraine majestye;
And thereon satt a woman gorgeous gay,
And richly cladd in robes of royaltye,
That never earthly prince in such aray
His glory did enhaunce and pompous pryde display.

His face right wondrous faire did seeme to bee,
That her broad beauties beam great brightness threw
Through the dim shade, that all men might it see:
Yet was not that same her owne native hew,
But wrought by art and counterfetted shew,
Thereby more lovers unto her to call;
Nath'lesse most hevenly faire in deed and vew
She by creation was, till she did fall;
Thenceforth she sought for helps to cloke her crime withall.

There as in glistring glory she did sitt,
She held a great gold chain ylincked well,
Whose upper end to highest heven was knitt,
And lower part did reach to lowest hell;
And all that preace did rownd about her swell,
To catchen hold of that long chaine, thereby
To climbe aloft, and others to excell:
That was Ambition, rash desire to sty,
And every linck thereof a step of dignity.

Some thought to raise themselves to high degree
By riches and unrighteous reward;
Some by close shouldring, some by flatteree;
Others through friendes, others for base regard;
And all by wrong waies for themselves prepard.
Those that were up themselves, kept others low,
Those that were low themselves, held others hard,
Ne suffered them to ryse or greater grow,
But every one did strive his fellow downe to throw.

The adventure closes with the passing of a river full of tormented souls, a river that reminds one in its foulness and horror of nothing less than Dante's Malebolge.

Although Guyon passes back to earth in safety he sinks down in a swoon-like death.

And is there care in heaven? And is there love
In heavenly spirits to these creatures bace,
That may compassion of their evilles move?
There is: else much more wretched were the cace
Of men then beasts. But O th' exceeding grace
Of Highest God, that loves his creatures so,
And all his workes with mercy doth embrace,
That blessed angels he sends to and fro,
To serve to wicked man, to serve his wicked foe!

How oft do they their silver bowers leave
To come to succour us, that succour want!
How oft do they with golden pineons cleave
The flitting skyes, like flying pursuivant,
Against fowle feendes to ayd us militant!
They for us fight, they watch and dewly ward,
And their bright squadrons round about us plant;
And all for love, and nothing for reward:
O why should hevenly God to men have such regard?

The palmer, who meanwhile had crossed the river at another
point, is hastened by the call of an angel to the side of Guyon,
but only that he may strive with pathetic futility to prevent
Cymochles and Pyrochles from despoiling their old foe whom
they suppose dead. Once more (unhappily for the last time)
Spenser prepares a perfect entrance for Magnanimity, Prince
Arthur, and the narrative moves upward once more, with some-
thing near to repetition, in the curious spiral structure which,
could Spenser have continued it to perfection, would never
have aroused a murmur from the critics. The battle in which
Prince Arthur slays Cymochles and Pyrochles, though it owes
something to Orlando's combat with Gradasso in Ariosto and
to Arthur's combat with Accolon in Malory, is an admirable
piece of sustained work full of sudden vicissitudes and worthy
of any martial poet. It is almost the last great duel in *The
Faërie Queene.*

In canto nine the narrative movement is quite becalmed and
we are made to pause over one of the most ingenious and absurd
pieces of elaborate allegory in *The Faërie Queene.* Arthur and
Guyon come to the House of Alma (Soul) which is surrounded
by an unruly mob (the Passions). There is little doubt that the
vivid picture that follows was painted right out of the wild life
which Spenser saw in Ireland.

Thus as he spoke, loe! with outragious cry
A thousand villeins rownd about them swarmd
Out of the rockes and caves adjoyning nye:
Vile caitive wretches, ragged, rude, deformd,
All threatning death, all in straunge manner armd;
Some with unwieldy clubs, some with long speares,

> Some rusty knifes, some staves in fier warmd,
>   Sterne was their looke, like wild amazed steares,
> Staring with hollow eies, and stiffe upstanding heares.

So the passions beleaguer the body which is the house of the
soul. Guyon and Arthur scatter them for a time and enter the
castle. The prevailing trouble with many critics who are so
constantly denying to Spenser the gift of realism is that they
are incapable of feeling the appropriateness of the allegory and,
at the same time, realizing that Spenser often turned to con-
temporary life in its full vigor and complexity for the models
of these same allegorical figures. There is an art in these
apparently contradictory processes that must be richly felt be-
fore one can hope fully to appreciate *The Faërie Queene.* On
the other hand Spenser occasionally drifts into the over-elabor-
ate, the over-ingenious as in the physiological allegory which
follows, which is even more mechanical than all its innumerable
quaint and starched medieval sources.[40] It was this strange
canto alone—such was the domination of Spenser over some
of his earlier followers—which gave Phineas Fletcher most of
the material for his fantastic religious quasi-epic, *The Purple
Island.* The frame of the House of Alma is described with a
curious kind of geometrical symbolism which, from the days of
the Pythagoreans, had a profound appeal for many serious
thinkers. As the soul was represented by the sphere, the most
perfect figure, the infinite circle of the heavens, while the
imperfect triangle symbolized the body, so the structure of

---

[40] What were Spenser's direct sources here we shall probably never
discover and prove. We may be sure that they were many and that his
individuality was great. Of the myriads of books on this subject we can
only list a few which are among those more likely to have influenced him
directly. Bishop Grosseteste's *Château d'Amour* or *Castel of Love* is the
body of Mary into which Christ enters. The castle of Inwyt in *Piers
Plowman* is a very plausible source of suggestion. Spenser may have seen
King Hart by Gavin Douglas in which the hero lives in an elaborate physio-
logical castle. Stephen Hawes in his *Passetyme of Pleasure* (Chap. XXIV)
has a similar classification of wits and senses, though he does not allegorize
them. In Lydgate's castle of Virtue in his *Assembly of Gods* there are
five posterns like Spenser's five bulwarks of the senses. It all goes back,
of course, to Prudentius and Bernard of Clairvaux and a jungle of church-
men who doubtless elaborated texts from the Bible in their characteristic
allegorical manner going, perhaps, especially to *The Wisdom of Solomon.*

Spenser's bizarre castle seemed "partly circulare and part
triangulare." The base of this "worke divine" was a quadrate,
"proportioned equally by seven and nine," that is to say, all
the powers of man.[41] Within the barbican was our friend the
tongue, of whom Spenser says gravely:

> His larumbell might lowd and wyde be hard,
> When cause requyrd, but never out of time;
> Early and late it rong, at evening and at prime.

Twice sixteen bright-armed yeomen we identify as the teeth. It
is all very diverting. There follows a solemn allegorization of
the functions of digestion worked out with painstaking complete-
ness. Then comes an early and popular version of the old
"faculty psychology," naïve, but hardly more naïve than that
which underlies the educational prescriptions of most contem-
porary American college professors. We arrive at the chamber
of one of the lady's three counsellors who dwell in the tower,
Phantastes, who surpassed Common Sense and Memory in that
he could foresee many things to come and to whom Spenser
rightly gives the place of honor.

> His chamber was dispainted all with in
> With sondry colours, in the which were writ
> Infinite shapes of thinges dispersed thin;
> Some such as in the world were never yit,
> Ne can devized be of mortal wit;
> Some daily seene, and knowen by their names,
> Such as in idle fantasies doe flit:
> Infernall hags, centaurs, feendes, hippodames,
> Apes, lyons, aegles, owles, fooles, lovers, children, dames.
>
> And all the chamber filled was with flyes,
> Which buzzed all about, and made such sound,
> That they encombred all mens eares and eyes,
> Like many swarmes of bees assembled round,

---

[41] All this was vital enough in the seventeenth century to stimulate Sir
Kenelm Digby to write his *Observations on the Twenty Second Stanza of
the Ninth Canto of The Second Book of The Faerie Queene*, in which he
explains in detail the hidden meanings of the poet, whom he calls "our
English Virgil," and whom he tells us he had pondered deeply and long.
The reader will find these observations most conveniently accessible in a
note to this stanza in Todd's edition, 1805, IV, 180 sq.

After their hives with honny do abound:
All those were idle thoughtes and fantasies,
Devices, dreames, opinions unsound,
Shewes, visions, sooth-sayes, and prophesies;
And all that fained is, as leasings, tales, and lies.

Emongst them all sate he which wonned there,
That hight Phantastes by his nature trew,
A man of yeares yet fresh, as mote appeare,
Of swarth complexion, and of crabbed hew,
That him full of melancholy did shew;
Bent hollow beetle browes, sharp staring eyes,
That mad or foolish seemd: one by his vew
Mote deeme him borne with ill-disposed skyes,
When oblique Saturne sate in the house of agonyes.

We may fairly leave Arthur and Guyon (in Canto X)
to peruse their long chronicles in peace. Arthur reads "of
Briton kings, from Brute to Uther's rayne." And dull reading
it is despite the poet's evident gusto and warm patriotism.
Although he doubtless found his precedent for this sort of thing
in Ariosto's flattery of the House of Este (which the Italian
poet had in turn worked out by using rather crudely the im-
pressive method of Virgil), Spenser's evident devouring of many
sources,[42] his genuine zest, his keen interest in curious details,
his freedom of treatment, and his almost unerring dilation of
the particular episodes which have appealed particularly to later
English poets from Shakespeare to Swinburne, reveal an en-
thusiasm which proves that there was no perfunctory versifying
here. At all events we must greet the critics, who seem bound
to talk about Spenser's lack of national fervor, with some
fervent lines.

...Deare countrey! O how dearely deare
Ought thy remembraunce and perpetual band
Be to thy foster childe, that from thy hand
Did commun breath and nouriture receave!
How brutish is it not to understand
How much to her we owe, that all us gave,
That gave unto us all, what ever good we have!

---

[42] See Miss Carrie Anna Harper's *The Sources of The British Chronicle
History in Spenser's Faerie Queene* (Philadelphia, 1910).

In the eleventh canto Spenser recaptures some of the sustained and spirited narrative power that makes this book unique in *The Faërie Queene,* but he does not regain the headlong speed that was so marked in some of the earlier cantos. The wild rout of Passions attacks the House of Alma at the bulwarks of the senses. The first part of the narrative is too elaborately allegorical. I shall have occasion, presently, to urge that Spenser was often more realistic in proportion as he became more allegorical and less purely romantic. But here we must admit that the allegory is a little too starched at first. Soon, however, in the account of Arthur's fight with the outlandish leader, Maleger, despite the evident influence of Ariosto's Orillo and the borrowing from the old story of Antaeus, we find much vigor and uncouth variety.

Then comes the gorgeous close, the adventure in the Bowre of Blisse, with its "celestial thieving" from Tasso and its incomparable originality. The voyage of Guyon and the palmer recalls the *Odyssey* and doubtless derived even more direct impulse from Tasso's account of the sailing of Carlo and Ubaldo to seek Rinaldo in Armida's bower; but Spenser's originality is beyond cavil. Allegory is here the perfect comrade of reality. The mind is haunted by the vision of the Gulf of Greediness with the rock near by

> ... whose craggie clift
> Depending from on high, dreadfull to sight,
> Over the waves his rugged armes doth lift,''

and the griesly mouth "sucking the seas into his entralles deep." Finally the rock looms terribly close and stark. Whirlpools and quicksands swim dizzily by. The rolling waves are filled with the "sea-shouldering whales" which delighted the awakening Keats, and monsters more uncouth and appalling, "such as Dame Nature selfe mote feare to see," "scolopendraes," "monoceros," "all dreadfull pourtraicts of deformitee," sea-satyrs, and

> The dreadfull fish, that hath deserv'd the name
> Of Death, and like him lookes in dreadfull hew.

These apparitions vanish and we hear the song of the mermaids.

> With that the rolling sea, resounding soft,
> In his big base them fitly answered,
> And on the rocke the waves breaking aloft,
> A solemne meane unto them measured,
> The whiles sweet Zephyrus lowd whisteled
> His treble, a straunge kinde of harmony;
> Which Guyons senses softly tickeled,
> That he the boteman bad row easily,
> And let him heare some part of their rare melody.

At last they land. The poet describes nature with a riot of erotic symbolism: the spacious plain is like "a pompous bride"; hanging grapes are like full, laughing, and inviting lips; groves tremble as though with desire. "He seems to feel with his eyes," cries Yeats. Guyon pauses in his delight like any healthy youth.

> One would have thought, (so cunningly the rude
> And scorned partes were mingled with the fine,)
> That Nature had for wantonesse ensude
> Art, and that Art at Nature did repine;
> So striving each th' other to undermine,
> Each did the others worke more beautify;
> So diff'ring both in willes agreed in fine:
> So all agreed through sweete diversity,
> This gardin to adorne with all variety.

> And in the midst of all a fountaine stood,
> Of richest substance that on earth might bee,
> So pure and shiny that the silver flood
> Through every channell running one might see:
> Most goodly it with curious ymageree
> Was overwrought, and shapes of naked boyes,
> Of which some seemd with lively jollitee
> To fly about playing their wanton toyes,
> Whylest others did them selves embay in liquid joyes.

> And over all, of purest gold was spred
> A trayle of yvie in his native hew:
> For the rich metall was so coloured,
> That wight, who did not wel advis'd it vew,
> Would surely deeme it to bee yvie trew:
> Low his lascivious armes adown did creepe,
> That themselves dipping in the silver dew,
> Their fleecy flowres they tenderly did steepe,
> Which drops of christall seemd for wantones to weep.

Infinit streames continually did well
Out of this fontaine, sweet and faire to see,
The which into an ample laver fell,
And shortly grew to so great quantitie,
That like a litle lake it seemd to bee;
Whose depth exceeded not three cubits hight,
That through the waves one might the bottom see,
All pav'd beneath with jaspar shining bright,
That seemd the fountaine in that sea did sayle upright.

And all the margent round about was sett
With shady laurell trees, thence to defend
The sunny beames, which on the billowes bett,
And those which therin bathed mote offend.
As Guyon hapned by the same to wend,
Two naked damzelles he therein espyde,
Which, therein bathing, seemed to contend
And wrestle wantonly, ne car'd to hyde
Their dainty partes from vew of any which them eyd.

Sometimes the one would lift the other quight
Above the waters, and then downe againe
Her plong, as over maystered by might,
Where both awhile would covered remaine;
And each the other from to rise restraine;
The whiles their snowly limbes, as through a vele,
So through the christall waves appeared plaine:
Then suddenly both would themselves unhele,
And th' amorous sweet spoiles to greedy eyes revele.

As that faire starre, the messenger of morne,
His deawy face out of the sea doth reare,
Or as the Cyprian goddesse, newly borne
Of th' oceans fruitfull froth, did first appeare,
Such seemed they, and so their yellow heare
Christalline humor dropped downe apace.
Whom such when Guyon saw, he drew them neare,
And somewhat gan relent his earnest pace;
His stubborne brest gan secret pleasaunce to embrace.

The wanton maidens, him espying, stood
Gazing a while at his unwonted guise;
Then th' one her selfe low ducked in the flood,
Abasht that her a straunger did avise:
But thother rather higher did arise,
And her two lilly paps aloft displayd,
And all, that might his melting hart entyse
To her delights, she unto him bewrayd:
The rest, hidd underneath, him more desirous made.

With that the other likewise up arose,
And her faire lockes, which formerly were bownd
Up in one knott, she low adowne did lose:
Which, flowing long and thick, her cloth'd arownd,
And th' yvorie in golden mantle gownd:
So that faire spectacle from him was reft,
Yet that which reft it no lesse faire was fownd:
So hidd in lockes and waves from lookers theft,
Nought but her lovely face she for his looking left.

Withall she laughed, and she blusht withall,
That blushing to her laughter gave more grace,
And laughter to her blushing, as did fall.
Now when they spyde the knight to slacke his pace,
Them to behold, and in his sparkling face
The secret signes of kindled lust appeare,
Their wanton meriments they did encreace,
And to him beckned to approch more neare,
And shewd him many sights, that corage cold could reare.

The two wanton damsels are from Tasso. But turn to the original and see how Spenser has translated. Tasso, for all his cunning, has no cadences equal to those in the delicious line,

Withal she laughèd, and she blusht withall.

The palmer rebukes Guyon's wandering eyes; but his words are drowned by a voluptuous symphony.

Eftsoones they heard a most melodious sound,
Of all that mote delight a daintie eare,
Such as attonce might not on living ground,
Save in this paradise, be heard elsewhere:
Right hard it was for wight which did it heare,
To reade what manner musicke that mote bee:
For all that pleasing is to living eare
Was there consorted in one harmonee;
Birds, voices, instruments, windes, waters, all agree.

The joyous birdes, shrouded in chearefull shade,
Their notes unto the voice attempred sweet:
Th' angelicall soft trembling voyces made
To th' instruments divine respondence meet:
The silver sounding instruments did meet
With the base murmure of the waters fall:
The waters fall with difference discreet,
Now soft, now loud, unto the wind did call:
The gentle warbling wind low answered to all.

The whiles some one did chaunt this lovely lay:—
Ah! see, who so fayre thing doest faine to see,
In springing flowre the image of thy day;
Ah! see the virgin rose, how sweetly shee
Doth first peepe foorth with bashfull modestee,
That fairer seemes, the lesse ye see her may;
Lo! see soone after, how more bold and free
Her bared bosome she doth broad display;
Lo! see soone after how she fades and falls away.

So passeth, in the passing of a day,
Of mortall life the leafe, the bud, the flowre,
Ne more doth florish after first decay,
That earst was sought to deck both bed and bowre
Of many a lady, and many a paramowre.
Gather therefore the rose, whilest yet is prime,
For soone comes age, that will her pride deflowre:
Gather the rose of love, whilest yet is time,
Whilest loving thou mayst loved be with equall crime.

Every one should read in this connection John Addington Symonds' charming essay on "The Pathos of the Rose in Poetry" with its lovely chain of translations from Ausonius, Catullus, Lorenzo de Medici, Poliziano, Ariosto, and Tasso.[43] I can give but a few extracts that sketch the growth of this theme, a theme which a futurist would shun because it is old, but a theme over which any number of masters have grown ardent because it is great.

It remained for Ausonius, in the crepuscular interspace between the sunset of the antique and the night which came before the sunrise of the modern age, to develop thus elaborately the motive of fragility in rose life and in human loveliness.... [In the renaissance Lorenzo wrought his version.] Here we have the *Collige virgo rosas*, "Gather ye roses while ye may," translated from the autumn of the antique to the April of modern poetry, and that note is echoed through all the love-literature of the Renaissance.... [Compare with Lorenzo's version the lyric of Poliziano.] Lorenzo is minute in detail, sober in reflection; Poliziano employs slighter touches with an airier grace and a freer flight of fancy. The one produces a careful study from nature by the light of his classical models; the other sings a new song, soaring high above the beaten track of imitation....

Thus the Florentine poets used the rose as a reminder to girls that they should enjoy their youth in season. The graver simile of Catullus was not

---

[43] *Essays Speculative and Suggestive*, II.

to their purpose.   It first makes its entrance into Italian poetry in these
stanzas of Ariosto, which are closely copied from the Latin. . . . Tasso, while
expanding in the main the motive of Ausonius, borrowed a touch from
Catullus. . . . Spenser's magnificent paraphrase from Tasso follows the orig-
inal closely, but omits, whether intentionally or not, to dwell upon the line
derived through Ariosto from Catullus.

Whether intentional or not, we may be sure that it was thor-
oughly characteristic of Spenser, for all his high-seriousness, to
omit here the graver trace of Catullus.   It is characteristic of
Tasso that he should admit one troubled touch to give evidence
of his morbid hesitancy between delight and disgust.   It is
equally characteristic that Spenser's picture is almost innocent
in its frank and full joy.   Professor Mackail makes a strange
contrast with Ariosto and says:

But with one or two exceptions, there is hardly anything in the *Orlando
Furioso* that is not suitable to be read aloud, even according to the taste
of the present day; the same cannot be said of *The Faerie Queene*.

But one may challenge any reader who has both poems fresh in
his mind to find a single stanza in Spenser as vicious and as
ugly as the adventure of Angelica and the hermit.   Against
those careless words of Mackail let us put the graver words of
Milton in the *Arcopagitica:*

I cannot praise a fugitive and cloistered vertue, unexercised and un-
breathed, that never sallies out and sees her adversary, but slinks out of
the race where that immortal garland is to be run for not without dust
and heat.   Assuredly we bring not innocence into the world, we bring
impurity much rather: that which purifies us is Triall, and Triall is by
what is contrary.   That vertue therefore which is but a youngling in the
contemplation of evill, and knows not the utmost that Vice promises to
her followers, and rejects it, is but a blank Vertue, not a pure; her white-
ness is but an excrementall whiteness: which was the reason why our sage
and serious Poet Spenser, whom I dare be known to think a better teacher
than Scotus or Aquinas, describing true Temperance under the person of
Guyon, brings him in with his Palmer through the Cave of Mammon and
the Bowre of Earthly Blisse, that he might see, and know, and yet abstain.

Let us then look at Acrasia herself and remember, as we
read the following stanzas, that Spenser was describing a pas-

sion far different from those earlier apparitions in this book, a
passion that is a virtue until excess or fickleness make it a vice.

> Upon a bed of roses she was layd,
> As faint through heat, or dight to pleasant sin,
> And was arayd, or rather disarayd,
> All in a vele of silke and silver thin,
> That hid no whit her alabaster skin,
> But rather shewd more white, if more might bee:
> More subtile web Arachne cannot spin,
> Nor the fine nets, which oft we woven see
> Of scorched deaw, do not in th' ayre more lightly flee.

> Her snowy brest was bare to ready spoyle
> Of hungry eies, which n'ote therewith be fild;
> And yet through langour of her late sweet toyle,
> Few drops, more cleare then nectar, forth distild
> That like pure orient perles adowne it trild;
> And her faire eyes, sweet smyling in delight,
> Moystened their fierie beames, with which she thrild
> Fraile harts, yet quenched not, like starry light,
> Which, sparckling on the silent waves, does seeme more bright.

> The young man, sleeping by her, seemd to be
> Some goodly swayne of honorable place,
> That certes it great pitty was to see
> Him his nobility so fowle deface:
> A sweet regard and amiable grace,
> Mixed with manly sternesse, did appeare,
> Yet sleeping, in his well proportiond face,
> And on his tender lips the downy heare
> Did now but freshly spring, and silken blossoms beare.

In that last stanza, the stanza on the youth, comes the recoil,
not brutal or prurient, but tender and firm and sure. In a
moment we see the men who, after Acrasia had become sated
with them, had been turned into beasts. Acrasia is bound and
her bower is torn down and burned. And, last of all, we shrink
from Gryll, the man who preferred his unnatural bestial form,
a lecher and a glutton who is allowed to remain in the guise of
a swine.

The structure of books one and two can be attacked at
occasional points. But if Spenser could have sustained their

architectonic strength and continuity throughout the six com-
pleted books of his immense poem his scheme would probably
have never been questioned.   For some reason or other he lost
his grip.   The most ridiculous theory is that his devotion to
allegory betrayed him.

"It is not to the existence of allegory in Spenser," writes Swinburne,
"that all save his most fanatical admirers object; it is to the fact that the
allegory like Mrs. Malaprop's 'on the banks of the Nile' is a 'rapacious
and insatiable imposter' who attracts and devours all living likenesses of
men and women within reach.   There is allegory also in Homer and Dante:
but prayers in Homer and qualities in Dante become vital and actual forms
of living and breathing creatures.   In Spenser the figure of a just man
melts away into the quality of justice, the likeness of a chaste woman is
dissolved into the abstraction of chastity.   Nothing can be more alien from
the Latin genius, with its love of clearness and definite limitation, than this
indefinite and inevitable cloudiness of depiction rather than conception
which reduces the most tangible things to impalpable properties, resolves
the solidest realities into smoke of perfumed metaphor from the crucible
of symbolic fancy, and suffuses with Cimmerian mist the hard Italian sun-
light. . . . The Tarpeian Muse of Spenser is not indeed crushed—there is too
much vigorous and supple vitality in her lovely limbs for that—but she
is heavily burdened if not sorely bruised by the ponderous and brilliant
weight of allegoric shields, emblazoned with emblematic heraldry of all
typic and chivalric virtues, which her poet has heaped upon her by way
of signs and bucklers of her high and holy enterprise in 'fairy lands for-
lorn,' through twilight woodlands and flowery wastes of mythical and moral
song.''

On the contrary, while many of Spenser's figures are vague
enough, the vagueness of his principal characters has been
absurdly exaggerated.   Miss Kate Warren makes a good point
when she says:

Spenser's mode, also of presenting his subject matter was not the
dramatic, but the *romantic* mode, in which incident and sentiment count
for more than individual characters.   Yet, in spite of these things, it
seems possible to discern, in several passages of the *Faerie Queene,* the
delineation of a character as distinct from the delineation of a type;
especially in the case of some of the women, certainly in the case of Brito-
mart.   Spenser's men are always less distinctive than his women, but
Arthegall, Calidore, Malbecco, Timias, and others have about them indi-
vidual touches.   But what there is of character drawing in the *Faerie
Queene* is rendered less vivid than it would be on account of the dreamlike

atmosphere and the lulling verse in which it is presented. It is only per-
haps when the scattered sayings and doings of a personage are drawn
together and viewed as a whole, somewhat apart from the mazy windings
of the verse in which they are involved, that it is possible to realize how
far Spenser could draw a lifelike character. Within certain limits, then,
it seems reasonable to say that Spenser could portray characters as well
as types.[44]

In Book Three, Britomart, who is the definite personification of
chastity, is distinctly human. As Professor Dowden says:

> When Spenser would present a patron knight of chastity, he chose a
> woman; and he made her no vestal vowed to perpetual maidenhood, but
> the most magnanimous of lovers. That is to say, the highest chastity is
> no cloistered virtue, but lives in a heart aflame with pure passion. Such a
> heart is no cold house swept and garnished; it is rather a sanctuary where
> a seraph breathes upon the altar coals.

In this same book it is Florimel, no allegorical figure at all, but
a typical romantic heroine, who is the colorless personage. The
first and second books, perfectly allegorical as they are, are not
"heavily burdened . . . with the weight af allegoric shields"
but move often with sustained and unbroken swiftness for cantos
at a time and are illumined with many touches of the richest
reality. There are some stirring episodes in Book Three, but
none so rapid and so graphic as the adventure with Despayre
or the deeds of Pyrochles. Finally, it is notable that in books
three and four we have an almost complete crumbling of the
general structure accompanied with a series of personages taken
mainly from romance and often with no allegory whatsoever,
while in the fifth book the allegory and the firmness of structure
return once more simultaneously. When the allegory wavers
the great framework totters and the characters grow paler.
Una, or Truth, and Britomart, or Chastity, are two of Spenser's
most human figures. Florimel, a mere imitation of Ariosto's
Angelica, without any of the comprehensible caprice of the
Princess of Cathay, is, except for a few moments, pallid and
saccharine. Samuel Crothers has the secret when he describes
The Faërie Queene as a "book of ethics from the point of view

---

[44] *The Faërie Queene*, III, Introduction, xiii–xiv.

of heroic youth, not an analysis of the virtues but an account
of the way in which they comport themselves in action.'' In
Book Three the romantic haze grows thicker and the figures
vaguer, less allegorical, less full of the poet's conviction, less
real.

What, then, is the real reason for the crumbling of the
structure? Not the *presence* of allegory, but the *weakening*
of allegory. And why does the allegory weaken? Because the
scheme was too mighty for human achievement? Partly, but
only partly. In Book Three *The Faërie Queene* reveals Spenser's
first disillusion over the course of English politics and religion.
Reality failed to follow this epic of the future. There is little
doubt that Spenser had not proceeded very far with Book Three
before Leicester died. Perhaps the masque of Cupid that now
stands as its culminating episode was written out either in the
form of a poem on the court of Cupid, which has commonly
been supposed to be lost, or even pretty much in its present
form. Doubtless other episodes were finished or at least vivid
before the writer's inner eye just as the episode of Mutabilitie,
a sort of digression but probably of great structural importance,
seems to have been completed before any of the main action
of the fragmentary seventh book was written or, at all events,
written out elaborately. But most of the episodes of the
third book seem loosely strewn about the several great ad-
ventures. And these great adventures are not goals or key-
stones. Britomart, the heroine, has no quest comparable to
St. George's or Guyon's. She merely seeks her lover. Her
achievement in the culminating canto is brilliant but casual,
the completing of a narrative strand introduced for the first
time in the eleventh canto. And where is Prince Arthur? In
the first canto he dashes madly after the exasperating Florimel.
He has no crowning action. Yet to have given him a crowning
action would have been far from difficult for Spenser with his
treasure-house of resources and his extraordinary ingenuity.
But Leicester was dead. And before his death, in 1588, his

highest hopes had been fast waning. Surely here is our reason. England was failing to become Utopia. Leicester was dead before the rich materials of the third book had been resolved into the intricate harmonies of which Spenser dreamed.

In the first canto Britomart enters almost immediately and overthrows Sir Guyon. In another moment Florimel flashes across the scene on her palfrey with a lustful forester in full pursuit and the whole structure of Book Three comes tumbling about our ears. At almost every one of her entrances Florimel rends the woof of the poem like a circus-rider tearing through a paper hoop and to about as little purpose. Arthur, Guyon, and Timias ride after her in all directions leaving Britomart to pursue her way quite sensibly, alone with her aged nurse who acts as squire. It is evident that, as I have said, Florimel is a pale replica of Ariosto's Angelica who allured Christian and Pagan, Orlando and Rinaldo, Sacripante and Ferrau, away from battle on the most fascinating and absurd goose-chases. But there is a vast difference between the animated complications in which the deliciously human Princess of Cathay involves vaunting Paynim and redoubted Paladin and upsets, at the most abrupt and impossible moments, a great international war between two civilizations and two religions a dozen times with her innocent and delightfully trivial mishaps, and finally marries a private soldier—there is a great difference between this bewitching coquette and the paper-doll creature of Spenser who turns sober knights into pompous clowns. How sadly misapplied is the refreshingly wilful current of Ariosto's fancy may be evident to all readers who turn from the *Orlando Furioso* and open *The Faërie Queene* at the point where Arthur, whom Spenser quite unintentionally makes forgetful of Gloriana, seems to have fallen in love with Florimel and is left like a querulous schoolboy, at the end of the fourth canto, launching an anticlimactic tirade against the dark night which impedes his pursuit. Spenser's confusion is further apparent in his neglect to bring in Duessa, whom, as his argument shows, he had provided for in the first canto of this book, as he doubtless had originally intended to introduce her at the beginning of each book, to make a link like that at the opening of Book Two and to give a certain continuity to the forces of evil that were to be crushed at the triumphant close of the whole epic.

But the first canto is redeemed at the close. For Britomart remains on the scene and allegory returns for an evanescent visitation. Professor Mackail wrote crassly that the model for Britomart, Ariosto's warrior-maiden Bradamante, "is as pure as Britomartis and ten times more lovable." Bradamante in her first meeting with Ruggiero as told in Bojardo's *Orlando Innamorato* is, I should say, ten times more lovable than the Bradamante of Ariosto, who did not have the advantage of portraying the first love-scene. And it is just in the first love-scenes, and even more in the longings awakened by the vision of the lover Artegall that Spenser surpasses both Ariosto and Bojardo. In brilliance and wit Ariosto was far superior to Spenser. In tenderness he was far inferior. Ariosto's tenderness, as for instance in the celebrated account of the death of Zerbino, is apt to be weakened by sentimentality. Bradamante, too, is intolerably addicted to jealousy. Britomart, as we shall see, has her acute pangs; but Bradamante has an almost chronic case. Britomart easily harmonizes sweetness and power in a way that is above all things womanly. Bradamante in her dealings with that other warrior-maiden, Marfisa, is a repulsive virago while the savagery of Marfisa seems perfectly congruous and attractively barbaric. Marfisa is like a panther; Bradamante is like a quarreling fish-wife. Never has Ariosto approached the beauty of the episode in which Spenser describes the adventures of Britomart in the castle of the wanton Malecasta, who thinks her a man. When Britomart lifts her visor at the table (for she refuses to remove her helmet),

> As when fayre Cynthia, in darkesome night,
> Is in a noyous cloud enveloped,
> Where she may finde the substance thin and light
> Breakes forth her silver beames, and her bright hed

Discovers to the world discomfited;
Of the poore traveiler, that went astray,
With thousand blessings she is heried;
Such was the beautie and the shining ray,
With which fayre Britomart gave light unto the day.

The stanzas which so beautifully reconcile her masculine (not mannish) courage and her essential and ineradicable femininity should win for her the adoration of every reader.

Now whenas all the world in silence deepe
Yshrowded was, and every mortall wight
Was drowned in the depth of deadly sleepe,
Faire Malecasta, whose engrieved spright
Could find no rest in such perplexed plight,
Lightly arose out of her wearie bed,
And, under the blacke vele of guilty night,
Her with a scarlott mantle covered,
That was with gold and ermines faire enveloped.

Then panting softe, and trembling every joynt,
Her fearfull feete towards the bowre she mov'd,
Where she for secret purpose did appoynt
To lodge the warlike maide, unwisely loov'd;
And to her bed approching, first she proov'd
Whether she slept or wakte; with her softe hand
She softly felt if any member moov'd,
And lent her wary eare to understand
. If any puffe of breath or signe of sence shee fond.

Which whenas none she fond, with easy shifte,
For feare least her unwares she should abrayd,
Th' embroderd quilt she lightly up did lifte,
And by her side her selfe she softly layd,
Of every finest fingers touch affrayd;
Ne any noise she made, ne word she spake,
But inly sigh'd. At last the royall mayd
Out of her quiet slomber did awake,
And chaunged her weary side, the better ease to take.

Where feeling one close couched by her side,
She lightly lept out of her filed bedd,
And to her weapon ran, in minde to gride
The loathed leachour. But the dame, halfe dedd
Through suddein feare and ghastly drerihedd,
Did shrieke alowd, that through the hous it rong,

> And the whole family, therewith adredd,
> Rashly out of their rouzed couches sprong,
> And to the troubled chamber all in armes did throng.

> And those six knights, that ladies champions,
> And eke the Redcrosse Knight ran to the stownd,
> Halfe armd and halfe unarmd, with them attons:
> Where when confusedly they came, they fownd
> Their lady lying on the senceless grownd;
> On thother side, they saw the warlike mayd
> Al in her snow-white smocke, with locks unbownd,
> Threatning the point of her avenging blaed;
> That with so troublous terror they were all dismayd.

In the second canto Britomart, travelling with the Red Cross Knight, whom she had lately succoured from six knights, wins our allegiance even more completely. She sounds St. George about Artegall, the knight who has appeared in her visions, but naturally disguises her purpose in seeking him.

> "But mote I weet of you, right courteous knight,
> Tydings of one, that hath unto me donne
> Late foule dishonour and reprochfull spight,
> The which I seeke to wreake, and Arthegall he hight."

Then comes the charming recoil.

> The word gone out she backe againe would call,
> As her repenting so to have missayd.

The royal maid goes on, however, to persist in her abuse of Artegall in order to draw out more and more sweet-sounding eulogy of him from her generous comrade. It is all very captivating and quite free from that element of unconscious contempt that is generally latent in our admiration for such soubrettish performances. This lady is no Lynette, a mere bundle of zephyr-like prejudices. She has a strong arm to wield a sword; she has an intellect; her chastity is not a cowardly attribute or an earnest of property value; it is her natural choice and it is perfectly compatible with both her ardent love that sends her out in pursuit of her man and her delightful shyness when he woos her.

Then the story veers back and tells us how Britomart, a curious girl at the court of her father, King Ryence of South Wales, stole into her father's closet and saw in a marvelous crystal globe the revelation of the knight whose image broke her peace.

> Eftsoones there was presented to her eye
> A comely knight, all arm'd in complete wize,
> Through whose bright ventayle, lifted up on hye,
> His manly face, that did his foes agrize,
> And frends to termes of gentle truce entize,
> Lookt foorth, as Phoebus face out of the east
> Betwixt two shady mountaynes doth arize:
> Portly his person was, and much increast
> Through his heroicke grace and honorable gest.

> His crest was covered with a couchant hownd,
> And all his armour seemd of antique mould,
> But wondrous massy and assured sownd,
> And round about yfretted all with gold,
> In which there written was, with cyphres old,
> *Achilles armes, which Arthegall did win.*
> And on his shield enveloped sevenfold
> He bore a crowned litle ermilin,
> That deckt the azure field with her fayre pouldred skin.

The ensuing dialogue with Glauce, her nurse (an amusing and kindly creature who might have offered faint though rare suggestions to Shakespeare, had Shakespeare needed a new and somewhat finer-fibered nurse than Juliet's), Britomart's little self-revelations in the cave of Merlin as recounted in the following canto—all these things, though told somewhat too profusely, are full of sure and delicate and penetrating human touches. The description of Merlin's cave, to which Glauce and Britomart repair for counsel, is admirably fearsome.

> And if thou ever happen that same way
> To traveill, go to see that dreadfull place:
> It is an hideous hollow cave (they say)
> Under a rock, that lyes a litle space
> From the swift Barry, tombling downe apace
> Emongst the woody hills of Dynevowre:

> But dare thou not, I charge, in any cace,
> To enter into that same balefull bowre,
> For feare the cruell feendes should thee unwares devowre.
>
> But standing high aloft, low lay thine eare,
> And there such ghastly noyse of yron chaines
> And brazen caudrons thou shalt rombling heare,
> Which thousand sprights with long enduring paines
> Doe tosse, that it will stonn thy feeble braines;
> And oftentimes great grones, and grievous stowndes,
> When too huge toile and labour them constraines,
> And oftentimes loud strokes, and ringing sowndes,
> From under that deepe rock most horribly rebowndes.

We are pretty likely to be bored by the magician's long prophecy of Artegall's and Britomart's royal progeny which Spenser adapted from the chronicles, although it is told with somewhat more vigor than the similar excursus in Book Two. But there is no doubt of Spenser's enthusiasm. And one could make out an all but irrefutable case for the influence of several passages in it on Gray's "Bard."

Britomart's lovelorn moods grow decidedly tiresome. But before we have gone far with the fourth canto we are relieved by her encounter with Marinell, a knight whose chief value for poetry lies in the fact that he has a lovely sea-nymph for a mother and lives on a picturesque seashore strewn with gems. He has no apparent allegorical significance and he helps to weaken the structure. We leave him overthrown and wounded, in the charge of his mother, the "lilly handed Liagore," without much compunction. The canto ends, as we have noted before, with the pointless and Thopas-like adventures of Arthur and with the prince's quite unnecessary denunciation of night.

Canto Five, however, makes ample amends by introducing us to one of the most exquisite adventures in the poem, the meeting of Timias, Arthur's squire, a very human character, and the incomparable Belphoebe. Spenser's rich and ductile memories of romance were swarming only too readily for solace to his sorrowing and bewildered spirit. But the bloom on the adventure of Timias is still as dew-fresh as it was for the entranced poet himself. The forester, whom Timias had helped to scare away from the fleeing Florimell, was waiting in ambush for the squire, with two savage brothers. The fight at the ford, though rather conventional, has some of the vividness of the best combats in the second book. Timias, the victor, lying unconscious in his blood, is found by Belphoebe and nursed back to life only that he may pine for love of her. The story is to emerge later in two of the most enchanting bypaths and arbors of the mazeful stories of the later books.

The reintroduction of Belphoebe gives the poet an opportunity to draw in one of his most effective set-pieces, his picture of the Gardens of Adonis. I never read it without recalling some phrases about Spenser in Mr. Bailey's essay.

> The whole deliciousness of earth is in his poetry; when she makes her bed smoothest, when her outline is softest, it is not softer or smoother than the fall of his verse.

The myth of the birth of Belphoebe and her twin-sister Amoret is a fancy possible only to a poet who (however careless he may have been in his attention to specific things like English daisies[45]) was evidently a most tender and intimate and reverent son of nature with an intimate sense of her inscrutable fertility.

> It were a goodly storie to declare
> By what straunge accident faire Chrysogone
> Conceiv'd these infants, and how them she bare,
> In this wilde forrest wandring all alone,
> After she had nine moneths fulfild and gone:
> For not as other wemens commune brood
> They were enwombed in the sacred throne
> Of her chaste bodie, nor with commune food,
> As other wemens babes, they sucked vitall blood.
>
> But wondrously they were begot and bred,
> Through influence of th' hevens fruitfull ray,
> As it in antique bookes is mentioned.
> It was upon a sommers shinie day,

---

[45] ''Search ever so diligently, you will not find an English daisy in all his enchanted forests,'' says Alexander Smith in a charming essay which should be noted for its conventional but graceful and suggestive contrast of Spenser and Chaucer. See *Dreamthorp* (Edinburgh, 1881), 213–214.

When Titan faire his beames did display,
In a fresh fountaine, far from all mens vew,
She bath'd her brest, the boyling heat t' allay;
She bath'd with roses red and violets blew,
And all the sweetest flowres that in the forrest grew:

Till, faint through yrksome weariness, adowne
Upon the grassy ground her selfe she layd
To sleepe, the whiles a gentle slombring swowne
Upon her fell all naked bare display'd:
The sunbeames bright upon her body playd,
Being through former bathing mollifide,
And pierst into her wombe, where they embayd
With so sweet sence and secret power unspide,
That in her pregnant flesh they shortly fructifide.

Here the poet very adroitly works in the pleasant old story of the hue and cry of Venus after her son Cupid.[46]   The Cytherean meets Diana and her nymphs.

She, having hong upon a bough on high
Her bow and painted quiver, had unlaste
Her silver buskins from her nimble thigh,
And her lanck loynes ungirt, and brests unbraste,
After her heat the breathing cold to taste;
Her golden lockes, that late in tresses bright
Embreaded were for hindring of her haste,
Now loose about her shoulders hong undight,
And were with sweet ambrosia all besprinckled light.

Soone as she Venus saw behinde her backe,
She was ashamed to be so loose surpriz'd,
And woxe halfe wroth against her damzels slacke,
That had not her thereof before aviz'd,

---

[46] Spenser may have used one of his ''lost poems.'' He seems to have always been very thrifty with whatever he wrote, in spite of the fact that he was also so richly endowed and so prodigal. Professor Philo M. Buck Jr. (''Spenser's Lost Poems,'' *Publications of the Modern Language Association of America*, March, 1908), and Miss Helen Sandison (''Spenser's 'Lost' Works,'' *Publications of the Modern Language Association of America*, March, 1910), consider this theory of the earlier poem. Professor J. Douglas Bruce (*Modern Language Notes*, XXVII, no. 6) does not agree with them. He regards the passage not as expanded from the lost translation of Moschus mentioned by E. K. (Gloss to *March*), but as influenced by Tasso's prologue to the *Aminta*, itself an expanded paraphrase of the Moschus theme. It is not impossible, of course, to reconcile his idea with the earlier theories.

But suffred her so carelessly disguiz'd
Be overtaken. Soone her garments loose
Upgath'ring, in her bosome she compriz'd,
Well as she might, and to the goddesse rose,
Whiles al her nymphes did like a girlond her enclose.

The two goddesses find the two babes born of Chrysogone without pain in her sleep.   Diana takes Belphoebe and the love-goddess carries Amoret to her Gardens of Adonis.   There follows a description at once quaint and gorgeous, paradisal, but with the sweet odor of loam and the most earthly of the flowers about it.   Dreaming over Plato's *Phaedrus*, the poet fills the garden with all the unborn beings of the earth.

It sited was in fruitfull soyle of old,
And girt in with two walls on either side,
The one of yron, the other of bright gold,
That none might thorough breake, nor overstride:
And double gates it had, which opened wide,
By which both in and out men moten pas;
Th' one faire and fresh, the other old and dride:
Old Genius the porter of them was,
Old Genius, the which a double nature has.

He letteth in, he letteth out to wend,
All that to come into the world desire:
A thousand thousand naked babes attend
About him day and night, which doe require
That he with fleshly weeds would them attire:
Such as him list, such as eternall Fate
Ordained hath, he clothes with sinfull mire,
And sendeth forth to live in mortall state,
Till they agayn returne backe by the hinder gate.

Here, too, flits the quaint and incongruous old figure of Time, who is described with a curious blend of whimsicality and wistfulness.

Great enimy to it, and to all the rest,
That in the Gardin of Adonis springs,
Is wicked Tyme, who, with his scyth addrest,
Does mow the flowring herbes and goodly things,
And all their glory to the ground downe flings,
Where they do wither and are fowly mard:

He flyes about, and with his flaggy winges
Beats downe both leaves and buds without regard,
Ne ever pitty may relent his malice hard.

Yet pitty often did the gods relent,
To see so faire thinges mard and spoiled quight:
And their great mother Venus did lament
The losse of her deare brood, her deare delight:
Her hart was pierst with pitty at the sight,
When walking through the gardin them she saw,
Yet no'te she find redresse for such despight:
For all that lives is subject to that law:
All things decay in time, and to their end doe draw.

But were it not, that Time their troubler is,
All that in this delightfull gardin growes
Should happy bee, and have immortall blis:
For here all plenty and all pleasure flowes,
And sweete Love gentle fitts emongst them throwes,
Without fell rancor or fond gealosy:
Franckly each paramor his leman knowes,
Each bird his mate, ne any does envy
Their goodly meriment and gay felicity.

But the poet, with his characteristic passion for immortality, an immortality full of the warmest life, turns quickly to his dream of Adonis who still lives (for all the old, lying myth) and to those ponderings over mutability never long silent in his soul.

Right in the middest of that paradise
There stood a stately mount, on whose round top
A gloomy grove of mirtle trees did rise,
Whose shady boughes sharp steele did never lop,
Nor wicked beastes their tender buds did crop,
But like a girlond compassed the hight,
And from their fruitfull sydes sweet gum did drop,
That all the ground, with pretious deaw bedight,
Threw forth most dainty odours, and most sweet delight.

And in the thickest covert of that shade
There was a pleasaunt arber, not by art,
But of the trees owne inclination made,
Which knitting their rancke braunches part to part,
With wanton yvie twyne entrayld athwart,
And eglantine and caprifole emong,

Fashiond above within their inmost part,
That nether *Phoebus* beams could through them throng,
Nor Aeolus sharp blast could worke them any wrong.

. . . .

There wont fayre Venus often to enjoy
Her deare Adonis joyous company,
And reape sweet pleasure of the wanton boy:
There yet, some say, in secret he does ly,
Lapped in flowres and pretious spycery,
By her hid from the world, and from the skill
Of Stygian gods, which doe her love envy;
But she her selfe, when ever that she will,
Possesseth him, and of his sweetnesse takes her fill.

And sooth, it seemes, they say: for he may not
For ever dye, and ever buried bee
In balefull night, where all things are forgot;
Al be he subject to mortalitie,
Yet is eterne in mutabilitie,
And by succession made perpetuall,
Transformed oft, and chaunged diverslie:
For him the father of all formes they call;
Therefore needs mote he live, that living gives to all.

Florimell evidently did not disturb the poet as much as she disturbed the structure of his epic, for she does not actually reappear until the seventh canto. Once more the allegory falls to the ground. The sojourn of Florimell in the witch's hut and the crude half-pathetic court paid the damsel by the witch's loutish and imbecile son are not without their picturesqueness, although they are paradoxically enough less lifelike than many of his most allegorical passages. There is, however, one stanza which describes the witch's son with rare quaintness and makes Florimell almost a woman with one luminous touch.

Oft from the forrest wildings he did bring,
Whose sides empurpled were with smyling red,
And oft young birds, which he had taught to sing
His maistresse praises sweetly caroled;
Girlonds of flowres sometimes for her faire hed
He fine would dight; sometimes the squirrell wild
He brought to her in bands, as conquered
To be her thrall, his fellow servant vild;
All which she of him tooke with countenance meeke and mild.

Florimell steals away. The witch conjures up an obscene and hideous monster to pursue her. The terrified maiden puts out to sea in a shallop with a sleeping fisherman, leaving her horse to be devoured by the sanguinary monster.

Sir Satyrane finds the horrible creature by the disemboweled palfrey and sees the girdle of Florimell lost in her flight. In his horror and anger he engages the monster vainly until, throwing away his sword, he grapples with him and binds him. The action increases in speed and merges into a lively and complicated scene into which, be it noted, allegory returns.

> Thus as he led the beast along the way,
> He spide far of a mighty giauntesse,
> Fast flying on a courser dapled gray
> From a bold knight, that with great hardinesse
> Her hard pursewd, and sought for to suppresse:
> She bore before her lap a dolefull squire,
> Lying athwart her horse in great distresse,
> Fast bounden hand and foote with cords of wire,
> Whom she did meane to make a thrall of her desire.

> Which whenas Satyrane beheld, in haste
> He left his captive beast at liberty,
> And crost the nearest way, by which he cast
> Her to encounter ere she passed by:
> But she the way shund nathemore forthy,
> But forward gallopt fast; which when he spyde,
> His mighty speare he couched warily,
> And at her ran: she having him descryde,
> Her selfe to fight addrest, and threw her lode aside.

> Like as a goshauke, that in foote doth beare
> A trembling culver, having spide on hight
> An eagle, that with plumy wings doth sheare
> The subtile ayre, stouping with all his might,
> The quarrey throwes to ground with fell despight,
> And to the batteill doth her selfe prepare:
> So ran the geauntesse unto the fight;
> Her fyrie eyes with furious sparkes did stare,
> And with blasphemous bannes High God in peeces tare.

The giantess Argante is what the student of abnormal psychology would call a nymphomaniac. She is the extreme and pathological personage among a series of unchaste antitypes who appear in this book in contrast to Britomart. Satyrane is stunned by the mace of the giantess but the first pursuer has gained so markedly that she is forced to relinquish both her young captives and flee this knight, whom she knows to be Palladine, a chaste warrior-maiden and therefore her irresistible bane. Satyrane crawls to his new friend lying half stunned in the road and finds that he is the Squyre of Dames.

There follows a tale that Spenser would never have dreamed of introducing into the first two or even the last two books of *The Faërie Queene.* The poet remembers Ariosto's twenty-eighth canto, the most clever and the most ugly libel ever launched against women. The faërie poet attempts a kind of humor which grows hard and cruel in his half-reluctant hands. And instead of Ariosto's callous and easy vivacity we find here a story so perfunctory that it is saved from dullness only by its brevity. In Ariosto two nobles, finding their wives unfaithful, go about the world seducing every woman with astounding case. Sated with conquests invariably so facile, they take a simple girl as common mistress. But even this artless creature contrives to grant her favors to a daring young Greek lover while she lies in bed with a paramour at each elbow. The two jolly noblemen are angry for a brief moment; then they laugh heartily and gaily admit the incontrovertible fact of woman's universal wantonness. Spenser's variation is very significant. The Squyre of Dames wooed the fair Columbell, who bade him travel for twelve months seducing all women and bringing their names and pledges as spoils to her. That was simple enough. But the wilful lady then imposed a most outrageous task: she commanded her faithful squire to find as many who refused his advances. He had travelled for three years and had found but three: a courtesan who rejected him because he could not give her sufficient money; a nun, because she feared he would not keep their secret; and third—and here Spenser quite artlessly forgets his cynicism and gives the story an incongruous and exquisite turn (though in the next stanza he comes back to his ugly moral)—

> The third a damzell was of low degree,
> Whom I in countrey cottage found by chaunce:
> Full litle weened I, that chastitee
> Had lodging in so meane a maintenaunce;
> Yet was she fayre, and in her countenaunce
> Dwelt simple truth in seemely fashion.
> Long thus I woo'd her with dew observaunce,
> In hope unto my pleasure to have won,
> But was as far at last, as when I first begon.

Along with this cynical vein which is to return once more in this book, along with the general looseness of structure and the frequent disappearance of allegory which mark the growth of Spenser's disillusion and faltering, we should not be surprised when we see a growing number of fickle and fraudulent people of the pettier type who fairly swarm in the eighth canto. We have had, of course, Duessa and Archimago. But even they are wicked on a large scale. And most of the Vices, Pride, Sansloy, Furor, Mammon, Acrasia and many more, seem foemen worthy of our respect so that we are fairly tempted to say that there is something admirable about them. Certainly we are not inclined to hesitate over our paradox when we read of these new and pettier figures: the false living image of Florimell, created for her son by the witch, but shortly captured and taken from him by Braggadochio; the old fisherman who would have violated Florimell but for the intervention of Proteus who, in his own turn, meditates a seduction which has not an atom of the dignity of the most capricious intrigues ascribed by the antique poets to Jove. Certainly, as we read of all these figures, so small, so sordid, we feel that they are drawn by a bewildered and a bitter hand. And more, some of the faërie knights themselves are represented as fickle and hard: Sir Paridell, for instance, who enters the story in this canto and becomes very soon a chief figure in one of Spenser's most sordid tales. Even the noble Sir Satyrane, once the chivalric protector of Una, has been laughing with cynical relish over the adventures of the Squyre of Dames.

The story of Malbecco and Paridell and Hellenore, which occupies cantos nine and ten, is Spenser's second and last incursion into the field of the Italian *novelle*. He begins with an apology influenced by a similar but mocking exordium which opens Ariosto's twenty-eighth canto. Satyrane and Paridell are refused admittance to the house of the old miser, Malbecco, who fears for the virtue of his pretty wife, Hellenore. Forced to take shelter from a violent storm in a shed near by, they are peremptorily invited to give up their cramped quarters by a third knight who has wandered hither. Paridell accepts the challenge. The poet is inspired by one of his most powerful similes.

> Tho, hastily remounting to his steed,
> He forth issew'd; like as a boystrous winde,
> Which in th' earthes hollow caves hath long ben hid,
> And shut up fast within her prisons blind,
> Makes the huge element, against her kinde,
> To move and tremble as it were aghast,
> Untill that it an issew forth may finde;
> Then forth it breakes, and with his furious blast
> Confounds both land and seas, and skyes doth overcast.

Paridell is overthrown, for the knight is none other than Britomart, whose lance, like that which Astolfo lent to Bradamante, was enchanted with mighty spells to overthrow all who felt its force. Ariosto would never have introduced a chaste Britomart into the midst of the scene that follows. But when the three knights have with fierce threats induced Malbecco to admit them, when Britomart doffs her helm in the midst of that ogling company, the contrasting effect is magical. The reader will remember that the earlier portrait of her, also in contrast, as she threatened the lovely but unchaste Malecaster, was very swiftly and briefly done. It was most happily planned to refrain from revealing her full beauty in an elaborate description until she sits down in this larger and lewder company: with the half-barbarous Sir Satyrane, with a rake, a wanton wife, and a miser.

And eke that straunger knight emongst the rest
Was for like need enforst to disaray:
Tho, wheneas vailed was her lofty crest,
Her golden locks, that were in tramells gay
Upbounden, did them selves adowne display,
And raught unto her heeles; like sunny beames,
That in a cloud their light did long time stay,
Their vapour vaded, shewe their golden gleames,
And through the persant aire shoote forth their azure streames.

Shee also dofte her heavy haberjeon,
Which the faire feature of her limbs did hyde,
And her well plighted frock, which she did won
To tucke about her short, when she did ryde,
Shee low let fall, that flowed from her lanck syde
Downe to her foot with carelesse modestee,
Then of them all she plainly was espyde
To be a woman wight, unwist to bee,
The fairest woman wight that ever eie did see.

Then follows the only episode in which Spenser even approaches real lubricity and this, like Chaucer's story of January and May, has its justification in its essential poetic justice. High-minded poets, almost as often as gay authors of Italian *novelle* and shrewd, hard authors of twentieth century problem plays, have expressed their disgust at the unnatural marriages of silly youth and selfish senility. The story of Hellenore is told with more vivacity, with a mirth less wan and flickering than the story of the Squyre of Dames. The abduction scene is one that Shakespeare may have remembered when he wrote *The Merchant of Venice*.

Darke was the evening, fit for lovers stealth,
When chaunst Malbecco busie be elsewhere,
She to his closet went, where all his wealth
Lay hid: thereof she countlesse summes did reare,
The which she meant away with her to beare;
The rest she fyr'd for sport, or for despight;
As Hellene, when she saw aloft appeare
The Trojane flames, and reach to hevens hight,
Did clasp her hands, and joyed at that dolefull sight.

This second Helene, fayre Dame Hellenore,
The whiles her husband ran with sory haste,
To quench the flames which she had tyn'd before,
Laught at his foolish labour spent in waste,
And ran into her lovers armes right fast;
Where streight embraced, she to him did cry
And call alowd for helpe, ere helpe were past,
For lo! that guest did beare her forcibly,
And meant to ravish her, that rather had to dy.

The wretched man, hearing her call for ayd,
And ready seeing him with her to fly,
In his disquiet mind was much dismayd:
But when againe he backeward cast his eye,
And saw the wicked fire so furiously
Consume his hart, and scorch his idoles face,
He was therwith distressed diversely,
Ne wist he how to turne, nor to what place:
Was never wretched man in such a wofull cace.

Ay when to him she cryde, to her he turnd,
And left the fire; love money overcame:
But when he marked how his money burnd,
He left his wife; money did love disclaime:
Both was he loth to loose his loved dame,
And loth to leave his liefest pelfe behinde,
Yet sith he n'ote save both, he sav'd that same
Which was the dearest to his dounghill minde,
The god of his desire, the joy of misers blinde.

Perhaps, from the point of view of the narrower moralist, the poet's chief mistake is that, in spite of himself, he lends to the figure of Malbecco a certain pathos that threatens the poetic justice of the situation. But the lover of Shakespeare will understand. He will understand why, as the wretched miser wanders about with the bullying coward Braggadochio and the crafty Trompart, who is planning to steal the niggard's bag of gold, Spenser's tenderness awakens our sympathy for even this muddy old rascal. In the meeting of Malbecco with Paridell, who had promptly abandoned the lady, and the adventure at night among the satyrs who have found the derelict Hellenore and made her a common wife, the poet occasionally drops into a jocular phrasing that reminds one of the incorrigible turns

in the *Decameron*. The night in the forest, the satyrs dancing
to shrill bagpipes and to their own strident shouts, the orgy
with Hellenore—all is extraordinarily vivid and rococo. The
poor man crawls near Hellenore, who sleeps by a satyr's side,
awakens her, and implores her in vain to return with him. But
Hellenore has found her own low happiness and we rejoice in
the fine sarcasm and perfect justice of the poet who leaves her
there. The striking metamorphosis at the end by which Mal-
becco becomes Jealousy incarnate is a vivid return to allegory.
Malbecco goes sorrowfully back to a place where, at the sug-
gestion of the designing Trompart, he had buried his bag of
gold. He finds it stolen and "with extreme fury" he becomes
"quite mad."

> And ran away, ran with him selfe away:
> That who so straungely had him seene bestadd,
> With upstart haire and staring eyes dismay,
> From Limbo lake him late escaped sure would say.

> High over hilles and over dales he fledd,
> As if the wind him on his winges had borne,
> Ne banck nor bush could stay him, when he spedd
> His nimble feet, as treading still on thorne:
> Griefe, and despight, and gealousy, and scorne
> Did all the way him follow hard behynd,
> And he himselfe himselfe loath'd so forlorne,
> So shamefully forlorne of womankynd;
> That, as a snake, still lurked in his wounded mynd.

> Still fled he forward, looking backward still,
> Ne stayd his flight, nor fearefull agony,
> Till that he came unto a rocky hill,
> Over the sea suspended dreadfully,
> That living creature it would terrify
> To looke adowne, or upward to the hight:
> From thence he threw him selfe dispiteously,
> All desperate of his fore-damned spright,
> That seemd no help for him was left in living sight.

> But through long anguish and selfe-murdring thought,
> He was so wasted and forpined quight,
> That all his substance was consum'd to nought,
> And nothing left, but like an aery spright,

That on the rockes he fell so flit and light,
That he thereby receiv'd no hurt at all;
But chaunced on a craggy cliff to light;
Whence he with crooked clawes so long did crall,
That at the last he found a cave with entrance. small.

Into the same he creepes, and thenceforth there
Resolv'd to build his balefull mansion,
In drery darkenes, and continuall feare
Of that rocks fall, which ever and anon
Threates with huge ruine him to fall upon,
That he dare never sleepe, but that one eye
Still ope he keepes for that occasion;
Ne ever rests he in tranquillity,
The roring billowes beat his bowre so boystrously.

Ne ever is he wont on ought to feed
But todes and frogs, his pasture poysonous,
Which in his cold complexion doe breed
A filthy blood, or humour rancorous,
Matter of doubt and dread suspitious,
That doth with cureless care consume the hart,
Corrupts the stomacke with gall vitious,
Croscuts the liver with internall smart,
And doth transfixe the soule with deathes eternall dart.

Yet can he never dye, but dying lives,
And doth himselfe with sorrow new sustaine,
That death and life attonce unto him gives,
And painefull pleasure turnes to pleasing paine.
There dwels he ever, miserable swaine,
Hateful both to himself and every wight;
Where he, through privy griefe and horrour vaine,
Is woxen so deform'd, that he has quight
Forgot he was a man, and Gelosy is hight.

Some have criticized this allegorical close as too fantastic after the realism of the preceding scene. As a matter of fact, the allegorical episode is even more realistic than any other part of the story. Every one who stops to think knows of some sinister character who is so dominated by an obsession that he becomes in time an allegorical character in the flesh. An old woman who has lived a life of unbroken selfishness, suspicion, slanderous hate may shrivel into malignance incarnate. To be

sure we are inclined to believe no longer in "humours" and
"master-passions." We talk well and wisely of "mixed mo-
tives" and of the infinite complexity and inconsistency of
character. And yet there are always in the world a few people
whose "humours" or "master-passions" or obsessions mould
and simplify them into genuine allegorical characters. They
are very few; they are generally pathological cases; but they
live.

Just as there is no continuity and no turning point in the
narrative of this third book, so there is no real culminating
episode. In the last two cantos Britomart, who rescues Amoret
from the castle of Busirane for Scudamour, is appropriately
prominent in the foreground. The last canto is one of the most
splendid eagle-flights in the whole poem. But the achievement
of Britomart's is the result of a chance encounter, not the ful-
filment of a quest. It is very important that we keep this
defect in mind, for in the evolution of the endings of the last
four books of *The Faërie Queene* lies much striking evidence
for my theory of Spenser's slow rising disillusion. The twelfth
canto remasters the allegory but only as a detached episode.
Britomart bursts through the flames which continually pour out
of the castle-gate and spends a day and night alone in the hold
of Busirane, gazing at the wonderful riot of amorous pictures,
and cautiously passing through room after room, through
silence after silence deepening our fears. Then comes thunder
and lightning and the masque of Cupid. This is doubtless Spen-
ser's revision of his early *Court of Cupid*, long thought lost,
here reappearing heavily crusted with the most mellow gold of
Spenser's maturity and doubtless, in its intricate allegory, much
more large and impersonal than the youthful vision if we may
judge from the tone of rather morbid and querulous subjectivity
that defaces his earlier love-poems. Here we have all the
elements of an elaborate psychology of loves, separated, con-
ceptualized, personified, and made astonishingly vivid as these
personages pour through the halls of the lustful wizard:

The first was Fansy, like a lovely boy,
Of rare aspect and beautie without peare,
Matchable ether to that ympe of Troy,
Whom Jove did love and chose his cup to beare,
Or that same daintie lad, which was so deare
To great Alcides, that, when as he dyde,
He wailed womanlike with many a teare,
And every wood and every valley wyde
He fild with Hylas name; the nymphes eke Hylas cryde.

His garment nether was of silke nor say,
But paynted plumes, in goodly order dight,
Like as the sunburnt Indians do aray
Their tawny bodies, in their proudest plight:
As those same plumes, so seemd he vaine and light,
That by his gate might easily appeare;
For still he far'd as dauncing in delight,
And in his hand a windy fan did beare,
That in the ydle ayre he mov'd still here and theare.

And him beside marcht amorous Desyre,
Who seemd of ryper yeares then th' other swayne,
Yet was that other swayne this elders syre,
And gave him being, commune to them twayne:
His garment was disguysed very vayne,
And his embrodered bonet sat awry;
Twixt both his hands few sparks he close did strayne,
Which still he blew, and kindled busily,
That soone they life conceiv'd, and forth in flames did fly.

Next after him went Doubt, who was yclad
In a discolour'd cote of straunge disguyse,
That at his backe a brode capuccio had,
And sleeves dependaunt Albanese-wyse:
He lookt askew with his mistrustfull eyes,
And nycely trode, as thornes lay in his way,
Or that the flore to shrinke he did avyse,
And on a broken reed he still did stay
His feeble steps, which shrunck when hard thereon he lay.

With him went Daunger, cloth'd in ragged weed,
Made of beares skin, that him more dreadfull made,
Yet his owne face was dreadfull, ne did need
Straunge horrour to deforme his griesly shade:
A net in th' one hand, and a rusty blade
In th' other was, this Mischiefe, that Mishap;
With th' one his foes he threatned to invade,
With th' other he his friends ment to enwrap:
For whom he could not kill he practizd to entrap.

Next him was Feare, all arm'd from top to toe,
Yet thought himselfe not safe enough thereby,
But feard each shadow moving too or froe,
And his owne armes when glittering he did spy,
Or clashing heard, he fast away did fly,
As ashes pale of hew, and wingyheeld;
And evermore on Daunger fixt his eye,
Gainst whom he alwayes bent a brasen shield,
Which his right hand unarmed fearefully did wield.

With him went Hope in rancke, a handsome mayd,
Of chearefull looke and lovely to behold;
In silken samite she was light arayd,
And her fayre lockes were woven up in gold;
She alway smyld, and in her hand did hold
An holy water sprinckle, dipt in deowe,
With which she sprinckled favours manifold
On whom she list, and did great liking sheowe,
Great liking unto many, but true love to feowe.

And after them Dissemblaunce and Suspect
Marcht in one rancke, yet an unequall paire:
For she was gentle and of milde aspect,
Courteous to all and seeming debonaire,
Goodly adorned and exceeding faire:
Yet was that all but paynted and pourloynd,
And her bright browes were deckt with borrowed haire:
Her deeds were forged, and her words false coynd,
And alwaies in her hand two clewes of silke she twynd.

But he was fowle, ill favoured, and grim,
Under his eiebrowes looking still askaunce;
And ever as Dissemblaunce laught on him,
He lowrd on her with daungerous eye-glaunce,
Shewing his nature in his countenaunce;
His rolling eies did never rest in place,
But walkte each where, for feare of hid mischaunse;
Holding a lattis still before his face,
Through which he stil did peep, as forward he did pace.

Then came Amoret, bleeding perpetually of lust's wound, and Love himself—Love is an evil passion—on a ravenous lion like Wrath. Behind them clanged the heavy brazen door so that Britomart could make no entrance till, at the second watch of the second night, it flew open and the bold warrior-maiden stole in.

So soone as she was entred, rownd about
She cast her eies, to see what was become
Of all those persons which she saw without:
But lo! they streight were vanisht all and some,
Ne living wight she saw in all that roome,
Save that same woefull lady, both whose hands
Were bounden fast, that did her ill become,
And her small waste girt rownd with yron bands,
Unto a brasen pillour, by the which she stands.

And her before, the vile enchaunter sate,
Figuring straunge characters of his art:
With living blood he those characters wrate,
Dreadfully dropping from her dying hart,
Seeming transfixed with a cruell dart;
And all perforce to make her him to love.
Ah! who can love the worker of her smart?
A thousand charmes he formerly did prove;
Yet thousand charmes could not her stedfast hart remove.

Suddenly Busirane saw the warrior-maiden. With knife upraised he leaped savagely towards her; but she, though wounded in the fray, struck him down with her bright blade. At Amoret's cry of warning Britomart stayed her avenging hand and forced the necromancer to read charms of reversal, charms so terrible that even her blood ran cold as she, halftrembling, held her sword over him.

Here followed, in Spenser's first published version of the third book, some beautiful stanzas recounting the reunion of Amoret and Sir Scudamour.

Lightly he clipt her twixt his armes twaine,
And streightly did embrace her body bright,
Her body, late the prison of sad paine,
Now the sweet lodge of love and deare delight:
But she, faire lady, overcommen quight
Of huge affection, did in pleasure melt,
And in sweete ravishment pourd out her spright:
No word they spake, not earthly thing they felt,
But like two senceles stocks in long embracement dwelt.

Had ye them seene, ye would have surely thought,
That they had beene that faire hermaphrodite,
Which that rich Romane of white marble wrought,
And in his costly bath causd to bee site:

> So seemd these two, as growne together quite,
> That Britomart, halfe envying their blesse,
> Was much empassiond in her gentle sprite,
> And to her selfe oft wisht like happinesse:
> In vaine she wisht, that fate n'ould let her yet possesse.

But when Spenser added his last three books and published them in 1596 he changed the close into two stanzas in which we are told that Scudamour, after waiting long with little hope, had gone away in despair. Undoubtedly Spenser wanted to extend the narrative strand into the following book. But we may be equally sure that his growing disillusion, his growing fear that England was not to become a Utopia, impelled him to close his first symphony on a desolate unresolved chord.

CHAPTER III

COMPLAINTS, ELEGIES. COLIN CLOUTS COME HOME AGAINE

Everyone remembers how on a certain immortal journey to Canterbury the bluff host, after a long interruption begun by the riotous outburst of the drunken miller, the irascible reve, and the boisterous cook with their ribald tales, turned a second time to the monk and, with no reverent exhortations, called for a new tale. The monk, though ruddy of face and anointed with nature's oils that come of much choice eating and much riding of good hunting horses, chose to edify the company with a catalogue of gloomy accounts of the deceitful fortunes and tragic falls of Lucifer, Adam, Hercules, "Petro, glorie of Spayne," Nero, Holofernes, and various others. We recall how he had barely finished with Croesus when he was politely but firmly interrupted by the knight and, more emphatically, by the host, who added:

> I preye yow hertely, telle us somwhat elles,
> For sikerly, nere clinking of your belles,
> That on your brydel hange on every syde,
> By heven king, that for us alle dyde,
> I sholde er this han fallen doun for slepe,
> Although the slough had never been so depe;
> Then had your tale al be told in vayn.
> For certeinly, as that thise clerkes seyn,
> "Where-as a man may have noon audience
> Noght helpeth it to tellen his sentence."

Despite the sly advice of Chaucer, however, these dreary and sacerdotal laments, which gave the Middle Ages so much lugubrious joy and were not utterly disdained by such as Boccaccio and Chaucer himself, persisted though Lydgate, Hoccleve, and other dull followers until, in the full dawn of the renaissance in England, they stirred the noble Sackville and his collaborators to write the *Mirror for Magistrates* and influenced Spenser and many of his followers.

Most of us will at first blush be inclined to extend the host's destructive criticism to the volume of Spenser's poems called *Complaints* which Ponsonby (probably at the desire of the author) collected and published in 1591. To most readers they are simply representative of an unworthy, querulous mood that is supposed to have been frequent with Spenser because (so it has been said) of the ungrateful and niggardly attitude of the court. I am convinced that this interpretation is quite false. To be sure the very title, *Complaints*, lends itself to the theory. But the word "complaints," as Spenser translated it from the French poets, had a connotation quite different from that of our age. With the Pléiade and with Spenser it was not necessarily associated with things petty and personal. It must be admitted that the modern reader of many of Spenser's *Complaints*, particularly "The Teares of the Muses," looks in vain for traces of the serene and deep-browed poet of the first three books of *The Faërie Queene* and finds much superficial morbidness that savors strongly of the "confessions of a second-rate sensitive mind." But if we examine this volume, in this place, at the expense of breaking the continuity of our study of *The Faërie Queene*, we shall catch the deeper continuity of Spenser's development and we shall find in the poet of the *Complaints* no sniveller, but a man under the influence of three noble moods: a sorrowful contemplation of that passing of beauty and grandeur which afflicts all high-minded men, but which Spenser was to master at the last in his philosophical cantos on Mutabilitie; a curious and graceful playfulness in contemplation of his own idealism which, at the moment, seemed almost fragile to him in the midst of a ruthless reality; and a spirited arraignment of the English court for its failure to emulate with swift success the high dream of the first books of *The Faërie Queene* and become a Utopia—a mood of fierce disillusion which was to sweep to a bitter climax at the close of the sixth book of his epic where his truculent imagination was to behold unleashed Slander, the Blatant Beast.

In answer to those who point out that the poems in this volume were probably written at wide intervals, from the days of *The Shepheards Calender* to perhaps within a few months of the date of publication, we may rejoin that some of them show signs of revision and that the three fundamental moods which I have described may well have colored them and dictated their publication or republication as Spenser returned in wrathful gloom to Ireland early in 1591. Undoubtedly the poet, enraged not so much at his personal disappointments but enraged magnanimously over what he deemed the purblind and perverse policies of the court, paused long enough to edge some of his hitherto suppressed attacks with a new and larger indignation and instructed Ponsonby to collect some other appropriate poems which we have commonly supposed to be lost.[1]

If we may then assume that the *Complaints* expresses three kindred moods it will be best to group Spenser's translations from French poetry, his "Visions of the Worlds Vanitie," his "Ruines of Time," and "Teares of the Muses" as of the first

---

[1] It would be out of proportion to enter here or elsewhere at length into the question of Spenser's "lost works." The shrewd learning of many critics has made it sufficiently clear that few of Spenser's works really found oblivion. The poet seems to have been very resourceful in revising them and in frequently incorporating them in larger works, especially *The Faërie Queene*. For the most part it will be enough to suggest important theories with an occasional venture of my own in notes at the proper places. Just here it is well to call attention to the two most important monographs. Professor Philo M. Buck ("Spenser's Lost Poems," *Publ. Mod. Lang. Assoc.*, 1908, XXIII) finds many of the "lost poems" in the *Complaints* which he believes to have been suddenly launched in wrath over personal disappointments. I have already agreed partially with this thesis but have explained Spenser's anger as being larger and more impersonal. My conception of Spenser is more in accord with Professor Greenlaw's brilliant and soundly supported theories which I have already noticed in my account of *The Shepheards Calender* and which I shall cite again and again. As for Professor Buck, much praise is due the care and ingenuity with which he has traced out the individual "lost works." He certainly deserves better treatment than is accorded him by Miss Helen E. Sandison ("Spenser's 'Lost' Works and their Probable Relation to his *Faërie Queene*," *Publ. Mod. Lang. Assoc.*, XXV, 1910), which contributes a very useful but rather carping examination of his results. In these two studies, particularly in the latter, the reader will find references to practically all the articles of any moment upon this subject.

mood, the sorrowful contemplation of the passing of beauty and grandeur. We may then consider "Virgils Gnat" and "Muiopotmos" as of the second mood where in mock-heroic he symbolizes (with a lightness that often attains to gaiety without ever quite losing sight of melancholy) the futility of his own idealism, at least as far as his immediate hopes of being followed as a seer are concerned. Finally we may consider the masterpiece of the volume, "Mother Hubberds Tale," as of the third mood, the fierce satire against the court that fell so far short of his utopian schemes that it shattered the vast looms of his epic dreams.

"The Ruines of Time," probably an English adaptation of Spenser's lost Latin poem, "Stemmata Dudleiana," is, as Professor Dodge says, "mainly official verse, melodious and uninspired, ... the one poem of the volume confessedly written to order—confessedly, in the frank and dignified letter of dedication." But it was easy enough for Spenser to celebrate Leicester and Sidney. And we may, without being too charitable, conceive that it was the genuine glow of his friendship for these that stirred his vaulting ambition to o'erleap itself and attempt to celebrate a whole family of varied abilities. The result seems insincere. The poet, roaming by "silver-streaming Thamesis," sees a sorrowful woman, the spirit of an ancient and forgotten city of Britain who bewails her own oblivion and rebukes the poet with his neglect to eternize his noble patrons. Artificial enough to be sure. Yet when the poet sings of Sidney we realize that in the midst of these perfunctory verses there sounds the true grief that was shaking the great fabric of *The Faërie Queene.* There is distress unfeigned in such lines as these:

> All is but fained, and with oaker dide,
> That everie shower will wash and wipe away,
> All things doo change that under heaven abide,
> And after death all friendship doth decaie.

Of that part of the poem which laments generally the instability of glory itself we may say with Professor Oliver Elton that "his lines gather up all the pessimism which besets the Renaissance itself, in the pauses of its exultation and energy, like a deep musical wail amidst the jubilation of a marching army.''[2]   If this philosophy of change sounds ungenuine it is only because of the formal occasion of the poem.   For as the poet remembers forgotten beauty and grandeur and as he contemplates more particularly the recent decay of a family whose most brilliant member, Sidney, had met death untimely, he must indeed have felt the first pangs of that real discouragement which, according to Dryden, inhibited the completion of *The Faërie Queene.*[3]   Yet Dryden, like all the innumerable critics who have contributed to the false notion that Spenser was in private life somewhat querulously self-centered, has overemphasized the sadness that fell on the Don Quixote of English poets.   What there is of real sorrow in ''The Ruins of Time'' did indeed rise to a crescendo of bitterness through the last three books of *The Faërie Queene.* The serene passages are but episodes; more insistent grows the *saeva indignatio.*   It will be noted that those idealistic passages of the sixth book which are most serene differ from those of the first three books in that they are more apart from life.   For what is Calidore's temporary disgust with the world of deeds, what is his life with wise old Meliboe and fairest Pastorella among the shepherds but a renaissance version of the philosophy of the ivory tower, a nature's palace of art hardly the less insidious because it gives sunlight and meadow and forest instead of warm perfumes and the gorgeous prison of tapestries? Spenser indeed realizes this and summons his hero once more to the world of deeds.   But he summons him with a visible reluctance.   And with the return to the world of deeds returns twofold the rush of bitterness so that the book closes with the futility of Calidore's quest.   It is the only book which ends harshly and uncompromisingly on the note of absolute defeat.

---

[2] *Modern Studies* (London, 1907), ''Literary Fame,'' pp. 56–58.

[3] It matters little that Dryden is somewhat muddled in his details.   He is no doubt right in considering that the death of Sidney as well as the death or disgrace of others of Spenser's heroes dealt mortal wounds to the epic.

Such is the full climax of the note of sorrow that sounds with only apparent artificiality in ''The Ruines of Time.'' But Dryden and most of Spenser's critics great and small err in two respects. In the first place, they have not heard so clearly the growing thunder of the poet's long philippic that they realize its large impersonality. His disillusionment transcends personal disappointments which are utterly lost in the fierce elevation of his sorrow over what seemed to him to be England's betrayal of her own attainable perfection. In the second place, the critics have all failed to appreciate fully Spenser's superb reconquest of faith in his last two poems: the last two *Hymnes,* the *Prothalamion,* and the marvellous fragment on Mutabilitie.

In ''The Ruines of Time'' Spenser not only seeks to eternize a fading family at the very moment he is lamenting the mortality of towns and palaces and monuments, but, with an approach to something of his proper power, he declaims against the English Philistines who, in his day, were perhaps most perfectly represented for better and for worse by Burghley. It is perhaps true, as Professor Greenlaw has suggested, that Burghley also represented for Spenser the sinister side of Machiavellism according to the hostile interpretation of Gentillet, ''the craft and temporizing and deceit of politicians'' which was as ''abhorrent to his high-souled idealism as it was to Sidney's.'' Certainly Spenser was not stung merely by Burghley's reputed coldness towards him or even by his active personal enmity, if such there really was. Irascibility of this pettier order was an impossibility for a man of Spenser's high-seriousness while he was communing with the muses. Yet we need not, just here, go so far in the other direction as to suppose that Burghley meant for Spenser that Satanic image of Machiavelli so current in Elizabethan England, or even the more sinister side of Machiavelli dwelt upon by Gentillet. Of Spenser's arraignment of those evils more later. If the verses at the climax of ''The Ruines of Time'' are really launched against Burghley, they portray him merely as the Philistine appears to the humanist in the latter's most high-strung moods.

Therefore in this halfe happie I doo read
Good Melibæ, that hath a poet got
To sing his living praises being dead,
Deserving never here to be forgot,
In spight of envie, that his deeds would spot:
Since whose decease, learning lies unregarded,
And men of armes doo wander unrewarded.

Those two be those two great calamities,
That long agoe did grieve the noble spright
Of Salomon with great indignities;
Who whilome was alive the wisest wight:
But now his wisedome is disprooved quite:
For he that now welds all things at his will
Scorns th' one and th' other in his deeper skill.

O griefe of griefes! O gall of all good hearts!
To see that vertue should dispised bee
Of him that first was raisde for vertuous parts,
And now, broad spreading like an aged tree,
Lets none shoot up, that nigh him planted bee.
O let the man of whom the Muse is scorned,
Not alive nor dead, be of the Muse adorned!

Spenser, had he been a Victorian, would have undoubtedly hurled the same denunciation at the complacent Macaulay whose facile and Saxon utilitarianism so frequently stung the humanist Arnold out of all kindly toleration for Philistinism.[4]

"The Teares of the Muses" applies Spenser's temporary pessimism more particularly to the state of poetry in what seemed to him to be an age of strife and Philistinism. Professor Mackail sketches its setting very effectively.

But the centre had for the time been lost. An iron age had displaced the golden time of Raphael and Ariosto and Erasmus. The brave attempt to breathe fresh life into the Middle Ages, and carry the old world alive and unbroken into the new age, had been made and had failed. The religious wars broke out before the middle of the sixteenth century. Thenceforth the whole of life became one vast field of battle between the revolutionary Reformation and the Catholic reaction. Those bitter enemies

---

[4] It is interesting to remember in this connection Macaulay's notorious emphasis on the tedium of *The Faërie Queene* in his conventional contrast of the allegories of Bunyan and Spenser, a model for all criticasters ever since. It is also interesting to recall the humanist Arnold's attack on Macaulay's own "pinchbeck" verse.

had one, and but one, disastrous feature in common, a fanatical hatred of the great and humane art. In Italy the sunset of the Renaissance lingered; but the shadow of the Catholic reaction is already visible in Tasso's romantic epic. In England the revolution which, in the historian's strik-ing words, laid its foundations in the murder of the English Erasmus, and set up its gates in the blood of the English Petrarch, left a long heritage of sombre restlessness, of doubt and gloom. It has often been remarked as strange, even as unaccountable, that throughout the earlier years of the Elizabethan age there is an all but universal cry that poetry is dead or dying, that barbarism and ignorance have flooded in. ''The Teares of the Muses,'' published by Spenser in 1591, and written not long before, is one prolonged complaint of this.

> ''Heaps of huge words uphoarded hideously
>   With horrid sound though having little sense,''

are all, he says, that is left of the palace of poetry. The truth was that, in her secular movement, poetry was breaking up and transforming herself. A new generation was already at the doors, one which was in turn to sweep up and put away the Renaissance, as the Renaissance had swept up and put away the Middle Ages.[5]

Perhaps it is better to modify the last sentence by saying that the later and richer renaissance was succeeding in England, the hope which the young Shakespeare felt with such a sense of exhilaration that he was probably impelled to gird at the pessimism of ''The Teares of the Muses'' when he made Theseus, on his wedding-day, bann all lugubrious pieces on

> The thrice three Muses mourning for the death
>   Of learning, late decease'd in beggary.

Shakespeare did well to smile Shakespearewise at a poem which appeared when the lark-songs were populous in the skies in an enchanting confusion. But we may judge that this, certainly Spenser's poorest poem, was written much longer before its appearance in the volume of *Complaints* than Professor Mackail would seem to imply; that it was thrust into the book by Spen-ser (or Ponsonby) merely because it was in a minor key. It was undoubtedly sincere for it has all the characteristic morbidity of the sensitive youth whom the crowds on the street impress daily more and more with an exaggerated conception of the

---

[5] *The Springs of Helicon* (London, 1909), pp. 100, 101.

world's indifference to poetry. Its main interest for us lies in
the fact that it may contain some of the materials that went to
the making of Spenser's prose work, *The English Poete,* an
essay that we could so ill afford to lose.[6] However it is not
utterly impossible to reconstruct, at least in outline, Spenser's
prose manifesto from what in Sidney's *Defence of Poesie* and
Spenser's other works we know to have been the views of the
coterie. Undoubtedly Spenser's essay was marked by two im-
portant general attitudes: an exultant idealism proclaiming
poetry to be of supreme importance in life, wedding the life of
the dreamer with that of the doer; and a very unfriendly
attitude, like Sidney's, towards practically all English poetry
since Chaucer, an attitude which he probably maintained till
about the time he wrote *Colin Clouts Come Home Again* wherein
he gave tardy recognition to his contemporaries and recognition
as inclusive and uncritical as that of Francis Meres.[7] For Spen-
ser's first attitude, the exultant idealism in the matter of the
function of poetry, we may go, with the guidance of E. K., to
"October" where it rings out trumpet-clear. For Spenser's
youthful pessimism as to the present condition of English poetry
we must dovetail the more sombre speeches of Cuddie in
"October" with "The Teares of the Muses." Professor Dodge's
condemnation of the latter poem says the last word.

The note of contempt... and of arrogance that one is glad to believe
youthful, the complaint of universal vulgarity, the cry that Ignorance and
Barbarism have quite laid waste the fair realms of the Muses—all this

---

[6] Professor Buck urges some plausible arguments for identifying *The
Teares of the Muses* with the lost nine comedies as well as with *The English
Poete.* His arguments are, however, severely and ably questioned by Miss
Sandison.

[7] See Meres' *Palladis Tamia* (1598) from which I quote one typical
sentence: "As Homer and Vergil among the Greeks and Latins are the
chiefe Heroic Poets: So Spenser and Warner be our chiefe heroicall
makers." Spenser he considers perfect in every *genre* but does not hesitate
to give praise almost as enthusiastic to such a motley assembly as Warner,
Breton, and even Gosson and Fraunce. Meres' chief purpose seems to have
been to marshal a huge array of English poets and proclaim them the peers
of the singers of classical and modern Europe. It is but one aspect of that
tragic nationalism which began in the Renaissance and culminated in the
debacle of August, 1914.

comes near, in the end, to seeming insufferable. If the Areopagus, the select literary club in which Sidney and Dyer and Spenser, with other young aristocratic spirits, discussed the condition of English letters and planned great reforms, if this *cénacle* is fairly represented by "The Teares of the Muses," it must have been, one thinks, a more than usually supercilious clique of young radicals.

That Spenser's sorrow over the passing of beauty and grandeur was sincere is further attested by the fact that his first extant poems and what are probably the last lines he ever wrote are full of this passionate contemplation. To be sure he was employed, as a poor schoolboy, to translate from Marot and from Du Bellay those stately visions that he rendered into irregular stanza forms and into blank verse. But later the poet, partly because of a thrift that is always found as a strange companion to his opulence and prodigality and partly because of his ceaseless meditation over the mortality of splendor and the despotism of Mutabilitie, revised these pieces casting them all in sonnet-form. One of the sonnets translated from Du Bellay will give the mood as felt in his school and college days with all the dark fervor so characteristic of lofty youth.

> On high hills top I saw a stately frame,
> An hundred cubits high by just assize,
> With hundreth pillours fronting faire the same,
> All wrought with diamond after Dorick wize:
> Nor brick, nor marble was the wall in view,
> But shining christall, which from top to base
> Out of her womb a thousand rayons threw
> On hundred steps of Afrike golds enchase:
> Golde was the parget, and the seeling bright
> Did shine all scaly with great plates of golde;
> The floore of jasp and emeraude was dight.
> O worlds vainesse! Whiles thus I did behold,
>> An earthquake shooke the hill from lowest seat,
>> And overthrew this frame with ruine great.

To my mind the sonnets revised from the earlier rhymed "epigrams" are generally somewhat more skilful than the first versions, but those, like the above, worked over from the blank verse are by no means superior in phrasing and are inferior in metrical versatility. Students of English versification should pay more attention to work most extraordinary for the year 1569.

> Sweetly sliding into the eyes of men.

Surely that is a remarkably cadenced line of blank verse for a schoolboy to write only eight years after *Gorbudoc* and at least fifteen years before the sweetly flexible lines of Peele. And in general, though there are in Spenser's first poems many wooden lines, there are traces of that purity which was mastered for English poetry about 1587 by the English Prometheus, the author of *Tamburlaine the Great*.

But all this is apart from our present consideration. The significant feature of these poems is their testimony to one of the dominating philosophical struggles of Spenser's life. Like many poets he was evidently more consistently pessimistic in early youth than in full maturity. As a boy he learned from the French poets to accept Mutabilitie with an almost hopeless resignation. Somewhat later, probably while in the university, he was to rephrase these laments with some added sonnets of his own in the same mood. Later, in a passing mood of general depression, he allowed these poems to appear among his *Complaints*. But, in striking contrast, as a lover at the age of forty, a lover by no means set and staid, he was to promise his mistress in the greatest of his *Amoretti* a proud immortality in the face of all the crushing power of Mutabilitie. And in the moment of ruin and amidst the crashing and falling of his Irish castle and his utopian dreams, on the very threshold of death, he was to wrestle with that titaness Mutabilitie, like Jacob with the angel, and he was to assure himself that she was to fall, prone and splendid, amid the splendors she had hurled down, conquered by the decree of the mightier "army of unalterable law." It lays bare the soul of Spenser if we read the sonnet, his own creation, that he added to the revised version of the "epigrams" which he translated from Marot when he reprinted them as *The*

Visions of Petrarch,[8] and if we read in contrast the last two
stanzas of *The Faërie Queene.*

> When I behold this tickle trustles state
> Of vaine worlds glorie, flitting too and fro,
> And mortall men tossed by troublous fate
> In restles seas of wretchednes and woe,
> I wish I might this wearie life forgoe,
> And shortly turne unto my happie rest,
> Where my free spirite might not anie moe
> Be vext with sights, that doo her peace molest.
> And ye, faire Ladie, iñ whose bounteous brest
> All heavenly grace and vertue shrined is,
> When ye these rhythmes doo read, and vew the rest,
> Loath this base world, and thinke of heavens blis:
>   And though ye be the fairest of Gods creatures,
>   Yet thinke, that death shall spoyle your goodly features.

It was a long ascent past gorges and glaciers to those far appa-
ritional peaks where we descry him beyond all morbid fears at
the end.

> When I bethinke me on that speech whyleare
> Of Mutability, and well it way,
> Me seemes, that though she all unworthy were
> Of the heav'ns rule, yet, very sooth to say,
> In all things else she beares the greatest sway:
> Which makes me loath this state of life so tickle,
> And love of things so vaine to cast away;
> Whose flowring pride, so fading and so fickle,
> Short Time shall soon cut down with his consuming sickle.

> Then gin I thinke on that which Nature sayd,
> Of that same time when no more change shall be,
> But stedfast rest of all things, firmely stayd
> Upon the pillours of eternity,
> That is contrayr to Mutabilitie:
> For all that moveth doth in change delight:
> But thence-forth all shall rest eternally
> With Him that is the God of Sabbaoth hight:
> O that great Sabbaoth God graunt me that Sabaoths sight!

It is probable that Spenser's translations of Du Bellay's
"Ruines of Rome" and his own "Visions of the Worlds Van-

---

[8] Marot's poem was a translation of one of Petrarch's *canzoni* under
the title of *Des Visions de Pétrarque.*

itie'' were written while at college along with his versions of his earliest poems. ''The Ruines of Rome'' gives little promise of that delicacy which enabled him in *The Faërie Queene* to translate and transfigure one of the most beautiful episodes in Tasso both by freshening Tasso's uneasy, sultry voluptuousness with a sensuality almost innocent and by rendering Tasso's trickery of phrase with the triumphant and easy grace which Tasso himself sought and, by the very feverishness of his search, just failed to master. ''The Ruines of Rome'' catches nothing of the finer pensiveness and troubled stateliness of Du Bellay's *Antiquitez,* nothing of its special beauties which Sainte Beuve praised as *intimes.* Spenser was but a youth pondering with hardly articulate thought over the inexplicable law which willed with such passionless ease the decay of the purple and marble of imperial Rome, ''the slowly-fading mistress of the world,'' and he did but paraphrase the grave French poet's solemn lines with a stammering tongue. ''The Visions of the Worlds Vanitie,'' in Spenser's own peculiar sonnet-form and in the then popular vein of emblem-writing, seems to have been nothing but a slightly more independent academic exercise. Almost all these sonnets are marked by a fantastic and grotesque insistence on the vanity of disregarding the small and weak.

> Soone after this I saw an elephant,
> Adorn'd with bells and bosses gorgeouslie,
> That on his backe did beare (as batteilant)
> A gilden towre, which shone exceedinglie;
> That he himselfe through foolish vanitie,
> Both for his rich attire and goodly forme,
> Was puffed up with passing surquedrie,
> And shortly gan all other beasts to scorne:
> Till that a little ant, a silly worme,
> Into his nosthrils creeping, so him pained,
> That, casting down his towres, he did deforme
> Both borrowed pride, and native beautie stained.
>   Let therefore nought, that great is, therein glorie,
>   Sith so small thing his happiness may varie.

So the little bird, the tedula, feeds in the grisly jaws of the crocodile; so the swordfish slays the leviathan; the worm kills the tall cedar; the wasp quells the lion; the spider conquers the dragon.

We may turn readily from these poems to the free para-phrase of the Virgilian *Culex* under the title "Virgils Gnat," in which, despite the fact that it is not an original poem, we may be sure that Spenser put a special symbolical fervor. In this curious fable the great merit of the small and the mean is exemplified by an account of how a gnat saved the life of a shep-herd. A menacing serpent approached the sleeping man. The poet describes the monster with an easy control of the *ottava rima* that shows an advance of years in metrical powers over the "Visions" and a marked approach towards the great Spen-serian stanza.

> Now more and more having himselfe enrolde,
> His glittering breast he lifteth up on hie,
> And with proud vaunt his head aloft doth holde;
> His crest above, spotted with purple die,
> On everie side did shine like scalie golde,
> And his bright eyes, glauncing full dreadfullie,
> Did seeme to flame out flakes of flashing fyre,
> And with sterne lookes to threaten kindled yre.

The gnat awakened the shepherd by stinging his eyelid. But the irate man, little knowing the worth of the deed, slew his rescuer with an impatient blow. Then, turning, he discovered the serpent; he trembled with terror; but, in desperate strength, he struck the monster a fatal blow. In the night that followed, the ghost of the gnat appeared to him, reproached him, and told of the sufferings of those in Hades, with a long series of pictures of the famous ministers and victims of Pluto that combine curiously an obvious delight in the epic phantasmagoria of the *Aeneid* with a certain feeling for the incongruous and the mock-heroic.

The reader might well imagine that Spenser was mainly con-cerned here with an epic study and that, dreaming of *The Faërie Queene,* he strove neither to make much of the mock-heroic element nor to give a new symbolical significance to the epic fable. But a dedicatory sonnet to Leicester, "late deceased"

(but probably written before Leicester died), is in a spirit of
complaint more intensely personal than any other poem in the
volume.

> Wrong'd, yet not daring to expresse my paine,
> To you (great Lord) the causer of my care,
> In clowdie teares my case I thus complaine
> Unto your selfe, that only privie are:
> But if that any Œdipus unware
> Shall chaunce, through power of some divining spright,
> To reade the secrete of this riddle rare,
> And know the purporte of my evill plight,
> Let him rest pleased with his owne insight,
> Ne further seeke to glose upon the text:
> For griefe enough it is to grieved wight
> To feele his fault, and not be further vext.
> But what so by my selfe may not be showen,
> May by this Gnatts complaint be easily knowen.

Some critics have accepted Spenser's warning not to "glose
upon the text" and have urged that a paraphrase could hardly
be very subjective. Yet Spenser's warning to the general reader
is only one of his characteristic half-serious attempts to disguise
a hidden message of unusual cogency. This sonnet was evidently
intended to point the moral very clearly to Leicester. Professor
Greenlaw has given us the setting and the attitude.

It must be remembered that... [Spenser] belonged to the circle which
included Sidney, Raleigh, and Fulke Greville, and that these men were not
town gallants but adventurous spirits who despised the vice and effeminacy
of the courtier class. There are in Spenser's works, in the *Mother Hub-
berds Tale*, in *Colin Clout*, in the *Faerie Queene*, too many passages that
pour contempt on those who loafed about the court, making a living by
their wits, aping the gallantries and affections of the French and Italians,
to make it conceivable that he wished to be of their number. No small
part of the task that confronted Elizabeth was the government of restless
and eager men like Drake, Gilbert, Raleigh, Sidney, who felt the intoxica-
tion of England's dawning greatness and like Tamburlaine sought to add
new realms to its domain. In 1576 Gilbert wrote the tract which first
suggested the duty of England to seize and colonize the lands across the
seas; two years later he received a charter authorizing him to fit out an
expedition to carry his project into execution: in 1583 he sailed with five
ships to plant a colony in Newfoundland. Raleigh was forbidden to accom-
pany him on this expedition, but in 1584 Virginia was named by him and

in the next few years he was ceaselessly employed in furthering the project of colonization. Sidney was sent to the Low Countries to prevent him from carrying out his project to curb the power of Spain through naval attacks and colonization; the testimony of Fulke Greville shows how persistently he warned Elizabeth of the danger from Philip and how earnest he was in urging his plan of defense and counter attack. Greville records his own dissatisfaction at being kept at court by the Queen and tells how he ran away repeatedly, only to be denied the gracious presence for months at a time when he crept back. When, therefore, Spenser, alert, young, eager, realized that his stay in Ireland meant that he was to be cut off from participation in these stirring projects, the revulsion of feeling, at first intense and terrible, found expression in his splendid protest to Leicester in *Virgils Gnat.*

Spenser, in other words, was reproaching his patron for allowing him to be exiled from what was to him the center of the universe, not, as earlier critics have supposed, because he had a feline hope of warming himself at the court, of writing pretty compliments, and of composing a very unreal epic sugared over with more compliments and smug sermons for the Philistines, while the flattered queen and her nobles showered him with lands and gold —no, not for such contemptible things as these, but because Sidney and Leicester had inoculated him with strange fires. Don Quixote that he was, he did not see the selfish and the treacherous side of Leicester, but saw only his own dazzled reading of him—"Magnificence." By the same token he could not see the virtues of Burghley because Burghley was a Philistine. Sidney and Leicester filled him full of a desire to make of England a Utopia. His *Faërie Queene* was to be no art for art's sake production, but a work of art that should be for great Englishmen a practical handbook of morality, politics, and philosophy. In his fiery and daring partisanship of his Prince Arthur he grew more and more militant until, with "Mother Hubberds Tale," he moved even his haughty patron to fear that such championship would do more harm than good. Leicester now lent a ready ear to the suggestion of a secretaryship with Lord Grey in Ireland in the summer of 1580. As Professor Greenlaw says: "Ireland, Brabant, the Low Countries, these were Siberias to which over-zealous persons might be sent if

needful. Leicester, Raleigh, Grey, even Sidney were subjected
to this 'cooling card'; Spenser was in distinguished company.''
Spenser felt that he had done something to save Leicester from
his serpent-foes; Leicester had impulsively sacrificed his too
zealous friend, who humbly imaged himself as a gnat; and so
Spenser was condemned to leave the scene where men wrought
largely—life as he saw it—to wander in a country which may
well have seemed to his then unknowing spirit a dreary Hades.
Wealth, to be sure, he might gain in Ireland. But in England,
only, so he felt at that moment, could he hope to help in building
that mighty city of human aspiration, that Camelot which

> They are building still, seeing the city is built
> To music, therefore never built at all,
> And therefore built for ever.

''Virgil's Gnat,'' then, is a poem in what I described as the
second mood of the volume, a mood in which the poet plays with
his idealism feeling it almost fragile in the midst of a ruthless
and half-blind reality. Though there is in the dedicatory sonnet
to Leicester a personal bitterness that seems to lend color to the
common theory that wherever Spenser turned from his luxuriant
dreams he was a sedulous and querulous courtier, we must re-
member that Spenser was grieving not over the loss of a comfort-
able court-position but over what he feared would be the death
of his knight-errantry for England and Elizabeth in the glitter-
ing and tumultous lists of London where beat the mighty heart
of a young empire. How bravely and efficiently he turned him-
self to his new duties in Ireland must be left for later consider-
ation. Suffice it to say that any tinge of moroseness must have
quickly disappeared and passed into the gay sunshine of such
a mood as that of the ''Muiopotmos: or The Fate of the Butter-
flie,'' wherein he once more symbolizes the tragic fate of the
dreamer, but this time with the consummate lightness of a mock-
heroic that touches the tragic storms of life only as a swift petrel
skims over a troublous sea catching but a flash of silver spray
from the agitated waves on the edge of its hurrying wings. If

the reader thinks this conception of the symbolism of the poem too fanciful I may remind him of the judgment of Lowell, who was certainly not inclined to be overzealous in his search for allegory in Spenser.

> He...shows his mature hand in the "Muiopotmos," the most airily fanciful of his poems, a marvel of delicate conception and treatment, whose breezy verse seems to float between a blue sky and golden earth in imperishable sunshine. No other English poet has found the variety and compass which enlivened the octave stanza under his sensitive touch. It can hardly be doubted that in Clarion the butterfly he has symbolized himself, and surely never was the poetic treatment so picturesquely exemplified.[9]

What Lowell fails to appreciate here is not the allegory, then, but the Alice-in-Wonderland mood of the poem. Lowell was unwilling to allow Spenser any humor to speak of and in consequence he missed a very delicate, elusive, but essential quality of the "Muiopotmos." Professor Dodge comes somewhat closer to the conception I would urge.

> Its subject is a mere nothing: it tells no story that could not be told in full in a stanza, it presents no situation for the delicate rhetoric of the emotions: it is a mere running frieze of images and scenes, linked in fanciful continuity. It is organized as a mock-heroic poem, but its appeal is essentially to the eye. Myths, invented or real, that seem to form themselves spontaneously into pictures, the landscape of the gardens, fantastic armor, the figured scenes of tapestry richly bordered, these are of a poetry akin to the plastic arts, such as one finds in the *Stanze* of Poliziano. Yet the temper of "Muiopotmos" is not that of the *Stanze* and their like. It is rather of the air than of the earth. One might think it an emanation

---

[9] For a brief and sufficient account of the unnecessary puzzlement of the critics over this poem—the theories of "Christopher North," Church, Lowell, Child, Craik, etc.—see Dr. Thomas William Nadal, "Spenser's *Muiopotmos*, in Relation to Chaucer's *Sir Thopas* and *The Nun's Priest's Tale*," *Publ. Mod. Long. Assoc. Amer.*, XXV (1910), 640 sq. Dr. Nadal's attempt to prove that the sources of "Muiopotmos" are to be found in Chaucer's two tales is hardly successful. I am inclined to believe, as my discussion of the mood of the poem will show, that "Sir Topas" had a real influence. But I am very sceptical about the "Nun's Priest's Tale." Enthusiasts in the pursuit of "scientific" investigations of sources and influences should not worship facts so devoutly until they have gone to the logic of science to find some sensible definition of the word "fact." Dr. Nadal's comparison of Aragnoll, the spider, and Russell, Chaucer's fox, his relating of Clarion and Chaunticleer is a good example of that "scientific" study of literature which should purge itself by a preliminary study of the general methodology of a Poincaré, a Mach, a Windelband, or a Bertrand Russell.

of the theme itself and fancy that the frail wings of the butterfly had been spread for the style, delicately colored, ethereal. The poet of the *Faery Queen* never more happily escaped into "delight with liberty" than here.

Still, graceful as this appreciation is, it does but come a shade nearer the point to be developed and it loses sight of what Lowell had partly seen: that the poem touches, like "Virgils Gnat," on the tragedy of idealism in this symbolic autobiography, rather lightly to be sure, but definitely enough, especially at the climax, to show us why Spenser and Ponsonby thought fit to include it in a volume called *Complaints*. We must always keep in mind, therefore, both the tragedy of idealism which Spenser could not keep out of even a mock-heroic poem, and a tenuous but exquisite humor which was always a potentiality in Spenser, but which he seldom cared to realize in writing. Spenser's poem does not fall in with the brilliant *genre* of which Pope's *Rape of the Lock* is a supreme example, but with the delicious foolery of Chaucer's *Sir Thopas*, with Drayton's *Ballad of Dowsabell* and his *Nymphidia*, with Alfred Noyes' *A Flower of Old Japan*. So delicate is the interplay of sly mirth and bright fancy in such poems as these that one reads them with the smile of a man who loves a jest and, at the same time, with the saucer-eyes of a child who loves a fairy-tale.

But there is one essential difference between the workmanship of the "Muiopotmos" and Drayton's *Nymphidia*. In Spenser the wonderful picture painting is as though done first with the infinite cunning of fairy miniature and then quaintly enlarged; in Drayton's poem we seem to have the reverse process, the reduction of a large painting, a manner for all its charm rather mechanical, ingenious, than artistic, fanciful.[10] Spenser's delicacy, together with an elusive humor, sparkles with a myriad of mischievous warm colors in the following stanzas. The butterfly Clarion is arming himself.

---

10 My notion of Drayton's manner gains color from a probability, never before noted, I think, that the climax of his poem, the combat between the two fairies, Pigwiggen and Oberon, seems to borrow important elements from Spenser's extravagant duel between the two knights, Cambal and Triamond, *F. Q.*, Bk. IV, C. III.

His breastplate first, that was of substance pure,
Before his noble heart he firmely bound,
That mought his life from yron death assure,
And ward his gentle corpes from cruell wound:
For it by arte was framed to endure
The bit of balefull steele and bitter stownd,
No lesse than that which Vulcane made to sheild
Achilles life from fate of Troyan field.

And then about his shoulders broad he threw
An hairie hide of some wilde beast, whom hee
In salvage forrest by adventure slew,
And reft the spoyle his ornament to bee:
Which, spredding all his backe with dreadfull vew,
Made all that him so horrible did see
Thinke him Alcides with the lyons skin,
When the Næmean conquest he did win.

Upon his head, his glistering burganet,
The which was wrought by wonderous device,
And curiously engraven, he did set:
The mettall was of rare and passing price;
Not Bilbo steele, nor brasse from Corinth fet,
Nor costly oricalche from strange Phœnice;
But such as could both Phœbus arrowes ward,
And th' hayling darts of heaven beating hard.

Therein two deadly weapons fixt he bore,
Strongly outlaunced towards either side,
Like two sharpe speares, his enemies to gore:
Like as a warlike brigandine, applyde
To fight, layes forth her threatfull pikes afore,
The engines which in them sad death doo hyde:
So did this flie outstretch his fearfull hornes,
Yet so as him their terror more adornes.

Lastly his shinie wings, as silver bright,
Painted with thousand colours, passing farre
All painters skill, he did about him dight:
Not halfe so manie sundrie colours arre
In Iris bowe, ne heaven doth shine so bright,
Distinguished with manie a twinckling starre,
Nor Junoes bird in her ey-spotted traine
So manie goodly colours doth containe.

Ne (may it be withouten perill spoken)
That Archer god, the sonne of Cytheree,
That joyes on wretched lovers to be wroken,
And heaped spoyles of bleeding harts to see,

Beares in his wings so manie a changefull token.
Ah! my liege lord, forgive it unto mee,
If ought against thine honour I have tolde;
Yet sure those wings were fairer manifolde.

Full manie a ladie faire, in court full oft
Beholding them, him secretly envide,
And wisht that two such fannes so silken soft
And golden faire, her love would her provide;
Or that, when them the gorgeous flie had doft,
Some one, that would with grace be gratifide,
From him would steale them privily away,
And bring to her so precious a pray.

Clarion's questing is described in a passage which pleased men as diverse as the neo-classical Shenstone and the romantic Lowell, a passage in which the delight in flowers combines the very ecstasy of the butterfly in poised flight with a quaint utilitarianism that Spenser loved to play with at times. It closes with some stanzas that would be perfectly congruous in any of the most sorrowful poems in the volume.[11]

Thus the fresh Clarion, being readie dight,
Unto his journey did himselfe addresse,
And with good speed began to take his flight:
Over the fields, in his franke lustinesse,
And all the champion he soared light,
And all the countrey wide he did possesse,
Feeding upon their pleasures bounteouslie,
That none gainsaid, nor none did him envie.

The woods, the rivers, and the medowes green,
With his aire-cutting wings he measured wide,
Ne did he leave the mountaines bare unseene,
Nor the ranke grassie fennes delights untride.
But none of these, however sweete they beene,
Mote please his fancie, nor him cause t' abide:
His choicefull sense with everie change doth flit;
No common things may please a wavering wit.

To the gay gardins his unstaid desire
Him wholly caried, to refresh his sprights:
There lavish Nature, in her best attire,
Powres forth sweete odors, and alluring sights;

Lowell quotes most of the passage after his eulogy noted above. Shenstone imitates the flower-stanzas rather closely in his description of the picturesque and quaintly utilitarian garden of his *School-Mistress*.

And Arte, with her contending, doth aspire
T' excell the naturall with made delights:
And all that faire or pleasant may be found
In riotous excesse doth there abound.

There he arriving, round about doth flie,
From bed to bed, from one to other border,
And takes survey, with curious busie eye,
Of everie flowre and herbè there set in order;
Now this, now that, he tasteth tenderly,
Yet none of them he rudely doth disorder,
Ne with his feete their silken leaves deface;
But pastures on the pleasures of each place.

And evermore with most varietie,
And change of sweetnesse (for all change is sweete)
He casts his glutton sense to satisfie;
Now sucking of that sap of herbe most meete,
Of of the deaw, which yet on them does lie,
Now in the same bathing his tender feete:
And then he pearcheth on some braunch thereby,
To weather him, and his moyst wings to dry.

And then againe he turneth to his play,
To spoyle the pleasures of that paradise:
The wholesome saulge, and lavender still gray,
Ranke smelling rue, and cummin good for eyes,
The roses raigning in the pride of May,
Sharp isope, good for greene wounds remedies,
Faire marigoldes, and beees-alluring thime,
Sweete marjoram, and daysies decking prime:

Coole violets, and orpine growing still,
Embathed balme, and chearefull galingale,
Fresh costmarie, and breathfull camomill,
Dull poppie, and drink-quickning setuale,
Veyne-healing verven, and hed-purging dill,
Sound savorie, and bazill hartie-hale,
Fat colworts, and comforting perseline,
Colde lettuce, and refreshing rosmarine.

And whatso else of vertue good or ill
Grewe in this gardin, fetcht from farre away,
Of everie one he takes, and tastes at will,
And on their pleasures greedily doth pray.
Then, when he hath both plaid, and fed his fill,
In the warme sunne he doth himselfe embay,
And there him rests in riotous suffisaunce
Of all his gladfulness and kingly joyaunce.

What more felicitie can fall to creature
Than to enjoy delight with libertie,
And to be lord of all the works of Nature,
To raine in th' aire from earth to highest skie,
To feed on flowres and weeds of glorious feature,
To take what ever thing doth please the eie?
Who rests not pleased with such happines,
Well worthie he to taste of wretchednes.

But what on earth can long abide in state,
Or who can him assure of happie day;
Sith morning faire may bring fowle evening late,
And least mishap the most blisse alter may?
For thousand perills lie in close awaite
About us daylie, to worke our decay;
That none, except a God, or God him guide,
May them avoyde, or remedie provide.

And whatso heavens in their secret doome
Ordained have, how can fraile fleshly wight
Forecast, but it must needs to issue come?
The sea, the air, the fire, the day, the night,
And th' armies of their creatures all and some
Do serve to them, and with importune might
Warre against us, the vassals of their will.
Who then can save what they dispose to spill?

So the poet comes to dwell quite soberly on the transitoriness of earthly bliss. The dominant tone of the *Complaints* sounds here indeed like a mellow gong—as though softened by distance yet genuinely sad still.

For even a frail and innocent lover of beauty like Clarion has his enemies. There was a spider, Aragnoll, an hereditary foe of all idealists, since he sprang of the race of that ill-fated maiden Arachne, whose proud and envious egoism moved her to vie in the weaving of tapestries with the goddess of wisdom. The poet dwells delightedly on the maiden's cunning, intoxicated with his memories of Ovid and Moschus. Arachne makes her "tapet" rich with the story of Europa carried to sea on the bull.

She seem'd still backe unto the land to looke,
And her play-fellowes aide to call, and feare
The dashing of the waves, that up she tooke
Her daintie feete, and garments gathered neare:

> But (Lord!) how she in everie member shooke,
> When as the land she saw no more appear,
> But a wilde wildernes of waters deepe!
> Then gan she greatly to lament and weepe.
>
> Before the bull she pictur'd winged Love,
> With his yong brother Sport, light fluttering
> Upon the waves, as each had been a dove;
> The one his bowe and shafts, the other spring
> A burning teade about his head did move,
> As in their syres new love both triumphing:
> And manie Nymphes about them flocking round,
> And manie Tritons, which their hornes did sound.

"Was not this picture painted by Paul Veronese?" cries Lowell. Then Minerva weaves a wondrous picture of the gods, a far-off, stately prevision of that assembly which Spenser was to limn with such a sublime anticipation of Milton in the cantos on Mutabilitie. But with a touch appropriate in this light poem Spenser makes the final enchantment of the tapestry an image of the butterfly.

> Emongst those leaves she made a butterfle,
> With excellent device and wondrous slight,
> Fluttring among the olives wantonly,
> That seem'd to live, so like it was in sight:
> The velvet nap which on his wings doth lie,
> The silken downe with which his backe is dight,
> His broad outstretched hornes, his hayrie thies,
> His glorious colours and his glistering eies.

"We can hardly doubt," says Lowell in one of his best and happiest moments, "that Ovid would have been glad to admit this exquisitely fantastic illumination into his margin."

But we must return with the poet to the tragedy, which is none the less real for all the poet's "delight in libertie" and his power to "raine in th' aire." Arachne saw in that image of the butterfly her own inferiority and her doom. She was changed into a spider whose posterity held ever after a venomous hatred of the butterfly and his kinship with divinity. The poem closes with a brief but vigorous account of the innocent dreamer's entrapping and death.

The poem that I have chosen to consider last among the *Complaints,* "Mother Hubberds Tale," was probably written some time during the years 1577–80 and was doubtless retouched and amplified most significantly during the very exciting and momentous court affairs of 1579–80· It is in what I have called the third mood of the *Complaints,* a mood in which the poet daringly abandoned himself to a haughty and spirited arraignment of a court and church which, in their corruption and their feuds, fell so far short of what the court of Gloriana and the Church of England should be. The satire is full of characteristic paradoxical moods in which Spenser champions with great violence his favorite doctrine of the golden mean. "Again and again," writes Professor Padelford of Spenser's general attitude, the poet "advocates the golden mean in the various relations and activities of life: the golden mean between communism and monopoly, between wealth and poverty, between abstinence and self-indulgence, between prudishness and wantonness, between the life of activity and the life of contemplation. I believe that he was also a consistent advocate of the golden mean in matters ecclesiastical."[12] In spite of certain breaks in the structure I do not hesitate to claim for "Mother Hubberds Tale," with its wonderful range from light mirth to bitter contempt, and from irony to blazing ferocity, a position almost as high as that of the satires of Dryden.

Professor Dodge has placed the poem excellently among earlier English productions of the same *genre.*

The most obvious characteristic of "Mother Hubberds Tale" is the range of its satire. The career of the Ape and the Fox is a kind of rogues' progress through the three estates to the crown. They begin among the common people, rise from thence to the clergy and from thence to the court, among the nobility; in the end they cap the climax of their villainies by making themselves king and prime minister. The satire is mainly concentrated, to be sure, upon life at the court and the intrigues of those in power, topics of direct personal concern to Spenser, yet the poem as a whole does survey, however imperfectly and unsymmetrically, some of the main conditions of life in the nation at large. In this it harks back unmistakably

---

12 "Spenser and the Puritan Propaganda," p. 22.

to *Piers Plowman*. Though the satiric scope is of Langland, however, there is much in the style to suggest the vein of Chaucer, and the *dramatis personae* and the stage-setting are those of *Reynard the Fox*. The combination results at times in curious contrasts. In their first sojourn at court, the Fox and the Ape are among lords and ladies, suitors, a world of men, from the midst of which emerges the figures of the ''brave courtier'': in their second sojourn there, this world is suddenly transformed; for lords and ladies, suitors, men, we have the animals of Caxton's book, the Wolf, the Sheep, the Ass, and their like; it is the court of King Lion. Yet so spontaneous and creative are the acts of the poet's imagination that at no point in the long range of this satire are we checked by the sense of incongruity. The strange succession of scenes and figures, all admirably alive, the variety of artistic effects ranging from grotesqueness to romantic beauty, the sudden eruptions of strong personal feeling from the levels of cool satire, the fluctuations of the style from crudity to masterliness, produce, in a small way, the sense of a world almost as real as that of the *Faery Queen*. This is mediæval satire at its best. The Italians, with whom Spenser was at this time rapidly becoming familiar, had already, for at least two generations, been cultivating the classic Roman form, and their lead had been followed by the head of the new English school, Sir Thomas Wyatt: one might expect that Spenser, who from boyhood had been steeped in the classics, should also adopt this revived form. Nothing shows better the independence of his artistic eclecticism, his gift for taking here, there, and everywhere whatever appeals to his imagination, than the mediævalism of this his one satire.

Our interest is redoubled when we see how Professor Greenlaw has shown that this satire is not only dramatic in execution but that it arises from circumstances in the poet's life not unlike the careers of gifted nobles who flashed across the horizon of Elizabethan England.

During the last few months of 1579 Spenser was probably finishing or retouching for the press his *Shepheards Calender,* as daring in its ecclesiastical and political satire as any privileged herald of chivalry hurling the defiance of a noble master in the face of tyrants. He had, so we learn from his own letters, won the regard of the chivalrous Sidney. He was an accepted and loyal follower of the great Leicester whose Puritan affiliations and brilliance blinded the young Don Quixote of English poetry to his lord's shortsightedness and selfishness and stirred him to find in Burghley, whose far-seeing policies were hidden in foxlike craft and cold hesitancy, nothing but the crawling

Philistine and, perhaps, the arch-traitor. Aglow with the ambition of his friends, full of a premonition of a fame that awaited the appearance of his pastoral, eager with devotion to a country whose coming greatness he saw and a queen whom he criticized boldly but worshipped as half divine, Spenser, like all supreme men, found the life of deeds and the life of dreams perfectly harmonious and was dazzled with the vision of the life of statesman and poet in which his own advancement would be but a part of the ascendancy of England. But against his master, Leicester, and apparently against all high hopes for his country Burghley loomed sinister. The court was in a ferment of frivolity. The duc D'Alençon was over from France as the queen's suitor. His master of the wardrobe, Simier, "a consummate courtier, steeped in the dissolute gallantry of the French Court," had apparently entranced the queen, who seemed to be abandoning herself to one of those very feminine and very frivolous moods to which she turned from the most cunning and far-seeing statecraft and with which she occasionally startled all England. Gayer and gayer grew one-half the court. The queen had labelled all her followers with a motley of fable-names. Burghley was a dromedary, Hatton a sheep, Leicester a lion or a bear, Alençon a frog, Simier an ape. The French guests avowed themselves charmed with her quaint whims. Their letters waxed Aesopian. Meanwhile it so chanced that Spenser had written, at least in part, a general satire in the medieval vein of the picturesque Reynard stories.[13] He saw a brilliant opportunity to exhort Leicester, who was still hopeful of winning Gloriana and the throne of England to save England from the domination of Burghley and France, from what might become a Catholic conquest. Spenser sought no mere "gaine or commoditie"; that is made clear in one of his confidential letters to Harvey. His was

---

[13] For an account of the purely literary origins of Spenser's poem see Professor Greenlaw's "The Sources of Spenser's 'Mother Hubberds Tale,'" *Modern Philology*, II, 411 sq. Professor Greenlaw attacks Grosart's theory that Spenser's source was *The Moral Philosophie of Doni* translated by Thomas North. His contention for the influence of the Reynard cycle is thoroughly convincing. His arguments against Grosart's theory are not absolutely conclusive.

that noble ambition which sees personal success and the public weal in one brave adventure. The only possible charge against him here is that his intellect did not rise above the mob-psychology of the moment. This is indeed a chronic frailty of poets and statesmen which is too often sentimentalized as "loyalty" by historians still innocent of the findings of liberal economics and of social psychology. It would be foolish to ascribe to Spenser any great critical acumen here. But it is important to exonerate him from ill-conceived charges of flunkeyism. Let me sum up Professor Greenlaw's ingenious theory with his own words.

These, then, are the conditions in this strange year 1579–80. The Queen, madly infatuated with her ''ape'' and her ''frog,'' adepts in love-making and compliment mongering, is in danger of letting her affections run away with her judgment. Burghley is thought by court and country to favor the match, while Leicester, madly jealous, yet fearful, blows hot and cold. But Leicester is the leader of the Puritan party, and the Puritans are panic-stricken at the danger. All the old hatred of the French ''Monsieurs Youths'' blazes out; contempt for their effeminate gallantry, for their subtlety, for their skill in making love. But Elizabeth, strange compound of statecraft, cunning, and mere woman, is happy. She adds the ape and frog to the ''number of her beasts,'' and they carry the affectation much farther. The court circle is made up of lions, apes, frogs, partridges, dromedaries, and all the rest of Aesop.

Near this charmed circle of the English Circe, but not yet of it, emboldened by the favor of the great earl and his brilliant nephew, ambitious to be a man of consequence, stands the youthful author of the *Shepheards Calender.* He is a disciple of Chaucer. Like Wyatt with his fable of town and country mice, also told in Chaucerian fashion, the new poet has in mind a tale of a fox and an ape. Perhaps it is already written in part when in this crisis it occurs to him to treat in allegorical fashion this Aesopian court, in order to show the danger threatening the Queen and his patron. *Mother Hubberds Tale* is the result.[14]

Spenser attributes his incendiary tale to the good old gossip Mother Hubberd. and hints, both at the beginning and the end,

---

[14] The main body of this theory is set forth in ''Spenser and the Earl of Leicester.'' I must repeat that I frequently make generalizations from Professor Greenlaw's suggestions and from bits of my own evidence that he himself might be unwilling to accept. Where the reader finds something he deems speculative rather than inductive it will be safer to blame me. Despite the strictures of Dr. Higginson and Dr. Long, already noted, Professor Greenlaw impresses me as an unusually sober as well as reflective observer.

that its rude style—does he not mean here its violence of tone?—
is due to his homely story-telling and to the fever from which
he was convalescing when he heard it. With this flimsy but
significant apology he launches into a satire which we may well
regard as astonishingly bold. Originally he may have intended
little more than a general satire on the idle and predatory sol-
diery, the gullible common people, the clergy, and the court.
But the poem in mid-career takes a turn which can be read in
but one way.[15]

At the outset, the fox (who becomes Burghley) and the ape
(who becomes Simier as the most cunning and militant of the
French gallants) are depicted as complaining in a manner which
is often uncritically attributed to Spenser, but which Spenser

---

[15] I quote two interestingly vague contemporary references to Spenser's
satire as late as the time of its appearance in the volume on *Complaints*.
These references are at least fair indications that "Mother Hubberds Tale"
was regarded as dynamite to be handled very gingerly even as late as ten
years after it was first written and that it still gave the poet's friends some
concern. Harvey wrote to Christopher Bird on September 4, 1592: "For
I must needes say, *Mother Hubberd* in the heat of choller, forgetting the
pure sanguine of her sweet *Fairie Queene* wilfully overshot her miscon-
tented selfe, as elsewhere I have specified with good leave of unspotted
friendship." Nashe made this material at once for his inveterate contempt
for Harvey and for his apparently genuine solicitude for Spenser: "Who
publickly accused of late brought *Mother Hubberd* into question, that thou
shouldst by rehersal rekindle against him [Spenser] the sparkes of dis-
pleasure that were quenched. Forgot hee the *pure sanguine of Fairy
Queene*, sayst thou? A pure sanguine sot art thou, that in vaine-glory to
have *Spencer* known for thy friend, and thou hast some interest in him,
censerest him worse than his deadliest enemie could do." *Works* (ed.
McKerrow, London, 1904), 1, 281 sq. Spenser's death does not seem to
have silenced the cryptic references. Nicholas Breton ("An Epitaph upon
Poet Spencer," *Melancholike Humours*, 1600), in a queer, bitter piece of
doggerel, thus refers to "Mother Hubberds Tale":

> As for Mother *Hubberts* Tale,
> Cracke the nut, and take the shale.

In 1604 Thomas Middleton published *Father Hubburds Tales or The Ant
and the Nightingale*, a satire in poetry and prose showing the distinct
influence of Spenser's poem. Every reader of this dramatist's *Game of
Chess* knows his tendency to make political satire daring and cryptic. That
the very title, however, of *Father Hubburds Tales* made him feel the
necessity of at least pretending innocence appears in his preface: "Why
I call these *Father Hubburds Tales* is not to have them called in again,
as the *Tale of Mother Hubburd*: the world would show little judgment in
that, i' faith; and I should say then, *plena stultorum omnia;* for I entreat
here neither ragged bears or apes . . . what is mirth in me, is as harmless
as the quarter-jacks in Paul's, that are up with their elbows four times an
hour, and yet misuse no creature living."

himself attributed to the idle and the sordid-minded, prototypes
of the ''get-rich-quick'' animals well known in our own epoch.

> ''Heare then my paine and inward agonie,''

cries the fox to the ape,

> ''Thus manie yeares I now have spent and worne,
> In meane regard, and basest fortunes scorne,
> Doing my country service as I might,
> No lesse I dare saie than the prowdest wight;
> And still I hoped to be up advaunced,
> For my good parts; but still it hath mischaunced.
> Now therefore that no longer hope I see,
> But froward fortune still to follow mee,
> And losels lifted up on high, where I did looke.''

The ape is made to reply in homely idiom and subtle self-pity
worthy of Chaucer.

> ''Deeply doo your sad words my wits awhape,
> Both for because your griefe doth great appeare,
> And eke because my selfe am touched neare:
> For I likewise have wasted much good time,
> Still wayting to preferment up to clime,
> Whilest others alwayes have before me stept,
> And from my beard the fat away have swept.''

Those who think that Spenser's celebrated episode of Artegal
and the giant shows his hatred of any democratic or other re-
form should compare it with some further words of the fox in
order to see that the poet was in reality only at odds with those
pseudo-socialists who demand redistribution with no real thought
of community, but with hypocritical selfishness.

> ''Let us our fathers heritage divide,
> And chalenge to our selves our portions dew
> Of all the patrimonie, which a few
> Now hold in hugger mugger in their hand,
> And all the rest doo rob of good and land.
> For now a few have all, and all have nought,
> Yet all be brethren ylike dearly bought.
> There is no right in this partition,
> Ne was it so by institution
> Ordained first, ne by the law of Nature,
> But that she gave like blessing to each creture,

> As well of worldly livelode as of life,
> That there might be no difference nor strife,
> Nor ought cald mine or thine: thrice happie then
> Was the condition of mortall men.''

The two rogues set out on their career disguised as a soldier and his dog. ''Be you the souldier,'' says the fox in a couplet which even Lowell, with his fixed idea of Spenser, admitted to be humorous,

> ''Be you the souldier, for you likest are
> For manly semblance, and small skill in warre.''

In this guise they met a simple husbandman (the Common People) of whom they besought employment. The kind-hearted man readily offered them a choice of tasks. But when the ape saw grave danger of honest labor

> He would have slipt the coller handsomly

and, pleading maimed limbs, begged for a lighter task. The naïve husbandman assigned them the care of his sheep. Daily they slew and despoiled.

> Thus is this Ape become a shepheard swaine,
> And the false Foxe his dog: (God give them paine),

cries the poet with a quick rush of anger that reminds us of Chaucer's personal outbursts. In the wanton slaughter and robbery of the sheep we have, perhaps, not only the original satire, but a glimpse at what Spenser felt would be the treatment of the innocent people if Burghley and the French gallants held sway in England. If, indeed, Spenser, in his satirical ferocity, prophesied murder and confiscation, it may seem to some that his condemnation of Burghley is unpardonable. But we must remember that such excesses were real in Spenser's day; that Spenser was, as always, sincere; and that, like all idealists, he was easily capable of hatred at once impersonal and violent. Similarly, in his *Veue of the Present State of Ireland* he appears as unquestionably an idealist even though afire with hatred, the exponent of a ruthless but dazzling imperialism.

The fox and the ape were presently fain to take flight when their master demanded his yearly account. From broken-down soldiers it was easy to fall lower and become ecclesiastical parasites, a profession which, says Spenser with a vicious home-thrust at the Elizabethan church, is

> Much like to begging, but much better named;
> For manie beg, which are thereof ashamed.

It was not long before the ape and the fox, in cassock and gown, met with a priest (the Church), Spenser's most subtle portrait, who stands in ugly contrast to the husbandman. Unlike the husbandman he has no spark of that cardinal virtue which, because of the modern degradation of the meaning of the English word, we are forced to call by its Latin name, *caritas*. Roughly he demanded of them why they disgraced their cloth by begging, but asked, with a shrewd afterthought, for their license. They readily produced a paper,

> Which when the Priest beheld, he vew'd it nere,
> As if therein some text he studying were,
> But little els (Got wote) could thereof skill:
> For read he could not evidence nor will,
> Ne tell a written word, ne write a letter,
> Ne make one title worse, ne make one better.

"All his care was," so we are told, "his service well to saine," and "to read homelies upon holidays." Here is a very bold and direct attack, as Professor Padelford points out, on "Elizabeth's distrust of preaching and prophesying." "Elizabeth," he adds, "did not argue: she simply said that 'it was good for the Church to have few preachers, and that three or four might suffice for a county, and that the reading of the homilies to the people was enough.' "[16] The modern reader may well agree with Elizabeth's desire for a paucity of clergy, though not on her grounds. There is no doubt that many features of her policy justified the poet's censure. For the priest's ignorance, which was the inevitable consequence of the regal coercion, Spenser makes a mordant ironical apology which is as daring as it is perfect.

---

[16] "Spenser and the Puritan Propaganda."

Of such deep learning little had he neede,
. Ne yet of Latine, ne of Greeke, that breede
Doubts mongst divines, and differences of texts,
From whence arise diversitie of sects,
And hatefull heresies, of God abhor'd.
But this good Sir did follow the plaine word.

At last the fox won the priest by tickling his pride; not through the cardinal virtue, *caritas*, but through the deadly sin, *superbia*. Indeed most of the seven deadly sins appear in the complacent and atrocious advice which the priest now glibly gave them at length. Under the guise of his thin idealism, the languid idealism of an automaton. and under a complacent satisfaction in the present as the best of all possible ages, there lurk spiritual sloth (*accidia*) and gluttony. There is, he says, no need to worry. We cannot feed men's souls. They must feed themselves, so smirks this Pharisee; we can but lay the meat before them. Christ is the shepherd and may be naturally expected to do all the hard work.

"We but his shepheard swaines ordain'd to bee.
Therefore herewith doo not your selfe dismay;
Ne is the paines so great, but beare ye may;
For not so great, as it was wont of yore,
It's now a dayes, ne halfe so streight and sore.
They whilome used duly everie day
Their service and their holie things to say,
At morne and even, besides their anthemes sweete,
Their penie masses, and their complynes meete,
Their dirges, their trentals, and their shrifts,
Their memories, their singings, and their gifts.
Now all those needlesse works are laid away;
Now once a weeke, upon the Sabbath day,
. It is enough to doo our small devotion,
And then to follow any merrie motion.
Ne are we tyde to fast, but when we list,
Ne to weare garments base of wollen twist,
But with the finest silkes us to aray,
That before God we may appeare more gay,
Resembling Aarons glorie in his place:
For farre unfit it is, that person bace
Should with vile cloaths approach Gods majestie,
Whom no uncleannes may approachen nie."

It may be an interesting practical demonstration of the enduring value of great literature to compare this passage with some dry and caustic sentences by Professor Thorstein Veblen, the most distinguished of liberal American economists, in which he points out the relation between clerical observances and those ideals of the "Leisure Class" which have done so much, since barbaric times, to retard the growth of modern democracy.

.   The most obvious bearing of these observances is seen in the devout consumption of goods and services. The consumption of ceremonial paraphernalia required by any cult, in the way of shrines, temples, churches, vestments, sacrifices, sacraments, holiday attire, etc., serves no immediate material end. All this material apparatus may, therefore, without implying deprecation, be broadly characterized as items of conspicuous waste. ... There is a striking parallelism, if not rather a substantial identity of motive, between the consumption which goes to the service of a gentleman of leisure—a chieftain or patriarch—in the upper class of society during the barbarian culture. Both in the case of the chieftain and in that of the divinity there are expensive edifices set apart for the behoof of the person served. These edifices, as well as the properties which supplement them in the service, must not be common in kind or grade; they always show a large element of conspicuous waste. It may also be noted that the devout edifices are invariably of an archaic cast in their structure and fittings. So also the servants, both of the chieftain and of the divinity, must appear in the presence clothed in garments of a special, ornate character.[17]

As the priest warmed up to his subject he noted that after sloth and gluttony a mild and pleasant degree of lechery is easy of justification.

> "Beside, we may have lying by our sides
> Our lovely lasses, or bright shining brides:
> We be not tyde to wilfull chastitie,
> But have the gospell of free libertie."

---

[17] Those students of literature who are not spoiled by the prevailing habit of teaching and studying literature in hot-house abstraction from life and from other branches of learning may be referred to Professor Veblen's entire book, *The Theory of the Leisure Class* (N. Y., Macmillan, 1912), particularly the chapters on "Pecuniary Canons of Taste" and "Devout Observances," which, however much they may overemphasize economic determinism, will exercise a most emancipating influence on many conventional esthetic and ethical modes of valuation and may well contribute to more progressive conceptions of art.

The priest went on to close his "ghostly sermon" with an appendix worthy of Iago on church and court.[18]

His shrewd hearers profited well by his advice for some time but, growing day by day more zealous in following out his precepts, they were presently constrained to flee once more. For a short time poverty gripped them till on a happy day they met a representative of the court,

> The Mule, all deckt in goodly rich aray,
> With bells and bosses, that full lowdly rung,
> And costly trappings, that to ground downe hung.
> Lowly they him saluted in meeke wise;
> But he through pride and fatnes gan despise
> Their meanesse; scarce vouchsafte them to require.

Presently, however, the mule condescended to give them news and advice. In an obscure and evidently somewhat carelessly revised passage we get the well-known allusion to Leicester's marriage which so infuriated Elizabeth; and with the survey of court life the satire grows more keen and more direct in its thrusts at Burghley and the French gallants whose shallow and dissolute allurements are set forth as the qualities with which the ape easily gulled the court.

> For he could play, and daunce, and vaute, and spring,
> And all that els pertaines to reveling,
> Onely through kindly aptness of his joynts.
> Besides he could doo manie other poynts,
> The which in court him served to good stead:
> For he mongst ladies could their fortunes read

---

[18] Throughout this entire episode it is clear that Spenser's quarrel is not with ritual, but with the corruption of the clergy. Compare this with the hint of sympathy for Catholicism, the old oak, in "Februarie," where he attacks not rituals as such, but what seem to him to be superstitions. Some plausible evidence could be collected to indicate that when Spenser could overcome his purely political fear of Catholicism he was inclined, without renouncing all aspects of Puritanism, to sympathize with the splendors of the church of Rome. See especially his concessions in the *Veue*:

"Next care in religion is to builde up and repayre all the ruinous churches, whereof the most part lye even with the grounde, and some that have been lately repayred are so unhandsomely patched and thatched, that men doe even shunne the places for the uncomeliness thereof; therefore I would wish that there were order taken to have them built in some better form, according to the churches of England; for the outward shew (assure your selfe) doth greatlye drawe the rude people to the reverencing and frequenting thereof, what ever some of our late nice fools saye, there is nothing in the seemely forme and comely orders of the churche."

> Out of their hands, and merie leasings tell,
> And juggle finely, that became him well:
> But he so light was at legier demaine,
> That what he toucht came not to light againe.

Yet the very abhorrence of such charlatanism is bound to kindle a spirit as naturally pure and serene as Spenser's with a memory of its opposite in such as Sidney, and the poet now spurns the base courtier for the more congenial task of portraying the perfect courtier, the English knight who, with the true democracy of a Prince Hal and of the male Cinderellas of English romance, disdains no more to bend the bow of the yeoman and wrestle like the sturdy rustic than to tilt at the ring and, like Chaucer's squire, passes readily from feats of arms to the gentle revelry of verse-making.

> Yet the brave courtier, in whose beauteous thought
> Regard of honour harbours more than ought,
> Doth loath such base condition, to backbite
> Anies good name for envie or despite.
> He stands on tearmes of honourable minde,
> Ne will be carried with the common winde
> Of courts inconstant mutabilitie,
> Ne after everie tattling fable flie.
>
> . . . .
>
> He will not creepe, nor crouche with fained face,
> But walkes upright with comely stedfast pace.
>
> . . . .
>
> And lotheful idlenes he doth detest,
> The canker worme of everie gentle brest;
> The which to banish with faire exercise
> Of knightly feates, he daylie doth devise:
> Now menaging the mouthes of stubborne steedes,
> Now practising the proofe of warlike deedes,
> Now his bright armes assaying, now his speare,
> Now the nigh aymed ring away to beare:
> At other times he casts to sew the chace
> Of swift wilde beasts, or runne on foote a race,
> T'enlarge his breath (large breath in armes most needfull)
> Or els by wrestling to wex strong and heedfull,
> Or his stiffe armes to stretch with eughen bow.

Thus when this courtly gentleman with toyle
Himselfe hath wearied, he doth recoyle
Unto his rest, and there with sweete delight
Of musicks skill revives his toyled spright;
Or els with loves and ladies gentle sports,
The joy of youth, himselfe he recomforts:
Or lastly, when the bodie list to pause,
His minde unto the Muses he withdrawes;
Sweete Ladie Muses, ladies of delight,
Delights of life, and ornaments of light:
With whom he close confers, with wise discourse,
Of Nature's workes, of heavens continuall course,
Of forreine lands, of people different,
Of kingdomes change, of divers government,
Of dreadfull battailes of renowmed knights;
With which he kindleth his ambitious sprights
To like desire and praise of noble fame,
The onely upshot whereto he doth ayme.
For all his minde on honour fixed is,
To which he levels all his purposis,
And in his princes service spends his dayes,
Not so much for to gaine, or for to raise
Himselfe to high degree, as for his grace,
And in his liking to winne worthie place,
Through due deserts and comelie carriage,

. . . .

Or else for wise and civill governaunce.
For he is practiz'd well in policie,
And thereto doth his courting most applie:
To learne the enterdeale of princes strange,

. . . .

T' enrich the storehouse of his powerfull wit,
Which through wise speaches and grave conference
He daylie eekes, and brings to excellence.
Such is the rightfull courtier in his kinde.

Here, indeed, we have Spenser's own code of action, a passionate code and, by itself alone, a refutation of that fallacious conception of Spenser as the querulous and fulsome seeker of affluence. Then in savage contrast comes the return to a consideration of the ways of the French gallants, of the ape.

A thousand wayes he them could entertaine,
With all the thriftles games that may be found;
With mumming and with masking all around,

> With dice, with cards, with balliards farre unfit,
> With shuttlecocks, misseeming manlie wit,
> With courtizans, and costly riotize,
> Whereof still somewhat to his share did rize:
> Ne, them to pleasure, would he sometimes scorne
> A pandares coate (so basely was he borne);
> Thereto he could fine loving verses frame,
> And play the poet oft. But ah! for shame,
> Let not sweete poets praise, whose onely pride
> Is vertue to advaunce, and vice deride,
> Be with the worke of losels wit defamed,
> Ne let such verses poetrie be named.

The fox, meanwhile, was busily engaged in financial activities which Spenser might well have sincerely attributed to the shrewd and avaricious Burghley.

> But the beste helpe, which chiefly him sustain'd,
> Was his man Raynolds purchase which he gain'd.
> For he was school'd by kinde in all the skill
> Of close conveyance, and each practise ill
> Of coosinage and cleanly knaverie,
> Which oft maintain'd his masters braverie.
> Besides, he usde another slipprie slight,
> In taking on himselfe, in common sight,
> False personages fit for everie sted,
> With which he thousands cleanly coosined:
> Now like a merchant, merchants to deceave,
> With whom his credite he did often leave
> In gage, for his gay masters hopelesse dett:
> Now like a lawyer, when he land would lett.
> Or sell fee-simples in his masters name,
> Which he had never, nor ought like the same:
> Then would he be a broker, and draw in
> Both wares and money, by exchange to win.

Besides all this (quite justifiable, no doubt, under that reverend maxim, "Business is business") Raynolds loved to beguile suitors. Here follows the famous passage which careless readers of Spenser, forgetful of his longer and far more passionate delineation of the perfect courtier, are fond of citing as the most personal passage in the poem.

> Full little knowest thou that hast not tride,
> What hell it is, in suing long to bide:

To loose good dayes, that might be better spent;
To wast long nights in pensive discontent;
To speed to day, to be put back to morrow;
To feed on hope, to pine with feare and sorrow;
To have thy Princes grace, yet want her Peeres;
To have thy asking, yet waite manie yeeres;
To fret thy soule with crosses and with cares;
To eate thy heart through comfortlesse dispaires;
To fawne, to crowche, to waite, to ride, to ronne,
To spend, to give, to want, to be undonne.
Unhappie wight, borne to desastrous end,
That doth his life in so long tendance spend!
Who ever leaves sweete home, where meane estate
In safe assurance, without strife or hate,
Findes all things needfull for contentment meeke,
And will to court, for shadowes vaine to seeke,
Or hope to gaine, himselfe will a daw trie:
That curse God send unto mine enemie!

Assuredly a home thrust; but not from the depths. Robert
Southey was absolutely right when he wrote of Spenser

> Yet not more sweet
> Than pure was he, and not more pure than wise;
> High priest of all the Muses' mysteries.

The half-suppressed fury of Spenser's verses, the abrupt, flam-
ing outburst of the last line—surely, say the critics, it is a
memory of some personal wrong from Burghley. A mere tinge
of the personal is there, perhaps. But I hope that the cum-
ulative evidence and interpretation in this book will leave the
reader sure that Spenser never could have stooped to the abject-
ness which he here assigns to the suitor. At a time when prac-
tically all the greatest and noblest in England's universities and
court and churches were tainted, the reader, who will ponder
carefully all the poetry of Spenser in the light of modern
perspective and modern investigations, can but marvel with
Southey more and more at Spenser's purity. Such men as he
may have their unworthy and querulous moments in the seclu-
sion of their closet with a friend and even by their hearth, but
never in their communion with the muses. An idealist of the
highest order does not complain; he hates with a large imper-
sonality not men but the vices of men.

Then it befel that once more ape and fox were unmasked and exiled. There follows a final episode which gives with special savagery a warning to Leicester and the queen, a warning in which there is no more cringing than there was in Sidney's bold letter to Elizabeth advising against the French marriage. To interpret Spenser's allegory too closely would be to misunderstand his Parthian method which was to keep within sight of a well-known incident of fable or romance and merely to color it with his observation of contemporary life. Here, however, as he was occasionally wont to do, he did not hesitate to prophesy and to suggest boldly a solution as yet not enacted. One day the exiled fox and ape found the lion sleeping in secret shade. At the exhortation of the fox the ape crept near the dread beast, tremblingly, and stole crown and scepter and lionskin. A quarrel for the supreme honors ensued between the conspirators. But the wily fox patched a compromise by virtue of which the ape was to be the imperial figurehead while he himself was, as counsellor, to be the brains of the kingdom. Once more they returned to court, this time to reach their apex of unscrupulous power. They buttressed up their despotism with a monstrous following of beasts "bred of two kinds:" griffons, minotaurs, crocodiles, dragons, centaurs. The fox became, in the more sinister sense, a machiavellian prince. We cannot but see the desperate lunge at Burghley in such lines as these:

> But the false Foxe most kindly plaid his part:
> For whatsoever mother wit or arte
> Could worke, he put in proofe: no practise slie,
> No counterpoint of cunning policie,
> No reach, no breach, that might him profit bring,
> But he the same did to his purpose wring.

But Jove, at last, looking down on the reign of terror that ensued, despatched Mercury to arouse the lion. The winged messenger, here the herald of the poet himself, exhorted the lion in language which, whether addressed to Elizabeth or Leicester, must seem to us surprisingly bold even after all the cool silence of these intervening centuries.

> "Arise," said Mercurie, "thou sluggish beast,
> That here liest senseles, like the corpse deceast,
> The whilste thy kingdome from thy head is rent,
> And thy throne royall with dishonour blent:
> Arise, and doo thy selfe redeeme from shame,
> And be aveng'd on those that breed thy blame."

The royal beast shattered the palace gates and restored justice but, with a fine contempt, punished the rogues only by cropping the ears and tail of the ape, stripping the fox, and banishing them.

Comments by such contemporaries as Harvey and Nashe, Breton and Middleton, show that Spenser's poem was regarded as bold and incendiary. Harvey evidently felt that his friend, in a moment of undue wrath, had tarnished the fair name which he celebrated in his epic as Gloriana. Nashe's words indicate quite clearly that Spenser had aroused some ireful remonstrances. Sidney had been dismissed from court for his letter of protest. Stubbs uttered the sentiment of the people and lost his right hand for his book, "The discovery of a gaping gulph, whereunto England is like to be swallowed by another French marriage, if the Lord forbid not the banns by letting her Majesty see the sin and punishment thereof." It is certain that Spenser allowed his poem to circulate at least in manuscript during the same year that Sidney and Stubbs suffered royal displeasure and that (though it was evidently hastily withdrawn, probably through the solicitude of the poet's friends) it attracted deadly attention. The poem, then, is not, as critics have so frequently said, based on a petty anger because Burghley (so the rumor runs) delayed the payment of the poet's pension. Professor Greenlaw states the case with temperate admiration.

We have seen that the Queen in the winter of 1579–80 was blind to what the Puritans regarded as a national peril, being completely infatuated with her dissolute and effeminate admirers. We have seen that there was a wide-spread fiction making the courtiers animals and the court an assembly of beasts—a beast-fable in application, appealing to the Elizabethan fondness for such allegories. With all this Spenser was familiar at first hand. He was in the service of Leicester, and at the very time of the crisis, in early October, was expecting to be sent on a mission for him. His patron, therefore, who had everything to lose by this marriage, since Burghley and not Leicester would rule the French favorites, should be warned of the danger; perhaps the Queen herself should be warned. So Spenser takes his imitation of Chaucer, written perhaps not long before, applies the beast-allegory to the crisis among Elizabeth's beasts, and with a daring not less great than Sidney's own, speaks his mind. Here we have reason for the traditional enmity of Burghley; we have also reason for Spenser's being shipped to Ireland the following summer; we have the grounds on which the poem was ''called in.'' Spenser was ambitious to succeed as Sidney was succeeding; his literary talents were to be a means for advancing him in the service of the powerful earl; at the same time he spoke sincerely the astonishment and terror of Englishmen at the imminence of the monstrous foreign alliance, to the dangers of which the Queen seemed through her passion utterly blind.

Leicester was in serious complications. In Professor Greenlaw's words: ''He was made a scape-goat for the failure of the marriage, as well as compelled to suffer the resentment of the Queen. Much of this resentment was due to the activities of Leicester's Puritan allies among whom was Spenser. And we can hardly doubt that 'Mother Hubberds Tale' was one of the slanderous documents to which objection was made.'' There was a convenient secretaryship with Lord Grey, another noble under royal displeasure. So the fervid and too loyal young poet was shipped to Ireland, whence he despatched some time later his protest which we have already studied in ''Virgils Gnat.''

When ''Mother Hubberds Tale'' was published or republished in the volume of *Complaints* in 1591 Burghley's star was falling. Perhaps Spenser was roused again by a furious eagerness to be in at the death of the fox. He was intimate with Essex and Raleigh, who were then actively at odds with Burghley. Perhaps as the poet turned towards Ireland for a second time he chose to help his friends by stirring up the old story of the French crisis in which the old treasurer had most assuredly offended many a stout Englishman.[19] It is supposed that the passage in Spenser's satire in which the fox is made to advance his own cubs to office is a reference, added about

---

[19] For whether Burghley actually favored the marriage or not he was thought by the public to have done so.

1591, to Burghley's recent advocacy of Sir Robert Cecil to the Privy Council and then to the secretaryship in succession to Walsingham. A passage in "The Ruines of Time"[20] is supposed to be a reference to the quarrel between Burghley and Essex and Raleigh that arose over Burghley's favoritism. "Mother Hubberd's Tale" was not, then, even in its second appearance three years after Leicester's death, an outburst of personal spleen against Burghley nor was it much less dangerous to publish it at this later date, as the words of Harvey and Nashe show.

Had Spenser been a cold and insincere office-seeker he might conceivably have been led by the native shrewdness of such characters to choose Burghley rather than Leicester as a patron. But he was evidently repelled by the great treasurer's sturdy philistinism and foxlike ways and was as truly blind to his merits and virtues as to Leicester's erratic mistakes and vices. Let us summarize once more with a compact paragraph from Professor Greenlaw.

> More subtle than the vigorous denunciations of Stubbs and the Puritan pulpits, *Mother Hubberds Tale* is not less daring. If it lacks the manly frankness of Sidney's letter, it has the same aim. Perhaps Spenser's motive was less pure, for he wished to serve Leicester and thereby advance himself; but there is no harm in a young man's seeking preferment through making himself honorably useful; and the ring of conviction, the sureness of touch which makes this satire a masterpiece. is proof of sincerity. Spenser allowed the caution revealed in his October letter to be overcome by the crisis.[21] The whole episode has that touch of the dramatic so characteristic of the times, not less interesting in that Spenser was not to be one of those who had prominent places among the *dramatis personae*. It meant success, or exile: he played for a high stake, and he lost.

We may turn quite naturally from the *Complaints* (with their great range from playful melancholy to savage bitterness) to kindred poems which complete a perfect circle of moods through which Spenser seems to have passed more than once— we may turn to the elegies with their gentler sadness and thence

---

[20] The stanza "O grief of griefs," quoted above.

[21] In a letter of October 5, 1579, to Harvey, Spenser shows great caution in his attitude towards his new friends of the court.

to *Colin Clouts Come Home Again*, which, except for a passage that seems to echo in temperate afterthought the satirical wrath of "Mother Hubberds Tale," is almost winsome in tone and closes on a characteristic note of gracious serenity.

Daphnaida, which seems to have appeared during the year in which the *Complaints* was published, is a graceful but rather perfunctory elegy on the death of Douglas Howard, daughter of Henry Lord Howard and wife of Spenser's gifted friend, Arthur Gorges. Its main distinction is its stanza in which, as Professor Dodge points out, Spenser, "by mere transposition of a line, . . . creates out of the orthodox rhyme royal a form of haunting cadence, almost as beautiful as the stanza of 'October.'" The poem has little other significance. The poet's reference to Elizabeth and to himself under his pastoral name is offensive and as near the fulsome and the vain as anything in Spenser. The dead girl is first lamented in fable and riddle as a beautiful young lioness, a fancy which has some quaint prettiness, but which is always on the verge of the rococo. A few of the stanzas grow hard with a peculiarly grotesque rhetoric that would be morbid if it were not so thoroughly artificial and extravagant. As a whole *Daphnaida* is merely a very formal lament with all the conventionalities of the renaissance elegy and with some borrowings, of dubious value, in general scheme and phrasing, from Chaucer's *Book of the Duchess*, which similarly mourns the death of the wife of John of Gaunt, the poet's friend.[22] Only once in the *Daphnaida* do we get a touch of pathos worthy of Spenser.

---

[22] Professor Henry Morley (*English Writers*, ed. 1892, IX, 370) was, I think, the first to suggest Spenser's general indebtedness to Chaucer's lament. Dr. Thomas William Nadal ("Spenser's *Daphnaida* and Chaucer's *Book of the Duchess*," *Publ. Mod. Lang. Assoc.*, XXIII, 1908) has made a detailed study of Spenser's indebtedness which is, for the most part, sound and useful, although he is overzealous and cites many passages which will hardly impress the impartial reader. When, moreover, he uses his material as significant of the lasting and pervasive influence of Chaucer and describes Spenser as "leaning hard on his master" in maturity he fails to see that this poem, though it may be as Professor Dodge has said "thoroughly characteristic," is not at all representative of Spenser's maturity in essential poetic quality.

She fell away in her first ages spring,
Whil'st yet her leafe was greene, and fresh her rinde,
And whil'st her braunch faire blossomes foorth did bring,
She fell away against all course of kinde:
For age to dye is right, but youth is wrong;
She fel away like fruit blowne downe with winde:
Weepe, shepheard, weepe, to make my undersong.

The last line of this lovely stanza is used as a refrain at the end of sections which seem to have been quite mechanically arranged in groups of seven stanzas to correspond with the stanzas of seven lines. But this refrain, at least, has an evasive beauty of its own appearing as it does at such infrequent intervals that it has all the glamor and wistfulness of a half-forgotten memory.

Astrophel, an elegy on Sidney, though it was not published until 1595, appears, so far as stanza and style and the facts of Spenser's life offer material for judgment, to have been composed at about the time that Spenser and Ponsonby were collecting the *Complaints.*[23] Though there can be no doubt of the perfect sincerity of its gentle sadness, it seems strangely pallid to the modern reader. When one remembers the relations of Spenser and Sidney and then examines into the quality of Spenser's many references to his dead young paragon, one feels that the poet was chilled by his sadness to an unwonted and uneasy self-consciousness closely akin to taciturnity. It is quite probable that the frigidity of *Astrophel* was partly due to the fact that it was composed in haste, after a long hesitation, as a prelude to a series of elegies most of which had been written some years before. Though some of these other poems had already appeared in anthologies or at least found record in the Stationers' Register, it seems likely that they had been turned over to Spenser for editorial supervision and for the prelude; and it is hardly fanciful to suppose that there was some disappointment among Sidney's most loyal friends at the delay. In "The Ruines of Time" Spenser upbraided himself for his

---

[23] See Professor Dodge's comments (Cambridge ed., p. 699).

long silence about Sidney. Yet the best amends he could make
was to revamp an old Latin occasional poem which he had com-
posed in a moment hardly worthy of his great admiration. How
then can we account for such apparent coldness towards the
man he loved and reverenced so profoundly unless we account
his a grief too deep alike for tears and song, one of those sorrows
that have at some time or other struck dumb many of the most
eloquent of poets? So, after long and mysterious delays, there
came forth the little volume of elegies with Spenser's prelude,
Astrophel, a poem artificial enough, yet not without the fragile
and lifeless beauty of a hothouse flower found dead and pale,
but almost perfect in some old favorite book.[24] For anything like
the true note one must turn from Spenser himself to another
lyric in the volume, by Matthew Royden, a poem which contains
at least one stanza worthy of immortality for the exquisite sure-
ness with which it makes vivid for us the spiritual beauty of the
dead hero.

> A sweet attractive kinde of grace,
> A full assurance given by lookes,
> Continuall comfort in a face,
> The lineaments of Gospell bookes;
>   I trowe that countenance cannot lie,
>   Whose thoughts are legible in the eie.

Colin Clouts Come Home Again is to the lover of Spenser
one of the richest and most suggestive of his minor poems. It
is, as Professor Trent has said, "perhaps the most remarkable
example in English of the blending upon an extensive scale of
occasional and familiar with essential poetry." Through the
silvery film of the pastoral manner and setting the reader may
easily discern all the significant impressions that came to Spen-
ser when in 1589 he made his journey to England with Raleigh,
taking with him the first three books of his epic to show to
Gloriana herself. Professor Dodge feels that this record "was

---

[24] Mr. Robert Schafer (*Mod. Lang. Notes,* XXVIII, 224–226) points
out that the artificiality of the poem may be due to some substantial and
inappropriate borrowings from Bion. This would, of course, be perfectly
compatible with my psychological reason suggested above.

obviously written not long after his return to Kilcolman,'' that is while his volume of *Complaints* and his *Daphnaida* were in Ponsonby's hands, although "about four years later, probably by way of revision, for the press, he made changes inspired by intervening events." The poem is then quite fitly a climax for this chapter and with it we may bring our poet back to Ireland (a place now no longer so hateful to him as many critics have supposed) to conjure forth the last three books of *The Faërie Queene*. And we can leave the poet in one of those characteristic gracious moods which were always for him, after great struggle and bitterness, the cadence; one of those gracious moods which inspired Keats to write:

> Spenser! thy brows are arched, open, kind,
> And come like a clear sun-rise to my mind.

No poem of Spenser's is more proudly and independently loyal and more serene. As in his quixotic championship of Grindal, Leicester, and Lord Grey, so here Spenser chose for his hero in Raleigh a man who was, at this time, out of favor with the court. Let any reader who will persist in classing Spenser crudely with the mere fortune-seekers contrast his consistent championship of his heroes in fair weather and foul and his consistent assault on their foe Burghley with Tasso's strange compound of pride and servility when he coquetted with the Medici, the enemies of his kindly patrons of Este, when he bargained for patrons with an epic. And let the advocates of art for art's sake contrast in this connection Tasso's decorous structure but intellectual caprice with Spenser's obviously faulty structure but firm integrity, the noble heights and sentimental, miasmal levels of the *Jerusalem Delivered* with *The Faërie Queene*, which is inferior in structure simply because, in his ardent utopianism, its poet sought to rear arches and spires that Tasso would not have dared even to contemplate. Surely—all things considered—Spenser made a greater poem in its sustained loftiness.

Raleigh certainly was not, at the moment, the best man

to introduce the poet to their great queen. Moreover Raleigh
was distrusted and disliked by Spenser's other friend and com-
mander, Lord Grey. There may be a few nowadays who will
question Spenser's taste in so profoundly admiring this brilliant
but wilful adventurer whom he so superbly named "the Shep-
heard of the Ocean." We may freely admit with Gardiner that
Raleigh was, "in his haste to be wealthy, his love of adventure,
his practical insight into the difficulties of the world, and his
unscrupulousness in dealing with peoples of different habits
and beliefs from his own, ... a representative Englishman."
We may sentimentalize over his picturesqueness and courage,
but we must also understand him as one of the first English
proponents of that tragic and sordid capitalism which makes
the quarrels of business *entrepreneurs* in a distant continent the
occasion for the decimation of whole armies of their less sophisti-
cated, romantic countrymen. We may also as freely maintain
that those qualities which were noblest in him, like those which
were noblest in Leicester, were precisely the qualities which fired
the emulous Spenser. The singer saw then as the careful his-
torian has seen today that "Raleigh's efforts were at least made
on behalf of a race whose own civilization and national inde-
pendence were at stake." That Raleigh was not, however, the
best man to introduce Spenser to the queen will be clear to those
who remember that Raleigh was at that time a victim of one of
the queen's gusts of anger. Of this circumstance Spenser does
not hesitate to speak plainly and, though he lauds Elizabeth and
emphasizes Raleigh's repentance, his partiality for the wayward
knight is perfectly clear.[25] Moreover, in the year that the
poem went through the press, Raleigh was certainly not basking
in the sunshine of his vain mistress. She had sent him to the
tower in 1591(2) for seducing and later marrying Elizabeth
Throckmorton, a medieval freedom and a sincerity both of which

---

[25] Note, for instance, the tone of these words which Colin claims to para-
phrase from Raleigh:

Ah! my loves queene, and goddesse of my life,
Who shall me pittie, *when thou doest me wrong?*

incensed the ever-jealous queen. In 1595 he was using his liberty, but lately granted, to sail on one of those expeditions which Elizabeth generally held in at best a dubious approval, and which sowed the first seeds of those complications that today fill with anguish the volumes of great English liberals like Hobson, Hobhouse, Wallas, and Russell and that confirm so-called practical statesmen in their cynical and fatalistic support of imperialism even after the romantic bloom has long worn away. Indeed it was not before 1597 that Raleigh was readmitted to court by the queen. It is only fair to the intelligence of our poet to assume that Spenser had some appreciation of that sinister ill-luck and royal anger which always hounded Raleigh's impetuosity at the heels and which was to culminate in his tragic relations with James I and with a puritanized public that no longer believed, like the Elizabethan mob, in gorgeous spendthrifts. We cannot too much emphasize the fact that the life of the Don Quixote of English poets was a series of bold defenses of the Don Quixotes of English politics coupled with frequent attacks on the Sancho Panzas. Only we must remember that Spenser, like the Don Quixote whom Cervantes has so subtly and fully portrayed, could be amazingly practical. Those who deny Spenser this attribute have not studied closely enough his Irish pamphlet and his political allegories or, perchance, they have not made a clear distinction between the practical man who sees issues keenly but in perspective and the grovelling "practical" man who worships common sense with a fervor which is but ignorance.

Yet *Colin Clouts Come Home Again* is a sumptuous compliment to Gloriana, or Cynthia as she is here called. To his English friends in Ireland—here made to masquerade as naïve shepherds—he tells of his voyage to the great queen in a mighty ship which he describes with a quaint awed picturesqueness which one might expect from an Aztec watching a Spanish galleon swing grandly round a headland. And the immense sea. The sea, sings Spenser, is

> A world of waters heaped up on hie,
> Rolling like mountaines in wide wildernesse,
> Horrible, hideous, roaring with hoarse crie.

Professor Elton thinks that "for an Englishman who wrote
when he did Spenser is strangely impressed with the hostility of
the sea, and its ghastliness, and the remarkable bravery of sea-
faring."[26]   But we must remember again that the poet here
assumes the rôle of a childlike shepherd addressing fellow
rustics.   And how superb seems the compliment when we learn
that this fearful realm is ruled by Cynthia, of whom Colin says
quaintly:

> Her heards be thousand fishes, with their frie,
> Which in the bosome of the billowes breed.
> Of them the shepheard which hath charge in chief
> Is Triton blowing loud his wreathed horne.

Everyone will remember Wordsworth's splendid theft of that
last line which, when it becomes the memorable close of a per-
fect sonnet, stands as an immortal refutation of that fear of
imitation or echo which warps those futurists who have mistaken
mere novelty in art for originality.   The praise of Cynthia
grows more and more extravagant until it reaches a climax in
some enchanting lines which have a delightful pastoral pseudo-
simplicity.

> Such greatnes I cannot compare to ought:
> But if I her like ought on earth might read,
> I would her lyken to a crowne of lillies,
> Upon a virgin brydes adorned head,
> With roses dight and goolds and daffadillies;
> Or like the circlet of a turtle true,
> In which all colours of the rainbow bee.

The passage hardens into rhetoric as it goes on.   Yet I for one
grow weary of the eternal girding at Spenser as exemplified by
Dean Church's conventional comments à propos of these same
lines and the less felicitous ones which follow: "He had already
too well caught the trick of flattery—flattery in a degree almost

---

[26] *Modern Studies:* "Colour and Imagery in Spenser."

inconceivable to us—which the fashions of the time, and the Queen's strange self-deceit, exacted from the loyalty and enthusiasm of Englishmen.'' If the reader, in turn, grows tired of my insistence on the fact that such ''flattery'' was transfigured by a real and rapturous faith in a queen who for all her ⱽ faults was one of the greatest women of renaissance Europe, let the reader remember that he is being visited with the sins of centuries of acrid criticism on this matter and that I am forced to react against a ''most damnable iteration'' with an equally ''damnable iteration.''

Afterwards Colin is brought to speak of himself when Alexis asks him how fared it at his introduction to the court by the Shepherd of the Ocean. But in another moment the poet forgets himself to praise the singers of England with a warmth which more than atones for his boyish pessimism in ''The Teares of the Muses,'' with a warmth indeed which tends towards that swashbuckling praise that prompted Meres to lump together poets of the first and the fourth order as the peers of the singers of the world and that is a part of that strange and terrible modern perversion of religion called ''nationalism.'' Not content with praising Sackville,

> ... good Harpalus, now woxen aged
> In faithfull service of faire Cynthia,

Colin must needs praise Alabaster, the pedantic author of a forgotten Latin poem on Elizabeth. He strikes the note that characterizes the criticism of the heydey of Elizabethan self-confidence :

> No braver poeme can be under sun.
> Nor Po nor Tyburs swans so much renowned,
> Nor all the brood of Greece so highly praised,
> Can match that Muse when it with bayes is crowned,
> And to the pitch of her perfection raised.

No better argument for the sincerity of the Elizabethans' praise of their queen exists than the uncritical but stirring rodomontade with which they hailed their poets great and small.

Such panegyrics were not flattery. They were a sincere and triumphant state of mind. And however contemptuous the selective critic may be in his general attitude he must be vinegar-visaged indeed to listen coldly to the gracious lines with which Colin hails his gifted younger contemporary, Samuel Daniel.

> And there is a new shepheard late up sprong,
> The which doth all afore him far surpasse:
> Appearing well in that well tuned song
> Which late he sung unto a scornfull lasse.
> Yet doth his trembling Muse but lowly flie,
> As daring not too rashly mount on hight,
> And doth her tender plumes as yet but trie
> In loves soft laies and looser thoughts delight.
> Then rouze thy feathers quickly, Daniell,
> And to what course thou please thy selfe advance:
> But most, me seemes, thy accent will excell
> In tragick plaints and passionate mischance.[27]

Presently Colin, recalling Astrophel, last among the poets who eternize Cynthia, is interrupted by an arch shepherdess.

> Then spake a lovely lasse, hight Lucida:
> ''Shepheard, enough of shepheards thou hast told,
> Which favour thee and honour Cynthia:
> But of so many nymphs which she doth hold
> In her retinew, thou hast nothing sayd;   .
> That seems, with none of them thou favor foundest,
> Or art ungratefull to each gentle mayd,
> That none of all their due deserts resoundest.''

---

[27] Critics have often said that Daniel, on his side, was very ungracious to Spenser. The famous sonnet beginning
    ''Let others sing of knights and paladins
    In agéd accents and untimely words''
does look like a fling at the romance and the archaisms of *The Faërie Queene*. But the young poet was more probably concerned with the hyperbolical protestation to Delia for which he was preparing. As a matter of fact it is easy to show that Daniel had the same rapturous faith that stirred Nashe and Meres to intemperate eloquence. In his dedication of *Cleopatra* he lamented that England is bounded by the ocean and longed that her songs might be known to other nations:
    ''Whereby great *Sydney* and our *Spencer* might
    With those *Po*-singers being equalled,
    Enchaunt the World with such a sweet Delight
    That their eternal Songs (for ever read)
    May shew what great Elisaes raigne hath bred.''

Whereupon the poet answers in a courtly passage paying tribute
first to his well-remembered Rosalind,

> The beame of beautie sparkled from above,
> The floure of vertue and pure chastitie,
> The blossome of sweet joy and perfect love,
> The pearle of peerlesse grace and modestie,

then to Urania, Sidney's sister,

> In whose brave mynd, as in a golden cofer,
> All heavenly gifts and riches locked are;
> More rich then pearles of Ynde, or gold of Opher,

and fair Marian,

> Faire Marian, the Muses onely darling:
> Whose beautie shyneth as the morning cleare,
> With silver deaw upon the roses pearling,

and many more, with last of all the poet's own kindred, "Phyllis,
Charillis, and sweet Amaryllis," the last of whom was to live
to receive from the young Milton the homage of the *Arcades*.

After another long eulogy of Cynthia which really is fulsome
in its extravagant rhetoric, Colin touches for a moment on the
satirical note of "Mother Hubberds Tale." He anticipates
the charge which some later critics have brought against him.

> "Shepheard," said Thestylis, "it seemes of spight
> Thou speakest thus gainst their felicitie,
> Which thou enviest, rather then of right
> That ought in them blameworthie thou doest spie."

But Colin retorts with plausibility that no personal wrong has
given him cause for "cancred will." Rather it is that he would
warn young shepherds not to abandon their more serene pur-
suits for the fever of the treacherous court. Then comes an
onslaught on slander, the Blatant Beast, who was to receive
such grim portrayal in the last two books of *The Faërie Queene*.

But from these dissonant notes Colin is soon diverted by
Hobbinol, who reminds him of the true men of the court, espe-
cially of Leicester, dead but unforgotten.

Then with a rare felicity Colin turns from the account of
the court to remember, at the close, Rosalind, his shepherdess,
and to discourse on love with a flash of that Platonic inspiration
that reached its climax in his last two *Hymnes*.

> "Of Loves perfection perfectly to speake,
> Or of his nature rightly to define,
> Indeed," said Colin, "passeth reasons reach,
> And needs his priest t' expresse his powre divine.
> For long before the world he was ybore,
> And bred above in Venus bosome deare:
> For by his powre the world was made of yore,
> And all that therein wondrous doth appeare.
> For how should else things so far from attone,
> And so great enemies as of them bee,
> Be ever drawne together into one,
> And taught in such accordance to agree?
> Through him the cold began to covet heat,
> And water fire; the light to mount on hie,
> And th' heavie downe to peize; the hungry to' eat,
> And voydnesse to seeke full satietie.
> So, being former foes, they wexed friends,
> And gan by litle learne to love each other:
> So being knit, they brought forth other kynds
> Out of the fruitfull wombe of their great mother."

It was just this "celestial rage of love" that always silenced
in Spenser his disappointment in the corruption of the court and
the greater sadness which came to him in that passionate con-
templation of change, the death of beauty, which dominates so
many of the *Complaints*.   In this chapter, then, we follow a
cycle of moods that is a perfect image of that larger cycle, the
life of Spenser, that came to a close with the *Hymne of Heavenly
Beautie* and the calm of the last two stanzas of *The Faërie
Queene*.

Plato's own visions were tainted by a luxurious arrogation
of contemplation to a mythological leisure-class and the visions
of the Christian Platonists are marked by that other-worldliness
which savors of defeat.   But Spenser, neither here nor in his
Platonic swan-songs, is a defeated man.   He is a serene self-
conqueror.   Spenser's pastoral, indeed, closes with that sweet-

ness which is peculiar to the greatest Elizabethan poets. After Colin has chanted his laud to Love, the shepherds and shepherdesses grow clamorous with their denunciation of the woman who rejected Love's very high-priest. Colin's answer, in his maturity, is in striking contrast to the morbid egoism of the amorous verses in the youthful *Shepheards Calender.*

> "Ah! shepheards," then said Colin, "ye ne weet
> How great a guilt upon your heads ye draw,
> To make so bold a doome, with words unmeet,
> Of thing celestiall which ye never saw.
> For she is not like as the other crew
> Of shepheards daughters which emongst you bee,
> But of divine regard and heavenly hew,
> Excelling all that ever ye did see.
> Not then to her, that scorned thing so base,
> But to my selfe the blame, that lookt so hie:
> So hie her thoughts as she her selfe have place,
> And loath each lowly thing with loftie eie.
> Yet so much grace let her vouchsafe to grant
> To simple swaine, sith her I may not love,
> Yet that I may her honour paravant,
> And praise her worth, though far my wit above.
> Such grace shall be some guerdon for the griefe
> And long affliction which I have endured:
> Such grace sometimes shall give me some reliefe,
> And ease of paine which cannot be recured.
> And ye, my fellow shepheards, which do see
> And heare the languours of my too long dying,
> Unto the world for ever witnesse bee,
> That hers I die, nought to the world denying
> This simple trophie of her great conquest."

There will be those who can never discern the wholesome fragrance in those lines because of that pastoral exaggeration which is to so many readers but an antiquated tongue. The salvation of such readers might well rest in a sincere unquietness at the thought that these verses which are to them at best but pretty trifling are to the initiated lovers of the poet's poet magical with a chivalry that no modern singer has recaptured.[28]

---

[28] At all events I feel sure that no reader of the foregoing pages will consider that M. Jusserand has caught the significant emphasis of the poem when he writes coldly and briefly: "The dazzling hopes of the first days [at court with Raleigh] and the final disappointment were echoed in a pastoral poem: 'Colin Clouts come home againe.'"

CHAPTER IV

AMORETTI AND EPITHALAMION

The vast star-dust of sonnets that swarmed and glittered in the wake of Petrarch has served little to justify the flaunting vanity of the poetasters or the arrogance of many true singers who believed with Gabriel Harvey that "it is no dishonour for the daintiest and divinest muse" to follow the lover of Laura and who assured lover and patron of an eternity outlasting brass and gold and marble. After a few hundred years of dubious popularity not untarnished by the irreverent lasciviousness of an Aretino, the mockery of a Berni, and the grotesque legal jargon of the "gulling sonnets" of a Sir John Davies, the Petrarchan love-sonnets found little more than oblivion in England until they were reread with the unquenchable enthusiasm of the nineteenth-century idolaters of Elizabethan poetry and, shortly after, were subjected to the more thorough researches of the colder scholar of our own hour. Petrarch's repentance for his own beautiful sonnets, "Nugellas meas vulgares ... juveniles ineptias," found in modern times a harsh Saxon approval from Lord Macaulay that has hardly brought denial from the lips of our weary and cynical investigators. Except for a few mellow humanists who can read Petrarch with learning enriched by the scientific method yet free from the esthetic paralysis that often comes with science, practically all of the minority of us who turn to the beauty and amorousness of the sonnets to Laura, sit grimly down in search of mere facts and devour scores of "sugared sonnets" with the automatic zeal of a person who, in the face of the first warnings of dyspepsia, tries to persuade himself that he has the appetite of a cow-boy. Now it is certain that the Petrarchists should be interpreted to our alien century by a man who is a scholar but who also can indulge the wholesome and capricious and luxurious tasting habit of the alert dilettante. Yet so great is the dyspepsia and paralysis that have resulted from scientific sophistication and romantic neurasthenia that even the sonnets of the supreme Petrarchan, Shakespeare, have been coldly tabulated for their conventionalities or ransacked for their allusions to mere facts, or patronizingly deplored for their frankness, their confessions of human weakness, their cries of anguish. And if Shakespeare has suffered, the lover of Spenser must not be surprised to find his master's most ambitious sonnets, though they were not written till the poet was forty and at the same time fathoms deep in his supreme poem, the object of the sharpest criticism from men of times and temperaments as diverse as William Drummond of Hawthornden, himself an ardent Petrarchan and perhaps a Spenserian as well, and Mr. Yeats, a modern Celt at war with the literary habits of a sophisticated society of any period.[1]

The most conventional attitude of present-day students of literature towards the Petrarchists in England is the result of certain investigations which culminated in the learned studies of Sir Sidney Lee, whose vast reading and sure memory have shown the Elizabethan sonnets to be ''a strange medley of splendour and dulness'' the full story of which is ''a suggestive chapter in the literary records of plagiarism.''[2] Sir Sidney Lee

[1] Drummond (Spingarn, *Critical Essays of the Seventeenth Century*, I, 215–217): ''As to that which *Spencer* calleth his *Amorelli*, I am not of their Opinion who think them his; for they are so childish that it were not well to give them so honourable a Father.''
Mr. Yeats says that Spenser wrote about his wife ''many intolerable sonnets'' and ''the most beautiful of all his poems, the *Epithalamium.*''

[2] Sir Sidney Lee's point of view should be studied in his edition of *Elizabethan Sonnets*, revised from the older *English Garner* of Professor Arber (New York, Dutton); in his chapter on Elizabethan Sonnets in the third volume of *The Cambridge History of English Literature;* in his *Life of Shakespeare*, ed. 5, chap. vii, and appendices K and X; in *Shakespeare's Sonnets, with Introduction and Bibliography* (Oxford, 1905); in *Great Englishmen of the Sixteenth Century*, ''Spenser''; and in *The French Renaissance in England*, Book IV, appendices I and II, especially pp. 261–263, which give an interesting contrast of Desportes, Spenser, and Daniel. Lee's work was anticipated by little worth attention. But see: Isaac Hermann, ''Wie weit geht die Abhängigkeit Shakespeare's von Daniel als Lyriker?'' *Shakespeare Jahrbuch* (1882), XVII, 165 sq.; Luigi De Marchi, ''L'influenza della italiana sulla lirica inglese nel secolo XVI,'' *Nuova Antologia*, IIId series (1895), LVIII, 136, a study which deals with Wyatt; Josef Guggenheim, *Quellen studien zu Samuel Daniels sonetten-egklus ''Delia''* (Berlin Dissertation, 1898, one of the first to note the

has had his answers. Mr. Arthur Symons, for example, himself a lyrist of rare delicacy, finds so much rare poetry in these Elizabethan sonneteers that he girds at their sources, "the graveyard of Desportes" in particular, and at Sir Sidney Lee.[3]   Again, Professor Neil Dodge, probably the most learned student of Spenser in America and certainly not blind to the foibles of Petrarchists, writes of the *Amoretti:* "Even a Petrarchist may draw from the life, and Spenser, to an unpreoccupied eye, would seem to have done just that."

It should be noted that in reacting against the disillusioned scholarship of Sir Sidney Lee his critics have not always done him justice.[4]   In many places he shows that his learning has not destroyed his taste or his zest.   Of Spenser he is ready to admit that the poet "rarely stoops to verbal translation" and that "a strand of autobiography is woven into the borrowed threads."[5]   To a few of the *Amoretti* he accords much praise.

---

influence of Desportes; and Emil Koeppel, "Studien zur Geschichte des englischen Petrarchizmus in 16ten Jahrhundert, *Romanische Forschungen* (1890), V, 65 sq.

[3] *A Pageant of Elizabethan Poetry*, arranged by Arthur Symons (London, 1906).   For Mr. Symons' criticism of Sir Sidney Lee the reader should examine the notes, pp. 383 sq.   There is a very brief but suggestive note on the *Amoretti* on p. 393.

[4] A good example of a thoroughly futile, carping review by a man who can write, at best, some very stimulating criticism is Mr. P. H. Frye's "The Elizabethan Sonnet," in his *Literary Reviews and Criticisms* (New York and London, 1908).   The most brilliant estimate of Lee's conclusions, mainly hostile, but with much valuable and felicitously phrased constructive criticism, will be found in *The Edinburgh Review*, "The Pléiade and the Elizabethans," CCV, 353–379.

On the other side, Professor L. E. Kastner, after Sir Sidney Lee, has been one of the most important champions of the scholarship that makes much of foreign influences.   See his articles in *The Athenaeum* (October 22 and 29, 1904), 552 sq., and 591 (the last of which shows that Lee and Kastner were at work on some important investigations, independently, at about the same time); articles by Kastner in *The Modern Language Review*, II, 155 sq.; III, 1–15, and 268–277; IV, 65 sq.; V, 40–53; and his edition of Drummond (Manchester, 1913).   See also Mr. James Fitzmaurice Kelley's "Note on Three Sonnets," *Revue Hispanique*, XII, 259–260; and Mr. George Wyndham's *Rosnard and la Pléiade* (London, 1906).

[5] Perhaps Sir Sidney Lee's greatest injustice was done to Sir Philip Sidney's *Astrophel*, which he seems to consider almost valueless as autobiography.   He has been ably answered by Professor Jefferson B. Fletcher (*The Religion of Beauty in Woman*, "Did 'Astrophel' love 'Stella'?" New York, 1911), though perhaps Professor Fletcher rides his own hobby —Platonism—too hard at times.

Yet he is primarily interested in unimpassioned scientific criticism and evidently assumes his readers to be, like himself, so safely endowed with an indestructible love of poetry that he chooses to invite a reaction dangerously and unnecessarily chilling. It is fair to say that though he has left little for the seeker of facts he has left much for the scholarship of interpretation. Such scholarship of interpretation, as superimposed on the scholarship of facts, has been felicitously applied to the sonnets of Shakespeare by Professor George Herbert Palmer, who brings to his work a gentle spirit saturated with the best poetry and philosophy and writes after years of meditation. It is just this rereading and unpreoccupied contemplation that is neglected too frequently by our present-day scholars. As a little manifesto, then, it is worth while to quote Professor Palmer on his own method.

In my early manhood a friend lived with me who was as greedy as I of sweet sounds and delicate diction. We made a compact that each of us should repeat one of these sonnets each morning at breakfast explaining why he had found it worthy of remark. We chose them merely in the order of our liking. In this way, during the otherwise unprofitable moments of dressing, I committed eighty to memory and my friend no fewer. Many years afterwards he told me that he believed himself to have derived more benefit from this exercise than from any two years of his college course.[6]

We find then, to go no further, a poet, a scholar, and a philosopher who can distil from at least the best of Elizabethan sonnets much wisdom and solace.[7] I propose to take the

---

[6] *Intimations of Immortality in the Sonnets of Shakespeare* (Boston and New York, 1912).

[7] It may be well to add here the recoil of another learned Elizabethanist from the scholarship of disillusion and mere facts. Professor F. C. Schelling (*The English Lyric*, Boston and New York, 1913) writes: ''It matters less than nothing whether Sidney loved Stella or not, whether Shakespeare unlocked his heart in the sonnets, or Spenser married the lady whom he courted so absolutely in accord with the canons of Petrarchan art. What does matter is that in the splendid body of Elizabethan sonnets and in the songs, pastoral, incidental to the drama, written to be set to music sacred and profane, we have as sincere, as spontaneous, as artistic, and as musical an outburst of lyrical poetry as any nation or time can boast. In view of this we may grant that the Elizabethan lyric is unequal, that it is more an art of great impact than of sustained effect, that there were a few in this prodigious chorus of sweet sound that could not sing and would not be silent. But in large, never has the gift of song been so widely diffused, so lavishly displayed, so crowded with definite artistic success.''

Amoretti very seriously as genuine love-poems which I have read countless times with very great pleasure, which I have found with Wordsworth to have always at least the magic of a ''glow-worm lamp,''[8] and which I have found often transcending Wordsworth's characterization because aglow with authentic passion.

Indeed the critics are very hardy who deny a man to be in love and who even venture to deny him true eloquence simply because he went freely to Petrarch and Ronsard and Tasso for jewelled phrases. We observe that when an Elizabethan made love he not infrequently turned to his Petrarch, found a sonnet in harmony with his mood, translated or paraphrased it, and sent it to his mistress. We do not make love in that way, so the literary critics tell us; and the Elizabethan lovers are called ungenuine. Nay, it is even averred that the mistresses who subjected them to slow torture were mere patrons or did not exist in the flesh. I wonder whether our young men, when they are seriously in love, never do anything as ungenuine as Spenser or even Barnabe Barnes? How refreshing in contrast to the words of these purblind critics is the gracious intuition of Charles Lamb. His words on Sidney's sonnets are equally applicable to the *Amoretti*.

They are stuck full of amorous fancies—far-fetched conceits, befitting his occupation; for True Love thinks no labour to send out Thoughts upon the vast, and more than Indian voyages, to bring home rich pearls, outlandish wealth, gums, jewels, spicery, to sacrifice self-depreciating similitudes, as shadows of true amiabilities in the Beloved. We must be Lovers —or at least the cooling touch of time, the *Circum praecordia frigus*, must not have so damped our faculties, as to take away our recollection that we were once so—before we can duly appreciate the glorious vanities, and graceful hyperboles, of the passion.[9]

---

[8] See Wordsworth's ''Scorn not the Sonnet.''
     ''A glow-worm lamp,
   It cheered mild Spenser called from Faery-land
   To struggle through dark ways.''

[9] Compare also in this connection some sensible arguments by Professor J. B. Fletcher in *Modern Language Notes* (1903), XVIII, 111 sq., ''Mr. Sidney Lee and Spenser's *Amoretti*.''

At all events we have, in this period of Spenser's, the well authenticated cases of William Drummond of Hawthornden, who loved deeply and lamented life-long a mistress untimely taken by death, yet who did not disdain to sing of his true love and grief in echoes and in rarely beautiful echoes of his beloved Petrarch. We may reprove Spenser's taste when he borrowed from the extravagant Desportes. But it would be rather sweeping to argue that a man who indulges bad taste cannot possibly be in love. It may be argued with some plausibility that because Spenser was forty years of age he was or should have been no calf-lover, but a sensible man who would scribble sonnets as at most mere toys to banter and entrap woman, a pretty slave. But the heroine was no more of a pretty slave than are the Atalantas of our day. In her exquisite combination of prìde and "humblesse," a harmony so rare and so perfect, she stands out at times, every full curve of her, more real than any of the other lovely children of Laura.

> Rudely thou wrongest my deare harts desire,
> In finding fault with her too portly pride:
> The thing which I doo most in her admire
> Is of the world unworthy most envide.
> For in those lofty lookes is close implide
> Scorn of base things, and sdeigne of foule dishonor;
> Thretning rash eies which gaze on her so wide,
> That loosely they ne dare to looke upon her.
> Such pride is praise, such portlinesse is honor,
> Such boldned innocence beares in hir eies,
> And her faire countenance, like a goodly banner,
> Spreds in defiaunce of all enemies.
> Was never in this world ought worthy tride,
> Without some spark of such self-pleasing pride.

Spenser, unlike all unpoetic people and in a greater degree than most poets, appreciated, as this sonnet shows with unique loveliness, the profound truth that the highest womanly beauty is associated with power. In the second place Spenser, like all true lovers at any time of life, was by no means beyond the influence of calf-love. But it was such a calf-love as that of which the memory inspired some of the most magnificent passages in the

stern epic of Dante's maturity. Those to whom this is unreal
and puerile are those who protest against healthy romantic love
because they confuse it with moonshine. Romantic love is the
only love worth the name. It can calculate sanely yet abhor
materialism. And unless we are muddy-minded enough to sur-
render this noble phrase, romantic love, to the memory of people
like Chateaubriand in his most unworthy moments, we may
add without paradox that romantic love abhors moonshine of
which there are comparatively few traces in Spenser's sonnets.
Dr. Percy W. Long has argued that the *Amoretti* are not
addressed to his real lover, Elizabeth Boyle, but to Lady Eliza-
beth Carey, a cousin to whom Spenser chose to pay compliment
as to a patron.[10] Critics have been too much influenced by
Drayton's swaggering impersonation in his Idea and by the
elder Giles Fletcher's preface to his sonnet-sequence, *Licia:*

> A man may write of love and not be in love, as well as of husbandry
> and not go to the plough, or of witches and be none, or of holiness and
> be flat profane.

Giles Fletcher is quite right. But it is just as plausible to fancy
that Drayton and he were disguising real loves under the cover
of abstractions or of imaginary ladies as to doubt the reality
of Spenser's passion. The weakness of contemporary criticism,
with its mania for explaining out of real existence all lovers
Elizabethan, comes out sufficiently in a *non-sequitur* perpetrated
by Sir Sidney Lee and used by most of his followers as a funda-
mental canon:

> The imitative character of Daniel's Muse renders it unnecessary to
> inquire, with former critics, into the precise identity of the lady to whom
> he affected to inscribe his miscellany.

---

[10] Professor Grosart, in his monumental edition of Spenser, was the
first to identify the heroine of the *Amoretti* with Elizabeth Boyle. I know
of no valid arguments against him. Dr. Long's article appeared in *The
Modern Language Review*, III, 257-267. He is one of the most ingenious
and sane of the American Spenser-scholars and this is the only occasion
on which I find myself clearly and firmly against him. See also in this
conection Mr. J. C. Smith's article in *The Modern Language Review*, V,
273-281.

But even Sir Sidney Lee has not cared to question the reality of Spenser's mistress. My quarrel with him is simply that his tone is partly responsible for the prejudices of his followers. Nevertheless Dr. Long has gained little following for his theory and it is not coxcombry for me to say roundly that I am quite convinced of Spenser's love when he wrote the *Amoretti* and that he was probably in love with the lady he married a few months before the sonnets were entered upon the Stationers' Register, November 19, 1594, the same lady to whom he wrote for the same volume the most magnificent and most tender epithalamium in the world.[11]

The freshness and reality of the *Amoretti* are enhanced by the uniqueness of Spenser's form. After some experimentation with sonnet-forms from his earliest known days of versifying to the days of his full powers Spenser settled into an almost unbroken use of the form which closely resembles his stanza in its cunning and caressing weaving of lines—ababbcbccdcdee— over the last line of which he occasionally lingers delightedly with the final alexandrine. It is only fair, I suppose, to preface my praise of the Spenserian sonnet-form with the words of an opponent as formidable as Leigh Hunt.[12]

This form of sonnet never became popular. It is surely not so happy as that of the Italian sonnet. The rhyme seems at once less responsive and always interfering; and the music has no longer its major and minor divisions. To my ear there is something in it of the teasing nature of Dante's *terza rima*, which is a chain that seems as if it would never end, and is dragged after him by the presumptuous poet through his next world, like a retribution.

Would it be too ungracious for a lover of Leigh Hunt to add that this essay is apparently hack-work, that it is certainly very uneven and capricious in the quality of its judgments, and that the poorer criticism of Leigh Hunt is everywhere recognized as being very poor indeed? It is not altogether safe to attribute

---

[11] Spenser's wedding-day was June 11, 1594. His sonnets were published by William Ponsonby in 1595.

[12] *The Book of the Sonnet* (Boston, 1878), pp. 70–74.

this sonnet-form entirely to Spenser despite its marked resemblance to the stanza which is his unquestioned, brilliant invention. His earliest definitely dated sonnet in this form is the one addressed to Harvey from "Dublin, this 18th of July, 1586." Now there are sonnets by Alexander Montgomerie (who was apparently the first of a long line of Scotch poets to show a decided preference for this identical form) which can be put at an earlier date. On this ground one investigator at least has claimed the honor of invention for the laureate of King James VI. Dr. O. Hoffman argued that Spenser imitated the form from certain sonnets of Montgomerie's printed in King James's *Essays of a Prentiss* in 1585.[18] But it may be argued that Spenser's famous sonnet to Leicester must have been written about 1580. At all events the apparent advantage of Montgomerie is inconclusive. It is true that scores of later Scotch poets with no vogue in England used this sonnet-form almost invariably. But, in England, except for a few scattered sonnets by Constable, by Taylor, the queer "water-poet," and a few other contemporaries, except for a few enthusiasts like Thomas Edwards in the eighteenth century and Thomas Hood in the nineteenth, the form, unlike the Spenserian stanza, has had little appeal. We may note too that the Scotch poets most closely allied with the English "fellows and followers" of Spenser, Sir Robert Aytoun and Sir William Alexander, used the close-woven form but a few times, and that Drummond of Hawthornden, the most versatile experimenter in sonnet-forms in all English and Scottish poetry, did not leave a single "Spenserian sonnet" on record. On the other hand Montgomerie's slight advantage in dates is unestablished and unimportant. Sonnets circulated freely in manuscript. Spenser was illustrious. Montgomerie seems to have been practically unknown

---

[18] "Studien zu Alexander Montgomerie," *Englische Studien* (1895), XX, 24–69. Stevenson, *Supplementary Volume*, Introduction, p. xlvii, thought that Montgomerie was the first to use the form, but that the development was independent. For these and other references see Lois Borland ("Montgomerie and Sixteenth-Century Poets," *Modern Philology*, 1913, XI) who considers that both Spenser and Montgomerie got their rudimentary suggestion from Marot.

in England, at least before James VI of Scotland had become James I of England. And although Montgomerie, in the complicated stanza of his *Cherrie and the Slae,* shows a good deal of ingenious rhyming skill, it pales before the extraordinarily various metrical virtuosity of Spenser. Under any circumstances Spenser was the first to do distinguished work with the form and the only poet of high quality who used it frequently. In his hands, too, it has a beauty that has never been given sufficiently explicit praise. It is difficult to see why it has not attracted many other illustrious singers, although it may be noted that it is really more difficult to write than even the most severe Italian sonnet; that a poetaster of the magazines can give you an *ignis fatuus* of distinction in the orthodox Petrarchan mould whereas he would probably expose himself with a "Spenserian sonnet." Spenser's favorite form is certainly inferior in range of expressiveness and in grave nobility to the forms made classical by Petrarch. But its peculiar echoing harmonies, though they could never perhaps be sounded greatly in an austere or a tragic key, are very rich in the hands of a master-lover, for the sonnet that woos, for the sonnet that combines tenderness and graciousness. The brooding rhymes seem indeed to caress each other and to cling to the sensuous moment they celebrate.

No critic has made capital of the fact that the *Amoretti* has a story made real by the very fact of its casual and truncated structure. Professor Dodge touches upon the point I wish to emphasize when he affirms that in reading the *Amoretti* "we are constantly within sight of fact, however trivial."

The poet, accustomed, it seems, to easy conquests, makes definite advances too soon, and is ignominiously beaten back; he is chidden by a friend for not pushing on more vigorously with his *Faery Queen,* and pleads the distractions of his suit; at the close of a visit, when he should be departing, there comes up a violent storm of rain, and he knows not whether to stay or go, or he walks with his mistress upon the beach and writes her name in the sand, whereupon the waves wash it out. Behind the graceful banalties of fancy, the imitations of previous imitators of Petrarch, almost inevitable in an Elizabethan sonnet sequence, one may read the history of a genuine courtship as clearly as in a set of old letters.

The only other critic I know who has struck the right note of appreciation in this connection is Professor John Erskine. When he says that "the individual sonnets have not the merit of the series as a whole," but that, "taking the sonnets as a whole, the critic must find in them the truest sequence of this decade," he hits the white.[14]   But more important, it seems to me, than the facts that these sonnets capriciously reveal is the unusual and most realistic progression of moods: the modulation from the mood of humble and patient chivalry to a mood of petulance and unmanliness that is little short of whining; then the modulation into the mood of tender victory; then, after this voluptuous paean, the queer, inartistic, but very real quirk at the end—a fierce gust of rage against certain venomous meddlers who have separated the two happy lovers leaving the poet with his loneliness and his ideal Platonic visions.   Then comes a capricious and quite natural silence, very unsymmetrical, however, for a pretty and artificial love-diary, for a carefully turned compliment to a patroness, but thoroughly understandable to the man who chooses to take these as genuine love-poems, a silence which is crudely filled in by the whimsical insertion of a handful of Spenser's trivial Anacreontics, and then—that sunburst, the *Epithalamion!*

It is in the first mood—of patient chivalry—that we see mirrored most clearly the stately image of madonna, a woman strong and beautiful for whom the phrase "huge brightnesse" has no grotesque connotation, a woman "more then most faire full of the living fire."   Through her eyes no pretty silly Cupid shoots his tiny arrows, as in the petulant and tawdry sonnets of the second mood, but "angels come, to lead fraile minds to rest."

> In that proud port which her so goodly graceth,
> Whiles her faire face she reares up to the skie,
> And to the ground her eie lids low embaseth,
> Most goodly temperature ye may descry:

---

[14] *The Elizabethan Lyric* (New York and London, 1903).

Myld humblesse mixt with awfull majesty.
For looking on the earth, whence she was borne,
Her minde remembreth her mortalitie:
What so is fayrest shall to earth returne.
But that same lofty countenance seemes to scorne
Base thing, and thinke how she to heaven may clime,
Treading downe earth as lothsome and forlorne,
That hinders heavenly thoughts with drossy slime.
Yet lowly still vouchsafe to looke on me;
Such lowlinesse shall make you lofty be.

In this sonnet there is a peculiar combination of warm earthiness and idealistic fervor that I find in no other but the poet of *The Faërie Queene*. The harmony of humility and pride, though not unknown to other poets of the renaissance, troubles Professor Dodge who, strangely enough, misses its point, its reality, its lovely perfection in Spenser. To appreciate the perfect reality of this harmony of humility and pride we must separate that pride which the medieval allegorist rightly made the most subtle demon of the Seven Deadly Sins and another kind of pride, a rare virtue that in the supreme souls of the renaissance·glowed easily in solution with true humility. Or if this seem fanciful, we may note, in the recent psychological terminology of Professor McDougall's *Introduction to Social Psychology* that "the instincts of self-abasement and of self-assertion" may blend in the "self-regarding sentiment." The climax of the first mood comes with a sonnet tinged with an earnest and beautiful piety.[15]

This holy season fit to fast and pray,
Men to devotion ought to be inclynd:
Therefore, I lykewise, on so holy day,
For my sweet saynt some service fit will find.
Her temple fayre is built within my mind,
In which her glorious ymage placed is,
On which my thoughts doo day and night attend,
Lyke sacred priests that never thinke amisse.
There I to her, as th' author of my blisse,
Will builde an altar to appease her yre;

---

[15] Sir Sidney Lee writes: "When he was in his most solemn mood Spenser invariably cast his anchor in a foreign port." Yet I must feel, for all our modern scholars' lists of parallels from Desportes and Petrarch, that Mr. Symons is right, who has it that in the *Amoretti* "there is a kind of piety which I find nowhere else."

> And on the same my hart will sacrifise,
> Burning in flames of pure and chast desyre:
> The which vouchsafe, O goddesse, to accept,
> Amongst thy deerest relicks to be kept.[16]

Before the poet is quite done with his gracious, quiet plead-
ings to his "faire flowre in whom fresh youth doth raine" there
comes a touch of the second, the petulant mood, unworthy, gen-
erally artificially expressed, yet real in its very inconsistency,
at first capricious and fitful but growing presently continuous.
As if the mood were hardly native to the author of *The Faërie
Queene* he imitates now with almost lurid extravagance, now in
a tone approaching perilously near a whine, the most tasteless
conceits of the Petrarchans. Like Petrarch and all his followers
he marvels over love's paradox: his mistress is ice, he is fire,
which but makes harder this extraordinary ice while he "fryes"
in "boyling sweat." His lady's eyes may not be compared with
sun or moon or stars or fire or lightning or crystal, but rather
"to the Maker selfe." Like all orthodox Petrarchists he com-
pares his mistress to the panther or the tiger. Her smiles allure
while her "bloody hands" slay or bathe with fierce joy in the
wounds her cruelty has inflicted. It has never been noted
that most of Spenser's least original sonnets fall into this second
mood, the unworthy mood, and that some of the worst of them

---

[16] Professor L. E. Kastner, in *The Modern Language Review*, IV, 65
sq., compares this poem with Sonnet XLIII of "Diane," *Oeuvres*, p. 31.
One might, with little profit, go back interminably along this trail as far
as the poets of the "Court of Love," who were fond of a religious veneer
at times. Mr. L. F. Mott (*The System of Courtly Love Studied as an Intro-
duction to the 'Vita Nuova' of Dante*, Boston, 1896) carries some of the
conventions of amorous poets to the early days of Italian sonneteering.
Readers would not find it too far afield to turn to Professor W. A. Neil-
son's study of the allegorical love poetry of the Middle Ages in his well
known *Origins and Sources of the Court of Love*. One of the most sug-
gestive essays connecting medieval and renaissance love-poetry is Vernon
Lee's "Medieval Love" in her *Euphorion* (ed. 2, London, 1895). As
a safeguard against the brilliantly argued obsession of this last essay
that adultery is invariably at the basis of chivalry one should add John
Addington Symonds' clear and persuasive exposition of the kindred ideal-
ism of Platonism and chivalric love (with its careful recognition, more
wholesome than Vernon Lee's, of the lawless origins and dangers of both),
in "The Dantesque and Platonic Ideals of Love," *In the Key of Blue*
(London and New York, 1893).

may be fathered on that coxcomb Desportes whose Indian sum-
mer of fame and notoriety grows daily as the followers of Sir
Sidney Lee trace back more and more of the poorest sonnets of
the Elizabethan English to his freakish influence. It was a
sorry day when the noble Don Quixote of English poetry went,
with his lesser countrymen, to the volumes of this French cuckoo.
Desportes wrote so many facile sonnets to aid Henry III
while he was seeking the favors of Renée de Rieux, "la belle
Chateauneuf," that the king retained him in his services after
the coronation to churn out his hard little shining conceits for
the court favorites. One persistent conceit in the second group
of the *Amoretti*, that of love conceived as a siege, is noted by
Professor Kastner as a particular favorite with Desportes. It
will be enough to close our exposition of this unworthy mood
of Spenser's—the false chivalry which so many mistake for the
true, quite blind as they are to the latent and lurking contempt
for women which is always an organic part of its protestations
—by contrasting one of his characteristic siege sonnets with some
rollicking verses of the following age.

> Retourne agayne, my forces late dismayd,
> Unto the siege by you abandon'd quite.
> Great shame it is to leave, like one afrayd,
> So fayre a peece for one repulse so light.
> Gaynst such strong castles needeth greater might
> Then those small forts which ye were wont belay:
> Such haughty mynds, enur'd to hardy fight,
> Disdayne to yield unto the first assay.
> Bring therefore all the forces that ye may,
> And lay incessant battery to her heart;
> Playnts, prayers, vowes, ruth, sorrow, and dismay;
> Those engins can the proudest love convert.
> And if those fayle, fall down and dy before her;
> So dying live, and living do adore her.''

We must turn to Sir John Suckling's happy lyric on the same
subject to be refreshed with the cavalier's frank abandonment of
the chivalrous veneer. He knows that if one must be contempt-
uous towards women it is best not to affect the chivalric at all,

and his keen cynical lightness, so much more wholesome than the almost feline hypocrisy of Spenser's sonnet, saves even this outworn conceit from falling drab.

> 'Tis now since I sat down before
>   That foolish fort, a heart,
> (Time strangely spent) a year or more,
>   And still I did my part:
>
> Made my approaches, from her hand
>   Unto her lip did rise,
> And did already understand
>   The language of her eyes.
>
> Proceeded on with no less art
>   (My tongue was engineer)
> I thought to undermine the heart
>   By whispering in the ear.
>
> When this did nothing, I brought down
>   Great cannon-oaths, and shot
> A thousand thousand to the town,
>   And still it yielded not.
>
>
> I then resolved to starve the place
>   By cutting off all kisses,
> Praying, and gazing on her face,
>   And all such little blisses.
>
> To draw her out, and from her strength,
>   I drew all batteries in:
> And brought myself to lie, at length,
>   As if no siege had been.
>
> When I had done what man could do,
>   And thought the place mine own,
> The enemy lay quiet too,
>   And smiled when all was done.
>
> I sent to know from whence and where
>   These hopes and this relief
> A spy informed, Honor was there,
>   And did command in chief.
>
> "March, march," quoth I, "the word straight give,
>   Let's lose no time, but leave her;
> That giant upon air will live,
>   And hold it out forever.

"'To such a place our camp remove
   As will no siege abide;
I hate a fool that starves her love,
   Only to feed her pride.''

But presently comes the great mood of the *Amoretti,* a mood
that Sir John Suckling could never have understood. At length
the poet find his lady gracious and he glorifies her.

> Coming to kisse her lyps, (such grace I found)
> Me seemd I smelt a gardin of sweet flowres,
> That dainty odours from them threw around,
> For damzels fit to decke their lovers bowres.
> Her lips did smell lyke unto gillyflowers;
> Her ruddy cheekes lyke unto roses red;
> Her snowy browes lyke budded bellamoures;
> Her lovely eyes lyke pincks but newly spred;
> Her goodly bosome lyke a strawberry bed;
> Her neck lyke to a bounch of cullambynes;
> Her brest lyke lillyes, ere theyr leaves be shed;
> Her nipples lyke yong blossomd jessemynes.
> Such fragrant flowres doe give most odorous smell,
> But her sweet odour did them all excell.

Ronsard has a similar sonnet (*Amours,* Livre I, cxl); but
though Ronsard excels all followers in his note of the wistful,
he falls far short of Spenser in these quaint raptures. Through-
out these sonnets in Spenser's third mood there is a beautiful
fleshliness which, with all its elaborateness, is light with that
peculiar naïveté or even innocence that colors so many of Spen-
ser's fleshly passages. His lady's breasts are at once "a lodging
of delight" and "fraught with vertues richest treasure." They
seem a goodly table of ivory "all spred with juncats fit to enter-
tayne"; yet they are, with perfect consistency in the nimble and
wholesome caprices of the poet, "the sacred harbour of that
hevenly spright." The poet's love can burn white with purity.

> The glorious image of the Makers beautie,
> My soverayne saynt, the idoll of my thought,
> Dare not henceforth, above the bounds of dewtie,
> T' accuse of pride, or rashly blame for ought.
> For being, as she is, divinely wrought,
> And of the brood of angels hevenly borne,

> And with the crew of blessed saynts upbrought,
> Each of which did her with theyr guifts adorne,
> The bud of joy, the blossome of the morne,
> The beame of light, whom mortal eyes admyre,
> What reason is it then but she should scorne
> Base things, that to her love too bold aspire?
> Such heavenly formes ought rather worshipt be,
> Then dare be lov'd by men of mean degree.

And when Spenser turns from such an ecstasy to one of those artificial but richly colored inventories of bodily charms and quaint flower catalogues that never cloy the true Spenserian, let the reader who feels incongruity or anticlimax remember that Spenser, at least by the time of his maturity, was a Puritan in the noblest sense of the word. Let the reader therefore question gravely his own logic of love. All the loveliness of the naked body evokes fancies from a vale unknown to prudes where "spotlesse Pleasure build her sacred bowre." Now and then, to be sure, desire burns itself momentarily into fever and there comes that great recoil of Saxon earnestness which saved England from being consumed by the blinding splendor of the renaissance and which, even more than Plato or Petrarch or any other influence, gave us three of the most impressive sonnets of renaissance Europe: Sir Philip Sidney's "Leave me, O Love, which reachest but to dust," where aspiration has struggled up to unimaginable heights; Shakespeare's "Poor soul, the centre of my sinful earth," the supreme master's *de profundis;* and Spenser's "Let not one sparke of filthy lustfull fyre," where the poet finds himself turning to the satyr as he gazes on the beauty of his mistress and he reels back with that moral terror which made not the grovelling prude but the Langlands and Bunyans of an iron race.

> Let not one sparke of filthy lustfull fyre
> Breake out, that may her sacred peace molest;
> Ne one light glance of sensuall desyre
> Attempt to work her gentle mindes unrest;
> But pure affections bred in spotlesse brest,
> And modest thoughts breathed from wel tempred sprites,
> Goe visit her in her chast bowre of rest,

Accompanyde with angelick delightes.
There fill your selfe with those most joyous sights,
The which my selfe could never yet attayne:
But speake no word to her of those sad plights,
Which her too constant stiffnesse doth constrayn.
Onely behold her rare perfection,
And blesse your fortunes fayre election.

We must not, however, fall into the prude's notion that a frank and delighted contemplation of the flesh conjures up inevitably the leer of the satyr. So innocent of both extremes is the poet's delighted contemplation that he finds it only natural to point his lady an amorous moral from what must have been to him one of the most terrific of religious truths.

Most glorious Lord of Lyfe, that on this day
Didst make thy triumph over death and sin,
And having harrowed hell, didst bring away
Captivity thence captive, us to win:
This joyous day, deare Lord, with joy begin,
And grant that we, for whom thou diddest dye,
Being with thy deare blood clene washt with sin,
May live for ever in felicity:
And that thy love we weighing worthily,
May likewise love thee for the same againe;
And for thy sake, that all lyke deare didst buy,
With love may, one another entertayne.
So let us love, deare love, lyke as we ought:
Love is the lesson which the Lord us taught.

The scholarship of disillusion here sends us again to Desportes, but this time to little purpose. Mr. James Ashcroft Noble, on the other hand, even after retailing the conventional pale depreciation of the *Amoretti* in general, pays this sonnet a unique and an interesting compliment:

Among them all there is only one which leaves on the mind any sharp impression, and that one has certainly a dignified movement and tender chastity of diction which makes it worthy of its high parentage. We may not all admit the perfect appropriateness of Lord Macaulay's characterization of Milton's ''Avenge, O Lord,'' as a ''collect in verse,'' but this sonnet of Spenser's has really a very appreciable affinity to the style of the collects—those unique jewels of devout aspiration.[17]

---

[17] *The Sonnet in England* (London, 1893).

In the midst of love's triumph pulses that great conviction of the permanence of song which Sir Sidney Lee, because of its conventionality, labels with unnecessary coldness the "immortality conceit" but of which Mr. Paul Elmer More writes with more essential truth in his essay on "Elizabethan Sonnets" and more particularly in his essay on "Shakespeare's Sonnets." Mr. More's words we may apply to Spenser with almost as much accuracy as we can to Shakespeare himself.

He was, after all, a child of his age. There was always present with him that sense of the eternal flux of things which is so characteristic of the Renaissance, but which, curiously enough, rarely appears in other Elizabethan sonneteers, however common it may be in the dramatists. It is safe to say that no single motive or theme recurs more persistently through the whole course of Shakespeare's works than this consciousness of the servile depredations of time, that "ceaseless lackey to eternity." As with other men of this period, this sense of brevity and mutability lay upon his mind like an obsession, and no small part of the tragic pathos in his plays arises from the jostling together of the insatiable desires of youth with the ever imminent perception of evanescence. One wonders whether Bacon could have had in recollection these apostrophes to time when he wrote in his *Essays:* "It is not good to look too long upon these turning-wheels of vicissitude, lest we become giddy."

Here is a sound explanation that is not disturbed or chilled by the verbal similarities that must needs come from a mighty obsession. We shall, in due time, see that when Spenser was meditating greatly about these things he was at the summit of his spiritual adventuring. It may be well to trace this "conceit" from Spenser to the Pléiade, from the Pléiade to Petrarch, from Petrarch to Pindar, and so ever backwards until we reach perchance some gibbering cave-man who first dared it in some strange carving of symbols. We are glad to know that Spenser was perhaps most directly influenced in this matter by "Ronsard and his disciples" who "had developed it with a complacency that gave it new life." "Complacency!" When we remember for a moment how intimately this sense of "the servile depredations of time" touches the most prosaic of us; when we feel more and more poignantly with a myriad rereadings the enchanting wistfulness of Ronsard's "Quand vous serez bien vieille, au soir, à la chandelle''; when we recall that of all the Elizabethans great and small who promised immortality to friend or patron or lover those two who dwelt most sorrowfully on mutability and who promised most passionately some memory after death were Shakespeare and Spenser, who dwelt on these things by divine right—when we have thought over all these things we must quarrel with Sir Sidney Lee for his phrase, ''the immortality conceit,'' and for that word ''complacency.'' And nowhere has this world-old hope been more humanly fused with its subtle comrade, sober doubt, than in this picture of the two lovers at their simple dalliance:

> One day I wrote her name upon the strand,
> But came the waves and washed it away:
> Agayn I wrote it with a second hand,
> But came the tyde, and made my paynes his pray.
> Vayne man, sayd she, that doest in vaine assay
> A mortall thing so to immortalize!
> For I my selve shall lyke to this decay,
> And eke my name bee wyped out lykewize.
> Not so (quod I) let baser things devize
> To dy in dust, but you shall live by fame:
> My verse your vertues rare shall eternize,
> And in the hevens wryte your glorious name;
> Where, whenas death shall all the world subdew,
> Our love shall live, and later life renew.

Had Spenser been concerned merely with turning out a dainty volume of poems arranged with graceful symmetry he would have brought his sonnet-sequence to a diapason closing full in the sensuous triumph of love. But abruptly we are confronted with a final fragmentary mood, a jet of unbridled rage against a ''venemous toung, tipt with vile adders sting,'' which has with ''false forged lyes'' stirred against him the undeserved ire of his lady. In a moment, too, the fury against the third person has modulated into a subdued and plaintive note as the poet counts the hours of his exile or compares himself to a dove lamenting a lost mate on a winter-lonely bough as bare as death.

Hereinafter the printer, Ponsonby, bundled three pretty, irrelevant Anacreontics.   Mr. More has written so significantly of the devastation wrought by this lighter mood in the amorous sonnets of singers less grave that I wish to quote him at length.

But another element has entered into the Elizabethan sonnets, which is utterly discordant with their Petrarchian basis, and which does much to produce the feeling of vacuity and insincerity inhering in them.   I mean the Anacreontic vein, which spread through the writings of the Pléiad after the publishing of the pseudo-Anacreon by Stephanes in 1554, and passed thence into England.   To Plato, as to all great writers of the early age, ''Eros, the son of Aphrodite, was a mighty god,'' and as such he appeared to Dante and Petrarch.   To attempt any fusion or juxtaposition of this great divinity, ''fairest among the immortal gods,'' as .Hesiod calls him, with the laughing mischievous boy of decadent Greece and Rome, was to show that inveracity of imagination which renders a work cold and meaningless.   I do not mean to condemn the Anacreontic poems in themselves.   Many of them in their airy Greek forms are exquisite trifles. That translucent little gem of Cupid and the bee, for instance, not even Tom Moore could vulgarize it in his translation, and we recognize its grace in Spenser's paraphrase. . . . There is something perfectly legitimate, even charming in the use of these delicate fancies in the proper place and in the proper metre, as when the same poet fashions this pretty conceit:

> I saw, in secret to my Dame
> How little Cupid humbly came,
>   And sayd to her ''All hayle, my mother!''
> But when he saw me laugh, for shame
> His face with bashfull blood did flame,
>   Not knowing Venus from the other.

That is well enough in a way, but any one can see how the introduction of such trifling into the idealism of Petrarchian love, with its life of melancholy abstinence and its visions of eternity, must mar and distort the fair image of truth.

What Mr. More does not make clear, although he seems not unaware of it. is that while a small man like Barnabe Barnes complacently allows his exquisite sonnet, ''Ah! sweet Content, where is thy mild abode?'' to be followed by a tawdry Anacreontic, to Spenser may be fairly attributed a reverence for the passionate autobiography in sonnets which, if it did not save him from the turgid rhetoric of Desportes, led him at least to realize the necessity of segregating his bright trivialities.   One may unhesitatingly add that Spenser's paraphrase of the "translucent little Gem of Cupid and the bee" is, with its pleasantly self-conscious quaintness and its homely whimsicalities, a bit of fragile workmanship which is too often forgotten.

Upon a day, as Love lay sweetly slumbring,
   All in his mothers lap,
A gentle bee, with his loud trumpet murm'ring,
   About him flew by hap.
Whereof when he was wakened with his noyse,
   And saw the beast so small:
"What's this," quoth he, "that gives so great a voyce,
   That wakens men withal?"
      In angry wize he flyes about,
      And threatens all with corage stout.

To whom his mother closely smiling sayd,
   Twixt earnest and twixt game:
"See, thou thy selfe like wise art lyttle made,
   If thou regard the same.
And yet thou suffrest neyther gods in sky,
   Nor men in earth to rest;
But when thou are disposed cruelly,
   Theyr sleepe thou doest molest.
      Then eyther change thy cruelty,
      Or give lyke leave unto the fly."

Nathelesse the cruell boy, not so content,
   Would needs the fly pursue,
And in his hand with heedlesse hardiment
   Him caught for to subdue.
But when on it he hasty hand did lay,
   The bee him stung therefore:
"Now out, alasse," he cryde, "and welaway!
   I wounded am full sore:
      The fly, that I so much did scorne,
      Hath hurt me with his little horne."

Unto his mother straight he weeping came,
   And of his griefe complayned:
Who could not chose but laugh at his fond game,
   Though sad to see him pained.
"Think now," quod she, "my sonne, how great the smart
   Of those whom thou dost wound:
Full many hast thou pricked to the hart,
   That pitty never found:
      Therefore, henceforth some pitty take,
      When thou doest spoyle of lovers make."

> She tooke him streight full pitiously lamenting,
>   And wrapt him in her smocke:
> She wrapt him softly, all the while repenting
>   That he the fly did mock.
> She drest his wound, and it embaulmed wel
>   With salve of soveraigne might:
> And then she bath'd him in a dainty well,
>   The well of deare delight.
>   Who would not oft be stung as this,
>   To be so bath'd in Venus blis?

> The wanton boy was shortly wel recured
>   Of that his malady:
> But he, soone after, fresh againe enured
>   His former cruelty.
> And since that time he wounded hath my selfe
>   With his sharpe dart of love:
> And now forgets the cruell careless elfe
>   His mothers heast to prove.
>   So now I languish, till he please
>   My pining anguish to appease.

And now the poet approaches us with a sacred intimacy that hushes all scholastic cynicism and fills the reader with an ecstasy that leaps to answer the wonderful lyric abandon with a fervent appreciation of it. The poet invokes the learned sisters with the charming unconscious familiarity of one who has brought them great glory and naturally calls them now to help him, like Orpheus, to sing his own bride. That the lady of the *Epithalamion* is the lady of the *Amoretti* will seem sufficiently likely to those who will but recall the noble sonnets describing the perfect harmony of "portly pride" and humility which I have already dwelt upon as the heritage of great souls, and who will recall the identical persistent phrases with which the poet visions his lady in the *Epithalamion*.

> Loe! where she comes along with portly pace,
> Lyke Phoebe, from her chamber of the east,
> Arysing forth to run a mighty race,
> Clad all in white, that seemes a virgin best.
> So well it her beseemes, that ye would weene
> Some angell she had beene.

Her long loose yellow locks lyke golden wyre,
Sprinckled with perle, and perling flowres atweene,
Doe lyke a golden mantle her attyre,
And being crowned with a girland greene,
Seeme lyke some mayden queene.
Her modest eyes, abashed to behold
So many gazers as on her do stare,
Upon the lowly ground affixed are;
Ne dare lift up her countenance too bold,
But blush to heare her prayses sung so loud,
So farre from being proud.
Nathelesse doe ye still loud her prayses sing,
That all the woods may answere, and your eccho ring.

So too her quiet pride and sober humility enthrall us as she waits the momentous words in the minster.

Behold, whiles she before the altar stands,
Hearing the holy priest that to her speakes,
And blesseth her with his two happy hands,
How the red roses flush up in her cheekes,
And the pure snow with goodly vermill stayne,
Like crimsin dyde in grayne:
That even th' angels, which continually
About the sacred altare doe remaine,
Forget their service and about her fly,
Ofte peeping in her face, that seemes more fayre,
The more they on it stare.
But her sad eyes, still fastened on the ground,
Are governed with goodly modesty,
That suffers not one looke to glaunce awry,
Which may let in a little thought unsownd.
Why blush ye, love, to give to me your hand,
The pledge of all our band?
Sing, ye sweet angels, Alleluya sing,
That all the woods may answer, and your eccho ring.

And not less, when laid in the nuptial couch in lilies and violets and odored sheets, does she seem to her awe-touched comrade to lie in "proud humility." The *Epithalamion* has to the highest degree what Coleridge so felicitously calls the "swan-like movement of Spenser." And Coventry Patmore, one of the subtlest of metrical adventurers, "was never tired of praising 'the great and gracious stanzas'" in which the *Epithalamion* was written.[18]   How delicately the sensuous heroic line is tempered with a light shy trimeter until, when the last trimeter has yielded to the full flow of another heroic, then follows the beloved final alexandrine, this time more wistful and clinging than ever, this time an echoing refrain swinging out like the long, undulant, falling crest of a wave spreading almost silently but masteringly along the gradual curves of the beach.

Once more we are impressed with the perfect union of fleshliness and innocence.   Like a sculptor with a childlike adoration of loveliness the poet seems to allow his hand to wander over his lady's body.

> Tell me, ye merchants daughters, did ye see
> So fayre a creature in your town before,
> So sweet, so lovely, and so mild as she,
> Adornd with beautyes grace and vertues store?
> Her goodly eyes lyke saphyres shining bright,
> Her forehead yvory white,
> Her cheekes lyke apples which the sun hath rudded,
> Her lips lyke cherryes charming men to byte,
> Her brest like to a bowle of creame uncrudded,
> Her paps lyke lyllies budded,
> Her snowie necke lyke to a marble towre,
> And all her body like a pallace fayre,
> Ascending uppe, with many a stately stayre,
> To honors seat and chastities sweet bowre.
> Why stand ye still, ye virgins, in amaze,
> Upon her so to gaze,
> Whiles ye forget your former lay to sing,
> To which the woods did answer, and your eccho ring?

The poet portrays her body like an opulent temple.   How easy then and how natural to pass with heightened ardor to a contemplation of those spiritual beauties which dwell within the temple of spotless pleasure!

> But if ye saw that which no eyes can see,
> The inward beauty of her lively spright,
> Garnisht with heavenly guifts of high degree,
> Much more then would ye wonder at that sight,

---

[18] Coventry Patmore's *Poems*, ''Introduction,'' p. xli, by Basil Champneys (London, 1906).

> And stand astonisht lyke to those which red
> Medusaes mazeful hed.
> There dwels sweet Love, and constant Chastity,
> Unspotted Fayth, and comely Womanhood,
> Regard of Honour, and mild Modesty;
> There Virtue raynes as queene in royal throne,
> And giveth lawes alone,
> The which the base affections doe obay,
> And yeeld theyr services unto her will;
> Ne thought of thing uncomely ever may
> Thereto approch to tempt her mind to ill.
> Had ye once seene these her celestial threasures,
> And unrevealed pleasures,
> Then would ye wonder, and her prayses sing,
> That al the woods should answer, and your echo ring.

For great souls this same larger consistency fuses and blends the severe Christian ecstasy and the warm Greek joy in life, a holy sensuousness.

> Open the temple gates unto my love,
> Open them wide that she may enter in,
> And all the postes adorne as doth behove,
> And all the pillours deck with girlands trim,
> For to receyve this saynt with honour dew,
> That commeth in to you.
> With trembling steps and humble reverence,
> She commeth in before th' Almighties vew:
> Of her, ye virgins, learne obedience,
> When so ye come into those holy places,
> To humble your proud faces.
> Bring her up to th' high altar, that she may
> The sacred ceremonies there partake,
> The which do endlesse matrimony make;
> And let the roring organs loudly play
> The praises of the Lord in lively notes,
> The whiles with hollow throates
> The choristers the joyous antheme sing,
> That al the woods may answere, and your eccho ring.

The praises of the Lord are followed by the crowning of God Bacchus with a coronal. Pagan and Christian emotion make yet richer symphony in the noble and frank joy of possession.

> Now cease, ye damsels, your delights forepast;
> Enough is it that all the day was youres:
> Now day is doen, and night is nighing fast:
> Now bring the bryde into the bridall boures.

The night is come, now soone her disaray,
And in the bed her lay;
Lay her in lillies and in violets,
And silken courteins over her display,
And odourd sheetes, and Arras coverlets.
Behold how goodly my faire love does ly,
In proud humility!
Like unto Maia, when as Jove her tooke
In Tempe, lying on the flowry gras,
Twixt sleepe and wake, after she weary was
With bathing in the Acidalian brooke.
Now it is night, ye damsels may be gon,
And leave my love alone,
And leave likewise your former lay to sing:
The woods no more shal answere, nor your echo ring.

In that august abandon of the lady of our supreme English idealist there is sounded a note heard never before or after. And to the close there is always this perfect tempering of Christian and pagan symbols, a sought-for harmony which in Italy often left fever and in the grim North the haggard restraint of Puritanism. And as the medieval dreamer of hushed cathedrals found it necessary to conjure up gargoyles to lurk like bats about the eaves, so Spenser shudders delightedly, like a child intoxicated with fairy stories, over the unreal elvish presences of night: Puck and "hob goblins, names whose sense we see not." Like Philodemus he looks out of his window to banter half-gravely with Cynthia, the moon.

Who is the same which at my window peepes?
Or whose is that faire face that shines so bright?
Is it not Cinthia, she that never sleepes,
But walkes about high heaven al the night?
O fayrest goddesse, do not thou envy
My love with me to spy:
For thou likewise didst love, though now unthought,
And for a fleece of woll, which privily
The Latmian shephard once unto thee brought,
His pleasures with thee wrought.
Therefore to us be favorable now:
And sith of wemens labours thou hast charge,
And generation goodly dost enlarge,
Encline thy will t' effect our wishfull vow,

> And the chaste wombe informe with timely seed,
> That may our comfort breed:
> Till which we cease our hopefull hap to sing,
> Ne let the woods us answere, nor your eccho ring.

This is just as exquisite, in its opposite way, as the perfectly simple and immortal lines of Catullus:

I would see a little Torquatus, stretching his baby hands from his mother's lap, smile a sweet smile at his father with his lips half parted.

> Torquatus volo parvulus
>   Matris e gremio suae
>   Porrigens teneras manus
> Dulce rideat ad patrem
>   Semhiante labello.[19]

When one constructs from the more distempered side of medieval literature the picture of an ascetic in the sultry twilight fallen prone in the dust in morbid fear and agony before the naked Cytherea, the last of the old pagans to haunt the evening, when one sees this ascetic, who may well have made the blasphemous tale about the ring given to Venus, recoiling from the goddess as she stands unashamed but with her immemorial smile half faded into a bewildered gaze at the man who supposes her a visitation from Lucifer—when one visualizes all this one sees that it is necessary for Spenser to invoke Cytherea, Cynthia, awful Juno, and Hymen free as well as the blessed saints who inherit tabernacles and the angels who continually remain about the throne in order that he may give us the full circle of goodness and beauty. And one likes to image Cytherea smiling once more at her new poet as she smiled long ago when the brown fields renewed their life and the young Romans chanted the *Pervigilium Veneris.*

The country quickens with love's delight, the country feels Venus' touch: Love himself, the child of Dione, is deemed country-born. Him while the field broke to birth, herself she took up into her bosom, herself nursed with the dainty kisses of flowers.

Tomorrow shall be love for the loveless, and for the lover to-morrow shall be love.[20]

---

[19] The translation is by Mr. F. W. Cornish.

[20] From Professor J. W. Mackail's translation.

THE FAËRIE QUEENE. BOOKS IV–VI

Through the adventures of the Don Quixote of English poets as through the career of a nation, of an age, of the universe there runs a rhythm now faint, now exultant. We have found this rhythm because we have put aside the narrow conceptions of gentle Spenser, Spenser the querulous, Spenser the flattering opportunist, Spenser at heart a hedonist, on the surface an allegorist. We have found that we must consider not only the serenity, the utopianism, the court-worship, the sensuousness of our poet, but also his independence, critical acumen, nationalism, spacious moral consciousness. It was willed that his last singing moments were to be in a rhythm comparable to the triumphant accents of the last moment of Beethoven's Ninth Symphony. But before the victorious hymns there came a period of profound depression, a complete unfaith to make firm and indestructible his ultimate faith.

As we approach the period of his deepest distress we must recall the long paths, the hills and the valleys of that part of his life which we now know. We must recall the youthful pastoral poem, drawing from a hundred diverse sources but strikingly original in technique and substance, full of varied metrical inventions, tentative but most ingenious in scheme, vivacious with homely fable and with something very close to popular song, afire in defense of trusted masters, Grindal, Young, bold if Parthian in its criticism of university, church, and queen, hymnlike in its hopes for poetry, for England, for Leicester, for the queen in her worthiest moments. More and more daring grew the poet, more and more uncompromisingly loyal in his hero-worship. At the moment of his highest hopes for England, his keenest interest in the great drama about him, and his legitimate desires to play an active and a noble part he was hurried off to Ireland with Lord Grey, the suspected, to share in a thankless, a terrible task. But he went on to dream, even in Ireland, of making of England a Utopia. He had confessed in *The Shepheards Calender* his groping epic aspirations. He had read Virgil, who tried to make a shadowy past flash a great searchlight into the future, but a future which had largely become present. Spenser planned to write an epic of the absolute future, not to celebrate history but to make it. He did not seek to turn Faërie Land into life, but life into Faërie Land. Two splendid books he perfected. But his hand faltered in the third. It was not due merely to the immensity of the scheme. The Phaeton-like genius of Elizabethan poetry was used to wrestling with angels. But court and nation seemed not to listen to his hope for them. Then Leicester died. Then the grim, narrow, noble Lord Grey was slandered by petty foes. The poet went back to England to publish his first three books. He was disappointed over his own career, but he was infinitely more sorrowful over the shipwreck of his impersonal ideals. Therefore he collected and published a series of poems which he had written in his bitterest moments. They are not splenetic as most critics have implied or asserted. In the very boyish fears for the future of poetry, in his lament for the noble family of Sidney and Leicester, in his mock-heroic reproach of Leicester, in his half-playful and brilliant symbolic poem on the futility of his own ideals and the immortality of malice, in his laments over the mortality of loveliness and grandeur, in his bold and savage satire on court and queen the notes of personal disappointment and personal bitterness are seldom audible. Indeed he was not personally unhappy. He could live with his own songs. And being like all supreme men both dreamer and doer, he entered with zest and shrewdness upon his political career in Ireland. Finally, he triumphed in love and turned aside from his epic to celebrate his lady and his wife with a fervor so noble and so warm that it must have done much to strengthen in him that victorious aspiration that carried him through the great depression, which we must now come to understand, to the summits on which we shall leave him when we listen to his swan-songs.

As the architectural lineaments of *The Faërie Queene* become, in the later books, more and more confused it would be an error for even the most acute and ingenious scholar to attempt to work out the supposed allegorical significance of every detail. To Spenser, after the death of Sidney and Leicester, as breathing personages faded from his worldly vision, the building of Utopia became necessarily less and less easy and many of his cloudy symbols must have become for him strange mocking runes written in wandering fires. As he strove courageously but tragically to fight against disillusioning realities, death and corruption, the allegory must have become at times but enigmatic gropings. Spenser had symbolized already the futility of his own idealism as far as his immediate hopes of being followed as a seer were concerned. And it is notable that the political allegory from now on becomes almost purely an account of past events, a celebration of Leicester's campaign in the Low Countries, for instance, or a touching memory of Leicester's quarrel with the queen, or a brave and chivalrous defense of the dead, disgraced Lord Grey of Wilton, almost never a prophetic allegory. The political allegory is hopelessly episodical; the moral allegory is capricious and, when vital, almost invariably bitter. At the same time the fantastic and almost meaningless romances which we saw increasing in the third book grow more and more numerous and elaborate and confusing.

But as we consider these things we must allow not only for disintegration in *The Faërie Queene* but for our own incapacity in reading Spenser and, instead of casting the old jeer at *The Faërie Queene*, Macaulay's, we should do well to listen to a brace of critics, an American and an Englishman. Half a century ago John S. Hart wrote:

Most persons who fail in the art of story-telling, do so from the want of imagination. They do not call a distant or past scene to mind, with that liveliness of apprehension which enables them to set it vividly before their hearers. Their own conceptions want freshness and distinctness, and consequently the narrative becomes heavy and dull. Spenser, as a story-teller, fails for the opposite reason. He has, if it be possible, too much imagination.[1]

And not long ago Mr. Bailey said a somewhat similar thing with great charm.

> When [Spenser] is dull . . . [it is because] he lets Memory, mother of the Muses, and Imagination, their eldest daughter, carry him away captive into strange countries, and delights his fancy in weaving story within story and adding episode to episode, he forgets that poetry, if it is to be a fine art, must dwell in Cosmos and not in Chaos, that order and limit are necessary parts of the constitution of the human mind, that the most poetical sort of confusion is still confusion and not creation, and that the end of confusion is weariness and sleep. Still these are faults that the rest of the world may envy. Just as we are not ethereal enough to live long with Shelley, we are not mobile enough, we have not enough of music in us to keep mind and ear long traveling with Spenser.

Yes, we do feel a languor in reading the fourth book of *The Faërie Queene,* though it is due partly to the fact that we are small folk and Spenser is a genius. When one contrasts the prologues of the early books, the epic exaltation of Book One, the defense of the reality of Faërie Land in Book Two, and in Book Three the hymn to chastity that probably gave Milton his lofty faith in *Comus* with the restless and angry attitude of self-defense at the opening of Book Four one feels immediately the great change. Recall the prelude to the adventures of Sir Guyon.

> Right well I wote, most mighty Soveraine,
> That all this famous antique history
> Of some th' aboundance of an ydle braine
> Will judged be, and painted forgery,
> Rather then matter of just memory;
> Sith none that breatheth living aire does know,
> Where is that happy land of Faery,
> Which I so much doe vaunt, yet no where show,
> But vouch antiquities, which no body can know.

---

[1] *An Essay on the Life and Writings of Edmund Spenser with a Special Exposition of The Fairy Queen* (New York and London, 1847).

But let that man with better sence advize,
That of the world least part to us is red:
And daily how through hardy enterprize
Many great regions are discovered,
Which to late age were never mentioned.
Who ever heard of th' Indian Peru?
Or who in venturous vessell measured
The Amazons huge river, now found trew?
Or fruitfullest Virginia who did ever vew?

Yet all these were when no man did them know,
Yet have from wisest ages hidden beene;
And later times thinges more unknowne shall show.
Why then should witlesse man so much misweene,
That nothing is, but that which he hath seene?
What if within the moones fayre shining spheare,
What if in every other starre unseene,
Or other worldes he happily should heare?
He wonder would much more; yet such to some appeare.

Of Faery Lond yet if he more inquyre,
By certein signes, here sett in sondrie place,
He may it fynd; ne let him then admyre,
But yield his sence to bee too blunt and bace,
That no'te without an hound fine footing trace.
And thou, O fayrest Princesse under sky,
In this fayre mirrhour maist behold thy face,
And thine owne realmes in lond of Faery,
And in this antique ymage thy great auncestry.

Now, after reading those stanzas with their half-smiling, patient
courtliness growing ever more serious until the faith glows out
clear and radiant at the close, turn to the half-discouraged,
uneasy defiance of men like Burghley culminating in an almost
pathetic appeal to the queen in whom the poet still believes,
since this faith, always mingled with the severest and frankest
criticism, was indestructible.

The rugged forhead that with grave foresight
Welds kingdomes causes and affaires of state,
My looser rimes (I wote) doth sharply wite,
For praising love, as I have done of late,
And magnifying lovers deare debate;
By which fraile youth is oft to follie led,
Through false allurement of that pleasing baite,
That better were in vertues discipled,
Then with vaine poemes weeds to have their fancies fed.

Such ones ill judge of love, that cannot love,
Ne in their frosen hearts feele kindly flame:
Forthy they ought not thing unknowne reprove,
Ne naturall affection faultlesse blame,
For fault of few that have abusd the same.
For it of honor and all vertue is
The roote, and brings forth glorious flowres of fame,
That crowne true lovers with immortall blis,
The meed of them that love, and do not live amisse.

Which who so list looke backe to former ages,
And call to count the things that then were donne,
Shall find, that all the workes of those wise sages,
And brave exploits which great heroes wonne,
In love were either ended or begunne:
Witnesse the father of philosophie,
Which to his Critias, shaded oft from sunne,
Of love full manie lessons did apply,
The which these Stoicke censours cannot well deny.

To such therefore I do not sing at all,
But to that sacred saint my soveraigne Queene,
In whose chast breast all bountie naturall
And treasures of true love enlocked beene,
Bove all her sexe that ever yet was seene:
To her I sing of love, that loveth best
And best is lov'd of all alive, I weene;
To her this song most fitly is addrest,
The queene of love, and prince of peace from heaven blest.

The first canto deepens our sense of the poet's depression. We are confronted by Duessa, whom the poet introduces in accordance with his evident scheme (neglected in Book Three) of bringing her into the first scene of each series of adventures. But this time Duessa is accompanied with the most loathsome and, we feel, the most invincible of her associates, Ate or Discord, a figure more potent than any of the Virtues who oppose her here. For, on the whole, this book might be justly said to celebrate discord, rather than the friendship or concord it professes to immortalize. Ate is an omnipresent apparition whose dwelling near the gates of hell is described with a gloomy eloquence which sounds the insistent theme of the *Complaints*.

Hard by the gates of hell her dwelling is,
There whereas all the plagues and harmes abound,
Which punish wicked men, that walke amisse.
It is a darksome delve farre under ground,
With thornes and barren brakes environd round,
That none the same may easily out win;
Yet many waies to enter may be found,
But none to issue forth when one is in:
For discord harder is to end then to begin.

And all within, the riven walls were hung
With ragged monuments of times forepast,
All which the sad effects of discord sung:
There were rent robes and broken scepters plast,
Altars defyl'd, and boly things defast,
Disshivered speares, and shieldes ytorne in twaine,
Great cities ransackt, and strong castles rast,
Nations captived, and huge armies slaine:
Of all which ruines there some relicks did remaine.

Here we have the dominating key of the book of friendship.
For friendship, or more properly, concord is celebrated here,
I repeat, in dim contrast to an almost omnipresent discord. The
petty quarrels of Paridell and Blandamour with each other,
with a host of new rogues, and with every noble knight they
meet recur again and again.

But Canto One is inlaid with one jeweled episode. Britomart
and Amoret came to a castle where each stranger knight must
win a lady or lie without the door. Britomart overthrew a
young knight and easily won her right to entrance; but, pitying
him in his misfortunes, she claimed first Amoret for her lady
and then, as a woman herself, claimed the unlucky youngster
as her knight.

With that, her glistring helmet she unlaced;
Which doft, her golden lockes, that were up bound
Still in a knot, unto her heeles downe traced,
And like a silken veile in compasse round
About her backe and all her bodie wound:
Like as the shining skie in summers night,
What time the dayes with scorching heat abound,
Is creasted all with lines of firie light,
That it prodigious seemes in common peoples sight.

Hitherto Amoret, ignorant of her savior's identity, had feared her as a rescuer perchance little better than Busirane himself. Now all the night they lay together and indulged their sweet sorrow in confidences over their unhappy loves.

But this evanescent mood quickly flees at the entrance of Blandamour and Ate, Paridell and Duessa. The contrasting figures of Cambell and Triamond, the two knightly friends, are the most tenuous among all the heroes of *The Faërie Queene* and, in spite of the chief part assigned them in the subtitle of this book, they prove to be but the heroes of two brief and casual episodes. Spenser was attempting to finish Chaucer's "Squire's Tale." Spenser evidently felt his own audacity and responsibility keenly and it led him into an extravagance so crude and turgid that it seems almost boyish and tempts the critic to suggest that this was the early fragment sent to Harvey, the fragment which stirred the Mentor to write contemptuously and cleverly of its inspiration as like "hobgoblin runne away with the garland from Apollo." The queer yarn of the two brothers whose souls pass, when their bodies have been riven by Cambell's sword, into the body of the third brother Triamond, the strange thrice-prolonged battle of Triamond with Cambell in which those two souls are once more dislodged from their new body by mortal strokes, the ridiculous climax where the two heroes are so exhausted that they care neither to strike or ward, but totter about with faint motions like mechanical toys which are nearly run down, all these absurdities on absurdities are but the events of a unique kind of tragic horse-play, a very boyish, saucer-eyed imitation of Ariosto's most brilliant triumphs in the bizarre-heroic. Now enters Cambina, sister of Triamond, who renders the heroes forgetful of their blind hate with a cup of Nepenthe which makes possible not only their great friendship but her marriage with Cambell and Triamond's with Canacee, the sister of his foe. This entrance is really effective in its spiritedness and strangeness.

Thereat the champions both stood still a space,
To weeten what that sudden clamour ment;
Lo! where they spyde with speedie whirling pace
One in a claret of straunge furniment
Towards them driving like a storme out sent.
The charet decked was in wondrous wize
With gold and many a gorgeous ornament,
After the Persian Monarks antique guize,
Such as the maker selfe could best by art devize.

And drawne it was (that wonder is to tell)
Of two grim lyons, taken from the wood,
In which their powre all others did excell;
Now made forget their former cruell mood,
T' obey their riders hest, as seeming good.
And therein sate a ladie passing faire
And bright, that seemed borne of angels brood,
And with her beautie bountie did compare,
Whether of them in her should have the greater share.

Cambell and Triamond play a conspicuous part in the tournament that follows, the tournament arranged by Satyrane for the girdle of Florimell. This, their last appearance, is very skilfully conceived. Cambell, fighting in his wounded friend's armor that Triamond may have the glory, Triamond, leaping from his bed, arming himself with Cambell's harness, and plunging to the rescue when he hears in the midst of his fever that Cambell is about to be captured by an overwhelming force of knights—these brilliant events stand out vivid in a fine throng of vicissitudes which, though conventional, move with startling change.[2]

The beauty contest of the ladies that crowns the tournament uses the old ballad motive of the girdle (which can be worn only

---

[2] This is perhaps the best place to call special attention to Professor John Erskine's "The Virtue of Friendship in the *Faërie Queene*," *Pub. Mod. Lang. Assoc.*, XXX, 1915, pp. 831 sq. Professor Erskine's main interest is historical and ethical, while mine is psychological at this point. His discussion of the meaning of the concept of friendship for Spenser and of Spenser's probable sources seems to be unanswerable. I am naturally dubious about his attempt to establish the artistic or logical continuity of the episode of the Marriage of the Thames and the Medway with the rest of Book Four. But it seems to me that our interpretations are, for the most part, harmonious allies.

by the chaste) with a faint touch of the cynicism which occasionally dominates Spenser at this period. The story closes with a skilful touch when the false Florimell chooses from among the bickering knights the cowardly Braggadochio above all champions. But the wholesale dissension which her perversity arouses is described with a tameness that falls leagues short of the scene from Ariosto it aims to imitate, the tumult of the pagan chiefs in the camp of Agramante.

This fifth canto is patched out at the end with a description of Scudamour's sleepless night at the abode of Care, an episode which, though somewhat overwrought in its grotesqueness, has at best a bizarre power that commands pause and must have meant much to Spenser, as his disillusion was gradually and relentlessly overcoming his great hopes for England. We can imagine it as one of the scenes which inspired the fanciful and brooding Burton to dub Spenser, in the *Anatomy of the Melancholy*, "our English Maro." Glauce and Scudamour come to "a little cottage, like some poore mans nest."

> Under a steepe hilles side it placed was,
> There where the mouldred earth had cav'd the banke;
> And fast beside a little brooke did pas
> Of muddie water, that like puddle stanke,
> By which few crooked sallowes grew in ranke:
> Wherto approaching nigh, they heard the sound
> Of many yron hammers beating ranke,
> And answering their wearie turnes around,
> That seemed some blacksmith dwelt in that desert ground.
>
> There entring in, they found the goodman selfe
> Full busily unto his worke ybent;
> Who was to weet a wretched wearish elfe,
> With hollow eyes and rawbone cheekes forspent,
> As if he had in prison long bene pent:
> Full blacke and griesly did his face appeare,
> Besmeard with smoke that nigh his eyesight blent;
> With rugged beard, and hoarie shagged heare,
> The which he never wont to combe, or comely sheare.
>
> Rude was his garment, and to rags all rent,
> Ne better had he, ne for better cared:

With blistred hands emongst the cinders brent,
And fingers filthie, with long nayles unpared,
Right fit to rend the food on which he fared.
His name was Càre; a blacksmith by his trade,
That neither day nor night from working spared,
But to small purpose yron wedges made;
Those be unquiet thoughts, that carefull minds invade.

In which his worke he had sixe servants prest,
About the andvile standing evermore,
With huge great hammers, that did never rest
From heaping stroakes, which thereon soused sore:
All sixe strong groomes, but one then other more:
For by degrees they all were disagreed;
So likewise did the hammers which they bore
Like belles in greatnesse orderly succeed,
That he which was the last the first did far exceede.

He like a monstrous gyant seem'd in sight,
Far passing Bronteus or Pyracmon great,
The which in Lipari doe day and night
Frame thunderbolts for Joves avengefull threate.
So dreadfully he did the andvile beat,
That seem'd to dust he shortly would it drive:
So huge his hammer and so fierce his heat,
That seem'd a rocke of diamond it could rive,
And rend a sunder quite, if he thereto list strive.

Sir Scudamour, there entring, much admired
The manner of their worke and wearie paine;
And having long beheld, at last enquired
The cause and end thereof: but all in vaine;
For they for nought would from their worke refraine,
Ne let his speeches come unto their care;
And eke the breathfull bellowes blew amaine,
Like to the northren winde, that none could heare:
Those Pensifnesse did move; and Sighes the bellows weare.

Nevertheless the puzzled knight would have stretched himself
out there for rest. But

...If by fortune any litle nap
Upon his heavie eye-lids chaunst to fall,
Eftsoones one of those villeins him did rap
Upon his headpeece with his yron mall,

> That he was soone awaked therewithall,
> And lightly started up as one affrayd,
> Or as if one him suddenly did call:
> So oftentimes he out of sleepe abrayd,
> And then lay musing long on that him ill apayd.

At last he fell to dreaming of the fancied perfidy of Amoret and her rescuer.

> With that, the wicked carle, the maister smith,
> A paire of redwhot yron tongs did-take
> Out of the burning cinders, and therewith
> Under his side him nipt, that, forst to wake,
> He felt his hart for very paine to quake,
> And started up avenged for to be
> On him the which his quiet slomber brake:
> Yet, looking round about him, none could see;
> Yet did the smart remaine, though he himselfe did flee.

Canto Six is devoted to one of the most splendid tales of romantic love in Elizabethan poetry. Scudamour and Artegall engage Britomart in joust. Both are overthrown. But Artegall, with sword drawn in a blind fury of revenge, slays the horse of Britomart with a stroke that glances from her helm. The combat on foot that ensues reminds us of Ariosto's description of the duel of Bradamante with her lover Ruggiero disguised in the arms of Leo. Ariosto is more obviously human. And never elsewhere does Ruggiero approach so near the heroic. Bradamante, importuned by her parents to marry Leo, desperate at Ruggiero's long and mysterious disappearance, has sworn never to yield her love to one who cannot withstand her martial prowess for a day. Leo has chivalrously rescued Ruggiero, his professed foe, from the prison of his countrymen. When, therefore, the magnanimous prince, knowing his own inability, calls upon Ruggiero to fight for him in his armor, the accepted lover of Bradamante feels constrained to ruin his own happiness in grateful devotion to his generous new friend, who does not dream that he is his rival. The account of Bradamante's ferocious attack, her growing desperation as the sun sinks, Ruggiero's agony of mind, as he withstands her showers of buffets with watchful ward but never a counterstroke—all these things make a superb ironic situation. But there is something in it of the caprice and brutality of medieval idealism. The combat in Spenser is far less realistic. The opening situations are much less elaborately conceived, much less richly human. But the dramatic disclosure of Britomart's sex, the sudden stunned adoration of Artegall, are described from a height to which Ariosto could never hope to attain. Sir Artegall, after having nearly exhausted Britomart with his cunning and deadly fence, suddenly gathered all his strength in a terrific stroke.

> The wicked stroke upon her helmet chaunst,
> And with the force which in it selfe it bore
> Her ventayle shard away, and thence forth glaunst
> Adowne in vaine, ne harm'd her any more.
> With that, her angels face, unseene afore,
> Like to the ruddie morne appeard in sight,
> Deawed with silver drops, through sweating sore,
> But somewhat redder then beseem'd aright,
> Through toylesome heate and labour of her weary fight.

> And round about the same, her yellow heare,
> Having through stirring loosd their wonted band,
> Like to a golden border did appeare,
> Framd in goldsmithes forge with cunning hand:
> Yet goldsmithes cunning could not understand
> To frame such subtile wire so shinie cleare.
> For it did glister like the golden sand,
> The which Pactolus, with his waters shere,
> Throwes forth upon the rivage round about him nere.

So Artegall dropped his sword, kneeled humbly, and "of his wonder made religion." Such a scene was equally impossible to medieval romancer, renaissance Italian, and mid-Victorian Englishman. Putting aside the artificial trappings, the joust, the clash of armor, literal battle, it is modern love, mutual conquest.

The stanza about Artegall's first wooing, with its frankness and its homely phrasing, is touched with the truest reverence growing out of its two essential elements: romantic passion and temperate calculation.

Yet durst he not make love so suddenly,
Ne thinke th' affection of her hart to draw
From one to other so quite contrary:
Besides her modest countenance he saw
So goodly grave, and full of pricely aw,
That it his ranging fancie did refraine,
And looser thoughts to lawfull bounds withdraw;
Whereby the passion grew more fierce and faine,
Like to a stubborne steede whom strong hand would restraine.

Only a delicacy utterly unknown to Ariosto could keep unsullied
the lofty dignity and unsoftened the beautiful power of Brito-
mart as we see her yield as well as conquer and as we see her
womanly solicitude grow when Artegall, like all of Spenser's
heroes, announces immediately that he must turn for a space
from the joys of true love to the stern pursuit of a great ad-
venture.

In all which time, Sir Artegall made way
Unto the love of noble Britomart,
And with meeke service and much suit did lay
Continuall siege unto her gentle hart:
Which being whylome launcht with lovely dart,
More eath was new impression to receive,
How ever she her paynd with womanish art
To hide her wound, that none might it perceive:
Vaine is the art that seekes it selfe for to deceive.

So well he woo'd her and so well he wrought her,
With faire entreatie and sweet blandishment,
That at the length unto a bay he brought her,
So as she to his speeches was content
To lend an eare, and softly to relent.
At last, through many vowes which forth he pour'd,
And many othes, she yeelded her consent
To be his love, and take him for her lord,
Till they with mariage meet might finish that accord.

Tho, when they had long time there taken rest,
Sir Artegall, who all the while was bound
Upon an hard adventure yet in quest,
Fit time for him thence to depart it found,
To follow that which he did long propound;
And unto her his congee came to take.

> But her therewith full sore displeased he found,
> And loth to leave her late betrothed make,
> Her dearest love full loth so shortly to forsake.
>
> .   .   .   .
>
> And by the way she sundry purpose found
> Of this or that, the time for to delay,
> And of the perils whereto he was bound,
> The feare whereof seem'd much her to affray:
> But all she did was but to weare out day.
> Full oftentimes she leave of him did take;
> And eft againe deviz'd some what to say,
> Which she forgot, whereby excuse to make:
> So loth she was his companie for to forsake.

The adventures in Canto Seven lead up to another very beautiful, very Spenserian romance—the quarrel of Timias and Belphoebe. While Britomart sleeps, the ill-fated Amoret, strolling at large through the woods, is seized by a monstrous savage, an incarnation of lust which shows very clearly that Spenser, though almost an apologist for sensuality in his enchanting portrait of Acrasia, made a sharp distinction between that sensuality which, as I have said before, is but virtue passed into excess, and mere lust which was to Spenser sheer bestiality. This savage, Lust, is described with a curious Celtic extravagance and grotesqueness which reminds one of the *Mabinogion* or of the Irish sagas.

> It was to weet a wilde and salvage man,
> Yet was no man, but onely one in shape,
> And eke in stature higher by a span,
> All overgrowne with haire, that could awhape
> An hardy hart, and his wide mouth did gape
> With huge great teeth, like to a tusked bore:
> For he liv'd all on ravin and on rape
> Of men and beasts; and fed on fleshly gore,
> The signe whereof yet stain'd his bloudy lips afore.
>
> His neather lip was not like man nor beast,
> But like a wide deepe poke, downe hanging low,
> In which he wont the relickes of his feast
> And cruell spoyle, which he had spard, to stow:
> And over it his huge great nose did grow,
> Full dreadfully empurpled all with bloud;

And downe both sides two wide long eares did glow,
And raught downe to his waste, when up he stood,
More great then th' eares of elephants by Indus flood.

Immured in the cave of this monster, Amoret learned from
Æmylia, another fair prisoner, how Lust daily violated, then
devoured a maiden. When the monster returned he rushed so
eagerly to his wonted orgy that he left the great stone away
from the mouth of the cave. Amoret fled but was easily re-
captured. It befell, however, that as the grinning savage was
returning he was confronted by Timias, the gentle squire of
Prince Arthur. The combat was unequal for the monster used
Amoret as a shield. But at last a shrewd thrust stung him into
hurling down his burden and seizing his huge glaive with both
hands. As Timias was defending himself with desperate courage
from this overwhelming assault Belphoebe appeared and the
monster fled, well knowing that in her chastity and in her cour-
age he read his doom. At the very entrance of his cave a swift
arrow thrilled in his throat "and all his hairy breast with gory
bloud was fild." The lovely huntress then ministered to the
prisoners.

Thence she them brought toward the place where late
She left the gentle squire with Amoret:
There she him found by that new lovely mate,
Who lay the whiles in swoune, full sadly set,
From her faire eyes wiping the deawy wet,
Which softly stild, and kissing them atweene,
And handling soft the hurts which she did get:
For of that carle she sorely bruz'd had beene,
Als of his owne rash hand one wound was to be seene.

Which when she saw, with sodaine glauncing eye,
Her noble heart with sight thereof was fild
With deepe disdaine, and great indignity,
That in her wrath she thought them both have thrild
With that selfe arrow which the carle had kild:
Yet held her wrathfull hand from vengeance sore,
But drawing nigh, ere he her well beheld,
"Is this the faith?" she said,—and said no more,
But turnd her face, and fled away for evermore.

Some critics have found in this story an allegory of Raleigh's amour with Elizabeth Throckmorton and the queen's anger. But Spenser would hardly have shadowed forth the woman whom Raleigh soon married as the lover of Scudamour by whom the poet doubtless meant some other nobleman at Elizabeth's court. I accept, rather, the conclusion of those who believe that in this particular passage Timias, Arthur's squire, like Arthur himself, symbolizes Leicester. When Leicester died it must have been perfectly natural for Spenser, as the vision of Arthur the resplendent slowly faded in the later books, to allow himself this inconsistency. His fond memory impelled him to write tenderly and delicately of some aberration of Leicester's which had excited the queen's wrath, but which to all hero-worshipping eyes had seemed quite innocent. To have described a quarrel of Arthur and Gloriana would have been to anticipate a dramatic meeting which, even in these days of disillusion, he probably still hoped to delay until he came to the last majestic scene of his epic. As the poet turned, however, from his allegorical prophecies to his scattered allegorical accounts of past events it is touching to read this reverent recollection and loyal defense of Leicester against the old gusts of regal anger. We must, with our poet, leave the exquisite conclusion and vindication for a moment, but we may anticipate the pretty idyl that immortalizes Leicester's grief and the reconciliation with a felicitous thought from Professor Greenlaw.

> Here is a charming picture of the quarrel of 1579 softened by time, and presenting in the happiest light the attachment of the Earl for his Queen. One wishes that Leicester might have seen it before the time, four days before he died, when he wrote that message on which Elizabeth penned the words, "His last letter."[3]

As we approach Canto Eight we remember that it was undoubtedly Spenser's original intention to make it the great

---

[3] "Spenser and the Earl of Leicester," pp. 560–561. I do not accept Professor Greenlaw's suggestion that Amoret is the Countess of Essex for the same reason that I turn from the theory that she was Elizabeth Throckmorton. It is more likely, it seems to me, that this episode refers to some quarrel rather less serious than that of 1579. Most probably it deliberately avoids specifying any.

turning point of each book where Arthur was always to appear the triumphant rescuer of the other heroes of each several adventure. But Arthur is introduced in the last stanzas of Canto Seven with a most significant casualness. He met Timias living alone in a rude cabin, wasted with sorrow, haggard, shaggy, dumb, unrecognizable. Arthur turned away, unknowing, to seek his long lost squire elsewhere and to achieve soon after an adventure of little distinction.

Meanwhile the story returns as though with wistful haste to the conclusion of the adventures of Timias. The story of the dove who ministers to the stricken squire is wrought out of a wonderfully delicate blending of the realistic and the fantastic, the pretty, the beautiful, and the homely. There is nothing to do but to allow Spenser to tell the fragile idyl himself with no blundering interruption from a critic who, with hands no matter how delicate, would but brush the gold dust from the butterfly wings of the narrative.

> Well said the wiseman, now prov'd true by this,
> Which to this gentle squire did happen late,
> That the displeasure of the mighty is
> Then death it selfe more dread and desperate.
> For naught the same may calme ne mitigate,
> Till time the tempest doe thereof delay
> With sufferaunce soft, which rigour can abate,
> And have the sterne remembrance wypt away
> Of bitter thoughts, which deepe therein infixed lay.
>
> Like as it fell to this unhappy boy,
> Whose tender heart the faire Belphoebe had
> With one stern looke so daunted, that no joy
> In all his life, which afterwards he lad,
> He ever tasted; but with penaunce sad
> And pensive sorrow pind and wore away,
> Ne ever laught, ne once shew'd countenance glad;
> But alwaies wept and wailed night and day,
> As blasted bloosme through heat doth languish and decay.
>
> Till on a day, as in his wonted wise
> His doole he made, there chaunst a turtle dove
> To come where he his dolors did devise,
> That likewise late had lost her dearest love,

Which losse her made like passion also prove.
Who seeing his sad plight, her tender heart
With deare compassion deeply did enmove,
That she gan mone his undeserved smart,
And with her dolefull accent beare with him a part.

Shee sitting by him, as on ground he lay,
Her mournefull notes full piteously did frame,
And thereof made a lamentable lay,
So sensibly compyld, that in the same
Him seemed oft he heard his own right name.
With that he forth would poure so plenteous teares,
And beat his breast unworthy of such blame,
And knocke his head, and rend his rugged heares,
That could have perst the hearts of tigres and of beares.

Thus, long this gentle bird to him did use
Withouten dread of perill to repaire
Unto his wonne, and with her mournefull muse
Him to recomfort in his greatest care,
That much did ease his mourning and misfare:
And every day, for guerdon of her song,
He part of his small feast to her would share;
That, at the last, of all his woe and wrong
Companion she became, and so continued long.

Upon a day, as she him sate beside,
By chance he certaine miniments forth drew,
Which yet with him as relickes did abide
Of all the bounty which Belphebe threw
On him, whilst goodly grace she did him shew:
Amongst the rest a jewell rich he found,
That was a ruby of right perfect hew,
Shap'd like a heart yet bleeding of the wound,
And with a litle golden chaine about it bound.

The same he tooke, and with a riband new,
In which his ladies colours were, did bind
About the turtles necke, that with the vew
Did greatly solace his engrieved mind.
All unawares the bird, when she did find
Her selfe do deckt, her nimble wings displaid,
And flew away, as lightly as the wind:
Which sodaine accident him much dismaid,
And looking after long, did marke which way she straid.

But when as long he looked had in vaine,
Yet saw her forward still to make her flight,

His weary eie returnd to him againe,
Full of discomfort and disquiet plight,
That both his juell he had lost so light,
And eke his deare companion of his care.
But that sweet bird departing flew forth right
Through the wide region of the wastfull aire,
Untill she came where wonned his Belphoebe faire.

There found she her (as then it did betide)
Sitting in covert shade of arbors sweet,
After late weary toile, which she had tride
In salvage chase, to rest as seem'd her meet.
There she alighting, fell before her feet,
And gan to her her mournfull plaint to make,
As was her wont, thinking to let her weet
The great tormenting griefe that for her sake
Her gentle squire through her displeasure did pertake.

She her beholding with attentive eye,
At length did marke about her purple brest
The precious juell, which she formerly
Had knowne right well, with colourd ribbands drest:
Therewith she rose in hast, and her addrest
With ready hand it to have reft away:
But the swift bird obayd not her behest,
But swarv'd aside, and there againe did stay;
She followd'd her, and thought againe it to assay.

And ever when she nigh approcht, the dove
Would flit a litle forward, and then stay,
Till she drew neare, and then againe remove;
So tempting her still to pursue the pray,
And still from her escaping soft away:
Till that at length into that forrest wide
She drew her far, and led with slow delay,
In th' end she her unto that place did guide,
Whereas that wofull man in languor did abide.

Eftsoones she flew unto his fearelesse hand,
And there a piteous ditty new deviz'd,
As if she would have made her understand
His sorrowes cause, to be of her despis'd,
Whom when she saw in wretched weedes disguiz'd,
With heary glib deform'd, and meiger face,
Like ghost late risen from his grave agryz'd,
She knew him not, but pittied much his case,
And wisht it were in her to doe him any grace.

Only after his pitiful lament did Belphoebe recognize her squire and accord him grace. It is well to repeat that one of the most touching things in Spenser is this courageous and most knightly habit of defending with memories like sunsets of pure golden mist the honor of dead heroes for whom he had once defied the queen herself. Here, practically, vanishes Spenser's most adorable woman; and Timias reappears long after only to suffer from the ulcerous wounds inflicted by Slander, the Blatant Beast, and to fall conquered under the club of Disdain.

Again Arthur has an absolutely casual entrance, this time to meet, to comfort, and escort Æmylia and Amoret.

> So when that forrest they had passed well,
> A litle cotage farre away they spide,
> To which they drew, ere night upon them fell;
> And entring in, found none therein abide,
> But one old woman sitting there beside,
> Upon the ground, in ragged rude attyre,
> With filthy lockes about her scattered wide,
> Gnawing her nayles for felnesse and for yre,
> And there out sucking venime to her parts entyre.

It is well to insist on the contrast between such figures as this hag, Sclaunder, so characteristic of the books of disillusion, and the figures of Pride and Acrasia in the first books, or even the figure of Duessa, who is not hideous at all times but more often alluring to the outward eye. We have in Sclaunder's description the first ugly notes of a theme that we shall find growing into a terrible obsession in the last books. Spenser, who set out to restore the Golden Age through the inspiration and the allegorical prophecies of his epic, now recalls the imagined, irrecoverable past with something of the disillusioned fervor that warmed like the dying sun the loveliest and saddest lines in Milton's remembrance of Eden.

> But antique age, yet in the infancie
> Of time, did live then like an innocent,
> In simple truth and blamelesse chastitie,
> Ne then of guile had made experiment,

But voide of vile and treacherous intent,
Held vertue for it selfe in soveraine awe:
Then loyall love had loyall regiment,
And each unto his lust did make a lawe,
From all forbidden things his liking to withdraw.

. . . .

Then beautie, which was made to represent
The great Creatours owne resemblance bright,
Unto abuse of lawlesse lust was lent,
And made the baite of bestiall delight:
Then faire grew foule, and foule grew faire in sight,
And that which wont to vanquish God and man
Was made the vassall of the victors might;
Then did her glorious flowre wex dead and wan,
Despisd and troden downe of all that overran.

And now it is so utterly decayd,
That any bud thereof doth scarse remaine,
But if few plants, preserv'd through heavenly ayd,
In princes court doe hap to sprout againe,
Dew'd with her drops of bountie soveraine,
Which from that goodly glorious flowre proceed,
Sprung of the auncient stocke of princes straine,
Now th' onely remnant of that royall breed,
Whose noble kind at first was sure of heavenly seed.

Powerfully bizarre is the picture of Sclaunder following the
Prince and the two ladies through the forest shrieking out foul
lies about them. Magnificence has no longer his epic dignity,
his stately entrances; he seems to ride unheroic, prosaic, shrink-
ing, with bowed head.

This scene suddenly melts into one more outlandish, in
which, for an instant, Arthur rises to something of his old heroic
stature. A squire comes fleeing and after him a most barbarous
giant mounted on a swiftly shambling dromedary. But the
giant, the lustful Corflambo, proves an easy victim for the
Prince. There is little to recall the prolonged and stirring
climaxes of the first two books. And the narrative quickly turns
to the rescued squire's tale, a pretty but rather outworn and
very loosely constructed romance of two friends, Amyas and
Placidas, whose absolute similarity of appearance made it pos-

sible for Placidas to assume voluntary imprisonment that he
might save Amyas from the wanton importunities of Pœana,
the daughter of Corflambo. The story closes (with characteristic
romantic irresponsibility) with the reunion of Amyas and
Æmylia, with the rapid and facile consolation of the bewildered
and envious Pœana, her convenient reformation, and her mar-
riage with Placidas.[4]

The celebration of true friendship is promptly and char-
acteristically followed by a contrasting scene of discord in which
Paridell and Blandamour, Druon and Claribell (two more
bickering nondescripts) fight in a strange, anarchic battle over
the false Florimell, whom they had all lost in the recent tourna-
ment. The situation, which involves a capricious changing of
sides in the very midst of the combat, would have been capital
for Ariosto or even for Spenser himself in his more successfully
grotesque vein of Book Two. But here it is described with un-
alloyed heavy seriousness. The situation is presently complicated
by the united attack of the four rogues on Scudamour and
Britomart and is immediately followed by the interference of
Prince Arthur. So the strange cavalcade sheathe swords and
listen to Scudamour's account of his winning of Amoret.

The winning of Amoret in the great Temple of Venus im-
presses us, still full as we are of memories of the magnificence
of the Masque of Cupid and of Britomart's conquest of Busirane,
with something of the effect that we might expect from a painter
trying, in an old age made premature by audacious excesses of
imagination, to fill a huge canvass with a faltering copy of a
great picture of his youth, a picture with immense perspectives,
riotous colors, a tumult of figures, now reproduced once more
but without the old impetuosity of stroke. Or we may say that
the episode of the Temple of Venus is a faded but beautiful
replica of the Masque of Cupid, a replica in most of its essentials
with all the pathos about it of an artist going back to retouch
one of his old masterpieces as if in despair of dealing with new

---

[4] See "The *Faërie Queene* and *Amis and Amiloun*," by Professor Harry
Morgan Ayres. *Modern Language Notes*, XXIII, 177–180.

miracles. But Sir Scudamour's adventures have something of
the old haunting qualities. After long wandering he came to
a Temple of Venus, the most stately and renowned of all her
dwellings.

> And it was seated in an island strong
> Abounding all with delices most rare,
> And wall'd by nature gainst invaders wrong,
> That none mote have accesse, nor inward fare,
> But by one way, that passage did prepare.
> It was a bridge ybuilt in goodly wize,
> With curious corbes and pendants graven faire,
> And, arched all with porches did arize
> On stately pillours, fram'd after the Doricke guize.

In an open plain before the Temple he found the Shield of
Love and won it brilliantly by overthrowing twenty knights.
Through a gate he ventured, past Doubt with double face, past
the crafty and garrulous enchantress Delay to a second gate,
the Gate of Good Desert, past Danger,

> An hideous giant, dreadfull to behold,
> That stopt the entraunce with his spacious stride.

One discerns the flagging creative energy of Spenser here in the
unusual conventionality and closeness with which he follows
old literary traditions. The Masque of Cupid reveals models
but remains full of originality, new power. This episode leans
very heavily on the fixed literary habits of medieval literature.
Yet for all its formality it is touched with the very immortality
of the elaborate Court of Love *genre* that permitted the most
artificial literature in the world to live on through a thousand
slightly varied variations. Beyond all perils, Sir Scudamour
found himself in an earthly paradise.

> Fresh shadowes, fit to shroud from sunny ray;
> Faire lawnds, to take the sunne in season dew;
> Sweet springs, in which a thousand nymphs did play;
> Soft rombling brookes, that gentle slomber drew;
> High reared mounts, the lands about to vew;
> Low looking dales, disloignd from common gaze;

Delightfull bowres, to solace lovers trew;
False labyrinthes, fond runners eyes to daze;
All which by Nature made did Nature selfe amaze.

And all without were walkes and alleyes dight
With divers trees, enrang'd in even rankes;
And here and there were pleasant arbors pight,
And shadie seates, and sundry flowring bankes,
To sit and rest the walkers weare shankes;
And therein thousand payres of lovers walkt,
Praysing their god, and yeelding him great thankes,
Ne ever ought but of their true loves talkt,
Ne ever for rebuke or blame of any balkt.

The old promenades of lovers and loving friends listed with such eternal gusto by hundreds of medieval poets and here listed once more seem to be lighted by a faint, new spring sunshine in these Spenserian arbors and alleys and seats. Beyond the outworks of the fortress and beyond these alluring walks the knight found the sacred harborage upon the porch of which sat Lady Concord attired in cloth of gold, "poudred with pearle and stone," and with a crown "much like unto a Danisk hood." Her commandment tempered two young men, Love and Hate, who stood by her hand in hand though Hate often averted his face, bit his lips, and gnashed his teeth in impotent "despight." Regardless of the menacing club of Hate, Sir Scudamour passed on.

"Into the inmost temple thus I came,
Which fuming all with frankensence I found,
And odours rising from the altars flame.
Upon an hundred marble pillors round
The roofe up high was reared from the ground,
All deckt with crownes, and chaynes, and girlands gay,
And thousand pretious gifts worth many a pound,
The which sad lovers for their vowes did pay;
And all the ground was strow'd with flowres, as fresh as May.

"An hundred altars round about were set,
All flaming with their sacrifices fire,
That with the steme thereof the temple swet,
Which rould in clouds to heaven did aspire,

And in them bore true lovers vowes entire: .
And eke an hundred brasen caudrons bright,
To bath in joy and amorous desire,
Every of which was to a damzell hight;
For all the priests were damzels, in soft linnen dight.

"Right in the midst the goddesse selfe did stand
Upon an altar of some costly masse,
Whose substance was uneath to understand:
For neither pretious stone, nor durefull brasse,
Nor shining gold, nor mouldring clay it was;
But much more rare and pretious to esteeme,
Pure in aspect, and like to christall glasse,
Yet glasse was not, if one did rightly deeme,
But being faire and brickle, likest glasse did seeme.

"But it in shape and beauties did excell
All other idoles which the heathen adore,
Farre passing that which by surpassing skill
Phidias did make in Paphos isle of yore,
With which that wretched Greeke, that life forlore,
Did fall in love: yet this much fairer shined,
But covered with a slender veile afore;
And both her feete and legs together twyned
Were with a snake, whose head and tale were fast combyned.

"The cause why she was covered with a vele
Was hard to know, for that her priests the same
From peoples knowledge labour'd to concele.
But sooth it was not sure for womanish shame,
Nor any blemish, which the worke mote blame;
But for, they say, she hath both kinds in one,
Both male and female, both under one name:
She syre and mother is her selfe alone,
Begets and eke conceives, ne needeth other none.

"And all about her necke and shoulders flew
A flocke of litle loves, and sports, and joyes,
With nimble wings of gold and purple hew,
Whose shapes seem'd not like to terrestriall boyes,
But like to angels playing heavenly toyes;
The whilest their eldest brother was away,
Cupid, their eldest brother: he enjoyes
The wide kingdome of Love with lordly sway,
And to his law compels all creatures to obay."

Among the hosts of lovers who lay scattered about her altar complaining, some one sang her praise.

   ' ''Great Venus, queene of beautie and of grace
      The joy of gods and men, that under skie
      Doest fayrest shine, and most adorne thy place,
      That with thy smyling looke doest pacifie
      The raging seas, and makst the stormes to flie;
      Thee, goddesse, thee the winds, the clouds doe feare,
      And when thou spredst thy mantle forth on hie,
      The waters play, and pleasant lands appeare,
And heavens laugh, and al the world shews joyous cheare.

   ' ''Then doth the daedale earth throw forth to thee
      Out of her fruitfull lap aboundant flowres;
      And then all living wights, soone as they see
      The Spring breake forth out of his lusty bowres,
      They all doe learne to play the paramours:
      First doe the merry birds, they prety pages,
      Privily pricked with thy lustfull powres,
      Chirpe loud to thee out of their leavy cages,
And thee their mother call to coole their kindly rages.'

    . . . .

   ''So did he say: But I with murmure soft,
      That none might heare the sorrow of my hart,
      Yet inly groning deepe and sighing oft,
      Besought her to graunt ease unto my smart,
      And to my wound her gratious help impart.
      Whilest thus I spake, behold! with happy eye
      I spyde where at the idoles feet apart
      A bevie of fayre damzels close did lye,
Wayting when as the antheme should be sung on hye.

   ''The first of them did seeme of ryper yeares
      And graver countenance then all the rest;
      Yet all the rest were eke her equall peares,
      And unto her obayed all the best.
      Her name was Womanhood, that she exprest
      By her sad semblant and demanure wyse:
      For stedfast still her eyes did fixed rest,
      Ne rov'd at randon, after gazers guyse,
Whose luring baytes oftimes doe heedlesse harts entyse.

   ''And next to her sate goodly Shamefastnesse,
      Ne ever durst her eyes from ground upreare,
      Ne ever once did looke up from her desse,
      As if some blame of evill she did feare,

That in her cheekes made roses oft appeare:
And her against sweet Cherefulnesse was placed,
Whose eyes, like twinkling stars in evening cleare,
Were deckt with smyles, that all sad humors chaced,
And darted forth delights, the which her goodly graced.

Thus sate they all around in seemely rate.
And in the midst of them a goodly mayd,
Even in the lap of Womanhood, there sate,
The which was all in lilly white arayd,
With silver streames amongst the linnen stray'd;
Like to the Morne, when first her shyning face
Hath to the gloomy world it selfe bewray'd;
That same was fayrest Amoret in place,
Shyning with beauties light and heavenly vertues grace.''

Sir Scudamour hesitated in awe but when he showed the Shield of Love he was allowed to take Amoret by the hand. As Edward Dowden puts it,

Spenser's thought seems to have been that, glorious in power, freedom, and beauty as virginity may be, such a state is only for rare natures elected to it, and that the true ideal of womanhood, as such, is only attained through love which leads to wedlock. Amoret, more than any other of his heroines, presents us with Spenser's conception in its purest form of the ''Ewig Weibliche,'' the eternal feminine principle, which assumes a myriad different forms and finds its highest embodiment in perfect woman. She is to Spenser what Eve was to Milton, the pure type of her sex, the general mother. Hence when her lover finds Amoret, it is in the Island of Love, and not in the island merely, but at the foot of the image of the goddess. To this veiled goddess—veiled not because of shame, but to shadow from profane eyes the mystery of her double sex, both male and female—a troop of lovers chant the great hymn of praise taken from the Roman poet's proemium, the ''Alma Venus'' of Lucretius. The ecstasy of love in all nature—in bird, and beast, and the sea, and the daedal earth—is celebrated, and last in human kind.

''Thou art the root of all that joyous is,
Great god of men and women, queen o' the air,
Mother of laughter, and well-spring of bliss.''

Mystical joy and courage stole over Sir Scudamour even while awe still held him.

''And evermore upon the goddesse face
Mine eye was fixt, for feare of her offence:
Whom when I saw with amiable grace
To laugh at me, and favor my pretence,

I was emboldned with more confidence,
And nought for nicenesse nor for envy sparing,
In presènce of them all forth led her thence,
All looking on, and like astonisht staring,
Yet to lay hand on her not one of all them daring.

"She often prayd, and often me besought,
Sometime with tender teares to let her goe,
Sometime with witching smyles: but yet, for nought
That ever she to me could say or doe,
Could she her wished freedome fro me wooe;
But forth I led her through the temple gate,
By which I hardly past with much adoe:
But that same ladie, which me friended late
In entrance, did me also friend in my retrate."

If the poet's imagination seems, in the adventure of Sir Scudamour, to be too dependent at times upon a group of his innumerable models he proves to us in the next canto that he is holding still for our future surprise new treasures most radiantly his own. The story turns to Marinell and to the maiden who has so lóng loved him without hope, to Florimell imprisoned in the hall of Proteus under sea. Marinell, at last healed of the wound inflicted by Britomart, came to the hall of Proteus where the Thames and the Medway were about to wed. Spenser had doubtless brooded over this quaint and haunting academic myth as a boy at Cambridge and he had attempted it soon after in his lost poem, the *Epithalamium Thamesis*, written undoubtedly in one of those classical measures with which Harvey, Sidney, Dyer, and others imitated classical prosody heavily, falteringly. and, in Spenser's particular case, half heartedly. All that was poetic in that poem Spenser doubtless used here when he suppressed that perverse effusion. Here, at the close of the fourth book where she should have been rising to the celebration of some culminating achievement by the alleged heroes, Cambell and Triamond, Spenser sought solace for his bewildered spirit by wandering along the bypaths of episode in which flowed old memories of Greek myths and university legends that had made him dream happily in his

early youth. Structurally it is all very weak. Yet it reassures
us of Spenser's inexhaustible opulence. For we are sure that
only a poet in a maturity most rich and at the same time beyond
all danger of decay could conjure up this procession with its
symphonic dignity and with its touches of studied quaintness
that suggest not a mere reproducing of early verses but a wistful
and happy groping back to those fancies of boyhood which
solaced him now, memories richer than the earlier realizations,
those memories which are the eternal innocence of the artist.

> First came great Neptune with his three-forkt mace,
> That rules the seas, and makes them rise or fall;
> His dewy lockes did drop with brine apace,
> Under his diademe imperiall:
> And by his side his queene with coronall,
> Faire Amphitrite, most divinely faire,
> Whose yvorie shoulders weren covered all,
> As with a robe, with her owne silver haire,
> And deckt with pearles, which th' Indian seas for her prepaire.

Among the sea-gods and goddesses famous in classical poetry
came also Albion, a son of Neptune whom the antique poets did
not know, England's divinity, with (most appropriately) old
Ocean and his aged dame and their wisest and most venerable
son, Nereus, who loved alike to prophesy the fall of vast empires
and to play with wanton nymphs.

> And after him the famous rivers came,
> Which doe the earth enrich and beautifie:
> The fertile Nile, which creatures new doth frame;
> Long Rhodanus, whose sourse springs from the skie;
> Faire Ister, flowing from the mountaines hie;
> Divine Scamander, purpled yet with blood
> Of Greekes and Trojans, which therein did die;
> Pactolus glistring with his golden flood,
> And Tygris fierce, whose streames of none may be withstood;
>
> Great Ganges, and immortal Euphrates,
> Deepe Indus, and Maeander intricate,
> Slow Peneus, and tempestuous Phasides,
> Swift Rhene, and Alpheus still immaculate;
> Ooraxes, feared for great Cyrus fate;
> Tybris, renowmed for the Romaines fame;

> Rich Oranochy, though but knowen late;
> And that huge river, which doth beare his name
> Of warlike Amazons, which doe possesse the same.

The musical pomp of that procession of names and the thought
of those great mysterious rivers of the New World exalts the
poet into digressing a moment in a defense of Raleigh's pro-
jected expedition to Guiana which shows a flash of the old
quixotic fire and of the imperialistic dreams which Spenser
shared with Drake and Sidney.

> Joy on those warlike women, which so long
> Can from all men so rich a kingdome hold!
> And shame on you, O men, which boast your strong
> And valiant hearts, in thoughts lesse hard and bold,
> Yet quaile in conquest of that land of gold!
> But this to you, O Britons, most pertaines,
> To whom the right hereof it selfe hath sold;
> The which, for sparing litle cost or paines,
> Loose so immortall glory, and so endlesse gaines.[5]

Love of native country glows warmly also in his description of
the bridegroom and the attendant English rivers all heralded
by Arion.

> Then there was heard a most celestiall sound
> Of dainty musicke, which did next ensew
> Before the spouse: that was Arion crownd;
> Who, playing on his harpe, unto him drew
> The eares and hearts of all that goodly crew,
> That even yet the dolphin, which him bore
> Through the Agaean seas from pirates vew,
> Stood still by him astonisht at his lore,
> And all the raging seas for joy forgot to rore.
>
> So went he playing on the watery plaine.
> Soone after whom the lovely bridegroome came,
> The noble Thamis, with all his goodly traine;
> But him before there went, as best became,
> His auncient parents, namely th' auncient Thame:
> But much more aged was his wife then he,
> The Ouze, whom men doe Isis rightly name;
> Full weake and crooked creature seemed shee,
> And almost blind through eld, that scarce her way could see.

---

[5] See Professor Greenlaw's comments in ''Spenser and British Imper-
ialism,'' p. 7.

Therefore on either side she was sustained
Of two smal grooms, which by their names were hight
The Churne and Charwell, two small streames, which pained
Them selves her footing to direct aright,
Which fayled oft through faint and feeble plight:
But Thame was stronger, and of better stay;
Yet seem'd full aged by his outward sight,
With head all hoary, and his beard all gray,
Deawed with silver drops, that trickled downe alway.

And eke he somewhat seem'd to stoupe afore
With bowed backe, by reason of the lode
And auncient heavy burden which he bore
Of that faire city, wherein make abode
So many learned impes, that shoote abrode,
And with their braunches spred all Britany,
No lesse then do her elder sisters broode.
Joy to you both ye double noursery
Of arts! but, Oxford, thine doth Thame most glorify.

But he their sonne full fresh and jolly was,
All decked in a robe of watchet hew,
On which the waves, glittering like christall glas,
So cunningly enwoven were, that few
Could weenen whether they were false or trew.
And on his head like to a coronet
He wore, that seemed strange to common vew,
In which were many towres and castels set,
That it encompast round as with a golden fret.

Like as the mother of the gods, they say,
In her great iron charet wonts to ride,
When to Joves pallace she doth take her way,
Old Cybele, arayd with pompous pride,
Wearing a diademe embattild wide
With hundred turrets, like a turribant.
With such an one was Thamis beautifide;
That was to weet the famous Troynovant,
In which her kingdomes throne is chiefly resiant.

And round about him many a pretty page
Attended duely, ready to obay;
All little rivers, which owe vassallage
To him, as to their lord, and tribute pay:
The chaulky Kenet, and the Thetis gray,
The morish Cole, and the soft sliding Breane,
The wanton Lee, that oft doth loose his way,
And the still Darent, in whose waters cleane
Ten thousand fishes play, and decke his pleasant streame.

On came stately Severn and storming Humber, speedy Tamar
and Avon proud of his adamants,

> And there came Stoure with terrible aspect,
> Bearing his sixe deformed heads on hye.
>
> .   .   .   .
>
> Next him went Wylibourne with passage slye,
> That of his wylinesse his name doth take,
>
> .   .   .   .
>
> And Mole, that like a nousling mole doth make
> His way still underground, till Thamis he overtake.

No wonder that this canto, this mere episode out of all
Spenser's incomparable wealth, was sufficient to stimulate
Michael Drayton, that sturdy yeoman-poet, to celebrate all the
rivers and almost every square foot of his country in his immense
geographical epic, the *Poly-Olbion*. Like Spenser, Drayton was
impressed, with true renaissance sensitiveness, by the ruins of
time. But, unlike Spenser, he did not yield, as a result, to
melancholy visions of the world's vanity. His ardent eye caught
the rich glow of England's past, legendary and historical. But
he saw no reason for lamenting at length its broken splendors.
He himself lived in lordly certainty of eternal fame. So he set
himself the task of garnering the immense riches of chronicle
and romance into a lasting shrine. The towering and shapeless
monument is grotesque at a distance. On nearer view the
curious may discover, among many crude carvings indicative
of a certain grandeur of mind in spite of their frailties, certain
pieces of rare workmanship. Let the irreverent listen to the
magniloquent promises of his preface. You are to walk

... into the Temple and fields of the Muses; where, throughout most delight-
ful groves the birds shall steal thee to the top of an easy hill, where in
artificial caves cut out of the most natural rock, thou shalt see the ancient
people of this isle delivered thee in their lively images; from whose height
thou may'st behold both the old and the later times, as in thy prospect lying
far under thee; then conveying thee down by a soul-pleasing descent
through delicate embroidered meadows veined with gentle-gliding brooks;
in which thou may'st fully view the dainty nymphs in their simple naked
beauties, bathing them in crystalline streams, which shall lead thee to

most pleasant downs, where harmless shepheards are, some exercising their
pipes, some singing roundelays to their grazing flocks.

Drayton was quite drunk with Spenser's spirit of fancy. Unfor-
tunately he was not impressed by Spenser's profound moral
purpose and by the allegorical method which, in spite of its
inadequate working-out and in spite of the harsh sentence of
certain critics from Reynolds and Davenant to Lowell and
even Jusserand, saves *The Faërie Queene* from that damning
anarchy of fancy that ruins such works as the *Poly-Olbion* and
the *Brittania's Pastorals*. But Drayton has his own answer to
those of us who scoff. Let us listen and remain to pray. "If,
as I say, thou hadst rather (because it asks thy labour) remain
where thou wert, than strain thyself to walk forth with the
Muses, the fault proceeds from thy idleness, not from any want
in my industry."

And assuredly, as the true lover of poetry returns again
and again to idle an hour over the pages of the *Poly-Olbion* he
will thank the prodigal Spenser for creating, besides his own
Faërie Queene, the spendthrift Drayton, who learns from certain
charmed allusions, over which his master paused in his account
of the gorgeous procession of rivers, to exalt his country. Again
and again a river pauses in her stately course to declare her
supreme right to sing the praise of an Arthur or a Bevis. Dert
shows her eld and nobility by telling of Britain-founding Brute's
flight from Italy and arrival in England and how she was pre-
destinate to meet him. Drayton imitates his master with a series
of river-weddings. In the Seventh Song, for example, the
wood-nymphs rush "with locks uncomb'd for haste," to see the
marriage of the Wye and the Lug. If there is no legendary
or historical association or if Drayton cannot create a myth,
he adopts Spenser's third device and praises his river by an
account of some prosperous city or beautiful grove which it
caresses, or its products: health-giving salts, fish, whatever the
river yields to inspire his Anglo-Saxon industrialism. Thus
the rivers near Lincoln inspire an exuberant list of their fishes,
all of which is suggested by Spenser's two compact lines

> And Lindus, that his pikes doth most commend
> Of which the auncient Lincolne men doe call.

But Drayton's enthusiasm and industry are as garrulous as the pride of a local gossip.

> The faster-feeding cod, the mackerel brought by May,
> The dainty sole and plaice, the dab, as of their blood,
> The conger finely sous'd, hot summer's coolest food,
>
> . . . .
>
> The sturgeon cut to keggs (too big to handle whole)
> Gives many a dainty bit out of his lusty jowl;
>
> . . . .
>
> Amongst whose sundry sorts, since thus far I am in,
> I'll of our shell-fish speak, with those of scales and fin:
>
> . . . .
>
> The scallop cordial judg'd, the dainty wilk and limp,
> The periwincle, prawn, the cockle and the shrimp,
> For wanton women's tastes or for weak stomachs bought.

And Drayton apostrophizes Cambridge University because Spenser in this mood of momentary forgetfulness of his disillusion had sung how

> ... The plenteous Ouse came far from land,
> By many a city, and by many a towne,
> And many rivers taking under hand
> Into his waters, as he passeth downe,
> The Cle, the Were, the Grant, the Sture, the Rowne,
> Thence doth by Huntingdon and Cambridge flit,
> My mother Cambridge, whom as with a crowne
> He doth adorne, and is adorn'd of it
> With many a gentle muse, and many a learned wit.

To compare Drayton's dilution with Spenser's original is to take the best possible means of writing an appreciation of one of Spenser's most fascinating cantos first, by giving Drayton his seldom given due, then, by emphasizing the vitality of these fancies of Spenser and Drayton in the days of Elizabeth, and finally, by showing the superiority of the master over his sturdy but garrulous pupil. To see this at a glance turn to the Eighteenth Song of the *Poly-Olbion* where we are told that Erix, the son of Neptune, marshalled the Nereids to "Loving Land."

Next Proto wondrous swift lead all the rest the way,
Then she that makes the calms the mild Cymodoce,
With god-like Dorrida and Galatea fair
With dainty nets of pearl, cast on their braided hair.

So Drayton gossips on for lines and lines. Now contrast the perfect stanzas in which Spenser concludes his procession. Here too throng the Nereids. But, in significant contrast to the diverting but very wordy and shambling lines of his pupil, Spenser compresses his stanzas into almost a bare enumeration of names such as even Milton never matched. For the faërie poet was well aware that the enchanting music thus produced was itself the richest kind of song-wine with dissolved pearl. The crowded stanzas give too a wonderful sense of the infinite life of the sea. Note further how, in contrast to Drayton's careless clauses, the sparsely chosen single epithets of Spenser are complete in their pictorial effect and blend in subtle intoxication of alliteration and of vowel sounds with the proper names to which they are wedded.

Swift Proto, milde Eucrate, Thetis faire,
Soft Spio, sweete Eudore, Sao sad,
Light Doto, wanton Glauce, and Galene glad,

White hand Eunica, proud Dynamene,
Joyous Thalia, goodly Amphitrite,
Lovely Pasithee, kinde Eulimene,
Light foote Cymothoe, and sweete Melite,
Fairest Pherusa, Phao lilly white,
Wondred Agave, Poris, and Nesæa,
With Erato, that doth in love delite,
And Panopæ, and wise Protomedæa,
And snowy neckd Doris, and milkewhite Galathæa.

Since the fourth book closes with the story of Florimell, we must expect the weakest conclusion of all. Yet this is the last book to close on a note of triumph. The adventures of Artegall and Calidore that follow are crowned with success, but branded with futility. Here in the twelfth canto of the strange medley we have just reviewed we are confronted with a beautiful but rather capricious and parasitical woman whose sufferings, so intensely personal and so casually touched upon, do not impress us as deeply as those of Una with her strength and her steadfast aspiration. The exaggerated helplessness, the timorousness, the hothouse quality of Florimell lower her before our eyes half-blinded by the radiant Britomart. But the tenderness which proves itself a kind of power to win the wayward love of Marinell, to reconcile his mother Cymodoce, half persuades us that the lady is, after all, a heroine who must have her own place in the bower where dwell Una and Britomartis, Belphœbe and Amoret and Pastorella.

Book Four, so chaotic in structure, is like a sky confused with cloud masses through which ever and anon come clean shafts and pillars of the sunshine of a young and wilful spring. Book Five is serried in structure, most sternly unified in its mood of proud and implacable scorn, but luminous only with that uncanny light that struggles and shifts through a sky of unbroken grey. We feel the gusts of bitterness which have hitherto come so capriciously, uniting and strengthening themselves with sinister quiet, ever lurking over us with oppressive imminence and we know that they will come at last with the vulture-swoop of a storm-wind.

In the fifth book there is little prophecy, little splendor of remembered triumphs. It is a sublimated political pamphlet and its poetry is to be found mainly in a feverish earnestness and lofty scorn; it is a defense of that paternalistic kind of government which was always hated by the English at home but recommended always for their alien subjects, a kind of government which Mr. Hilaire Belloc called the ''Servile State'' in his book of that name and which he has prophesied, with an accuracy that is becoming too terribly clear, to be the prevalent government of the immediate future. Much of Spenser's doctrine here will seem painfully narrow in its ruthless imperialism to all but incurable romanticists or hard-headed, bigoted economic determinists. But this poetry of Spenser, even to a people who see the fallacy and the fatality of imperialism, will ring clear to many who will find in its defense of Lord Grey of

Wilton an exploit more knightly than the deeds of any of Spen-
ser's heroes.   There is little splendor, I have said.   The poet
sternly denies himself his special pleasure of lingering over
warmly colored scenes and informs the reader that this book
is a "treatise."   He touches, in Canto Three, on the "spousals
of faire Florimell," but of the feasting and the gorgeous
costumes he has little to say.

> To tell the glorie of the feast that day,
> The goodly service, the devicefull sights,
> The bridegromes state, the brides most rich aray,
> The pride of ladies, and the worth of knights,
> The royall banquets, and the rare delights
> Were worke fit for an herauld, not for me:
> But for so much as to my lot here lights,
> That with this present treatise doth agree,
> True vertue to advance, shall here recounted bee.

He hastens on to tell of the fierce jousting and to dwell with
special savagery on the final disgrace of Braggadochio wrought
by the noble and pitiless Artegall.   There is a flash of sensuous
beauty in the last portrait of Florimell, but only in order that
in the act of winning back her long lost girdle she may bring
more shame to that false Florimell who, with the many other
charlatans thronging in the last two books, had already deceived
so many knights and ladies good and bad.   We have here, as
Miss Warren well says, "a piece of the best kind of allegory,
where the meaning is as clear as it is deep."

> So forth the noble ladie was ybrought,
> Adorn'd with honor and all comely grace:
> Whereto her bashfull shamefastnesse ywrought
> A great increase in her faire blushing face;
> As roses did with lillies interlace.
> For of those words, the which that boaster threw,
> She inly yet conceived great disgrace.
> Whom when as all the people such did vew,
> They shouted loud, and signes of gladnesse all did shew.

> Then did he set her by that snowy one,
> Like the true saint beside the image set,
> Of both their beauties to make paragone,
> And triall, whether should the honor get.

Streight way so soone as both together met,
Th' enchaunted damzell vanisht into nought:
Her snowy substance melted as with heat,
Ne of that goodly hew remayned ought,
But th' emptie girdle, which about her wast was wrought.

As when the daughter of Thaumantes faire
Hath in a watry cloud displayed wide
Her goodly bow, which paints the liquid ayre;
That all men wonder at her colours pride;
All suddenly, ere one can looke aside,
The glorious picture vanisheth away,
Ne any token doth thereof abide:
So did this ladies goodly forme decay,
And into nothing goe, ere none could it bewray.

In this book, as I have already said, there is little prophecy. Lord Grey of Wilton had been disgraced by a hesitant and suspicious government and by slanderous colleagues in Ireland. The fifth book was probably completed in the very year of Artegall's death and was in truth an impassioned and bitter *adagio lamentoso* on a past that could not be mended, on a hero who had been crucified in spirit but who would never on this earth have a resurrection.

It is hard for us to find the essential poetry in Spenser's hero-worship of Lord Grey. We must grow gloomy and storm-swept with a berserker-rage like Carlyle's against Mammonist and Dilettante, against an unscrupulous selfishness like that of so many of our own "Captains of Industry," and against an apathy at court exactly like that of many of our contemporaries who live, careless of the grim problems of our poor and unemployed, on the incomes of their great-grandfather's intellects; we must turn, as Carlyle turns, to glorify a grim figure like William the Conqueror or John Knox, a darkly splendid fanatic like Mahomet or Cromwell, in order to feel the rush of exaltation that came to Spenser as it should come to us when we contemplate his bigoted and terrible and noble hero. We must, in short, assume the mood which all occidental countries today seem to be rapidly assuming in vigorous emulation of each other, the mood precisely which today we choose to call "Prussian." Lord Grey's administration, Spenser's pitiless machiavellian politics, Carlyle's neo-aristocracy, the twentieth-century "Servile State" all seem to a few irreconcilables today, alike for Ireland in the sixteenth century and for the lasting social well-being of the world in the twentieth century, appallingly futile. But there is inspiration in the destructive action and thought of these men, there is a doom-trumpet nobility that is immortal in its elevating influence.

Dean Church in his chapter on "Spenser in Ireland" gives us an account which, though slightly warped by its author's zeal to be just into an excess that becomes injustice to Spenser and Lord Grey, is the most brilliant and fair-minded and vivid of all narrations of the poet's years of service to imperial politics. Dean Church quotes from the *Calendar of State Papers* Lord Grey's report of the destruction of the Spanish garrison at Smerwick—a report perhaps written out by Spenser, the secretary—which should be read by every adventurer in Spenser's Faërie Land before he opens the volume at the fifth book. The garrison had asked for a parley. Then, so runs the report of Lord Grey:

There was presently sent unto me one Alexandro, their camp master; he told me that certain Spaniards and Italians were there arrived upon fair speeches and great promises, which altogether vain and false they found; and that it was no part of their intent to molest or take any government from your Majesty; for proof, that they were ready to depart as they came and deliver into my hands the fort. Mine answer was, that for that I perceived their people to stand of two nations, Italian and Spanish, I would give no answer unless a Spaniard was likewise by. He presently went and returned with a Spanish captain. I then told the Spaniard that I knew their nation to have an absolute prince, one that was in good league and amity with your Majesty, which made me to marvell that any of his people should be found associate with them that went about to maintain rebels against you.... And taking it that it could not be his king's will, I was to know by whom and for what cause they were sent. His reply was that the king had not sent them, but that one John Martinez de Ricardi, Governor for the king at Bilboa, had willed him to levy a band and repair with it to St. Andrews (Santander), and there to be directed by this their colonel here, whom he followed as a blind man, not knowing whither. The other avouched that they were all sent by the Pope for the defence of the *Catholica fede.* My answer was, that I would not greatly have marvelled if men being commanded by natural and absolute princes did sometimes take in hand wrong actions, but that men, and that of account as some of them made show of, should be carried into unjust, desperate, and wicked actions, by one that neither from God or man could claim any princely power or empire, but (was) indeed a detestable shaveling, the right Antichrist and general ambitious tyrant over all right principalities, and patron of the *Diabolica fede*—this I could not but greatly rest in wonder. Their fault therefore far to be aggravated by the vileness of their commander; and at my hands no condition or composition they were to expect, other than they should render me the fort, and yield their selves to my will for life or death. With this answer he departed; after which there was one or two courses to and fro more, to have gotten a certainty for some of their lives: but finding that it would not be, the colonel himself about sunsetting came forth and requested respite with surcease of arms till the next morning, and then he would give a resolute answer.

Finding that to be but a gain of time to them, and a loss of the same to myself, I definitely answered I would not grant it, and therefore presently either he took my offer or else return and I would fall to my business. He then embraced my knees simply putting himself to my mercy, only he prayed that for that night he might abide in the fort, and that in the morning all should be put into my hands. I asked hostages for the performance; they were given. Morning came; I presented my companies in battle before the fort, the colonel comes forth with ten or twelve of his chief gentlemen, trailing their ensigns rolled up, and presented them unto me with their lives and the fort. I sent straight certain gentlemen in, to see their weapons and armour laid down, and to guard the munition and victual there left for spoil. Then I put in certain bands, who straight fell to execution. There were six hundred slain. Munition and victual great store: though much wasted through the disorder of the soldier, which in that fury could not be helped. Those that I gave life unto, I have bestowed upon the captains and gentlemen whose service hath well deserved.... Of the six hundred slain, four hundred were as gallant and goodly personages as of any (soldiers) I ever beheld. So hath it pleased the Lord of Hosts to deliver your enemies into your Highnesses' hand, and so too as one only accepted, not one of yours is either lost or hurt.

So the grim story goes on, reënacted by the English with the Boers, by American soldiers in the Philippines, by Germans in Belgium, by Russians in Poland. Here, indeed is Sir Artegall in the flesh, terrible enough for the most Calvinistic hero-worshipper and the most enthusiastic imperialist. Let us not forget, for one thing, that his tactics were quite common

and orthodox in his day. And today it is clear that we have
not advanced much beyond this kind of national piety even in
our most peaceful modern communities. But the man who is
not shaken at the horror and the infamy of Lord Grey's report
and yet somewhat stirred with Spenser's barbaric hero-worship
of Artegall is a man who can hardly hope to see the nobility
on this earth because he must needs see earthly good, in some
unreal existence, divorced from its swart comrade, evil. That
reader is purblind indeed who would allow his hatred of the
memory of Lord Grey to destroy his admiration for Spenser
who wrote this fifth book, his impassioned defense of the name
of this dead and disgraced friend whose friendship, even in
memory, could bring the poet little but reproach. For Spen-
ser hurled this defense like an iron gauntlet in the teeth of the
court.

The whole book is tense with scorn. It begins, not with
joyous prophecy, but with a challenge to the whole age.

> So oft as I with state of present time
> The image of the antique world compare,
> When as mans age was in his freshest prime,
> And the first blossome of faire vertue bare,
> Such oddes I finde twixt those and these which are,
> As that, through long continuance of his course,
> Me seemes the world is runne quite out of square
> From the first point of his appointed sourse,
> And being once amisse, growes daily wourse and wourse.
>
> . . . .
>
> Let none then blame me, if in discipline
> Of vertue and of civill uses lore,
> I doe not forme them to the common line
> Of present dayes, which are corrupted sore,
> But to the antique use which was of yore,
> When good was onely for it selfe desyred,
> And all men sought their owne, and none no more;
> When Justice was not for most meed outhyred,
> But simple Truth did rayne, and was of all admyred.
>
> For that which all men then did vertue call
> Is now cald vice; and that which vice was hight,
> Is now hight vertue, and so us'd of all:
> Right now is wrong, and wrong that was is right,

> As all things else in time are chaunged quight.
> Ne wonder; for the heavens revolution
> Is wandred farre from where it first was pight,
> And so doe make contrarie constitution
> Of all this lower world, toward his dissolution.

Most of the allusions to present and future are meager and hope-
less or intensely bitter. Artegall, we are told, was brought up
in infancy by Justice herself, the fair Astræa, who gave him
Chrysaor, the very sword with which Jove quelled the Titans.
Then comes a stanza thoroughly characteristic of these last
books.

> Now when the world with sinne gan to abound,
> Astræa loathing longer here to space
> Mongst wicked men, in whom no truth she found,
> Return'd to heaven, whence she deriv'd her race;
> Where she hath now an everlasting place,
> Mongst those twelve signes which nightly we doe see
> The heavens bright-shining baudricke to enchace;
> And is the Virgin, sixt in her degree,
> And next her selfe her righteous ballance hanging bee.

Here is the key of the book, omnipresent, never a modulation,
grimly monotonous to the last episode where Artegall faces
Slander. One wonders whether Wordsworth, who loved Spenser
so reverently and deeply, could have ever appreciated this side
of the man when he could write those expressive but most nar-
rowly expressive lines in *The Prelude*.

> And that gentle Bard,
> Chosen by the Muses for their Page of State—
> Sweet Spenser, moving through his clouded heaven
> With the moon's beauty and the moon's soft pace,
> I called him Brother, Englishman, and Friend.[6]

It is this scorn with which Book Five is so tense, rather than
any desire to conjure into oblivion the harsher side of Lord
Grey, that moved Spenser to give Sir Artegall his strange com-
rade Talus, the Man of Iron, who massacres routs of men after
his master judges. Miss Warren says ingeniously:

---

[6] *The Prelude*, Book III, ll. 278–282.

[Spenser] makes Artegall ... a striking and a noble figure, but all the most unpleasant results and the useless slaughters which follow from his judgments or action are taken in hand by Talus, the Iron Man. This would seem to say that Spenser felt the cruelties involved in Gray's government of Ireland to be incompatible with the ideal of a Knight of Justice. Several times in the poem he makes Artegall forbid the slaughter which Talus is carrying out with such grim pleasure, though it is plain from history that Lord Grey made no attempt to stop the massacres in Ireland. Talus, as the groom of Artegall, is usually supposed to stand for the executive power which carries out the decrees of justice, and as such he has some rightful place in the story; but that an Iron Man, incapable of human feeling, should be the sole attendant upon Justice is a woeful limitation to impose upon our conception of the virtue which Aristotle thought the most perfect of all.

I fear, however, that Spenser cannot be credited even with a desire to free Lord Grey, with this allegorical quibble, from the memory of his most horrible exploits. Spenser has told us explicitly that Talus, the soulless wielder of the iron flail, was the cherished groom of Astraea herself. We cannot defend Spenser's hero in this way. In Canto Two, for instance, it is Artegall who jousts on the perilous bridge with Pollente, the rapacious official who plunges with the unwary through the trapfall into the turbulent stream where he is as much at ease as on land and where he has overcome many knights. Thus Spenser finds something of the heroic in an allegory which tells of the triumph of Justice over a political ''boss.'' The whole passage, perhaps because of its close dependence on Ariosto's account of the fight of Rodomonte and Brandimarte, is very spirited. And when Spenser comes to recount the destruction of Munera (Bribery), the daughter of Pollente, his scorn surges up resistless and Talus comes into the foreground not because Spenser would exonerate Artegall from the charge of cruelty, but because he would turn over mean work to mean hands.

> Eftsoones his page drew to the castle gate,
> And with his iron fiale at it let flie,
> That all the warders it did sore amate,
> The which erewhile spake so reprochfully,
> And made them stoupe, that looked earst so hie.
> Yet still he bet and bounst upon the dore,

And thundred strokes thereon so hideouslie,
That all the peece he shaked from the flore,
And filled all the house with feare and great uprore.

With noise whereof the lady forth appeared
Uppon the castle wall; and when she saw
The daungerous state in which she stood, she feared
The sad effect of her neare overthrow;
And gan entreat that iron man below
To cease his outrage, and him faire besought,
Sith neither force of stones which they did throw,
Nor powr of charms, which she against him wrought,
Might otherwise prevaile, or make them cease for ought.

But when as yet she saw him to proceede,
Unmov'd with praiers or with piteous thought,
She ment him to corrupt with goodly meede;
And causde great sackes with endlesse riches fraught,
Unto the battilment to be upbrought,
And powred forth over the castle wall,
That she might win some time, though dearly bought,
Whilest he to gathering of the gold did fall.
But he was nothing mov'd nor tempted therewithall;

But still continu'd his assault the more,
And layd on load with his huge yron flaile,
That at the length he has yrent the dore,
And made way for his maister to assaile.
Who being entred, nought did then availe
For wight, against his powre them selves to reare:
Each one did flie; their hearts began to faile;
And hid them selves in corners here and there;
And eke their dame halfe dead did hide her selfe for feare.

Long they her sought, yet no where could they finde her,
That sure they ween'd she was escapt away:
But Talus, that could like a limehound winde her,
And all things secrete wisely could bewray,
At length found out whereas she hidden lay
Under an heape of gold. Thence he her drew
By the faire lockes, and fowly did array,
Withouten pitty of her goodly hew,
That Artegall him selfe her seemeless plight did rew.

Yet for no pitty would he change the course
Of justice, which in Talus hand did lye;
Who rudely hayld her forth without remorse,
Still holding up her suppliant hands on hye,

And kneeling at his feete submissively.
But he her suppliant hands, those hands of gold,
And eke her feete, those feete of silver trye,
Which sought unrighteousnesse, and justice sold,
Chopt off, and nayled on high, that all might them behold.

Her selfe then tooke he by the sclender wast,
In vaine loud crying, and into the flood
Over the castle wall adowne her cast,
And there her drowned in the durty mud:
But the streame washt away her guilty blood.
Thereafter all that mucky pelfe he tooke,
The spoile of peoples evill gotten good,
The which her sire had scrap't by hooke and crooke,
And burning all to ashes, powr'd it downe the brooke.

And lastly all that castle quite he raced,
Even from the sole of his foundation,
And all the hewen stones thereof defaced,
That there might be no hope of reparation,
Nor memory thereof to any nation.
All which when Talus throughly had perfourmed,
Sir Artegall undid the evill fashion,
And wicked customes of that bridge refourmed:
Which done, unto his former journey he retourned.

To be sure the poet speaks tersely here of Artegall's pity, but he brushes it aside as tersely in the next line. Similarly, in the next adventure, Artegall merely argues loftily with the revolutionary giant while it is Talus, who seems almost the embodiment of Artegall's contempt grown silent, who shoulders the huge demagogue off the cliff and slaughters the mutinous rabble of auditors whose blood is too base to soil Chrysaor. Here, indeed, the zealous defender of Spenser would like to apologize, even with a quibble, for Artegall. But Artegall has already stained himself. Artegall's whole behavior reminds one of nothing so much as a smug adherent of the Manchester school of economics explaining why all I. W. W.'s are fools and criminals. The giant, with his false scales, is an impersonation of that levelling-down tendency which we all recognize as the supreme danger of democracy. He is indeed a sophist. But so is Artegall. And Artegall is the cheaper sophist of the two.

This whole episode is a capital instance of Spenser's noble narrowness. But we must approach it precisely as we would approach Carlyle's *Past and Present.* We can be stirred by the fine destructive criticism of democracy which is here set forth with great sweep of scornful poetic imagination. And Spenser's remedy, precisely the same as Carlyle's neo-feudal hero worship, although bigoted and impossible, has in it a fervid hatred of revealed evils that contains a positive philosophical value.

The most interesting adventure in Book Five, the encounter with the Amazon Radigund, seems to our age to be weighted down with the same narrowness. But to call this episode, as it has been called by all critics who have discussed it, an allegorical attack on the doctrine of "woman's rights" is pretty thoroughly to misinterpret it with a half-truth. It is strange that this should have been said, since the figures of Radigund and Britomart are thrown together with such vivid contrast—and yet, after all, it is not so utterly strange since it is here where Spenser's hand falters somewhat in the portrayal of his greatest heroine. We must analyze the whole series of incidents carefully.

Artegall has saved Terpin from the hands of Radigund's warrior women and is to meet the queen herself in single combat. At morn the beautiful Amazon comes forth in barbaric majesty to the deafening sound of trumpets and shawms.

> All in a Camis light of purple silke
> Woven uppon with silver, subtly wrought,
> And quilted uppon sattin white as milke,
> Trayled with ribbands diversely distraught,
> Like as the workeman had their courses taught;
> Which was short tucked for light motion
> Up to her ham, but when she list, it raught
> Downe to her lowest heele, and thereuppon
> She wore for her defence a mayled habergeon.
>
> And on her legs she painted buskins wore,
> Basted with bends of gold on every side,
> And mailes betweene, and laced close afore:
> Uppon her thigh her cemitare was tide,

> With an embroidered belt of mickell pride;
> And on her shoulder hung her shield bedeckt
> Uppon the bosse with stones, that shined wide
> As the faire moone in her most full aspect,
> That to the moone it mote be like in each respect.

In the stubborn duel she proves herself for long time his equal
and wounds him grievously with her scimitar.   But a coun-
terstroke interrupts her savage boasts and shatters her shield
to bits.

> Having her thus disarmed of her shield,
> Upon her helmet he againe her strooke,
> That downe she fell upon the grassie field,
> In sencelesse swoune, as if her life forsooke,
> And pangs of death her spirit overtooke.
> Whom when he saw before his foote prostrated,
> He to her lept with deadly dreadfull looke,
> And her sunshynie helmet soone unlaced,
> Thinking at once both head and helmet to have raced.

> But when as he discovered had her face,
> He saw, his senses straunge astonishment,
> A miracle of Natures goodly grace
> In her faire visage voide of ornament,
> But bath'd in bloud and sweat together ment;
> Which, in the rudenesse of that evill plight,
> Bewrayd the signes of feature excellent:
> Like as the moone, in foggie winters night,
> Doth seeme to be her selfe, though darkned be her light.

Overcome with pity and fascination the knight throws aside
his sword and bends over her.   In a moment her swoon passes.
Leaping fiercely to her feet she rushes upon him and forces
him, all unarmed as he is, to yield.   Like Omphale she clothes
him in woman's garb and sets him to spinning.   The poet's
observations seem, for the nonce, "anti-feministic" enough.

> Such is the crueltie of wemen kynd,
> When they have shaken off the shamefast band,
> With which wise Nature did them strongly bynd,
> T' obay the heasts of mans well ruling hand,
> That then all rule and reason they withstand,
> To purchase a licentious libertie.

> But vertuous women wisely understand,
> That they were borne to base humilitie,
> Unlesse the heavens them lift to lawfull soveraintie.

Talus, meanwhile, easily escapes and carries the news to Britomart, who is chafing over Artegall's long absence with a growing jealousy of a kind once considered quite necessary but now growing a little tiresome to modern readers. Just here Ariosto influences Spenser to his cost. The picture of Brada-mante stuffing the bed-clothes into her mouth to stifle her loud weeping is one of those fine homely touches in which the Italian poet is quite matchless. We respect Bradamante none the less for these outbursts, but we recoil from Britomart because such petty squalls are not in character. Spenser should have re-mained with his own ideal but most human and plausible visions. In the interview between Talus and Britomart the Iron Man proves himself not only more intelligent but positively more human. Britomart, like a spoiled soubrette rather than a truly "womanly woman," interrupts his explanations and perverts them to her own angry whim. We are forced to choke down our disgust and our utter astonishment over this new and quite unbelievable side of her character by seeking solace in a delightfully homely simile which, judged on its own merits as a detached picture rather than as a figure, is the one thing that makes the passage endurable.

> Like as a wayward childe, whose sounder sleepe
> If broken with some fearefull dreames affright,
> With froward will doth set him selfe to weepe;
> Ne can be stild for all his nurses might,
> But kicks, and squals, and shriekes for fell despight;
> Now scratching her, and her loose locks misusing;
> Now seeking darknesse, and now seeking light;
> Then craving sucke, and then the sucke refusing:
> Such was this ladies fit, in her loves fond accusing.

We remember the wonderful picture of Britomart in her smock threatening with drawn sword the lewd and sentimental Male-casta, we remember her giving herself to Sir Artegall, but only

in mutual conquest, and we try to forget this vagary. We should
expect her to have unreasonable faults a plenty. But when we
read of how she grows weary over her delirium of grief aroused
by her own perversely mendacious interpretation of the half-told
story of Talus and how she returns in ''mylder mood'' to learn

> The certaine cause of Artegals detaine;
> And what he did, and in what state he stood,
> And whether he did woo, or whether he were woo'd

we realize that Spenser is only nodding and that in his half-
somnolent state he is simply confusing his own Britomart with
some one perilously like a heroine of Jane Austen's or a ''Mrs.
Newly Wed'' in a cheap American ''comic'' paper. When,
however, she sallies forth and girds herself to answer with deeds
the defiance of a recreant knight on the bridge of Pollente she
is made at once, with one superb stroke, a woman, but such a
woman as only heroes may woo.

> Strange were the words in Britomartis eare;
> Yet stayd she not for them, but forward fared,
> Till to the perillous bridge she came, and there
> Talus desir'd that he might have prepared
> The way to her, and those two losels scared.
> But she thereat was wroth, that for despight
> The glauncing sparkles through her bever glared,
> And from her eies did flash out fiery light, .
> Like coles that through a silver censer sparkle bright.

This is not the kicking and squalling of a pretty feather-
brain; this is the wrath of Britomart and, in spite of Mr.
Frederick Harrison and his followers, it is, as the creators of
Artemis, Atalanta, Brunhilde, yes, and Isolde well knew, a
most ''womanly'' wrath.

Spenser was led to belie and contradict his own better
instinct and judgment by his memories of the age of chivalry.
Spenser's own chivalry, the real chivalry, is always, at its best,
above that strange institution which, though it did much to
liberate woman from her humiliating position in the strictly
feudal period, was so often associated with a latent contempt

for women and with corruption. Spenser realized, in his best moments, the true chivalry of which the troubadours and romancers only dreamed confusedly and half-sincerely. Unfortunately, the more faltering conceptions of chivalry, which Spenser shared in his weaker moments, are still current today in this still more than half-feudalistic age. One has only to talk sustainedly with the average contemporary advocate of "chivalry" to perceive that he implies a definition of it which makes us wish that we could believe with Edmund Burke (although in a mood the opposite of Burke's) that the days of chivalry were gone. You will apprehend always, if you listen for only a few moments to an impassioned harangue from the alarmist who prophecies that the "new woman" will destroy man's natural "chivalry," that his sentiments are tinged with that patronizing attitude towards women that always accompanied the protestations of the advocates of "chivalry" even in the days when the troubadour wrote an amorous virelay to his mistress and avowed himself prepared to run disguised in wolf-skins before the hounds if his lady's whim so desired it. When the "primitive" man whom Lucretius admired so much wooed his lady he knocked her down with a club or a stone. The method of the advocate of chivalry, whether he be troubadour or minnesinger or prosaic gentleman of the twentieth century with an ugly derby instead of a splendid helmet—the method of the advocate of chivalry is almost precisely the same as that of the heroic ruffian of the Roman poet. Both the "primitive" man and the "chivalric" man show an equal contempt for women. Civilization, however, has made it necessary for the "chivalric" man to be rather more cunning. He pretends a greater respect for feminine whims. But his contempt is uncompromisingly revealed in his very belief that woman must have whims so outrageous as to require him to masquerade in a wolf-skin or to execute predatory business campaigns in order to . load her with furs. At the risk of all charges of sermonizing and digressing, I must develop this point in order that we may clearly discern and distinguish both the false and the true

chivalry in Spenser. We find that while Spenser had no
difficulty in imagining a woman who could be at once beautiful
and courageous, learned in life's ways and noble, many modern
advocates of what they call "chivalry" would jealously guard
the creatures they consider so fragile not only from the slums
or the battlefield but from the relatively innocent and peaceful
life in comradeship with men on a college campus. For most
of these advocates of "chivalry" fear that the frail creatures
whom they have made in the fantastic image that once amused
them will "wither into intellectual womanhood" and "grow
coarse" in their comradeship with young men who turn out
after all to have some points of difference from Watt's sicken-
ing picture of Sir Galahad. One remembers that insipid and
insufferable company which Tennyson described in the insipid
and insufferable "Prologue" and "Conclusion" of *The Princess*
(a poem which is the only considerable blot on Tennyson's great
name), one remembers in the midst of that company Lilia—a
most appropriate name—taking no part in the dispute about
woman's position, but like a perfect mid-Victorian lady showing
by her silent "showerful glance" that she was converted without
a struggle and without an idea. It will be no small compensation
to some of the more callous of us, when women through the
"coarsening" influences of coeducation, suffrage, economic inde-
pendence, etc., "wither into intellectual womanhood," that the
wearisome "showerful glance" will be almost completely dried
up. "Wither into intellectual womanhood," "grow too coarse
to nourish a people's offspring"! What do these phrases really
mean? They mean that the female bundle of whims, prophecies,
prejudices, divine truths, vulgarisms, insipidities, and fine in-
tuitions which man in his "chivalric" mood uncritically classi-
fies all together as woman's "angelic intuition" and in his
contemptuous mood classifies all together as woman's "absurd
whims" is being purified by knowledge and reason which will
separate false superstitions and prejudices and feline desires
from that true intuition which can endure the test of reason.
"Wither into intellectual womanhood," "grow too coarse to

nourish a people's offspring''! These quasi-oracular utterances
mean simply that the "cute" girl may, thank heaven, soon cease
to be. They mean that the best women of the new generations
are becoming more like Atalanta and less like Helen, more like
Britomart and less like Florimell, that is to say, more truly and
divinely womanly than ever before except in a few of the highest
imaginings of the loftiest poets.

Britomart, once more herself, overcomes the ruffians who
oppose her and journeys to the Temple of Isis, one of the most
fascinating and outlandish of the gorgeous habitations that
spring up with such delightful suddenness along the dim paths
of *The Faërie Queene.*

> There she received was in goodly wize
> Of many priests, which duely did attend
> Uppon the rites and daily sacrifize,
> All clad in linnen robes with silver hemd;
> And on their heads, with long locks comely kemd,
> They wore rich mitres shaped like the moone,
> To shew that Isis doth the moone portend;
> Like as Osyris signifies the sunne:
> For that they both like race in equall justice runne.

> The championesse them greeting, as she could,
> Was thence by them into the temple led;
> Whose goodly building when she did behould,
> Borne uppon stately pillours, all dispred
> With shining gold, and arched over hed,
> She wondred at the workemans passing skill,
> Whose like before she never saw nor red;
> And thereuppon long while stood gazing still,
> But thought that she thereon could never gaze her fill.

> Thence forth unto the idoll they her brought,
> The which was framed all of silver fine,
> So well as could with cunning hand be wrought,
> And clothed all in garments made of line,
> Hemd àll about with fringe of silver twine.
> Uppon her head she wore a crowne of gold,
> To shew that she had powre in things divine;
> And at her feete a crocodile was rold,
> That with his wreathed taile her middle did enfold.

One foote was set uppon the crocodile,
And on the ground the other fast did stand,
So meaning to suppresse both forged guile
And open force: and in her other hand
She stretched forth a long white sclender wand.
Such was the goddesse; whom when Britomart
Had long beheld, her selfe uppon the land
She did prostrate, and with right humble hart,
Unto her selfe her silent prayers did impart.

To which the idoll as it were inclining,
Her wand did move with amiable looke,
By outward shew her inward sence desining.
Who well perceiving how her wand she shooke,
It as a token of good fortune tooke.
By this the day with dampe was overcast,
And joyous light the house of Jove forsooke:
Which when she saw, her helmet she unlaste,
And by the altars side her selfe to slumber plaste.

A weird and repulsive dream reassures her of her marriage with
Artegall and of their mutual enthronement.   Hardily she goes
forth and slays Radigund.   In the great moment when she
stands over the body of the Amazon you realize (as Spenser in
his highest moods clearly realized) the essential difference be-
tween the feminists who are anomalies (the mannish women
who have appeared as anomalies in substantial numbers in
every age) and the sane feminist, more womanly than ever.   To
be sure Spenser nods once more when he describes Britomart's
short protectorate among the Amazons.

So there a while they afterwards remained,
Him to refresh, and her late wounds to heale:
During which space she there as princes rained,
And changing all that forme of common weale,
The liberty of women did repeale,
Which they had long usurpt; and them restoring
To mens subjection, did true justice deale:
That all they, as a goddesse her adoring,
Her wisedome did admire, and hearkned to her loring.

But in the exquisitely conceived meeting of Britomart and her
humiliated lover, in the description of her finely blended sym-

pathy and reproach you perceive Spenser's clearer insight, his
conception of two comrades who are essentially equal even
though one for the moment has erred as the other some time may
err, a comradeship that calls for that sympathy which is above
pity since it recognizes a true hero even at this moment of shame.

Here is the woman of loveliness and strength, dowered with
intuition and reason, whom George Meredith sought. Tenny-
son's notorious lawn party, which has become a part of the
irrecoverable Gilded Age, may cause many to lament its pass-
ing. But this younger contemporary of Tennyson wrote, less
than twenty years after the appearance of *The Princess,* a poem
that sounded the death-knell of mid-Victorianism. George Mere-
dith's *Modern Love* tells the story of a beautiful, ineffectual girl
who married a man and ceased to love him with perfect feminine
unreason. The strange but most natural complications and the
tragic close of her story called from Meredith a powerful and
a harrowing poem. "Their senses with their subtleties are
mixed," he cries of women, "more brain, O God, more brain!"
That cry of his for a more rational sense was vaguely but deeply
at Spenser's heart and has been echoed by many of the greatest
writers of today. As a result, we have a new generation of girls
developing keen rational powers. And with these qualities they
are retaining and developing quite as much or more womanly
charm than the beauties of the older generations. Jane Austen's
pretty and petty heroine is giving place to Diana of the Cross-
ways, once thought impossible, now growing up, under our very
eyes, in imperial beauty.

Should we pause here to deal with any one who thinks that
Meredith's poem was also the death-knell of romantic love?
Neither Meredith's *Modern Love* nor such works as Ibsen's
Doll's House breathe a syllable against romantic love. But they
all denounce moonshine. Spenser, in his silly and effeminate
description of Britomart's causeless jealousy, is momentarily
false to true romantic love of which he shows, at his best, a per-
fect understanding. Romantic love, real romantic love that
does not fear the presence of the intellectual and the rational,

that is vigorous enough to endure without disillusion the sudden
apparition of an Artegall reduced to toiling with a distaff, that
can idealize not only in the evening in the salon but at the
breakfast table on the morning after—real romantic love scorns
the pseudo-realism called cynicism equally with the pseudo-
idealism which is sentimentalism, and is always healthily sus-
picious of that subtle compound of shrewd wisdom and myopic
ignorance which is denominated common sense.[7]   It is not too
much to maintain, when we remember Britomart as the mortal
foe of both the lewd and sentimental Malecasta and the hard
and capricious Radigund, that Spenser (for all his inconsistency)
caught and partly mastered this essential truth.   Here, indeed,
in the creator of Britomart in her loftiest moods and in the
creator of Diana of the Crossways, not in those who believe that
woman's fine qualities are so perishable that they must be hot-
housed from the dust and even the dew, here indeed we have the
true chivalry which, without sickly and insincere angel worship,
believes in the new and wonderful potentialities of women as
mothers and as "world-builders."

The remainder of Book Five, until we reach the fierce and
bitter close, falls in interest.   Canto Nine has been made noto-
rious by many critics on the score of its alleged flattery of
Elizabeth.   Artegall and Arthur come to the court of Mercilla
(Mercy, Queen Elizabeth), where they witness the trial of
Duessa (Mary Queen of Scots).   One notes a real defect in
the general structure in the way the stern Artegall outshines
Arthur, who is here rather sentimental in his facile pity.   Duessa
is proved worthy of death, but Mercilla withholds the sentence
and weeps over her.   Gross flattery and misrepresentation of
facts, say critics who are bent on proving Spenser a courtier
in the worst sense.   I hold the criticism of Miss Warren much
more fair.

---

[7] I may take this occasion to note that the best interpretation of the
character of Britomart, written by a liberal (and Britomart can be in-
terpreted properly only by a liberal or by a radical), is in Professor Padel-
ford's "Women in Spenser's Allegory of Love," *The Mid-West Quarterly*,
IV (January, 1917), 134–145.

It has been laid to Spenser's charge—by Professor Courthope and by Dean Church—that he grossly flattered Queen Elizabeth in the *Faerie Queene*. The witness of this Fifth Book helps to free him from that accusation. We have seen that he chooses for his hero a man disliked by Elizabeth and boldly commends him to her notice. But more than this. He introduces in canto nine a direct description of Elizabeth and her Court, making it quite unmistakable to whom he refers. Here was the finest opportunity for flattery. But what do we find? In a description of Elizabeth not a word of praise to which any real exception can be taken (unless the epithet "angel-like" may offend some). As a great Queen and a stately figure in the history of the time she deserved, even in her old age, all he says of her here, and the incident of her reluctance and tears at the condemnation of Mary Queen of Scots is said to be historical. In the introductory stanzas he commends her, but chiefly for her justice— "the instrument whereof loe here thy Artegall." If this was flattery, it was dashed with an audacity which risked something for its speaking.

Cantos Ten and Eleven celebrate Leicester's rather dubious expedition to the Low Countries. Prince Arthur is described as slaying Geryoneo (Spain) and freeing Belgae (the Netherlands) and her five surviving sons. The allegory is bald and patent. But it cannot be regarded as courtier-craft. For Leicester was dead. Rather it is but another of those examples of Spenser's constant and ardent remembrance of his dead friends, that persistent loyalty that puts my fundamental emphasis on his noble steadfastness and independence beyond cavil.

The last of the book tells of Artegall's adventures: first, how he rescues Burbon (Henry IV of France), who had laid aside his shield (the Protestant Faith) given him by the Knight of the Red Cross, and reconciles him to his contemptuous lady Flourdelis (France); then the narrative deals briefly with Artegall's achievement of his quest, the freeing of Irena (Ireland) and the slaying of Grantorto, who is Spain in another one of those protean apparitions with which the image of England's foe haunts this book. But the book closes with a terrible picture of Sir Artegall's encounter with the Blatant Beast that symbolizes boldly the slanderous ingratitude which hounded Lord Grey.

> Tho, as he backe returned from that land,
> And there arriv'd againe, whence forth he set,

He had not passed farre upon the strand,
When as two old ill favour'd hags he met,
By the way side being together set;
Two griesly creatures; and, to that their faces
Most foule and filthie were, their garments yet,
Being all rag'd and tatter'd, their disgraces
Did much the more augment, and made most ugly cases.

The one of them, that elder did appeare,
With her dull eyes did seeme to looke askew,
That her mis-shape much helpt; and her foul heare
Hung loose and loathsomely: thereto her hew
Was wan and leane, that all her teeth arew
And all her bones might through her cheekes be red;
Her lips were like raw lether, pale and blew,
And as she spake, therewith she slavered;
Yet spake she seldom, but thought more, the lesse she sed.

Her hands were foule and durtie, never washt,
In all her life, with long nayles over raught,
Like puttocks clawes: with th' one of which she scracht
Her cursed head, although it itched naught;
The other held a snake with venime fraught,
On which she fed and gnawed hungrily,
As if that long she had not eaten ought;
That round about her jawes one might descry
The bloudie gore and poyson dropping lothsomely.

This creature, Envy, was accompanied by the hag, Detraction,
and by the Blatant Beast. Envy hurled her half-devoured ser-
pent at the knight and both hags shrieked out against him
charges that he had slain Grantorto with treachery.

Thereto the Blatant Beast, by them set on,
At him began aloud to barke and bay,
With bitter rage and fell contention,
That all the woods and rockes nigh to that way
Began to quake and tremble with dismay,
And all the aire rebellowed againe,
So dreadfully his hundred tongues did bray:
And evermore those hags them selves did paine
To sharpen him, and their owne cursed tongs did straine.

The first and second books closed with a triumph. At the
end of the third book we read how Britomart achieved brilliantly

but crowned no long-sought quest. The fourth book ended with a pageant and with the consummation of the loves of two minor personages, a wistful escaping from all contemplation of those great and serious issues which were no longer promising to befall as the poet had dreamed. Book Five rises to this bitter outcry at the futility of great deeds. But there is a fine dignity in Artegall's scorn here as fiery and as self-contained as ever.

> Yet he past on, and seem'd of them to take no keepe.

And we may note last of all that in this profound bitterness our knightly poet allows no tinge of personal complaint, no reference to his own thwarted ambitions which his critics are so constantly seeking to detect in his works. His one grief was for his maligned friend, of whose return to "Faery court," despite a faintly hopeful promise, made perhaps when he dreamed that Artegall would achieve ultimately due praise, Spenser never wrote. For Artegall's death followed not far after his disgrace and even before this book could appear as a fearless champion.

> The waies, through which my weary steps I guyde,
> In this delightfull land of Faery,
> Are so exceeding spacious and wyde,
> And sprinckled with such sweet variety
> Of all that pleasant is to eare or eye,
> That I, nigh ravisht with rare thoughts delight,
> My tedious travell doe forget thereby;
> And when I gin to feele decay of might,
> It strength to me supplies, and chears my dulled spright.

This stanza, which has haunted for over three centuries men as different as Thomas Wharton and Mr. Maurice Hewlett, sounds the most lovely note of Book Six, always a favorite with those who are not, like Macaulay, too purely Anglo-Saxon. There is, in this book, scene after scene that has a pastoral serenity most alluring, yet most deceptive too, most deceptive because the serenity is only on the surface.

This poet, so often falsely called above all things serene, is only trying to escape from his growing disillusion. The hero,

Sir Calidore, Courtesy,[8] though pale, is one of the most attractive heroes in *The Faërie Queene*. As the probable allegorical semblance of Essex, who came into Spenser's life to comfort him somewhat for the loss of his other heroes, he seems to lend a note of cheerfulness. But terribly vivid is his foe, the Blatant Beast, Slander, the object of the fiercest hate of most great poets. That hatred is also of the kind at once impersonal and intense of which only great poets are capable. Lord Grey had suffered. Leicester had suffered—from Spenser's point of view—unjustly. The plea often expressed in Spenser's dedicatory sonnets and in others of his poems against the slander that sends songs to oblivion was a plea intended as much to save his ideals, his dreams, and his heroes from misrepresentation.

Sir Calidore's quest is recounted capriciously and perfunctorily. The poet and the hero escape together, at every opportunity, from the sordid issue. In the first two cantos, to be sure, Sir Calidore has appropriate adventures which might have lead effectively to a climax in the final discomfiture of Slander. The discourteous and brutal Crudor, who would have for his lady a mantle lined with beards of knights and locks of ladies, falls before the hero's impetuous bravery. And Sir Calidore rewards the champions of courtesy. He sees a slender squire battling with a full armed knight.

> Him stedfastly he markt, and saw to bee
> A goodly youth of amiable grace,
> Yet but a slender slip, that scarse did see
> Yet seventeene yeares, but tall and faire of face,
> That sure he deem'd him borne of noble race.
> All in a woodmans jacket he was clad
> Of Lincolne greene, belayd with silver lace;
> And on his head an hood with aglets sprad,
> And by his side his hunters horne he hanging had.
>
> Buskins he wore of costliest cordwayne,
> Pinckt upon gold, and paled part per part,

---

[8] Dr. Percy W. Long ("Spenser's Sir Calidore," *Englische Studien*, XLII, 53–60) skilfully explodes the old theory that Sir Calidore represents Sir Philip Sidney. And Dr. Long makes out a plausible case for an identification of Calidore and Essex.

> As then the guize was for each gentle swayne;
> In his right hand he held a trembling dart,
> Whose fellow he before had sent apart;
> And in his left he held a sharpe bore-speare.

This is young Tristram. When the squire slays the warrior, to revenge a lady most foully used, Sir Calidore knights him.

> There he him causd to kneele, and made to sweare
> Faith to his knight, and truth to ladies all,
> And never to be recreant, for feare
> Of perill, or of ought that might befall:
> So he him dubbed, and his squire did call.
> Full glad and joyous then young Tristram grew,
> Like as a flowre, whose silken leaves small,
> Long shut up in the bud from heavens vew,
> At length breakes forth, and brode displays his smyling hew.[9]

In the third canto Sir Calidore pursues the Blatant Beast. But in this same canto there abruptly begins the love story of Serena and Calepine, which often turns the fond poet from the chief adventure. From this episode there jets, fountainlike, romance after romance, irrelevant, clear, and sweet. Nothing in *The Faërie Queene* is more quaintly attractive than the account of Sir Calepine's rescue of a babe from a bear and the humorous, tender picture of the knight forgetting his sorrow over his lost Serena to play clumsily at being a father.

> Then tooke he up betwixt his armes twaine
> The little babe, sweet relickes of his pray;
> Whom pitying to heare so sore complaine,
> From his soft eyes the teares he wypt away,
> And from his face the filth that did it ray,
> And every litle limbe he searcht around,
> And every part that under sweathbands lay,
> Least that the beasts sharpe teeth had any wound
> Made in his tender flesh; but whole them all he found.

---

[9] Mr. Edgar A. Hall (*Pub. Mod. Lang. Assoc.*, XXVIII, December, 1913, 539 sq.) argues that Spenser "drew materials directly from two French romances of the Grail-Perceval cycle for the episodes of the first two cantos of Book VI." He warns us against the current over-emphasis of Malory as a source. And he observes that "Malory, unlike both the mediaeval writers and Spenser, had small sense for the spiritual values with which external events may be invested."

Prince Arthur enters in Canto Five, but not as the resplendent super-hero, merely as the escort of Serena, whom he leads to an old hermit, a thoroughly characteristic figure for Book Six.

> And soothly it was sayd by common fame,
> So long as age enabled him thereto,
> That he had bene a man of mickle name,
> Renowmed much in armes and derring doe:
> But being aged now and weary to
> Of warres delight and worlds contentious toyle,
> The name of knighthood he did disavow,
> And hanging up his armes and warlike spoyle,
> From all this worlds incombraunce did himselfe assoyle.

Sir Calidore disappears in wild pursuit of the Blatant Beast in Canto Three and does not reappear until Canto Nine, where he is portrayed as forgetful of his quest in the midst of a shepherd's paradise to which Spenser turns with a relief as evident as that which he attributes to his hero. In Canto Eight Arthur is the chief figure as he was evidently originally intended to be at precisely this point in each book. But he appears only to vanquish for a futile moment a foe unworthy of his steel, Disdain, and to aid the victim maid Mirabell, a sorry heroine, "with her little hard and shallow heart," who is doing absurd penance for her absurd cruelty to her lover.

The most beautiful cantos of Book Six are the ninth and tenth, where Sir Calidore abandons his quest to live in a pastoral earthly paradise and where the poet, for the only time in his epic, introduces himself. In Spenser's youth, when he wrote his *Shepheards Calendar,* his visions of Arcadia and the Golden Age were seldom wistful for long. His eager spirit filled shepherd-land with raucous contemporary voices. But here, where in his masterwork the crescendo of bitterness in his *Complaints* and in his last three books grows faint and almost disappears, the poet gives us a pure idyllic gold that is perhaps only possible when the wistful singer dreams of the irrecoverable. Yet we must remember, if we are to be unflinchingly true to Spenser in our appreciation of his own stern ideals, that this mood is not Spenser's greatest. I have already called Sir Calidore's pastoral retirement a renaissance version of the philosophy of the ivory tower, a nature's Palace of Art, hardly less insidious because it gives sunlight and meadows and groves instead of the warm perfumes and gorgeous prisons of tapestries.

We may well be deceived by the exquisite health and innocence and clean sensuousness of this Spenserian philosophy of the tower of ivory. The heroine has been compared with Perdita and she is worthy of the comparison. The splendid knight, flashing suddenly among the simple folk of the fields and sitting down to their homely fare,

> Saw a faire damzell, which did weare a crowne
> Of sundry flowres, with silken ribbands tyde,
> Yclad in home-made greene that her owne hands had dyde.

> Upon a litle hillocke she was placed
> Higher then all the rest, and round about
> Environ'd with a girland, goodly graced,
> Of lovely lasses, and them all without
> The lustie shepheard swaynes sate in a rout,
> The which did pype and sing her prayses dew,
> And oft rejoyce, and oft for wonder shout,
> As if some miracle of heavenly hew
> Were downe to them descended in that earthly vew.

> And soothly sure she was full fayre of face,
> And perfectly well shapt in every lim,
> Which she did more augment with modest grace
> And comely carriage of her count'nance trim,
> That all the rest like lesser lamps did dim:
> Who, her admiring as some heavenly wight,
> Did for their soveraine goddesse her esteeme,
> And caroling her name both day and night,
> The fayrest Pastorella her by name did hight.

And if this lady leads Sir Calidore for a time from duty, whereas even glorious Britomart could not for a moment turn Artegall aside from his quest, if the poet is himself turning from his own quest, yet Pastorella is one of the ladies of *The Faërie Queene* who inspire most the beautiful reflections with which Edward Dowden has begun his essay on the "Heroines of Spenser."

Spenser's manner of portraiture differs much from that of Chaucer, whom he names his poetical master. Ambling Canterburyward, with his eyes on the ground, the earlier poet could steal sprightly glances at every member of the cavalcade—glances which took in the tuft of hairs on the Miller's nose, the sparkle of pins in the Friar's tippet, and the smooth forehead and little rosy mouth of Madam Eglantine. We should know the Wife of Bath, if we met her, by the wide-parted teeth, the dulness of hearing, the bold laugh, the liberal tongue; we should expect to see the targelike hat, the scarlet stocking, and the shining shoes. Spenser's gaze dwelt longer on things, in a more passive luxury of sensation or with reverence more devout. His powers of observation are, as it were, dissolved in his sense of beauty, and this again is taken up into his moral idealism and becomes a part of it. To Chaucer a beautiful woman is a beautiful creature of this good earth and is nothing more; her beauty suddenly slays the tender heart of her lover, or she makes glad the spirit of man as though with some light, bright wine. She is more blissful to look on than "the new perjonette tree," and softer than the wether's wool; her mouth is sweet as "apples laid in hay or heath"; her body is gent and small as any weasel. For Spenser behind each woman, made to worship or to love, rises a sacred presence—womanhood itself. Her beauty of face and limb is but a manifestation of the invisible beauty, and this is of one kin with the Divine Wisdom and the Divine Love.

We must grasp this inconsistency of Spenser's. Here is one the poet's most blessed saints leading the hero into a life of sin, venial, but sin. Such an interpretation, you will say, is puritanical. You must, I agree, abandon yourself to the sensuous charm of these scenes. But you must also be ready to recoil from them; you must be a Don Quixote with his outlandish helmet of Mambrino replaced with something suspiciously like a shovel hat to appreciate Spenser here to the full. In the dialogue between Sir Calidore and old Meliboe, the foster-father of Pastorella, one hears the beautiful poetry of defeat.

> "How much," sayd he "more happie is the state,
> In which ye, father, here doe dwell at ease,
> Leading a life so free and fortunate
> From all the tempests of these worldly seas,
> Which tosse the rest in daungerous disease;
> Where warres, and wreckes, and wicked enmitie
> Doe them afflict, which no man can appease!
> That certes I your happinesse envie,
> And wish my lot were plast in such felicitie."

    "Surely, my sonne," then answer'd he againe,
    "If happie, then it is in this intent,
      That, having small, yet doe I not complaine
      Of want, ne wish for more it to augment,
      But doe my selfe, with what I have, content;
      So taught of nature, which doth litle need
      Of forreine helpes to lifes due nourishment:
      The fields my food, my flocke my rayment breed;
No better doe I weare, no better doe I feed.

  . . . .

    "To them that list, the worlds gay showes I leave,
      And to great ones such follies doe forgive,
      Which oft through pride do their owne perill weave,
      And through ambition downe themselves doe drive
      To sad decay, that might contented live.
      Me no such cares nor cumbrous thoughts offend,
      Ne once my minds unmoved quiet grieve,
      But all the night in silver sleepe I spend,
And all the day, to what I list I doe attend.

  . . . .

    "The time was once, in my first prime of yeares,
      When pride of youth forth pricked my desire,
      That I disdain'd amongst mine equall peares
      To follow sheepe, and shepheards base attire:
      For further fortune then I would inquire,
      And leaving home, to roiall court I sought;
      Where I did sell my selfe for yearely hire,
      And in the princes gardin daily wrought:
There I beheld such vainenesse, as I never thought.

    "With sight whereof soone cloyd, and long deluded
      With idle hopes, which them doe entertaine,
      After I had ten yeares my selfe excluded
      From native home, and spent my youth in vaine,
      I gan my follies to my selfe to plaine,
      And this sweet peace, whose lacke did then appeare.
      Tho backe returning to my sheepe againe,
      I from thenceforth have learn'd to love more deare
This lowly quiet life, which I inherite here."

Then, when the hero has abandoned himself to this winning gospel of defeat, he is given a glimpse of the Graces, of Colin Clout, and of the poet's lady of the *Epithalamion* in that most bewitching scene in which the poet croons himself into a lyric ecstasy of forgetfulnss of all his disillusionings.

It was an hill plaste in an open plaine,
That round about was bordered with a wood
Of matchlesse hight, that seem'd th' earth to disdaine;
In which all trees of honour stately stood,
And did all winter as in sommer bud,
Spredding pavilions for the birds to bowre,
Which in their lower braunches sung aloud;
And in their tops the soring hauke did towre,
Sitting like king of fowles in majesty and powre.

And at the foote thereof, a gentle flud
His silver waves did softly tumble downe,
Unmard with ragged mosse or filthy mud;
Ne mote wylde beastes, ne mote the ruder clowne
Thereto approch, ne filth mote therein drowne:
But nymphes and faeries by the bancks did sit,
In the woods shade, which did the waters crowne,
Keeping all noysome things away from it,
And to the waters fall tuning their accents fit.

And on the top thereof a spacious plaine
Did spred it selfe, to serve to all delight,
Either to daunce, when they to daunce would faine,
Or else to course about their bases light;
Ne ought there wanted, which for pleasure might
Desired be, or thence to banish bale:
So pleasauntly the hill with equall hight
Did seeme to overlooke the lowly vale;
Therefore it rightly cleeped was Mount Acidale.

They say that Venus, when she did dispose
Her selfe to pleasaunce, used to resort
Unto this place, and therein to repose
And rest her selfe, as in a gladsome port,
Or with the Graces there to play and sport;
That even her owne Cytheron, though in it
She used most to keepe her royall court,
And in her soveraine majesty to sit,
She in regard hereof refusde and thought unfit.

"What the poet of Faerie Land especially loves," writes Edward Dowden on Spenser's favorite landscapes, "are those select spots devised by nature for delight, sacred and secure, where nature, as it were, vies with art, and where men in instinctive gratitude would fain build an altar on the green sward to the mild genius of the place."

Unto this place when as the Elfin knight
Approcht, him seemed that the merry sound
Of a shrill pipe he playing heard on hight,
And many feete fast thumping th' hollow ground,
That through the woods their eccho did rebound.
He nigher drew, to weete what mote it be;
There he a troupe of ladies dauncing found
Full merrily, and making gladfull glee,
And in the midst a shepheard piping he did see.

He durst not enter into th' open greene,
For dread of them unwares to be descryde,
For breaking of the daunce, if he were seene;
But in the covert of the wood did byde,
Beholding all, yet of them unespyde.
There did he see, that pleased much his sight,
That even he him selfe his eyes envyde,
An hundred naked maidens lilly white,
All raunged in a ring, and dauncing in delight.

All they without were raunged in a ring,
And daunced round; but in the midst of them
Three other ladies did both daunce and sing,
The whilest the rest them round about did hemme,
And like a girlond did in compasse stemme:
And in the middest of those same three was placed
Another damzell, as a precious gemme
Amidst a ring most richly well enchaced,
That with her goodly presence all the rest much graced.

Looke how the crowne, which Ariadne wore
Upon her yvory forehead that same day
That Theseus her unto his bridale bore,
When the bold Centaures made that bloudy fray
With the fierce Lapithes, which did them dismay,
Being now placed in the firmament,
Through the bright heaven doth her beames display,
And is unto the starres an ornament,
Which round about her move in order excellent:

Such was the beauty of this goodly band,
Whose sundry parts were here too long to tell:
But she that in the midst of them did stand
Seem'd all the rest in beauty to excell,
Crownd with a rosie girlond, that right well
Did her beseeme. And ever, as the crew
About her daunst, sweet flowres, that far did smell,
And fragrant odours they uppon her threw;
But most of all, those three did her with gifts endew.

> Those were the Graces, daughters of delight,
> Handmaides of Venus, which are wont to haunt
> Uppon this hill, and daunce there day and night:
> Those three to men all gifts of grace do graunt,
> And all that Venus in her selfe doth vaunt
> Is borrowed of them. But that faire one,
> That in the midst was placed paravaunt,
> Was she to whom that shepheard pypt alone,
> That made him pipe so merrily, as never none.

> She was, to weete, that jolly shepheards lasse,
> Which piped there unto that merry rout;
> That jolly shepheard which there piped was
> Poore Colin Clout (who knowes not Colin Clout?)
> He pypt apace, whilest they him daunst about.
> Pype, jolly shepheard, pype thou now apace
> Unto thy love, that made thee low to lout;
> Thy love is present there with thee in place,
> Thy love is there advaunst to be another Grace.

Colin reveals the symbolism of those three dancing Graces to the courteous knight in a stanza that is the very essence of this pathetic protest against the main theme of this book, malice, a protest that leads him into these wayward episodes.

> Therefore they alwaies smoothly seeme to smile,
> That we like wise should mylde and gentle be,
> And also naked are, that without guile
> Or false dissemblaunce all them plaine may see,
> Simple and true, from covert malice free:
> And eeke them selves so in their daunce they bore,
> That two of them still froward seem'd to bee,
> But one still towards shew'd her selfe afore;
> That good should from us goe, then come, in greater store.

Thus this delicate passage, this happy pastoral, proves to be like a haunting secondary or contrasting theme in some vast, sombre movement of a symphony, a contrasting theme which by itself is perfection and absolute purity, but which seduces us from the greater significance of the whole by transporting us for too long a period of delightful and innocent somnolence from the fundamental mood of fierce denunciation.

But in another moment the tale takes a tragic turn that leads the poet and his hero back into the stern and sordid reality that

is overweighting the great ideal epic.	There proves to be no
ultimate escape in the gentle poetry of defeat, in sweet forget-
fulness, however lovely and innocent.	Pastorella is torn away
by robbers and in their quarrels over her old Meliboe is slain.
The hero comes to the rescue and leads her to the castle ,of an
aged knight and lady who prove to be her father and mother.
But in these last bitter hours Sir Calidore has remembered the
Blatant Beast.	Short is the time for plighting troth.	The hero
must hasten away to complete his quest.

And this book, like the fifth book, ends with a note of bitter-
ness, with a sense of futility greater than ever before.	The
course of Book Six is as though we had been ascending a great
mountain around many long and warm-colored slopes and val-
leys full of brooding sunlight and dotted with many fragrant
groves and clear streams alluring us to stay forever; then, of a
sudden, emerging from some caressing shelter around a graceful
shoulder of slope, we totter at the very edge of a gorge beyond
which we see above us, bare, stark, and terribly near, the gaunt
and awful peak which stands before us like a silent curse.
Spenser grows most bitter as he describes the ravages of the
monster, a squalid trail by which Sir Calidore hounds him.

> Through all estates he found that he had past,
> In which he many massacres had left,
> And to the clergy now was come at last;
> In which such spoile, such havocke, and such theft
> He wrought, that thence all goodnesse he bereft,
> That endlesse were to tell.	The Elfin knight,
> Who now no place besides unsought had left,
> At length into a monastere did light,
> Where he him found despoyling all with maine and might.

> Into their cloysters now he broken had,
> Through which the monckes he chaced here and there,
> And them pursu'd into their dortours sad,
> And searched all their cels and secrets neare;
> In which what filth and ordure did appeare
> Were yrkesome to report; yet that foule beast,
> Nought sparing them, the more did tosse and teare,
> And ransacke all their dennes from most to least,
> Regarding nought religion, nor their holy heast.

From thence into the sacred church he broke,
And robd the chancell, and the desks downe threw,
And altars fouled, and blasphemy spoke,
And th' images, for all their goodly hew,
Did cast to ground, whilest none was to rew;
So all confounded and disordered there.
But seeing Calidore, away he flew,
Knowing his fatall hand by former feare;
But he him fast pursuing, soone approached neare.

Him in a narrow place he overtooke,
And fierce assailing forst him turn againe:
Sternely he turnd againe, when he him strooke
With his sharpe steele, and ran at him amaine
With open mouth, that seemed to containe
A full good pecke within the utmost brim,
All set with yron teeth in raunges twaine,
That terrifide his foes, and armed him,
Appearing like the mouth of Orcus griesy grim.

And therein were a thousand tongs empight,
Of sundry kindes, and sundry quality;
Some were of dogs, that barked day and night,
And some of cats, that wrawling still did cry,
And some of beares, that groynd continually,
And some of tygres, that did seem to gren
And snar at all that ever passed by:
But most of them were tongues of mortall men,
Which spake reprochfully, not caring where nor when.

And them amongst were mingled here and there
The tongues of serpents with three forked stings,
That spat out poyson and gore bloudy gere
At all that came within his ravenings,
And spake licentious words and hatefull things
Of good and bad alike, of low and hie;
Ne kesars spared he a whit, nor kings,
But either blotted them with infamie,
Of bit them with his banefull teeth of injury.

Sir Calidore captures Slander, but the monster soon escapes and, so the unhappy poet tells us, is still spreading his poison and disrupting all noble institutions. Who could dream of completing a great epic of prophecy with the Blatant Beast abroad and so venomous? No other book closes so uncompromisingly on the note of arid futility. As we have seen, the first two books

recount the complete success of the Red Cross Knight and of
Sir Guyon. The original conclusion of Book Three narrated
not only Britomart's brilliant if somewhat detached exploit, but
the reunion of Amoret and Sir Scudamour. But when it was
reissued with the last three books in the period of disillusion
those stanzas of triumph were struck out not only to weave the
strands of the romance of Amoret far into the confused tapestry
of the other glimmering episodes but, we may well believe,
because of the poet's growing feeling that his dreams were fail-
ing to come true in the life of the court and the life of his nation.
Book Four closes with the happy but inconsequential conclusion
of the adventures of the shadowy and almost insignificant Flori-
mell and the son of Cymodoce. Book Five ends with the success
of Artegall but also with the bitter detraction which the irony
of life and the ingratitude of even high-minded sovereigns willed
as his guerdon. Book Six ends with stark futility.

> Thus was this monster, by the maystring might
> Of doughty Calidore, supprest and tamed,
> That never more he mote endammadge wight
> With his vile tongue, which many had defamed,
> And many causelesse caused to be blamed:
> So did he eeke long after this remaine,
> Untill that, whether wicked fate so framed,
> Or fault of men, he broke his yron chaine,
> And got into the world at liberty againe.
>
> Thenceforth more mischiefe and more scath he wrought
> To mortall men, then he had done before;
> Ne ever could, by any, more be brought
> Into like bands, ne maystred any more:
> Albe that long time after Calidore,
> The good Sir Pelleas him tooke in hand,
> And after him Sir Lamoracke of yore,
> And all his brethren borne in Britaine land;
> Yet none of them could ever bring him into band.
>
> So now he raungeth through the world againe,
> And rageth sore in each degree and state;
> Ne any is, that may him now restraine,
> He growen is so great and strong of late,

Barking and biting all that him doe bate,
Albe they worthy blame, or clear of crime:
Ne spareth he most learned wits to rate,
Ne spareth he the gentle poets rime,
But rends without regard of person or of time.

Ne may this homely verse, of many meanest,
Hope to escape his venemous despite,
More then my former writs, all were they cleanest
From blamefull blot, and free from all that wite,
With which some wicked tongues did it backebite,
And bring into a mighty peres displeasure,
That never so deserved to endite,
Therefore do you, my rimes, keep better measure,
And seeke to please, that now is counted wisemen's threasure.

The last stanza undoubtedly refers to "Mother Hubberds Tale" and to the daring admonitions to queen and lords and nation in *The Faërie Queene* itself. The last two lines hiss with the dry sneer of despair. Hereafter, my muse, says Spenser in effect, let us write nothing but pretty versicles intended to give pleasure by their empty gaudiness and their flattery. Essay no more epics to beacon the future. The age desires not nectar but treacle. These last stanzas quoted, a veritable cry of distress, are the last stanzas of the last completed book of *The Faërie Queene*. We are to get later a glimpse of Spenser, serene with the serenity that comes only after such a bitter disillusioning as this if one can but at last rise above it victorious, on the summit. But in this last book the great stream of *The Faërie Queene* recoils like a river that has long flowed majestic through wonderful tropical forests towards a sea which grows ever more and more harshly near and defiant and which hurls the river back at its mouth with acrid and roaring breakers. Here, after flashes of bitterness growing more and more frequent but relieved by the most exquisite utopian and pastoral moods he ever felt, Spenser's passionate indignation at last flares forth like a conflagration. Here the poet stands for the moment pale, intense, sorrowful over his splendid but futile hopes and ideals like a knight bestriding on a battlefield a dead comrade still radiant in his blazing armor.

CHAPTER VI

SPENSER'S SWAN-SONGS

It is generally an ascent beyond the reach of all but the loftiest dreamers who read poetry to toil upward with the most august singers to those soaring peaks where in their last utterances they walk still restlessly but within all-hail of peace among the stars. Yet I stoutly believe that the humblest reader, if he will but woo the muses long in thoughtful perusal and severe vigil can slowly develop that strenuous devotion to song which will give him from those supreme poets' very lips the ultimate revelation. Some of the greatest poets have indeed taken pride, half austere, half grimly humorous, in their unfathomable heights and depths. Yet when Dante says

> Ye that have set out in a little skiff . . .
> Turn back, to see once more your native land,
> Venture not out to open sea; lest haply,
> Unable to follow me, ye might get lost,

it should be but a challenge to even the lowliest reader with any iron in him and it should be a challenge to the critic to be an eloquent guide to all readers as Virgil was to Dante himself.[1]

---

[1] The translation from Dante is by Professor Jefferson B. Fletcher, "A Study in Renaissance Mysticism: Spenser's 'Fowre Hymnes,'" *Publ. Mod. Lang. Assoc.*, XXVI (1911), 3. This and the same author's *The Religion of Beauty in Woman*, especially the chapter on "Benivieni's Ode of Love and Spenser's 'Fowre Hymnes'" are by all odds the most learned and suggestive articles yet published on Spenser's Platonic hymns. Miss Lilian Winstanley's edition of *The Fowre Hymnes* (Cambridge, England, 1907) contributes most valuable information in the introduction and notes especially in the way of citing practically all the important parallel passages in Plato, Ficino, and Bruno. Her main points are succinctly and lucidly summarized by Professor Courthope, *Cambridge History of English Literature*, III, chap. 12, "Spenser." The most elaborate treatise is by Dr. John Smith Harrison, *Platonism in English Poetry* (N. Y., 1903), a pioneer work by no means rendered negligible by the later essays already cited. See *passim* but especially the chapters on the "Theory of Love" and "God and the Soul." Professor Frederick Morgan Padelford, in "Spenser and the Theology of Calvin," *Modern Philology* (May, 1914), pp. 1–18, and in "Spenser's Fowre Hymnes," *Jour. Eng.*

Of one of the most noble and magnificent passages in Spen-
ser's Platonic hymns Taine wrote: "We touch here the sublime
sharp summit where the world of mind and the world of sense
unite; where man, gathering with both hands the loveliest
flowers of either, feels himself at the same time a pagan and a
Christian." Such was the mood of Spenser in the little volume
of *Fowre Hymnes* which appeared in 1596. As we stand with
Spenser on the summit we may consider also his gracious song,
the *Prothalamion*, published in the same year, and his marvel-
lous fragment on "Mutabilitie," written, it must have been, last
of all, and published for the first time in 1609, ten years after
his death, with the first folio edition of *The Faërie Queene* as
appearing "for forme and matter...to be parcell of some
following booke" of the immense, unfinished epic.

But we left Spenser writing the last lines of the sixth book
in passionate despair. When he was writing most of the poetry
we are about to consider he must have been oppressed not only
with the sordid reality of the court but with the savagery of
Ireland which was to blast him with such horrors as must have
done much to crack a mighty and a gentle heart, not merely
because of personal injuries, but equally because of the debacle
of his political ideals. We cannot grant much plausibility to
later stories of his starvation or even of his bereavement. But
let us open Landor and see through his delicate and stately
style the poet in his hour of deepest agony.

Essex. Instantly on hearing of thy arrival from Ireland, I sent a
message to thee, good Edmund, that I might learn, from one so judicious
and dispassionate as thou art, the real state of things in that distracted

---

Ger. Phil, XIII (1914), 418–433, calls attention to some very plausible re-
semblances between the last two *Hymnes* and the *Institutes of the Christian
Religion* and emphasizes in general an important current of thought in
Spenser. Nor should the reader fail to examine a long and very interesting
footnote, *Shelburne Essays,* by Mr. Paul Elmer More, ser. 6, "Plato,"
pp. 337 sq., which compares pagan and Christian virtues in "a scholastic
table" pointing out how easy it was for Platonism and Christianity "to
melt together into a religion which possessed something of the free idealism
of the former and the personal enthusiasm of the latter," a combination
"exquisitely fresh and lovely" that forms "the avowed theme of Spenser's
Hymne of Heavenly Beautie."

country; it having pleased the Queen's Majesty to think of appointing me her deputy, in order to bring the rebellious to submission.

Spenser. Wisely and well considered; but more worthily of her judgment than her affection. May your lordship overcome, as you have ever done, the difficulties and dangers you foresee.

Essex. We grow weak by striking at random; and knowing that I must strike and strike heavily, I would fain see exactly where the stroke shall fall.

Now what tale have you for us?

Spenser. Interrogate me, my lord, that I may answer each question distinctly, my mind being in sad confusion at what I have seen and undergone.

Essex. Give me thy account and opinion of these very affairs as thou leftest them; for I would rather know one part well than all imperfectly; and the violences of which I have heard within the day surpass belief.

Why weepest thou, gentle Spenser? Have the rebels sacked thy house?

Spenser. They have plundered and utterly destroyed it.

Essex. I grieve for thee, and will see thee righted.

Spenser. In this they have little harmed me.

Essex. How! I have heard it reported that thy grounds are fertile, and thy mansion large and pleasant.

Spenser. If river and lake and meadow-ground could render any place the abode of pleasantness, pleasant was mine, indeed!

On the lovely banks of Mulla I found deep contentment. Under the dark alders did I muse and meditate. Innocent hopes were my gravest cares, and my playfullest fancy was with kindly wishes. Ah! surely of all cruelties the worst is to extinguish our kindness. Mine is gone: I love the people and the land no longer. My lord, ask me not about them: I may speak injuriously.

Essex. Think, rather, then, of thy happier hours and busier occupations; these likewise may instruct me.

Spenser. The first seeds I sowed in the garden, ere the old castle was made habitable for my lovely bride, were acorns from Penshurst. I planted a little oak before my mansion at the birth of each child. My sons, I said to myself, shall often play in the shade of them when I am gone; and every year shall they take the measure of their growth, as fondly as I take theirs.

Essex. Well, well; but let not this thought make thee weep so bitterly.

Spenser. Poison may ooze from beautiful plants; deadly grief from dearest reminiscences. I *must* grieve, I *must* weep; it seems the law of God, and the only one that men are not disposed to contravene. In the performance of this alone do they effectually aid one another.

Essex. Spenser! I wish I had at hand any arguments or persuasions of force sufficient to remove thy sorrow; but really I am not in the habit of seeing men grieve at anything except the loss of favour at court, or of a hawk, or of a buck-hound. And were I to swear out condolences to a man of thy discernment, in the same round, roll-call phrases we employ with one another upon these occasions, I should be guilty, not of insincerity, but of insolence. True grief hath ever something sacred in it; and, when it visiteth a wise man and a brave one, is most holy.

Nay, kiss not my hand: he whom God smiteth hath God with him. In his presence what am I?

Spenser. Never so great, my lord, as at this hour, when you see aright who is greater. May He guide your counsels, and preserve your life and glory!

Essex. Where are thy friends? Are they with thee?

Spenser. Ah where, indeed! Generous, true-hearted Philip! where art thou, whose presence was unto me peace and safety; whose smile was contentment, and whose praise renown? My lord! I cannot but think of him among still heavier losses: he was my earliest friend, and would have taught me wisdom.

Essex. Pastoral poetry, my dear Spenser, doth not require tears and lamentations. Dry thine eyes; rebuild thine house: the Queen and Council, I venture to promise thee, will make ample amends for every evil thou hast sustained. What! does that enforce thee to wail still louder?

Spenser. Pardon me, bear with me, most noble heart! I have lost what no Council, no Queen, no Essex, can restore.

Essex. We will see that. There are other swords, and other arms to yield them, beside a Leicester's and a Raleigh's. Others can crush their enemies, and serve their friends.

Spenser. O my sweet child! And of many so powerful, many so wise and so beneficent, was there none to save thee? None! none!

Essex. I now perceive that thou lamentest what almost every father is destined to lament. Happiness must be bought, although the payment may be delayed. Consider: the same calamity might have befallen thee here in London. Neither the houses of ambassadors, nor the palaces of kings, nor the altars of God himself, are asylums against death. How do I know but under this very roof there may sleep some latent calamity, that in an instant shall cover with gloom every inmate of the house, and every far dependent?

Spenser. God avert it!

Essex. Every day, every hour of the year, do hundreds mourn what thou mournest.

Spenser. Oh, no, no, no! Calamities there are around us; calamities there are all over the earth; calamities there are in all seasons: but none in any season, none in any place, like mine.

Essex. So say all fathers, so say all husbands. Look at any old mansion-house, and let the sun shine as gloriously as it may on the golden vanes, or the arms recently quartered over the gateway or the embayed window, and on the happy pair that haply is toying at it: nevertheless, thou mayest say that of a certainty the same fabric hath seen much sorrow within its chambers, and heard many wailings; and each time this was the heaviest stroke of all. Funerals have passed along through the stout-hearted knights upon the wainscot, and amid the laughing nymphs upon the arras. Old servants have shaken their heads, as if somebody had deceived them, when they found that beauty and nobility could perish.

Edmund! the things that are too true pass by us as if they were not true at all; and when they have singled us out, then only do they strike us. Thou and I must go too. Perhaps the next year may blow us away with its fallen leaves.

Spenser. For you, my lord, many years (I trust) are waiting: I never shall see those fallen leaves. No leaf, no bud, will spring upon the earth before I sink into her breast for ever.

Essex. Thou who art wiser than most men, shouldst bear with patience, equanimity, and courage what is common to all.

Spenser. Enough, enough, enough! Have all men seen their infant burnt to ashes before their eyes?

Essex. Gracious God! Merciful Father! what is this?

Spenser. Burnt alive! burnt to ashes! burnt to ashes! The flames dart their serpent tongues through the nursery-window. I cannot quit thee, my Elizabeth! I cannot lay down our Edmund! Oh these flames! They persecute, they enthrall me; they curl round my temples; they hiss upon my brain; they taunt me with their fierce, foul voices; they carp at me, they wither me, they consume me, throwing back to me a little of life to roll and suffer in, with their fangs upon me. Ask me, my lord, the things you wish to know from me: I may answer them; I am now composed again. Command me, my gracious lord! I would yet serve you: soon I shall be unable. You have stooped to raise me up; you have borne with me; you have pitied me, even like one not powerful. You have brought comfort, and will leave it with me, for gratitude is comfort.

Oh! my memory stands all a tip-toe on one burning point: when it drops from it, then it perishes. Spare me: ask me nothing; let me weep before you in peace,—the kindest act of greatness.

Essex. I should rather have dared to mount into the midst of the conflagration than I now dare entreat thee not to weep. The tears that overflow thy heart, my Spenser, will staunch and heal it in their sacred stream; but not without hope in God.

Spenser. My hope in God is that I may soon see again what he has taken from me. Amid the myriads of angels, there is not one so beautiful; and even he (if there be any) who is appointed my guardian could never love me so. Ah! these are idle thoughts, vain wanderings, distempered dreams. If there ever were guardian angels, he who so wanted one—my helpless boy—would not have left these arms upon my knees.

Essex. God help and sustain thee, too gentle Spenser! I never will desert thee. But what am I? Great they have called me! Alas, how powerless then and infantile is greatness in the presence of calamity!

Come, give me thy hand: let us walk up and down the gallery. Bravely done! I will envy no more a Sidney or a Raleigh.

Exaggerated stories of Spenser's calamities swarmed among his countrymen grown acrid with the bitterness of the following generation. Sir John Ware's tale of certain last books of *The Faërie Queene,* lost "by the disorder and abuse" of Spenser's servant, and Phineas Fletcher's lament over his master's poverty sound sufficiently absurd. Ben Jonson's assertion that one of Spenser's children perished in the flames remains unsubstantiated but plausible. At all events Landor's dialogue, though it depends largely on the most tragic of these legends for its climax, is essentially true in its portrayal of the sorrow-stricken poet to whom Lord Grey Wilton's failure and the failure of the court to grow utopian were of themselves sources of the most poignant grief. The facts in Landor's dialogue are the least of the matter. With his restraint marmoreal yet rose-ensanguined with tenderness, Landor sounds the true overtones of this tragic occurrence, the sorrowful strength of the Don Quixote of English poets, the mastery of himself. Only, remember that the earl's "too gentle Spenser" is at best but a half-truth; it was Spenser, gentle and mighty. For neither Landor nor any other writer has emphasized with sufficient point Spenser's final ascent to a summit which, if the quietude due his years and his achievements in deeds and song had been granted him, would have been to him and to the entranced world an ineffable Prospero-mood. Even as it is, though the notes are few, they are strangely clear with that almost supernatural clearness that sounds like a voice beyond the world and beyond the restless seas of space.

On the first of September, 1596, only two years and one month before his flight from Ireland and less than three years before his death, Spenser wrote a sensitive and courtly epistle dedicatory for his *Hymnes* to "the right honorable and most vertuous Ladies, the Ladie Margaret Countess of Cumberland, and the Ladie Marie Countess of Warwicke." The first two hymns were written, he tells us, "in the greener times of my youth," probably in the days when as a shepherd poet he wooed Rosalind. Many critics have expressed their puzzlement over the poet's stern condemnation of these earlier hymns which, he says, "too much pleased those of like age and disposition, which, being too vehemently caried with that kind of affection, do rather sucke out poyson to their strong passion, then hony to their honest delight." The poet, unable to recall completely these amorous lyrics, put them forth with two new poems, "An Hymne of Heavenly Love" and "An Hymne of Heavenly Beautie" in the first of which he writes:

> Many lewd layes (ah, woe is me the more!)
> In praise of that mad fit which fooles call love,
> I have in th' heat of youth made heretofore,
> That in light wits did loose affection move.
> But all those follies now I do reprove,
> And turned have the tenor of my string,
> The heavenly prayses of true love to sing.

"Lewd"? Assuredly not in our modern sense. We may agree with Lowell that Spenser had ever "a purity like that of thrice-bolted snow" though "with none of its coldness." Was Spenser then, as so many think, recoiling with a Bunyan-like repentance? I cannot think so if Bunyan-like repentance implies, as it generally does, the remorse of a large soul for venial sins. No, I believe that in the judgment of the supreme court of the muses Spenser had sinned most grievously against that high seriousness with which he, in common with a very few poets, had been specially entrusted. It is extremely probable that the first two hymns, as we have them, are retouched with the purer severer gold of a Fra Angelico background. They are certainly noble in tone. Yet, in a few places uncensored, in common with certain lovelorn laments which we found to be the least distinctive passages in *The Shepheards Calender*, in common with the second, the querulous mood in the *Amoretti* when Spenser lapsed into his most marked imitations of the cuckoo Desportes, these first hymns retain brief passages hectic with the same morbid fever, a mood human enough but one which certainly no poet of Spenser's stately equipoise could in his highest moments quite tolerate. And as he rose, despite the torment of his own troublous affairs, despite the savage mutterings of the "wild kerns and gallowglasses" of Ireland, despite the shattering of his impatient utopian dreams for England, to the summit where we now find him, what else was there for him but a noble and fiery intolerance of the morbid and narrowly selfish melancholy of his youthful love-making? He was now to turn with that sublimated selfishness with which, like men as different as St. John and Dante and Shakespeare and Milton in their last years, he was to inspire the most audacious of questing-spirits with the greatest of intellectual adventures. Having fought his good fight on earth he was gone, impetuously before death took him, on the adventure of God-seeking.

The youthful hymns which he probably revised as more earthy preludes to his God-seeking, though still tinged with the old febrile mood, must have been, too, from the first, noble with that love which he sought in Plato more ardently than any other English poet except Shelley. Spenser would certainly have revoiced, at any period of his life, the old saying: "If Jove should descend to the earth he would speak in the style of Plato." And from many dwellers in Plato's academe throughout the thought-heavy centuries, from the Neo-Platonists, from some of the Church fathers in the Dark Ages, from Dante and his circle, and from the Renaissance mystics he learned directly or indirectly the passion for fusing Platonism and Christianity into that "combination exquisitely fresh and lovely" which should appeal alike to believer and unbeliever. For we should feel as these Platonists themselves are urged by Walter Pater to have felt: "The essence of humanism is that belief...that nothing which has ever interested living men and women can wholly lose its vitality—no language they have spoken, nor oracle beside which they have hushed their voices, no dream which has once been entertained by actual human minds, nothing about which they have ever been passionate, or expended time and zeal." And those Platonists whom Pater had particularly in mind when he wrote that beautiful sentence were as much to Spenser as Plato himself—Bruno and Ficino, Benevieni, and

Pico della Mirandola, the last perhaps the most picturesque of all, a youth whose whole pure life-passion remains only dimly in his commentary on Benevieni's hymn, but a youth whose quaint biography and Pater's essay have kept flower-fresh for us, "of feature and shape seemly and beauteous, of stature goodly and high, of flesh tender and soft, his colour white, intermingled with comely reds, his eyes grey, and quick of look, his teeth white and even, his hair yellow and abundant," so that when he came on his ardent pilgrimage to Ficino the older mystic "seems to have thought there was something not wholly earthly about him." We can easily visualize the young Spenser passing readily, even in youth, from his earthly love to contemplate the arcane powers and we may quote Lowell's words on the earlier hymns without essential qualification:

Nowhere does his genius soar and sing with such continuous aspiration, nowhere is his phrase so decorously stately, though rising to an enthusiasm which reaches intensity while it stops short of vehemence, as in his Hymns to Love and Beauty, especially the latter. There is an exulting spurn of the earth in it, as of a soul just loosed from its cage. I shall make no extracts from it, for it is one of those intimately coherent and transcendentally logical poems that "moveth altogether if it move at all," the breaking off a fragment from which would maim it as it would a perfect group of crystals.

Yet despite Lowell's warning I must attempt by analysis and quotation to give a glimpse of these poems too little read. "The Hymne in Honour of Love" begins with the censored minor key.

> Love, that long since hast to thy mighty powre
> Perforce subdude my poore captived hart,
> And raging now therin with restlesse stowre,
> Doest tyrannize in everie weaker part;
> Faine would I seeke to ease my bitter smart
> By any service I might do to thee,
> Or ought that else might to thee pleasing bee.

He passes quickly through this less felicitous, plaintive note to that mood of sensuous innocence which is always so winning but which is still of the earth earthy.

Come then, O come, thou mightie God of Love,
Out of thy silver bowres and secret blisse,
Where thou doest sit in Venus lap above,
Bathing thy wings in her ambrosiall kisse,
That sweeter farre then any nectar is;
Come softly, and my feeble breast inspire
With gentle furie, kindled of thy fire.

But in a moment the poet is dreaming on philosophical heights over that speech of Socrates in the *Symposium* which describes the mysterious origins of Love begotten of Plenty and Penury. Spenser remembers also that Phaedrus called Love the eldest of the gods, while Agathon made him the youngest and the poet strives, with Ficino, to reconcile the two ideas since everything in Plato must be gospel. Nowadays, for those purblind people who think that they have outgrown myth-making, it is difficult to realize how important this problem was. Ficino and Spenser solved it by identifying the gods of Greece with the angels. The Creator gave life to these radiant cohorts with a love that was the most ancient of primal forces and gods; but when the angelic Love flowed back to the supreme Maker the new force was the youngest of divine beings. Spenser's bare intellectual contribution to these doctrines is sometimes ingenious but almost always slight. But his imaginative contribution is always fervid and as we watch him ascend the great Platonic stairway which leads, according to Benevieni, in six great stages of increasing and dazzling exaltation to the Sabbath vision, we feel that the ecstasy of the English poet was emotionally at a higher stage than that of any Platonist since Dante had learned the same divine wisdom from ·Beatrice in Paradise.

With Socrates, Spenser watches Love the great first Cause, move men, in their turn, to beget children for the sake of immortality. Spenser is characteristically more severe than Socrates (who grants the same motive-power to animals) in saying that animals are moved merely by lust. But man, with still a bit of heaven in him,

> ... Is enlumind with that goodly light,
> Unto like goodly semblant to aspyre:
> Therefore in choice of love, he doth desyre
> That seemes on earth most heavenly, to embrace;
> That same is Beautie, borne of heavenly race.
>
> For sure, of all that in this mortall frame
> Contained is, nought more divine doth seeme,
> Or that resembleth more th' immortall flame
> Of heavenly light, then Beauties glorious beame.
> What wonder then, if with such rage extreme
> Fraile men, whose eyes seek heavenly things to see,
> At sight thereof so much enravisht bee?

For a moment the thought of Beauty, whom the poet has not yet seen in mystical purity, allures him once more into his old wilful complaints and conjures up not the Eros whom Plato saw, but the mischievous Anacreontic Cupid, rejoicing in vain pranks with man as soon as he sees him in quest of Beauty.

> Which well perceiving, that imperious boy
> Doth therwith tip his sharp empoisned darts;
> Which, glancing through the eyes with countenance coy
> Rest not till they have pierst the trembling harts,
> And kindled flame in all their inner parts,
> Which suckes the blood, and drinketh up the lyfe
> Of carefull wretches with consuming griefe.

Here, indeed, we are at the heart of that unworthy mood that Spenser, remembering the supreme courts of the muses and their special gift to him of high-seriousness, would fain have altogether erased but was forced to send forth, chastened a little perhaps, and accompanied by the last two soaring hymns with their pure white fire. Yet just here, for the moment, doubt has assailed the poet. Is Love a truly benignant force or is not Love a pitiless wanton god who laughs at the grief his caprices cause. Here is no forgotten conceit but a question that haunts every man as much today as ever. Our poet sets himself earnestly to understand this apparent injustice and soon sees that it is well. For, while ignoble love comes with every gust of whim, the highest Love cannot be invoked with a moment's

fancy. As with a rush of radiant wings there comes to the
singer that ἐνθουσιασμός which thrilled him first in the bright
trumpet-tones of "June."

> For love is Lord of truth and loialtie,
> Lifting himselfe out of the lowly dust
> On golden plumes up to the purest skie,
> Above the reach of loathly sinfull lust,
> Whose base affect, through cowardly distrust
> Of his weake wings, dare not to heaven fly,
> But like a moldwarpe in the earth doth ly.

Who but Spenser could scorn Lust with such exultation? In
Milton and Dante there is mingled a good deal of haughty bitter-
ness. In Spenser there is only joy in the superb condemnation
of Lust, a creature so crawling, so unreal!

> His dunghill thoughts, which do themselves inure
> To dirtie drosse, no higher dare aspyre,
> Ne can his feeble earthly eyes endure
> The flaming light of that celestial fyre,
> Which kindleth love in generous desyre,
> And makes him mount above the native might
> Of heavie earth, up to the heavens hight.

Such is the impetuosity of true passion that it refashions the
mind more near the holy heart's desire.

> Such is the powre of that sweet passion,
> That it all sordid basenesse doth expell,
> And the refyned mynd doth newly fashion
> Unto a fairer forme, which now doth dwell
> In his high thought, that would it selfe excell;
> Which he beholding still with constant sight,
> Admires the mirrour of so heavenly light.

Love, as in the *Symposium*, is as a clarion that calls to heroic
questing the ardent lover; it has its pragmatic criterion, what-
ever its ultimate meaning may prove to be.

> Then forth he casts in his unquiet thought,
> What he may do, her favour to obtaine;
> What brave exploit, what perill hardly wrought
> What puissant conquest, what adventurous paine,
> May please her best, and grace unto him gaine:

He dreads no danger, nor misfortune feares;
His faith, his fortune, in his breast he beares.
Thou art his god, thou art his mightie guyde,
Thou, being blind, letst him not see his feares,
But cariest him to that which he hath eyde,
Through seas, through flames, through thousand swords and
    speares:
Ne ought so strong that may his force withstand,
With which thou armest his resistlesse hand.

But, alas, even love victorious is intolerant of a rival and
man grows bitter with jealous fears.   The poet evidently recalls
his own sad vigils with such fervor that even in the severer days
of mature revision he has not quite cared to banish the phantom
Rosalind.   Nevertheless the monster Jealousy is but the storm
before the sun.   And the poet turns presently to a lovely vision
of happy lovers in Elysium, a vision once more in that mood of
innocent sensuousness which, though less severe than the mood
of the last two hymns, could hardly have caused him the repen-
tance that surely grew solely out of the occasional tone of morbid
complaint.   In other words, as any philosophic student of Plato
could testify, Spenser had no categorical imperative to repent
or refrain from sensuousness, but it was his duty to reject·
subjectivism.

There thou them placest in a paradize
Of all delight and joyous happie rest,
Where they doe feede on nectar heavenly wize,
With Hercules and Hebe, and the rest   .
Of Venus dearlings, through her bountie blest,
And lie like gods in yvorie beds arayd,
With rose and lillies over them displayd.

There with thy daughter Pleasure they doe play
Their hurtlesse sports, without rebuke or blame,
And in her snowy bosome boldly lay
Their quiet heads, devoyd of guilty shame,
After full joyance of their gentle game;
Then her they crowne their goddesse and their queene,
And decke with floures thy altars well beseene.

The "Hymne in Honour of Beautie" is still full of the low
·sun that makes the color; but it is the low sun of dawn upleap-

ing not the low sun of evening. This is by all odds the most beautiful, stylistically, of the *Fowre Hymnes.* After a brief invocation to Aphrodite, mother of Love and queen of Beauty, whom he implores both to help him praise herself and to win his lady so that

> It may so please, that she at length will streame
> Some deaw of grace into my withered hart,
> After long sorrow and consuming smart,

the poet plunges into speculations philosophical and harmonizes Ficino's notion that beauty is the "lively grace" of God's light with the brilliant theory of Plato in the *Timaeus* that beauty is a great unchangeable pattern from which the supreme Artificer modeled the world. This beauty, beyond the reach of the dread goddess Mutabilitie of whom Spenser was going to sing with such awed splendor, is infused into those lovely changing things of earth that make us happy and sad.

> What time this worlds great workmaister did cast
> To make al things such as we now behold,
> It seemes that he before his eyes had plast
> A goodly paterne, to whose perfect mould
> He fashioned them as comely as he could,
> That now so faire and seemely they apeare,
> As nought may be amended any wheare.
> . . . .
> Thereof as every earthly thing partakes
> Or more or lesse, by influence divine,
> So it more faire accordingly it makes,
> And the grosse matter of this earthly myne,
> Which clotheth it, thereafter doth refyne,
> Doing away the drosse which dims the light
> Of that faire beame which therein is empight.
>
> For through infusion of celestial powre
> The duller earth it quickneth with delight,
> And life-full spirits privily doth powre
> Through all the parts, that to the lookers sight
> They seeme to please. That is thy soveraine might,
> O Cyprian queene, which flowing from the beame
> Of thy bright starre, thou into them doest streame.

Against any conception of the mere physiological externality of beauty the poet urges with alluring persuasiveness the sub-tleties of Bruno and Ficino.

> How vainely then doe ydle wits invent
> That Beautie is nought else but mixture made
> Of colours faire, and goodly temp'rament
> Of pure complexions, that shal quickly fade
> And passe away, like to a sommers shade;
> Or that it is but comely composition
> Or parts well measurd, with meet disposition!

Could mere red and white have the mighty influence we find in beauty?

> Why doe not then the blossomes of the field,
> Which are arayd with much more orient hew,
> And to the sense most daintie odours yield,
> Worke like impression in the lookers vew?
> Or why doe not faire pictures like powre shew,
> In which oft-times we Nature see of Art
> Exceld, in perfect limning every part?

But when all outward semblances have changed and decayed there yet lives Beauty, the soul, the source.

> For that same goodly hew of white and red,
> With which the cheekes are sprinckled, shal decay,
> And those sweete rosy leaves, so fairely spred
> Upon the lips, shall fade and fall away
> To that they were, even to corrupted clay.
> That golden wyre, those sparckling stars so bright
> Shall turne to dust, and loose their goodly light.
>
> But that faire lampe, from whose celestiall ray
> That light proceedes which kindleth lovers fire,
> Shall never be extinguisht nor decay;
> But, when the vitall spirits doe expyre,
> Unto her native planet shall retyre;
> For it is heavenly borne and can not die,
> Being a parcell of the purest skie.

Like Benevieni, Spenser describes the passing of the soul down to earth. Prometheus-like it passes with some of the divine fire of the sun, a power which can wonderfully transform the corporeal frame which the soul assumes.

> Thereof it comes that these faire soules, which have
> The most resemblance of that heavenly light,
> Frame to themselves most beautifull and brave
> Their fleshly bowre, most fit for their delight,
> And the grosse matter by a soveraine might
> Tempers so trim, that it may well be seene
> A pallace fit for such a virgin queene.

Ah, but wherein did the Potter's hand shake? Why is it
that some unmistakably beautiful souls dwell immured in a
deformed corporeal tabernacle? What gentle poet would not
sorrow over this? It is because the soul found perchance sub-
stance too lawless and stubborn for its beauty, for all its divinity.
And, more unhappily still, it often befalls that beauty, for all
its "celestiall hew," becomes the "bait of sinne."

> Yet nathemore is that faire Beauties blame,
> But theirs that do abuse it unto ill:
> Nothing so good, but that through guilty shame
> May be corrupt, and wrested unto will.
> Nathelesse the soule is faire and beauteous still,
> However fleshes fault it filthy make:
> For things immortall no corruption take.
>
> But ye, faire dames, the worlds deare ornaments,
> And lively images of heavens light,
> Let not your beames with such disparagements
> Be dimd, and your bright glorie darkned quight,
> But mindfull still of your first countries sight,
> Doe still preserve your first informed grace,
> Whose shadow yet shynes in your beauteous face.
>
> Loath that foule blot, that hellish fierbrand,
> Disloiall lust, faire Beauties foulest blame,
> That base affections, which your eares would bland,
> Commend to you by loves abused name;
> But is indeede the bondslave of defame;
> Which will the garland of your glorie marre,
> And quench the light of your bright shyning starre.

These ardent lines flame up directly, perhaps, from the crabbed
commentary of Pico della Mirandola and ultimately, no doubt,
from the speech of Pausanias in the *Symposium*. There follows
in Spenser a passage so perfect that it must speak entirely for

itself.   Like the modern psycho-analyst he sees that impulses
are not to be crushed but ''sublimated.''

> But gentle love, that loiall is and trew,
> Will more illumine your resplendent ray,
> And adde more brightnesse to your goodly hew,
> From light of his pure fire, which, by like way
> Kindled of yours, your likenesse doth display,
> Like as two mirrours, by opposd reflexion,
> Doe both expresse the faces first impression.
>
> Therefore, to make your beautie more appeare,
> It you behoves to love, and forth to lay
> That heavenly riches which in you ye beare,
> That men the more admyre their fountaine may;
> For else what booteth that celestiall ray,
> If it in darknesse be enshrined ever,
> That it of loving eyes be vewed never?
>
> But, in your choice of loves, this well advize,
> That likest to your selves ye them select,
> The which your forms first sourse may sympathize,
> And with like beauties parts be inly deckt:
> For if you loosely love without respect,
> It is no love, but a discordant warre,
> Whose unlike parts amongst themselves do jarre.
>
> For love is a celestiall harmonie
> Of likely harts composed of starres concent,[2]
> Which joyne together in sweete sympathie,
> To worke ech others joy and true content,
> Which they have harbourd since their first descent
> Out of their heavenly bowres, where they did see
> And know each other here belov'd to bee.
>
> Then wrong it were that any other twaine
> Should in loves gentle band combyned bee
> But those whom Heaven did at first ordaine,
> And made out of one mould the more t' agree:
> For all that like the beautie which they see
> Streight do not love: for love is not so light,
> As streight to burne at first beholders sight.

---

[2] ''According to Ficino, true lovers are those whose souls have departed
from heaven under the same astral influences and who, accordingly, are
informed with the same idea in imitation of which they frame their earthly
bodies.''—Harrison, p. 115.
See also Miss Winstanley, Introduction, iii.

Truly an answer at once sober and rapturous to Marlowe's fine audacity,

> Where both deliberate the love is slight:
> Whoever lov'd that lov'd not at first sight?

and Shakespeare's charmed echo in *As You Like It*. But Spenser's love here must inevitably transcend the sweetness of the breathing person.

The next stanza carries us into pure renaissance Platonism. In phrases somewhat similar to those in Benevieni's *Ode of Love* he tells us that the true lover beholds the person of the beloved only to evolve from the inspiration of her presence "a more refyned forme . . . voide of all blemishment," the "first perfection" that is to say, the pure Idea, free from the "fleshes frayle infection."

> And then conforming it unto the light,
> Which in it selfe it hath remaining still,
> Of that first sunne, yet sparckling in his sight,
> Thereof he fashions in his higher skill
> An heavenly beautie to his fancies will,
> And it embracing in his mind entyre,
> The mirrour of his owne thought doth admyre.

Thus the mind remembers, even though half-numbed by the flesh, the only half-forgotten beauty it once contemplated in heaven.

But if the reader is not yet ready to ascend up the great stairway of aspiration, in this mood of sublimated egoism, he will for a little while find a comrade in the poet whose eternal youth, even under the censorious eye of mature revision, will not allow him to pass yet beyond a luxurious cherishing of what all lovers may clearly see in their lady's fleshly countenance,

> In which how many wonders doe they reede
> To their conceipt, that others never see!
> Now of her smiles, with which their soules they feede,
> Like gods with nectar in their bankets free,
> Now of her lookes, which like to cordials bee;
> But when her words embassade forth she sends,
> Lord, how sweete musicke that unto them lends!

Sometimes upon her forhead they behold
A thousand graces masking in delight;
Sometimes within her eye-lids they unfold
Ten thousand sweet belgards, which to their sight
Doe seeme like twinckling starres in frostie night;
But on her lips, like rosy buds in May,
So many millions of chaste pleasures play.

And Spenser closes with an earth-warm prayer to Aphrodite, "fresh flowre of grace," to grant him a yielding mercy from his mistress.

One need not be a mere literary man, under suspicion of irresponsible hedonism, to feel some sense of regret as Spenser passes on to an uncompromising Platonic mysticism. One may admire Plato and yet feel quite soberly (with those philosophers of today who would help rather than hinder science to emancipate us) that the epistemological games of leisure-class Greek academicians have checked progress for centuries quite as definitely as they have aided it. Nobody has described the reactionary side of Plato's permanent influence better than Professor Horace M. Kallen.

> The heart of the idealistic movement of which he is the father lies in the hope of saving mankind from this terror of chaos and destruction. In it, hence, the eternities are again reasserted, only indeed in a supra-sensible heaven to which fallen man might philosophically aspire, and by whose aid he might escape the elusive world of flux. Despite appearances, the good, the beautiful, the real, the noble things which enriched human life must not be touched by death. The ideas must be eternal, comforting harbingers of life from the source of life, God, the Good, in seeking and contemplating whom the soul lives and moves and has its being. So the happy hunting grounds, Valhalla and Elysium, were refined and intellectualized, but human survival, as the myth of the Phaedrus shows, was still among such objects and activities as on earth were most certain and most delightful."[3]

Like Plato, Spenser was fain to escape from his chilly heaven of logical universals into an equally mythical happy hunting grounds (or happy loving grounds). But the ascetic side and

---

[3] "A Pragmatic Interpretation of the History of Philosophy," *The Mid-West Quarterly*, IV (October, 1916), 78.

the antinaturalism of Plato dominate in the last two hymns. Such a mood, for all its mystical ecstasies, is next-door neighbor to the restless and intrepid pessimism of Calvin, whose influence on the *Fowre Hymnes* has been so clearly traced by Professor Padelford. Such a kinship is still apparent even in academic American philosophy of to-day as Mr. George Santayana has shown in his brilliant account of "The Gentile Tradition." But because the logical implications of Platonic idealism and Calvanistic pessimism are so amazingly similar we must be wary of attempting too explicitly to sift and run down these influences in detail. Let us rather recur to them as little as possible, let us cease all censorship of Spenser as reactionary mystic, let us seek to understand him sympathetically, to appreciate the heroic self-conquest of these last works which, when compared with the last stanzas of the sixth book of *The Faërie Queene*, are assuredly more full of victory than of defeat.

In the "Hymne of Heavenly Love" the pilgrim soul seeks immediately its manumission from the bondage of earth.

> Love, lift me up upon thy golden wings,
> From this base world unto thy heavens hight,
> Where I may see those admirable things
> Which there thou workest by thy soveraine might,
> Farre above feeble reach of earthly sight,
> That I thereof an heavenly hymne may sing
> Unto the God of Love, high heavens king.[4]

As the poet pauses only long enough to spurn his own earlier "lewd lays" and quite forgets not only Rosalind but even his

---

[4] We must note again briefly a common heresy about these last two hymns, since, in this context, the reader ought to be in a position to see readily its utter sophistry. It is given typical expression in Miss Sheavyn's *The Literary Profession in the Elizabethan Age* (1909), 170–171, in which we are told that because "sober Englishmen" distrusted poetry, Spenser "acquiesced humbly in the judgment which condemned his beautiful and innocent poems on Love and Beauty, writing in atonement, though rather perfunctorily, two other hymns on Heavenly Love and Heavenly Beauty." Such a criticism is the too facile product of one, who approaching a subject from a special angle, fails utterly to see its logical implications and exposes herself to a suspicion of knowing far too little about the fervor of renaissance Platonism. It is likely that "sober Englishmen," before the Civil Wars gave such religious intensity to both Cavaliers and Puritans, would have found Spenser's mysticism far more dubious than his amorousness.

wedded Elizabeth in his eagerness for union with God, we must
not confuse his mood with the world-weariness or defeat that
we saw in his last bitter stanzas against the Blatant Beast at
the close of the sixth book of *The Faërie Queene.* The overtones
of holy and courageous calm sound. so majestically in his last
poems that, for all the evil that came upon him, his swan-songs
must have intoned the mood that was dominant to the end.
And so this desire for God was not the desire for an ivory tower
far from a hated life, but rather the natural impatience of a
mighty harmonist to hurry over the last years of the hampered
life and to project into eternity his fiery idealistic quest; not to
abjure poetic achievement, not to give up all hope of making a
Utopia of England, but to include these in a vastly expanded
hope seen at last from the infinite heights where there might be
something like peace through divine insight but assuredly no
grovelling rest. Let us follow then, unfalteringly, this hymn
which praises God with that richer, deeper music that was to
reach its large perfection in the sublime cantos on Mutabilitie.

> Before this worlds great frame, in which al things
> Are now containd, found any being place,
> Ere flitting Time could wag his eyas wings
> About that mightie bound, which doth embrace
> The rolling spheres, and parts their houres by space,
> That high eternall Powre, which now doth move
> In all these things, mov'd in it selfe by love.

Spenser's aristocratic fervor assumes here a fierce Calvin-
ism, strange but not irreconcilable concomitant for Platonism,
and promises for the Elect, the perfect lover, the gift of
Heavenly Love, the idea of Christ's "pure glorie," and the
gift of Heavenly Beauty, "the divine reality behind that Idea,
Christ's 'pure glorie' as it is in itself."[5] By a brave if odd
synthesis the humanists of the renaissance sought to reconcile
through Plotinus and other Neo-Platonists, as well as some of
the more sympathetic Church Fathers, the flower of Greek
thought and the doctrines of Christianity. The three ultimate

---

[5] Fletcher, *Fowre Hymnes,* p. 457; Harrison, pp. 167 sq.

Neo-Platonic principles—the Good, Intellect, and Soul were identified with the three Persons of the Trinity. To prepare us for this Spenser in his first religious hymn explains the creation entirely in terms of love. The Creating Power which first "mov'd in it selfe by love," loved its own beauty and begot of itself the Son.

> With him he raignd, before all time prescribed,
> In endlesse glorie and immortall might,
> Together with that third from them derived,
> Most wise, most holy, most almightie Spright,
> Whose kingdomes throne no thought of earthly wight
> Can comprehend, much lesse my trembling verse
> With equall words can hope it to reherse.

Plato's wonderful woman, Diotima, had taught the culminating wisdom about love as a desire of birth in beauty, and highest love as a desire of birth in the absolute beauty. To the Christian, God is love. How easy then for Spenser to identify God with the absolute beauty of Plato! Spenser goes on to tell how God, "pregnant still with powreful grace," created the bright Angels, "an infinite increase" to keep the "heavens illimitable hight."

But pride fired the most radiant Angel to marshall hosts in awful revolt. The Almighty swept them to Hell with His "consuming yre."

> But that Eternall Fount of Love and grace,
> Still flowing forth his goodnesse unto all,
> Now seeing left a waste and emptie place
> In his wyde pallace, through those angels fall,
> Cast to supply the same, and to enstall
> A new unknowen colony therein,
> Whose root from earths base groundworke shold begin.

Then man also, the new creation, sinned so grievously that he would have perished had not the Son of God offered to redeem him.

> In flesh at first the guilt committed was,
> Therefore in flesh it must be satifyde:
> Nor spirit, nor angell, though they man surpas,

> Could make amends to God for mans misguyde,
> But onely man himselfe, who selfe did slyde.
> So, taking flesh of sacred virgins wombe,
> For mans deare sake he did a man become.[6]

The poet is stirred to a medieval intensity by the "huge and most unspeakeable impression" of Christ "nayled on a gallow-tree." For this supreme sacrifice the Deliverer asked the simple reward of man's mercy and charity to man.

It is easy for the purblind to make this broken reasoning the subject of that wan, flickering mirth which is supposed by the second rate thinker to be the necessary concomitant of sound rationalism. There are those too who will gird at what they are wont to call the other-worldiness of this Christian hope which, they will feel, blasphemes man's sacred duty upon earth. Spenser does "renounce" all earthly love. He does say that earth's glory will seem dirt and dross after the purification. Yes, but the quest that men follow on earth which is greater even than the love which inspires it and the glory that applauds it, even that highest earthly glory, "that last infirmity of noble minds," this quest only renounces earthly love and earthly fame in order to make them parts of a larger vision. By themselves they may well appear as dross, warped visions which take the changing parts for the unchangeable whole which man at last, after severe purification, will comprehend. It should be possible, then, for Christian and Agnostic and metaphysician to feel the lure in that inward glance into the mind, the mirror of thought, which will reveal the vision of the man-Christ's pure glory, that is to say, God-Christ.

But we must seek paths more dizzy. It remains now to rise from that introspective contemplation of God-Christ to actual mystical possession. In the "Hymne of Heavenly Beautie" the poet, who has been at the foot of the stairway to eternity lifting his hands often in exalted adoration but often turning to look earthward, now begins to ascend with eager reverence.

---

[6] Professor Fletcher, "Fowre Hymnes," p. 455 n, calls attention to the "interestingly analogous argument in Dante, *Paradiso*, Book VII, ll. 85–120."

> Rapt with the rage of mine own ravisht thought,
> Through contemplation of those goodly sights,
> And glorious images in heaven wrought,
> Whose wondrous beauty, breathing sweet delights,
> Do kindle love in high conceipted sprights,
> I faine to tell the things that I behold,
> But feele my wits to faile, and tongue to fold.

It is like the last movement of a violin *concerto* where, after the musician has made his violin sob with the voluptuous melodies of an *andante,* he sweeps suddenly into a brilliant melody richly overlaid with flute-like harmonics. The verses, though aestuous, are rich as well in those overtones of the calm that comes with the supreme adventure on the heights within all-hail of peace, yet eternally restless in the wondrous quest now fully understood. This is no shamed palinode flaming against the two youthful hymns. It takes the best from them and goes on. This is not quietism. All well-read men know that the supreme men of action are dreamers. This is mysticism which lurks in all men on tiptoe for its own evocation.

Spenser begins the main movement of his last hymn by bidding us take our start with the world we know and so rise upward to heaven on heaven.

> First, th' earth, on adamantine pillers founded,
> Amid the sea, engirt with brazen bands;
> Then th' aire, still flitting, but yet firmely bounded
> On everie side, with pyles of flaming brands,
> Never consum'd, nor quencht with mortall hands;
> And, last, that mightie shining christall wall,
> Wherewith he hath encompassed this All.
>
> By view whereof, it plainly may appeare,
> That still as everything doth upward tend,
> And further is from earth, so still more cleare
> And faire it growes, till to his perfect end
> Of purest Beautie it at last ascend:
> Ayre more then water, fire much more than ayre,
> And heaven then fire appeares more pure and fayre.
>
> Looke thou no further, but affixe thine eye
> On that bright shynie round still moving masse,
> The house of blessed gods, which men call skye,

All sowd with glistring stars more thicke then grasse,
Whereof each other doth in brightnesse passe;
But those two most, which, ruling night and day,
As king and queene, the heavens empire sway;

And tell me then, what hast thou ever scene
That to their beautie may compared bee?
Or can the sight that is most sharpe and keene
Endure their captains flaming head to see?
How much lesse those, much higher in degree,
And so much fairer, and much more then these,
As these are fairer then the land and seas?

For farre above these heavens, which here we see,
Be others farre exceeding these in light,
Not bounded, not corrupt, as these same bee,
But infinite in largenesse and in hight,
Unmoving, uncorrupt, and spotlesse bright,
That need no sunne t' illuminate their spheres,
But their owne native light farre passing theirs.

And as these heavens still by degrees arize,
Untill they come to their first movers bound,
That in his mightie compasse doth comprize
And carrie all the rest with him around,
So those likewise doe by degrees redound,
And rise more faire, till they at last arive
To the most faire, whereto they all do strive.

Faire is the heaven where happy soules have place,
In full enjoyment of felicitie,
Whence they doe still behold the glorious face
Of the Divine Eternall Majestie;
More faire is that where those Idees on hie
Enraunged be, which Plato so admyred,
And pure Intelligences from God inspyred.

Yet fairer is that heaven, in which doe raine
The soveraine Powres and mightie Potentates,
Which in their high protections doe containe
All mortall princes and imperiall states;
And fayrer yet whereas the royall Seates
Of heavenly Dominations are set,
From whom all earthly governance is fet.

"Yet farre more faire be those bright Cherubins"—so the
song soars to visions fairer and fairer, as in Dante's audacious

Paradiso, where one heaven overtops another "continually increasing in light, in beauty and in happiness,"[7] until we throw ourselves down in the presence of the very God, where

> With the great glorie of the wondrous light
> His throne is all encompassed around,
> And hid in his owne brightnesse from the sight
> Of all that looke thereon with eyes unsound:
> And underneath his feet are to be found
> Thunder, and lightning, and tempestuous fyre,
> The instruments of his avenging yre.

In God's bosom rests Sapience, she whom the Greeks called Venus Urania, Beauty Intellectual, she whose presence was felt by Shelley, the greatest myth-maker of our time, whose famous hymn must be placed here in contrast with Spenser's.

> The awful shadow of some unseen Power
>   Floats though unseen among us, visiting
>   This various world with as inconstant wing
> As summer winds that creep from flower to flower;
> Like moonbeams that behind some piny mountain shower,
>   It visits with inconstant glance
>   Each human heart and countenance;
> Like hues and harmonies of evening;
>   Like clouds in starlight widely spread,
>   Like memory of music fled,
>   Like aught that for its grace may be
> Dear, and yet dearer for its mystery.
>
> Spirit of beauty, that dost consecrate
>   With thine own hues all thou dost shine upon
>   Of human thought or form, where art thou gone?
> Why dost thou pass away, and leave our state,
> This dim vast vale of tears, vacant and desolate?—
>   Ask why the sunlight not forever
>   Weaves rainbows o'er yon mountain river;
> Why aught should fail and fade that once is shown;
>   Why fear and dream and death and birth
>   Cast on the daylight of this earth
>   Such gloom; why man has such a scope
> For love and hate, despondency and hope.
>
> . . . .

---

[7] Miss Winstanley, p. 71.

> Love, Hope and Self-Esteem, like clouds, depart,
>   And come, for some uncertain moments lent.
>   Man were immortal and omnipotent,
> Didst thou, unknown and awful as thou art,
> Keep with thy glorious train firm state within his heart.
>   Thou messenger of sympathies
>   That wax and wane in lovers' eyes!
> Thou, that to human thought art nourishment,
>   Like darkness to a dying flame,
>   Depart not as thy shadow came!
>   Depart not, lest the grave should be,
> Like life and fear, a dark reality!
>
>   .   .   .   .
>
> I vowed that I would dedicate my powers
>   To thee and thine—have I not kept the vow?
>   With beating heart and streaming eyes, even now
> I call the phantoms of a thousand hours
> Each from his voiceless grave: they have in visioned bowers
>   Of studious zeal or love's delight
>   Outwatched with me the envious night—
> They know that never joy illumed my brow
>   Unlinked with hope that thou wouldst free
>   This world from its dark slavery,—
>   That thou, O awful Loveliness,
> Wouldst give whate'er these words cannot express.

But mortality still clings to Shelley. Spenser has taken on immortality before his physical death and sees Sapience with the clearness that marks uncompromising mysticism.[8] Spenser, despite the far graver tragedies to his person and to his ideals for his fatherland that were shutting in on him, catches no melancholy glimpses of Intellectual Beauty, Sapience, a fitful apparition. He beholds her with calm certainty and permanence. It is a mysticism a little too professional for the wise man of today. It fails to appreciate, as Shelley did, the inade-

---

[8] Fletcher (*Fowre Hymnes*, p. 473): "Benevieni's friend and commentator, Pico della Mirandola, explains indeed that there are two deaths through which the heart may pass to life. In the first 'death,' the soul is released from the body, but not the body from the soul. The animal body lives on, while the soul goes on a heavenly excursion. As Milton puts it: leaving the body behind,

> '... the deep transported mind may soar
> Above the wheeling poles, and at Heaven's door
> Look in.'"

quacy of mere words.   But in no poet, not even in Michelangelo, did the mystical interpretation of the Platonic idea come more beautifully and clearly to make its avatar than in Spenser.

There in ... [God's] bosome Sapience doth sit,
The soveraine dearling of the Deity,
Clad like a queene in royall robes, most fit
For so great powre and peerelesse majesty,
And all with gemmes and jewels gorgeously
Adornd, that brighter then the starres appeare,
And make her native brightnes seem more cleare.

And on her head a crowne of purest gold
Is set, in signe of highest soveraignty;
And in her hand a scepter she doth hold,
With which she rules the house of God on hy,
And menageth the ever-moving sky,
And in the same these lower creatures all,
Subjected to her powre imperiall.

Both heaven and earth obey unto her will,
And all the creatures which they both containe;
For of her fulnesse, which the world doth fill,
They all partake, and do in state remaine,
As their great Maker did at first ordaine,
Through observation of her high beheast,
By which they first were made, and still increast.

The fairenesse of her face no tongue can tell;
For she the daughters of all wemens race,
And angels eke, in beautie doth excell,
Sparkled on her from Gods owne glorious face,
And more increast by her owne goodly grace,
That it doth farre exceed all humane thonght,
Ne can on earth compared be to ought.

This is Spenser's old facile allegorizing habit, you say.   But let us study Professor Fletcher's apt quotations and ingenious interpretation.

"There are three," says St. John, "that bear record in heaven, the Father, the Word, and the Holy Ghost." Christian writers from the earliest times have often identified the Holy Ghost with Wisdom. Theophilus of Antioch conceived the Trinity as *Theos, Logos, Sophia*,—God, the Word, Wisdom. So Irenaeus. So St. Gregory Thaumaturgus. So Athanasius, who says further that to possess the Holy Ghost is to possess God. And St. Paul: "The kingdom of God ... is joy in the Holy Ghost."

Spenser's Sapience is then Venus Urania, Beauty Intellectual, or what all Christians call the Holy Ghost, quite fervently real to our poet. Shelley, with his hatred of formalism, is, most of us think at first blush, more comprehensible. But Spenser is the truer mystic because more direct, more aglow with a sense of immediacy in spite of his taint of verbal literalness.

A strange seventeenth century reference to the *Hymnes* by Edward Bolton in his *Hypercritica* is by no means merely curious. Bolton was one of the first to react against the plesio-saurian sentences and the parti-colored diction of the Eliza-bethans in favor of more sober ideals for prose style. In a zealous search for models for good historical prose-writing he pored over many of our old poets and prosemen. We are at first startled to note that, although he will have none of most of the antique poets and condemns the "old outworn words" of most of Spenser's poems, "as for practick English," he recommends the *Hymnes* only less strongly than the poetry of Jonson and the prose of Bacon as stylistic models for the historian who would be lucid. It is a fact worth pondering over with this old student of our prose that Spenser, in his most abandoned mysti-cism, approached nearer to a workaday style (without dropping in poetic quality) than he did anywhere else.[9]

I have repeatedly insisted that Spenser's renunciation of his lover and the world does not imply a complete and final abjuration of the love of a beautiful woman and the making of England a Utopia. These things are to be wrought into a larger scheme of things. The permanence, then, in which Spen-ser and not a few mystics of every age believe is a projection of the vital elements of our ideal lives here into an eternal quest within all-hail of peace (since we shall then know something of the larger significance of the universe), but never utterly scorning the things of earth and always restless with exalted aspiration. Marlowe, though a sceptic, caught, for a moment, the true insight.

---

[9] Bolton's *Hypercritica* was completed about 1618 but first published by Anthony Hall at the end of his *Nicolai Triveti Annalium Continuatio* (Oxford, 1722).

Nature, that framed us of four elements
Warring within ourselves for regiment,
Doth teach us all to have aspiring minds:
Our souls—whose faculties can comprehend
The wondrous architecture of the world,
And measure every wandering planet's course,
Still climbing after knowledge infinite,
And always moving as the restless spheres—
Will us to wear ourselves and never rest.

It was characteristic of Spenser's most tender humanity that he could turn even in the hour of his earthly sorrow and his contemplation of heavenly beauty to write a gorgeous interlude for two pairs of youthful lovers—the *Prothalamion*. Professor Palgrave, perhaps influenced by the notable critical acumen of Tennyson, and, in America, Professor Trent have been inclined to prefer the technique of this lyric to that of the *Epithalamion*. But in sheer passion and in sumptuous imagery the earlier lyric is certainly superior. And after all, as Professor Trent says, ''to prefer the *Prothalamion* to the *Epithalamion* is much like preferring the moon to the sun.'' Professor Trent's phrase is very happy in connotations. We have here indeed the serene, aloof, but kindly moon, not the triumphant wooing of the life-giving sun.

There are two lovely and evanescent visitations of personal melancholy, delicate wraiths of that sadness and disillusion that came with a fierce and poignant outcry at the close of the sixth book of *The Faërie Queene*. The first visitation is in the first stanza.

Calme was the day, and through the trembling ayre
Sweete breathing Zephyrus did softly play,
A gentle spirit, that lightly did delay
Hot Titans beames, which then did glyster fayre:
When I, whom sullein care,
Through discontent of my long fruitlesse stay
In princes court, and expectation vayne
Of idle hopes, which still doe fly away,
Like empty shaddowes, did afflict my brayne,
Walkt forth to ease my payne

> Along the shoare of silver streaming Themmes;
> Whose rutty bancke, the which his river hemmes,
> Was paynted all with variable flowers,
> And all the meades adornd with daintie gemmes,
> Fit to decke maydens bowres,
> And crowne their paramours,
> Against the brydale day, which is not long:
> Sweete Themmes, runne softly, till I end my song.

But at the very same moment the poet is turning to his gracious
fancy of the meadows by the banks of sweet Thames crowded
with nymphs with loosened locks.

> And each one had a little wicker basket,
> Made of fine twigs entrayled curiously,
> In which they gathered flowers to fill their flasket;
> And with fine fingers cropt full featously
> The tender stalkes on hye.
> Of every sort, which in that meadow grew,
> They gathered some; the violet pallid blew,
> The little dazie, that at evening closes,
> The virgin lillie, and the primrose trew,
> With store of vermeil roses,
> To decke their bridegromes posies
> Against the brydale day, which was not long:
> Sweete Themmes, runne softly, till I end my song.

The poet is celebrating the visit of two maidens to their
betrothed at the Essex House. As their barges sail up the silken
current of the Thames they seem to Spenser like two swans and
he plays with the fancy throughout the entire poem—a *scherzo*
tinged with a pensiveness unusual to the bright form, but none
the less jocund for all its delicate restraint—a curious kind of
grave and sincere cajolery.

> With that I sawe two swannes of goodly hewe
> Come softly swimming downe along the lee;
> Two fairer birds I yet did never see:
> The snow which doth the top of Pindus strew
> Did never whiter shew,
> Nor Jove himselfe, when he a swan would be
> For love of Leda, whiter did appear:
> Yet Leda was, they say, as white as he,
> Yet not so white as these, nor nothing neare:
> So purely white they were,

> That even the gentle streame, the which them bare,
> Seem'd foule to them, and bad his billowes spare
> To wet their silken feathers, least they might
> Soyle their fayre plumes with water not so fayre,
> And marre their beauties bright,
> That shone as heavens light,
> Against their brydale day, which was not long:
> Sweete Themmes, runne softly, till I end my song.

Here indeed "we have a picture such as Botticelli might have painted."[10]

Except for the two brief moments of personal sadness the poet seems to be smiling always with a wonderful kindliness. Surely I was right when I insisted in my discussion of the *Fowre Hymnes* that he had not altogether abjured the world even to behold Sapience. He could now turn once more to adore the beauty of the world, the happiness of others at least, and with a new quietude that almost forgets the Blatant Beast. For the moment he is with Shakespeare. With a joy like a child's he sees the nymphs marvel at the swans and run to greet them with flowers.

> Then forth they all out of their baskets drew
> Great store of flowers, the honour of the field,
> That to the sense did fragrant odours yeild,
> All which upon these goodly birds they threw,
> And all the waves did strew,
> That like old Peneus waters they did seeme,
> When downe along by pleasant Tempes shore,
> Scattred with flowres, through Thessaly they streeme,
> That they appeare, through lillies plenteous store,
> Like a brydes chamber flore.

He hears one nymph improvise an exquisite lay to bless "loves couplement," to invoke peace, and to wish for fruitful issue, sweet earthly immortality. He sees swarms of the smaller craft flock about the flower-decked barges and follow the maidens up the river.

As the dear familiar lines of London grow real on the horizon and in the poet's dream, the second evanescent visitation

---

[10] Professor E. B. Reed, *English Lyric Poetry* (Yale University Press, 1912), p. 184.

of melancholy is bound to come with reminiscence—lightly—for a moment only. It is charged with Spenser's sorrow for the dead Leicester, his Prince Arthur. Here, even in the last years, is that proud independence that we saw from the first when in *The Shepheards Calender* he defended Grindal against the popular clergy, when in "Mother Hubberds Tale" he scored Alençon and Burghley, when he uttered his reverence for Harvey in a sonnet amidst the shrill jeers of the popular writers, when, in the fifth book of *The Faërie Queene*, he hurled his lofty praise of Lord Grey Wilton in the teeth of the snarling court. Here he pours out his gratitude, his admiration, and his mourning for the dead lord of the house once called Leicester House in the face of his still living patron, for whom it was now named Essex House. And Essex, though of a generous tendency, was often a victim of jealousy. The younger lord's sensitive, emulous nature, spoiled as it was by his dazzling success, must have winced at this note of grief in an hour which he might well claim for untempered rejoicing.

> At length they all to mery London come,
> To mery London, my most kindly nurse,
> That to me gave this lifes first native sourse;
> Though from another place I take my name,
> An house of auncient fame.
> There when they came, whereas those bricky towres,
> The which on Themmes brode aged backe doe ryde,
> Where now the studious lawyers have their bowers,
> There whylome wont the Templer Knights to byde,
> Till they decayd through pride:
> Next whereunto there standes a stately place,
> Where oft I gayned giftes and goodly grace
> Of that great lord which therein wont to dwell,
> Whose want too well now feeles my freendles case:
> But ah! here fits not well
> Olde woes, but joyes to tell,
> Against the bridale daye, which is not long:
> Sweete Themmes, runne softly, till I end my song.

Again, as you see, the poet turns quickly to his kindly delight over the beauty of his young friends and their happiness to come

soon. And in a moment more the old hope of *The Faërie Queene*
rings out trumpet-clear in a belated but stirring praise of Essex,
who had but recently returned from the expedition into the jaws
of Spain: the burning of the Spanish fleet in a Spanish harbor
and the capture and sacking of Cadiz.

> Yet therein now doth lodge a noble peer,
> Great Englands glory and the worlds wide wonder,
> Whose dreadfull name late through all Spaine did thunder,
> And Hercules two pillors standing neere
> Did make to quake and feare.
> Faire branch of honor, flower of chevalrie,
> That fillest England with thy triumphes fame,
> Joy have thou of thy noble victorie,
> And endlesse happinesse of thine owne name
> That promiseth the same:
> That through thy prowesse and victorious armes
> Thy country may be freed from forraine harmes;
> And great Elisaes glorious name may ring
> Through al the world, fil'd with thy wide alarmes,
> Which some brave Muse may sing
> To ages following,
> Upon the brydale day, which is not long:
> Sweete Themmes, runne softly, till I end my song.

The trumpet-call dies away. The poem closes with a quiet
and smiling blessing as the two maidens alight and meet their
two bachelors.

We can accompany our poet's poet for only a brief dream-
while longer. We know that we cannot leave him even at the
portal of some high mountain fortalice where he is to find rest.
He is to go on unceasingly.

> He's for the morning.
> . . . . .
> He was a man born with thy face and throat,
> Lyric Apollo!
> . . . . .
> He said, "What's time? Leave Now for dogs and apes!
> Man has Forever!"

> Did not he magnify the mind, show clear
>   Just what it all meant?
> He would not discount life, as fools do here,
>   Paid by instalment,
> He ventured neck or nothing—heaven's success
>   Found, or earth's failure:
> "Wilt thou trust death or not?" He answered "Yes!
>   Hence with life's pale lure!"
> That low man seeks a little thing to do,
>   Sees it and does it:
> This high man, with a great thing to pursue,
>   Dies ere he knows it.
> That low man goes on adding one to one,
>   His hundred's soon hit:
> This high man, aiming at a million,
>   Misses an unit.
> That, has the world here—should he need the next,
>   Let the world mind him!
> This, throws himself on God, and unperplexed
>   Seeking shall find him.

We must leave Spenser, shortly,

> ...where meteors shoot, clouds form,
>   Lightnings are loosened,
> Stars come and go! Let joy break with the storm.

It has often been urged that death has been kind to the repu-
tation of certain great poets. Marlowe's streaming lightning
might have hardened with maturity into the lifeless glistening
lava of rhetoric. Shelley's ethereal song might have faded to
a silver tenuity. So some critics think. Whether they are right
or not in these instances it is clear that had the promised later
books of *The Faërie Queene* sustained even fitfully the new
grandeur of the cantos on Mutabilitie they would have placed
their poet on a more triumphant peak and very near to Shake-
speare. They would have been the utterance of a clairvoyant
and unimaginable Prospero-mood.[11] All the morbid bitterness

---

[11] It is hardly worth while to pause here to lay the ghost of theory that
these cantos do not belong to *The Faërie Queene*. Those interested in the
controversy may consult Sebastian Evans in *Macmillan's Magazine*, XLII;
Grosart's answer, *Spenser*, I, Appendix U; Trent, *Longfellow and Other
Essays*, pp. 60–61n; and Dodge, *Cambridge Edition*, p. 131.

that we heard sounding with plangent monotony in the *Complaints*, all the fever that has fascinated and devoured hundreds of singers remembering forgotten beauty, mourning and mocking over the snows of yesteryear, crying out in sharp pain that "dust hath closéd Helen's eyes," all that special sorrow of poetry was healed for Spenser in a vision of the Titaness Mutabilitie, terrible yet no longer revolting, wondrously beautiful and, for all her crushing might, lowering her imperial head before the supreme laws of a benignant universe.

Spenser's last victory was peculiarly illustrious because of all poets he was most intensely haunted by the sorrow of change common to his craft. The idea was, however, an omnipresent and sinister portent to his whole age—this notion of the instability of man and his works and even of the vast works of nature and the universe. As Audrey De Vere puts it:

> In the remotest parts of Europe omens of change were heard, like those vague murmurs in the polar regions which announce the breaking up of the ice; and in Ireland unfriendly echoes of those voices muttered near and nearer around that ruined mansion, one of Desmond's hundred castles, within whose walls some strange fortune had harboured the gentlest of England's singers.[12]

No wonder then that the poet should cry:

> What man that sees the ever-whirling wheele
> Of Change, the which all mortall things doth sway,
> But that thereby doth find, and plainly feele,
> How Mutability in them doth play
> Her cruell sports, to many mens decay!
> Which that to all may better yet appeare,
> I will rehearse that whylome I heard say,
> How she at first her selfe began to reare
> Gainst all the gods, and th' empire sought from them to beare.

More than two centuries were to elapse before that new courageous attitude which accepts change and yet bows no servile knee to it but aims to control it was to find expression in Darwin

---

[12] *Essays Chiefly on Poetry*, I, "Spenser as a Philosophic Poet." See pp. 74 sq. from which I make several quotations and which, to a certain extent, I follow for a short space in outline though I find a number of points for difference.

and Huxley and Bateson, in James and Dewey.   Even in his maturest years, even in his great moments of self-conquest, Spenser was fain to adopt the helpless attitude of the traditionalist towards change, to explain it into non-existence with a noble sophistry.

But from Spenser's youth to maturity there is none the less, a marked evolution towards healthiness and courage that seems almost to pass from timid transcendentalism to militant naturalism.   The poet in the youthful, morbid days of his *Complaints* would have visioned this Mutabilitie as a loathsome spreading disease but now he eyes her with a courage as calm as Jove's and finds her beautiful, majestic, a mightier warrior than her armored sister, Bellona, and more darkly terrible than her other sister, Hecatè.   What wonder then that this Titaness, the most radiant offspring of that old shadowy hierarchy of gods that reigned with Saturn vast, should claim the suzerainty over the upstart usurpers?   First she conquered the earth with deadly ease.   She shattered the great ordinances and statutes which Nature had founded; she transformed earth's very frame: that is, as the student of modern science beholds it: "The seas had left dry their beds at her command, continents had sunk beneath the waves, mountains had fleeted like clouds, rivers had filled their mouths with desert sands, kingdoms had risen and fallen, and the languages which recorded their triumphs had died." Among men, too, she had taken those vague but half-divine visions of Justice and Polity and perverted wrong into right, bad into good.   Haughty with success she scaled high heaven moving naturally first to the circle of the changeful moon, Cynthia.

> Her sitting on an ivory throne shee found,
> Drawne of two steeds, th' one black, the other white,
> Environd with tenne thousand starres around,
> That duly her attended day and night;
> And by her side there ran her page, that hight
> Vesper, whom we the evening-starre intend:
> That with his torche, still twinkling like twylight,
> Her lightened all the way where she should wend,
> And joy to weary wandring travailers did lend.

The discerning reader will see in the curious blend of fancy and sublimity in this stanza the quality, peculiar to these last cantos, that Mr. Paul Elmer More very happily calls the "elfin gravity" of Spenser. But that is not the highest harmony here. We pass swiftly to sheer sublimity as we read how Cynthia, "bending her horned browes, did put her back," but Mutabilitie strode forward to hurl the "radiant and inviolate divinity" from her glorious chariot-throne. There follows a passage which awed critics have often compared with Milton for its sublimity.

> Yet nathemore the Giantesse forbare:
> But boldly preacing-on, raught forth her hand
> To pluck her downe perforce from off her chaire;
> And there-with lifting up her golden wand,
> Threatned to strike her if she did withstand.
> Where-at the starres, which round about her blazed,
> And eke the Moones bright wagon, still did stand.
> All beeing with so bold attempt amazed,
> And on her uncouth habit and sterne looke still gazed.

> Meane-while the lower world, which nothing knew
> Of all that chaunced here, was darkned quite;
> And eke the heavens, and all the heavenly crew
> Of happy wights, now unpurvaide of light,
> Were much afraid, and wondred at that sight;
> Fearing least Chaos broken had his chaine,
> And brought againe on them eternall night.

The gods themselves, hardly less fearful, hastened before the father Jove who, "doubting least Typhon were again upreard," despatched Mercury down to the circle of the Moon to learn whether their once dreaded enemies were plunging upward through the ancient blind night with their old horrid clangor. The winged-footed one came to the scene of the struggle, mastered a sudden seizure of fear of the presumptuous Titaness,

> And there-with-all, he on her shoulder laid
> His snaky-wreathed mace, whose awfull power
> Doth make both gods and hellish fiends affraid:
> Where-at the Titanesse did sternely lower,
> And stoutly answer'd, that in evill hower
> He from his Jove such message to her brought,
> To bid her leave faire Cynthias silver bower;
> Sith shee his Jove and him esteemed nought,
> No more then Cynthia's selfe; but all their kingdoms sought.

Jove heard the dire news in the full assembly of terrified gods, without change of awful countenance. He signed his cohorts to speak their counsel. But before they could formulate a definite plan the swift and terrible Visitant was among them with her audacious claims. As De Vere acutely says:

An inferior poet would have made this portent hideous as well as terrible, Spenser knew better. He knew that revolution and destruction wear often on their countenances a baleful loveliness of their own, for which many a victim, disinterested in madness, has willingly died. The following lines are in Homer's grandest vein—

> Whil'st she thus spake, the gods, that gave good eare
> To her bold words, and marked well her grace,
> Beeing of stature tall as any there
> Of all the gods, and beautiful of face
> As any of the goddesses in place,
> Stood all astonied; like a sort of steeres,
> Mongst whom some beast of strange and forraine race
> Unwares is chaunc't, far straying from his peeres:
> So did their ghastly gaze bewray their hidden feares.

Jove, alone imperturbable, answered with stately taunts at the destruction of her ancestry.

> "But now this off-scum of that cursed fry
> Dare to renew the like bold enterprize,
> And chalenge th' heritage of this our skie;
> Whom what should hinder, but that we likewise
> Should handle as the rest of her allies,
> And thunder-drive to hell?" With that, he shooke
> His nectar-deawed locks, with which the skyes
> And all the world beneath for terror quooke,
> And eft his burning levin-brond in hand he tooke.
>
> But, when he looked on her lovely face,
> In which faire beames of beauty did appeare,
> That could the greatest wrath soone turne to grace
> (Such sway doth beauty even in heaven beare)
> He staide his hand: and having chang'd his cheare,
> He thus againe in milder wise began:
> "But ah! if gods should strive with flesh yfere,
> Then shortly should the progeny of man
> Be rooted out, if Jove should doe still what he can."

Surely Mutabilitie, he thinks, is but lead astray by passing error. But she, undaunted, summons the Supreme One himself before a tribunal held by impartial Nature "and by nothing does the poet more subtly impress us with the magic power of this strange claimant, than by the Thunderer's consent to leave his Olympian throne, and stand her co-suitor before an alien potentate." As for us, today, as our hopes for young Russia grow, we feel that Mutabilitie's "loveliness" is not always so baleful as De Vere thought.

Spenser, for whom the breasts of the nymph in the brake never faded wherever he made his abode, chooses with unassuming certainty a mountain range of his own Irish country for the great rendezvous.

> ... Upon the highest hights
> Of Arlo-hill (Who knowes not Arlo-hill?)
> That is the highest head (in all mens sights)
> Of my old father Mole, whom shepheards quill
> Renowmed hath with hymnes fit for a rurall skill.

Then, as though resting his pinions from a flight unprecedented, he alleviates the sternness of his style, invokes Calliope in place of Clio, and turns with evident delight to people his beloved Irish landscape with nymphs and wood-gods and to make playful myth for his quarrelsome foster-country. The gay little tale of how "foolish god Faunus" bribed the simple river-nymph, Molanna, to conceal him where he might watch Cynthia bathe, how the irate goddess discovered him through his coxcomb laughter, and how her nymphs and hounds hunted him over hill and dale, is of special charm and significance as being one of the very few serene episodes in Spenser inspired by Irish influence. Certainly one of the most beautiful and illuminating functions of criticism is to imagine what might have been, and this little tale makes one wistful when one things what Spenser might have done with the glimmering lore of Ireland. It is not altogether unjust to say, as Mr. Yeats does, that Spenser was "one of many Englishmen to see nothing but what he was desired to see,'' though we must insist that Spenser's view was warped not through a base desire to curry favor at court, but through his hero-worship of Lord Grey Wilton even in the last hour of the stern governor's disgrace in England.   Mr. Yeats makes handsome amends for a snap judgment by adding gracefully: ''If he had gone there as a poet merely, he would have found among its poets more wonderful imaginations than even those islands of Phaedria and Acrasia.   He would have found many wandering story-tellers, not indeed his own power of rich, sustained description, for that belongs to lettered ease, but certainly all the kingdom of the Faerie, still unfaded, of which his own poetry was often but a troubled image.''   The ''troubled image'' is indeed present in the last stanza of even this sportive episode when, grown suddenly grave, he recounts in the last stanza, Cynthia's abandonment of Irish forests and mountains and rivers.

> Them all, and all that she so deare did way,
> Thence-forth she left; and parting from the place,
> There-on an heavy haplesse curse did lay,
> To weet, that wolves, where she was wont to space,
> Should harbour'd be, and all those woods deface,
> And thieves should rob and spoile that coast around.
> Since which, those woods, and all that goodly chase,
> Doth to this day with wolves and thieves abound:
> Which too-too true that lands in-dwellers since have found.

We may well add the words of Aubrey De Vere.

Those ''thieves'' were the original dwellers on Desmond's confiscated lands, who had taken refuge in the forests.   There is a profound pathos in the last line quoted, one which may possibly have been written but the day before those wild bands issued from the woods of Arlo, and wrapped in flame the castle of its poet, thus grimly closing the four wedded and peaceful years of his Irish life.

In the next canto the poet turns with that harmony of humility and pride, which he displayed even in his youthful *Shepheards Calender* and which he found in his wife Elizabeth, to press on to the very outrance of his ambitious philosophy.

> Ah! whither doost thou now, thou greater Muse,
> Me from these woods and pleasing forrests bring?
> And my fraile spirit (that dooth oft refuse
> This too high flight, unfit for her weake wing)
> Lift up aloft, to tell of heavens king
> (Thy soveraine sire) his fortunate successe,
> And victory in bigger noates to sing,
> Which he obtain'd against that Titanesse,
> That him of heavens empire sought to dispossesse?

He describes Dame Nature, the judge of Jove and Mutabilitie, with a cloudy grandeur that has in it the living essence of the crepuscular sublimity of his avowed pupil, Milton. Nature "is invested with attributes so mysterious, and tending so much towards the infinite as to suggest the thought that Spenser, in some of his lonely musings, had occasionally advanced to the borders of a philosophy little guessed of in his own time."

> Then forth issewed (great goddesse) great Dame Nature,
> With goodly port and gracious majesty,
> Being far greater and more tall of stature
> Then any of the gods or powers on hie:
> Yet certes by her face and physnomy,
> Whether she man or woman inly were,
> That could not any creature well descry:
> For, with a veile that wimpled every where,
> Her head and face was hid, that mote to none appeare.

> That, some doe say, was so by skill devized,
> To hide the terror of her uncouth hew
> From mortall eyes, that should be sore agrized;
> For that her face did like a lion shew,
> That eye of wight could not endure to view:
> But others tell that it so beautious was,
> And round about such beames of splendor threw,
> That it the sunne a thousand times did pass,
> Ne coulde be seene, but like an image in a glass.

For her pavilion, "in a fayre plaine upon an equall hill," Earth from her fruitful bosom makes to shoot up a mighty garland of "most dainty" blossoming trees which swayed a stately homage. Flowers swarmed about her like tapestry. Before the presence of this potent divinity who is at once terrible because she consumes all life and beautiful since "she is ever teeming with all things fair," Mutabilitie makes obeisance in great hope since these very qualities of Nature apparently resemble her own. But Nature with her beauty veiled seems to gods and men to be what their own souls really are. Often, before the days of Spenser and since, men have thought they discerned in the veiled lineaments of Nature an oracle for economic lawlessness and religious sentimentality.

> This great grandmother of all creatures bred,
> Great Nature, ever young yet full of eld,
> Still mooving, yet unmoved from her sted,
> Unseene of any, yet of all beheld.

Not without justification to a modern, arbiter, the Titaness charges Jove and all his fellows of having arrogated to themselves the divine power of Nature and of herself, Nature's most consistent viceregent. Then Mutabilitie recounts her sweeping conquests of earth and air, sea and fire and summons to witness the most magnificent pageant of the changing, thronging splendors of the seasons that was ever dreamed of in poetry.

> So forth issew'd the seasons of the yeare:
> First, lusty Spring, all dight in leaves and flowres
> That freshly budded and new bloosmes did beare
> (In which a thousand birds had built their bowres,
> That sweetly sung, to call forth paramours):
> And in his hand a javelin he did beare,
> And on his head (as fit for warlike stoures)
> A guilt engraven morion he did weare;
> That, as some did him love, so others did him feare.

Then came "jolly Sommer" in thin silken cassock with the sweat dropping from under his garland, Autumn in yellow with his sickle, and aged Winter blue-nosed and snow-bearded. The parti-colored Months followed riding on outlandish mounts: stern March on a ram, April, "wanton as a kid," flower-bedecked, upon the very bull which stole Europa in the springtime for amorous Zeus,

> Then came faire May, the fayrest mayd on ground,
> Deckt all with dainties of her seasons pryde,
> And throwing flowres out of her lap around:
> Upon two brethrens shoulders she did ride,
> The twinnes of Leda; which on eyther side
> Supported her like to their soveraine queene.
> Lord! how all creatures laught, when her they spide,
> And leapt and daunc't as they had ravisht beene!
> And Cupid selfe about her fluttred all in greene.

After these came the gorgeous midsummer months, then September laden with the spoil of harvests,

> Then came October full of merry glee:
> For yet his noule was totty of the must,
> Which he was treading in the wine-fats see,
> And of the joyous oyle, whose gentle gust
> Made him so frollick and so full of lust:
> Upon a dreadfull scorpion he did ride,
> The same which by Dianaes doom unjust
> Slew great Orion: and eeke by his side
> He had his ploughing-share and coulter ready tyde.

So they filed along till last of all came cold February, with pruning-knife to hasten a new spring, riding in a quaint wagon drawn through the river by two softly sliding fishes. Then came Night and Day and the chaste, ever-watchful Hours.

> And after all came Life, and lastly Death:
> Death with most grim and griesly visage seene,
> Yet is he nought but parting of the breath;
> Ne ought to see, but like a shade to weene,
> Unbodied, unsoul'd, unheard, unseene:
> But Life was like a faire young lusty boy,
> Such as they faine Dan Cupid to have beene,
> Full of delightfull health and lively joy,
> Deckt all with flowres, and wings of gold fit to employ.

In this last group one sees the close original of Milton's famous picture.

> ... The other Shape—
> If shape it might be called that shape had none
> Distinguishable in member, joint, or limb;
> Of substance might be called that shadow seemed,
> For each seemed either—black it stood as Night,

> Fierce as ten Furies, terrible as Hell,
> And shook a dreadful dart: what seemed his head
> The likeness of a kingly crown had on.

The similarity in suggestive vagueness and actual phrasing is striking. Equally striking is Milton's gloomy magnificence which blots out Spenser's original attitude of superb contempt towards death, an attitude as buoyant with the older poet as though he had already passed it in his vision of Heavenly Beauty and found it utterly unreal. By making Life the climax of all, by making February (with its hope of the new birth) the climax month, Spenser seems almost to pay joyous allegiance to Mutabilitie.

But the poet rouses himself and passes on to a debate, clever, but rather quibbling. Jove conjures up no pageants; he merely utters a maze of dialectic. Mutabilitie shows how the august procession by its very color and change proclaims her despotism in silent and visual eternally moving splendor. Jove answers like a modern Kantian turning Time into a comfortable *à priori* form of his own thought.

> "... Right true it is, that these,
> And all things else that under heaven dwell,
> Are chaung'd of Time, who doth them all disseise
> Of being: but who is it (to me tell)
> That Time himselfe doth move and stil compell
> To keepe his course? Is not that namely wee,
> Which poure that vertue from our heavenly cell
> That moves them all, and makes them changed be?
> So them we gods doe rule, and in them also thee."

Ah yes, but for all your plausible reasoning who can deny the testimony of the senses and who will find reality in shadowy dogmas? Thus, in effect, retorts the Titaness unleashing that subtle scepticism that floods all human veins like restless fire.

> "... The things
> Which we see not how they are mov'd and swayd
> Ye may attribute to your selves as kings,
> And say they by your secret powre are made:
> But what we see not, who shall us perswade?"

Nay, even the gods themselves change and die, for they, too, come of mortal parentage; they are, that is to say, but a beautiful and evanescent fancy of man's.

> "And first, concerning her that is the first,
> Even you, faire Cynthia, whom so much ye make
> Joves dearest darling; she was bred and nurst
> On Cynthus hill, whence she her name did take:
> Then is she mortall borne, how-so ye crake;
> Besides, her face and countenance every day
> We changed see, and sundry forms partake,
> Now hornd, now round, now bright, now brown and gray;
> So that *as changefull as the moone* men use to say."

The valiant Mars runs at times so far "out of square" that he seems to have lost his way and the poor "star-gazers" of earth are fain to "damne their lying bookes." So with keen thrusts of biting scepticism Mutabilitie traces the human origin and changeful caprices of every god, even Jove himself, whom she finds bound to man's illusions by specious ligatures that betray his unreality. Crude anthropomorphism! We are all confronted by that contemptuous finality of the modern naturalist.

> "Besides, the sundry motions of your spheares,
> So sundry waies and fashions as clerkes faine,
> Some in short space, and some in longer yeares;
> What is the same but alteration plaine?
> Onely the starrie skie doth still remaine:
> Yet do the starres and signes therein still move,
> And even it self is mov'd, as wizards saine.
> But all that moveth doth mutation love:
> Therefore both you and them to me I subject prove."

With what eloquent sadness could Spenser have enriched this argument if he had known the scientific theory that the moon was already dead and of the coming death of the sun!

> "Then since within this wide great universe
> Nothing doth firme and permanent appeare,
> But all things tost and turned by transverse:
> What then should let, but I aloft should reare
> My trophee, and from all the triumph beare?

> Now judge then (O thou greatest goddesse trew!)
> According as thy selfe doest see and heare,
> And unto me addoom that is my dew;
> That is the rule of all, all being rul'd by you.''

A triumph of cunning reasoning surely! For do we not discern in these last lines the hidden gleam of an ingenious sophistry that awaits only for Nature's ruling before it proves the subordination of Nature herself. For Nature herself, you see, is here defined as Mutabilitie.

Now Nature, though she has feasted her senses on the great pageant of change, makes no haste but pauses long to take counsel with her reason before she makes her momentous decision. Her answer is shrewd but we may well fear that it would be rightly dubbed by William James a ''metaphysical verbalism.''

> So having ended, silence long ensewed;
> Ne Nature to or fro spake for a space,
> But, with firme eyes affixt, the ground still viewed.
> Meane while, all creatures, looking in her face,
> Expecting th' end of this so doubtfull case,
> Did hang in long suspence what would ensew,
> To whether side should fall the soveraigne place:
> At length, she, looking up with chearefull view,
> The silence brake, and gave her doome in speeches few:

> ''I well consider all that ye have sayd
> And find that all things stedfastnes doe hate
> And changed be: yet being rightly wayd,
> They are not changed from their first estate;
> But by their change their being doe dilate:
> And turning to themselves at length againe,
> Doe worke their owne perfection so by fate:
> That over them Change doth not rule and raigne;
> But they raigne over Change, and doe their states maintaine.

> ''Cease therefore, daughter, further to aspire,
> And thee content thus to be rul'd by me:
> For thy decay thou seekst by thy desire:
> But time shall come that all shall changed bee,
> And from thenceforth none no more change shall see.''
> So was the Titaness put downe and whist,
> And Jove confirm'd in his imperiall see.
> Then was that whole assembly quite dismist,
> And Natur's selfe did vanish, whither no man wist.

One remembers the gloom-shattering trumpet song of Donne.

> Death, be not proud, though some have called thee
> Mighty and dreadful, for thou art not so;
> For those, whom thou think'st thou dost overthrow,
> Die not, poor Death, nor yet canst thou kill me.
> From rest and sleep, which but thy picture be,
> Much pleasure, then from thee much more must flow,
> And soonest our best men with thee do go,
> Rest of their bones, and soul's delivery.
> Thou'rt slave to Fate, chance, kings, and desperate men,
> And dost with poison, war, and sickness dwell,
> And poppy, or charms can make us sleep as well,
> And better than thy stroke; why swell'st thou then?
> One short sleep past, we wake eternally,
> And Death shall be no more; Death, thou shalt die.

In both these poets in their supreme moments the soul had its transfiguration before death. Aubrey De Vere writes conclusions that are nearly final though like most men of his type he leans more heavily towards quietism than any Elizabethan poet.

According to the philosophy of Spenser it was impossible that Mutability should enjoy a final triumph, because her true function is to minister through change to that which knows no change. Revolution is but a subordinate element in a system which includes a recuperative principle, and tends ever to the stable. To the undiscerning eye things seem to pass away; to the half-discerning they seem to revolve merely in a circle; but the motion is in reality upward as well as circular; as it advances, it ascends in a spiral line; and as it ascends it ever widens. When the creation has reached the utmost amplitude of which it was originally made capable, it must stand face to face with the Creator, and in that high solstice it must enter into the sabbath of His endless rest.

This seems an almost complete interpretation of what may have been the last lines that Spenser ever wrote.

> When I bethinke me on that speech whyleare
> Of Mutability, and well it way,
> Me seemes, that though she all unworthy were
> Of the heav'ns rule, yet, very sooth to say,
> In all things else she beares the greatest sway:
> Which makes me loath this state of life so tickle,
> And love of things so vaine to cast away;
> Whose flowring pride, so fading and so fickle,
> Short Time shall soon cut down with his consuming sickle.

> Then gin I thinke on that which Nature sayd,
> Of that same time when no more change shall be,
> But stedfast rest of all things, firmly stayd
> Upon the pillours of eternity,
> That is contrayr to Mutabilitie:
> For all that moveth doth in change delight:
> But thence-forth all shall rest eternally
> With Him that is the God of Sabbaoth hight:
> O that great Sabbaoth God graunt me that Sabbaoths sight!

De Vere adds what few seem to have appreciated: "This is the voice of a spirit wearied with the storms of our lower spheres, *but not daunted or weakened by them.*" But once more I must take issue with the conception of Sapience, of "that Sabbaoths sight," as "endless rest." Spenser does say that all shall rest eternally with God. But that is very different, in connotation at least, from De Vere's phrase, "endless rest." Spenser would have found much in common with the philosophy of Fichte. Spenser, like all Elizabethans, was ever a fighter. He had always a zest for the warm earth as the *Prothalamion* and the pageant of the Seasons show. He had, to the end, the lure of battle, since his last cantos rise to a description of the most stupendous of struggles. To him the "Sabbaoths sight" was not, I repeat, a fleeing from life into an ivory tower on earth or in heaven, but a projection of the great adventure into eternity where, cherishing all that was best in earthly life—love, beauty, chivalry—the pilgrim-soul might hurry on, exalted by a fuller understanding, within all-hail of peace, serene, but ever restless in its quest of unattainable perfection.

CHAPTER VII

CONCLUSION

No age, by its own resources alone, can appreciate the many sides of a supreme poet. How can we then escape from the inevitable narrowness of our times and gain a really large and adequate appreciation of our Titans? We cannot test the poet and our glittering generalities by the superior wisdom of unborn generations. But we can subject our opinions to a most severe examination in the light of the wisdom of a spacious past. Spenser, for instance, will be thoroughly appreciated for the first time when we learn what the men of consequence in his own days and since have thought of him and when we place our own ideas, warped by our times and our personalities, in a proper perspective. I purpose, therefore, to discuss the attitudes of Spenser's contemporaries and of subsequent ages towards the faërie poet, to sketch the opinions of certain of the more important critics and poets who were influenced by him in a particularly significant manner, as an elaborate and most searching test of my own conclusions which I must marshal and reiterate at the close of this chapter.[1]

Of the Golden Age of English literature, the Age of Enthusiasm, I need say little further in this book. We all understand it as the age in which Shakespeare could make the splendors of English history move in a vast, heroic pageant across a little wooden stage. It was the age of Spenser-worship because the English worshipped everything English. It has long been a popular superstition among the ignorant and the learned that great poets are not appreciated in their own day. It is true,

---

[1] For this purpose I combine and condense many passages from a series of monographs which I published in 1910, 1911, and 1912. I have removed most of the catalogue quality and all the minor citations of those dissertations here; I have dovetailed them in a new way; I have revised every passage and added many new ones at all points in the discussion.

as I have said, that they are not completely appreciated, but nothing could be more ill-supported by evidence than the notion that they are not appreciated by contemporaries within certain limits. It is true that the world often allows a great poet to go threadbare because the world has a habit of being loth to pay for what it can get free. But the world is liberal in the appreciation of truly great poets, even in their own period. As a matter of fact, poets are often more heartily if less shrewdly appreciated in their own day than later. Provided that he is supreme, provided that his worth is dazzlingly undeniable, the world has always been ready to nourish a starving poet with appreciation to the choking point. Whether Spenser could reasonably complain to his empty purse or even whether Spenser did actually complain to any serious extent about his empty purse are matters for emphatic doubt. As for appreciation, it was, as I have said, an age of Spenser-worship as it was the age of worship of all things English.

Then came the Age of Reason and England developed a real literary criticism for the first time. When we find Davenant and others complaining about certain defects in *The Faërie Queene* we must not say, as some have said, that Spenser had fallen into the hands of the Philistines. We must ask ourselves whether these censors had not just cause for complaint and whether their appreciation, if less enthusiastic, was not more true for all time. Of course we cannot date the Age of Reason any more than we can date any other age. We can only say that Ben Jonson stood in the very midst of the turbulent ocean of enthusiasm, scarred, sullen, but immovable, a prophet of the age at hand. We can only say that by about 1620 the seas of enthusiasm were becoming stagnant and that reason stood dominant but not triumphant. England needed an Age of Reason to develop certain essentials in literary criticism. And many of the words written about Spenser in those days will enrich, with no accompanying blight or pallor, our appreciation of the master.

But England had to pay a penalty for her Age of Reason. I think we may better understand the currents of English literature in the latter half of the seventeenth century if we call it the Age of Literary Anarchy.

Then came the Augustan Despotism. Wise scholars are slowly and painfully teaching us to appreciate how much the neo-classicists did for England when they finally brought a faith to the tortured sceptics and the hundred jarring sects. But it will take time to right the wrongs inflicted by the great romanticists in their youth. For Keats wrote of the Augustans:

> Yes, a scism
> Nurtured by foppery and barbarism,
> Made great Apollo blush for this his land.
> Men were thought men who could not understand
> His glories: with a puling infant's force
> They sway'd about upon a rocking horse,
> And thought it Pegasus. Ah dismal soul'd!
> The winds of heaven blew, the ocean roll'd
> Its gathering waves—ye felt it not. The blue
> Bar'd its eternal bosom, and the dew
> Of summer nights collected still to make
> The morning precious; beauty was awake!
> Why were ye not awake? But ye were dead
> To things ye knew not of,—were closely wed
> To musty laws lined out with wretched rule
> And compass vile: so that ye taught a school
> Of dolts to smooth, inlay, and clip, and fit,
> Till, like the certain wands of Jacob's wit,
> Their verses tallied. Easy was the task;
> A thousand handicraftsmen wore the mask
> Of Poesy. Ill-fated, impious race!
> That blasphem'd the bright Lyrist to his face,
> And did not know it,—no, they went about,
> Holding a poor, decrepid standard out
> Mark'd with most flimsy mottos, and in large
> The name of one Boileau!

If one ignores the outrageous libel against Boileau, there is, of course, much truth in this abuse. Nevertheless we are beginning to see that after all the Augustans were not heavy villains, but very useful ancestors. Their apologists, however, still make the mistake of thinking that they are not worth while unless they contain symptoms of romanticism, real or fancied. Too much current scholarship on eighteenth century England is a mad scramble in search of romanticism. I can show that the Augustans, with their purely classical ideals, have done much for a fuller appreciation of Spenser, if we would only listen to them.

But the principles of Augustanism, in their turn, served their purpose, were distrusted, and flung aside. Then came the Triumph of Romanticism. I do not need to rhapsodize the great days of the new faith. In spite of the pasteboard dragons of realism, science, and commercialism, romanticism still flourishes and is, in some aspects, a deadly menace. Poe, in his sonnet on science, voiced a thought still popular when he accused the men of scalpels and acids of driving the faun from the forest, the light of romance from men's eyes. As a matter of fact the romanticists, whatever they may have said by way of theory, have developed a highly organized method that may be often quite accurately termed ''scientific romanticism.'' Sometimes the romanticist makes of himself a delicately adjusted machine with works of fairy frailty that respond to the least shadow of a sensation and record it with painful accuracy. Man no longer merely rejoices. He is said to suffer in some glorious agony of delight. Like the seismograph, which registers to the watching scientist the least tremor of the earth, this sensation-loving scientific romanticist, with body and soul magnetized to the point of disease, shudders exquisitely and luxuriously at the dimmest adumbration of a feeling. Sometimes the romanticists have practically taken over the realistic methods of Zola. But instead of examining all human nature in a scientist's laboratory, as Zola advocates, they have confined themselves to society in those pathological aspects which now replace the older romantic passions or, more often still, they have confined themselves to an elaborate vivisection of the ego. Too often we misuse Spenser, who projected vaster, saner things, as a mere picture gallery or as an exotic drug to feed an already overdeveloped part of our organisms.

A sketch of the critics, poets, and ages filled with these currents of thought is not an impertinent or a grandiloquent, but an illuminating way for a critic to prelude and test his own final and personal impressions of Edmund Spenser.

I

I have said that Spenser's day was aglow. with ardent faith in everything English and therefore with Spenser-worship. At the very outset *The Shepheards Calender* was acclaimed with a full chorus of idolatrous panegyrics. To most of the best spirits it was nothing less than scripture to meditate upon. Those who, like Drayton and Phineas Fletcher and even Dr. Samuel Woodford toward the close of the seventeenth century, were less enthusiastic at first about *The Faërie Queene* were, in the main, those who were so enamored of Colin Clout's shepherd-poetry that they would brook no other *genre* from their idol. But those whose enthusiasm for *The Shepheards Calender* made them at first reluctant to see him retire to the heights of the epic poet, came forward, almost without exception, a little later, with the highest praise. And their hesitant protests had already been lost in a storm of laudation with which others had welcomed the poet's masterpiece. Even Harvey, though he has been sometimes recorded as a most uncompromising enemy of *The Faërie Queene*, appears, on investigation, to have recanted. We may safely quote, as his final verdict, from a letter of September 5, 1592, where he wrote to Christopher Bird of ''the pure sanguine of ... [the] sweete Fairie Queene,'' and a charming phrase from the *New Letter of notable Contents* (1593), ''is not the verse of M. Spencer in his brave Faery Queene the Virginall of the divinest Muses and gentlest Graces?''

The entire attitude of the Age of Enthusiasm may be best summed up in Tom Nash's swashbuckling eulogy:

And should the challenge of deepe conceit be intruded by any forrainer, to bring our English wits to the touchstone of Art, I would preferre divine Master *Spencer*, the miracle of wit to bandie line for line for my life in the honor of England, against Spaine, Fraunce, Italy, and all the world.

We have also noted before how Francis Meres wrote his *Palladis Tamia* (1598) to prove English poets the peers of the singers of all the world and how he ranked Spenser as excelling in all *genres*. So also Richard Carew, in his quaint *Epistle on the Excellency of the English Tongue*, remembers Spenser in the midst of a delightful fanfaronade.

I come nowe to the last and sweetest point of the sweetnes of our tongue, which shall appeare the more plainlye yf, like towe Turkeyes, or the *London Drapers*, wee match it with our neighboures. The Italyan is pleasante but without synewes, as to stillye fleeting water; the French delicate but over nice, as a woman scarce daring to open her lipps for feare of marring her countenaunce; the Spanishe maiesticall, but fullsome, running to much on the O, and terrible like the devill in a playe; the Dutch manlike, but withall very harshe, as one ready at every worde to picke a quarrell. Now wee in borrowing from them geve the strength of Consonantes to the Italyan, the full sounde of wordes to the French, the varietye of termi[na]cions to the Spanish, and the mollifieinge of more vowells to the Dutch; and soe (like bees) gather the honye of their good properties and leave the dreggs to themselfes.... Adde hereunto, that what soever grace any other Languadge carryeth, in Verse or Prose, in Tropes or Metaphors, in Ecclioes or Agnomintions, they maye all be lively and exactly represented in ours. Will you have *Platos* vayne? reede Sir *Thomas Smith: The Ionick?* Sir *Tho. Moor: Ciceros? Aschame: Varro? Chaucer: Demosthenes?* Sir *John Cheeke* (who in his treatise to the Rebells hath comprised all the figures of Rhetorick). Will yow reade *Virgill?* take the *Earll of Surrey: Catullus? Shakespeare,* and *Marlowes* fragment: *Ovid? Daniell: Lucane? Spencer: Martiall?* Sir *John Davis* and others. Will you have all in all for prose and verse? take the miracle of our age Sir *Philip Sydney....*

This is typical work of the Age of Enthusiasm, unbounded faith in England's language and men of letters, coupled with a grotesque lack of discrimination that is almost unparalleled except in time of war. We can see what a rare world of fine frenzy England had to lose before she learned how to be judicious. Even Michael Drayton's weighty *Epistle to Henry Reynolds of Poets and Poesie*, genial, sympathetic, and extraordinarily shrewd as it is in its judgment of contemporaries, has for Spenser nothing but hallelujahs.

> Grave morrall *Spencer* after these came on,
> Than whom I am perswaded there was none
> Since the blind *Bard* his *Iliads* up did make,
> Fitter a taske like that to undertake,
> To set downe boldly, bravely to invent,
> In all high knowledge surely excellent.

Again and again this enthusiasm, if it was fatal in its exuberant lawlessness to criticism, was the muse of no end of lovely poetry about the poet of poets. Among the many tributes we should never forget the exquisite sonnet by Richard Barnefield, a sensitive, somewhat decadent poet who fell suddenly and mysteriously silent in his youth but not before he had given us a glimpse of a young man's "best and happiest moments."

> If Musique and sweet Poetrie agree,
> As they must needes (the Sister and the Brother)
> Then must the Love be great, twixt thee and mee,
> Because thou lov'st the one, and I the other.
> *Dowland* to thee is deare; whose heavenly tuch
> Upon the Lute, doeth ravish humaine sense:
> *Spenser* to mee; whose deepe Conceit is such,
> As passing all Conceit, needs no defence.
> Thou lov'st to heare the sweete melodious sound,
> That *Phoebus* Lute (the Queene of Musique) makes:
> And I in deep Delight am chiefly drownd,
> When as himselfe to singing he betakes.
> One God is God of Both (as Poets Faigne)
> One Knight loves Both, and Both in thee remaine.

Certain of the early Spenserians, "well-languaged Daniell," the sensitive Barnefield, Rous with his boyish high dreams of chivalry, might be classed as the Gawains of poetry, goldentongued, courtly, rather passionless and languid, like the garrulous knights of Chretien's leisurely narratives. By way of contrast the group of Drayton seems to constitute the yeomanry of song, bending good English yew instead of Cupid's graceful bow. Drayton, William Browne, Wither, Davies of Hereford loved the very soil of merrie England, and mostly chose to naturalize the creatures of their fancy in their own tangible fatherland, not in the realms of Faërie. Theirs was the spirit of the young American poet, Drake, who strove to people the majestic scenery of his country with the beings of Old World legend. Drayton and Browne made their favorite rivers haunted by little fairy-folk, with something of the homely conviction of English peasants. Nymphs clasped hands with pretty peasant girls and danced around May-poles. The sombre Davies of Hereford, more partial to Spenser's allegorical personages, took them from the realms of Faërie and placed them in the narrow streets and taverns of his beloved London. Like the sturdy authors of Piers Plowman he made his allegorical Vices more tangible by an infusion of the coarse blood of London topers and rakes. Browne, the gentlest spirit of the group, was content to sing forever of his own river, the Tavy, a devotion which is rewarded, it is said, by the veneration of the Devonshire folk to this very day. He gives us quaint and most significant evidence of the Spenser-worship characteristic of his group in "Fido: an Epistle to Fidelia," where we find him, a most pensive lover, turning the pages of *The Faërie Queene* as a devout churchman would open his Bible, for some chance comfort and some divine inspiration to conduct.

> Sitting one day beside a silver brook,
> Whose sleepy waves unwillingly forsook
> The strict embraces of the flow'ry shore,
> As loathe to leave what they should see no more:
> I read (as fate had turn'd it to my hand)
> Among the famous lays of fairy land,
> Belphœbe's fond mistrust, whenas she met
> Her gentle Squire with lovely Amoret.
> And laying by the book, poor lad, quoth I,
> Must all thy joys, like Eve's posterity,
> Receive a doom, not to be chang'd by suit,
> Only for tasting the forbidden fruit?
> Had fair Belphoebe licens'd thee some time
> To kiss her cherry lip, thou didst a crime;
> But since she for thy thirst no help would bring,
> Thou lawfully might'st seek another spring;
> And had those kisses stol'n been melting sips,

Tn'en by consent from Amoret's sweet lips,
Thou might'st have answer'd, if thy love had spied,
How others gladly gave what she denied;
But since they were not such, it did approve
A jealousy not meriting thy love,
And an injustice offer'd by the maid
In giving judgment ere she heard thee plead.
I have a Love (and then I thought of you,
As heaven can witness I each minute do,)
So well assur'd of that once promis'd faith
Which my unmoved Love still cherisheth,

. . . .

I surely could believe, nay, I durst swear,
That your sweet goodness would not stoop to fear.

. . . .

Such were my thoughts of you, and thinking so,

. . . .

I in security was further gone,
And made a path for your suspicion
To find me out. Time being nigh the same,
When thus I thought, and when your letters came.
But, oh, how far I err'd, how much deceiv'd
Was my belief!

There are no records to tell us whether Browne's mistress was duly repentant for having knocked a few stars out of her poet's heaven, though it is to be feared that the high ideals which Browne often derived from ruminating over some choice morsel of *The Faërie Queene* were frequently battered by the work-a-day world even in the Arcadia that was reigned over by the good Queen Bess and by James the First, Apprentice in the Divine Art of Poesy. But whatever the man-in-the-street may have said to Browne, this poem typifies a steadfast attitude toward Spenser and toward life that throws much light on the Age of Enthusiasm. By some appropriate leisurely brook Browne read and reread *The Faërie Queene*. What some prying peasant might have supposed to be the soliloquies of a lonely imbecile were in reality conversations which the good poet was holding with Guyon or Timias or Calidore visible to him in the flesh. To him *The Faërie Queene* was Scripture wherewith to make love. And perhaps, if he had been a husbandman, he would have somehow derived from the same source practical precepts for farming. For his best known work, *Britannia's Pastorals*, he imported scenes, characters, and episodes from *The Faërie Queene* into Devonshire. He pillaged more widely than even Drayton, searching every page of his model with the industry of a bee. Like Drayton he was hopelessly irresponsible. But the formlessness of the *Poly-Olbion* is due to its poet's sturdy temperament, goading him to monstrous efforts. Browne lacked somewhat of this largeness and this clumsiness. The formlessness of *Britannia's Pastorals* is due to his gentle meditative spirit which led him to seek in *The Faërie Queene* the least austere, the most winding paths and lose his way, to make digressions which never end; similes within similes ever becoming less and less apt but more and more captivating.

We can pause no longer over the myriad voices of other poets, who, in sweet-singing hosts, threw their garlands at the feet of the great singer. Peele, Breton, Sir John Davies, William Basse, a legion, glowed with the most generous praise. We may best point the close of a passage on the Age of Enthusiasm and Spenser-worship by quoting the sonnet with which Sir Walter Raleigh flung down the gauntlet for Spenser in challenge to the memorable singers of the whole world.

> Me thought I saw the grave where Laura lay,
> Within that temple where the vestall flame
> Was wont to burne; and passing by that way,
> To see that buried dust of living fame,
> Whose tumbe faire Love, and fairer Vertue kept,
> All suddeinly 1 saw the Faery Queene:
> At whose approch the soule of Petrarke wept,
> And from thenceforth those graces were not seene.
> For they this Queene attended; in whose steed
> Oblivion laid him downe on Lauras herse:
> Hereat the hardest stones were seene to bleed,
> And grones of buried ghostes the hevens did perse:
> Where Homers spright did tremble all for griefe,
> And curst th' accesse of that celestiall theife.

II

While the Elizabethans were in the first rapture of self-discovery, extravagant mutual eulogy was to be expected. But when they dropped back to the C-major of this life and rodomontade ceased to be the fashion, a genuine literary criticism came to be born.

We may begin our study of the Age of Reason with a figure who reveals all the agitation of first self-doubting and little of the new conviction that came, for a while, to greater personages of the period. Joseph Hall, rough-and-ready satirist, and later bishop, has perplexed not a few critics with what they consider his inconsistent attitude toward Spenser.[2] He has been named as an admirer of Spenser, as an enemy of Spenser, as hopelessly, almost treacherously inconsistent. But with those who have found him at any time hostile lies the burden of proof. All the definite references to Spenser laud him. The harsh lines are deceptive and have been quoted too often without any explanation of their general context. But a careful examination of Hall's poems *in toto* makes his attitude perfectly clear. He called himself the first English satirist. A natural influence, before the Age of Reason was quite articulate and self-conscious, led him to believe that the age of creative poetry was at least temporarily over. His was an academic or bookish attitude common in many ages. The great writers have said it all. What is the use of writing feeble echoes? He believed in the half-truth that there is nothing new under the sun. So to Hall one of the supreme writers who had left nothing more to be done was Edmund Spenser. In 1597 he brought out his *Virgidemiarum* containing six books of satires. As a kind of

---

[2] Thus Dr. Grosart, *Hall's Poems* (ed. Manchester, 1879), p. xviii: ''I cannot help regretting his double-dealing treatment of Spenser as the most unpleasant alloy of the satires.'' Thomas Warton, too, was disturbed over the same problem. Other critics have conveyed unfortunate impressions by tearing fragmentary selections inconsiderately from Hall's references or possible references to Spenser without due consideration for the context.

preface he wrote a "Defiance of Envy," the seventh stanza of which has offended the admirers of Spenser. He asserted that he did not care to

> ... Scoure the· rusted swords of Elvish Knights,
> Bathed in Pagan blood; or sheath them new
> In misty morall Types, or tell their fights,
> Who mightie Giants, or who Monsters slew.
> And by some strange inchanted speare and shield,
> Vanquisht their foe and won the doubtful field.

This certainly seems, by itself, like girding at *The Faërie Queene*. But let us look at the poem as a whole. It begins humbly enough with the statement that the pines of Ida may fear the sudden fires of heaven. With his lowly shrubs, in their humble dales, he may safely feel secure. If his muse *did* attempt to "scoure the rusted swords of Elvish Knights," then Envy might attack him.

> But now such lowly Satyres here I sing,
> Not worth our Muse, not worth their envying.

The swords are rusted, then, because there is no Spenser to draw them. That is the point. The book is full of Spenserian phrases and ends with an unmistakable tribute. Hall dares try no high pastoral strain but throws his "yeelding reade" "at Collin's feete." Nor is it possible to urge that Hall loved *The Shepheards Calender* but thought meanly of *The Faërie Queene*. For elsewhere he writes:

> Th' eternall Legends of thy Faerie Muse,
> Renowned Spenser: whom no earthly wight
> Dares once to emulate, much ·less dares despight
> Salust of France and Tuscan Ariost
> Yeeld up the Lawrell garland ye have lost:
> And let all others willow wear with me
> Or let their undeserving Temples bared be.

Not a shadow of disapproval of Spenser. Only the satiety of a bookish mind, feeling but not understanding a new *Zeitgeist*.

> Whilome the sisters nine were Vestal maides,
> . . . .
> Now is Parnassus turned to a stewes.

The great poets have written; times are degenerate, thinks Hall. What seem like attacks on Spenser, as in the "Defiance of Envy," are but preludes to self-abasement. This is the characteristic attitude of the Jeremiah who thinks that all the beautiful things have been said; that the present is diseased. In a reference to the episode of the marriage of the Thames and the Medway in *The Faërie Queene* the satirist is specific in self-effacement before Spenser's muse.

> Or if we list [make lofty songs] what baser muse can bide,
> To sit and sing by Grantaes naked side?
> They haunt the tyded Thames and salt Medway
> Ere since the fame of their late Bridall day.

We must hasten on to Ben Jonson, the most significant of the first English writers of critical works. Unfortunately he gave us no well-rounded estimate of Spenser although he was liberal with tantalizing allusions. With Spenser's stanza he was clearly out of tune. He told Drummond that "Spenser's stanzaes pleased him not, nor his matter." But Jonson was grumbling almost unintermittently at that symposium. And perhaps Drummond tinged his record more deeply with his own evident conception of Ben's perennial surliness. Jonson all but contradicted this recorded dictum on Spenser's "matter" in his *Discoveries* (1625–1635?) when he said: "Spenser in effecting the Ancients writ no Language. Yet I would have him read for his matter, but as Virgil read Ennius." And he all but contradicted his attack on Spenser's archaisms in another part of his *Discoveries* where he says, somewhat inconsistently: "Words borrow'd of Antiquity doe lend a kind of Majesty to style, and are not without their delight sometimes."

In his Masque, *The Golden Age Restored*, Jonson introduces Chaucer, Gower, Lydgate, and Spenser as the far-famed and sanctified singers of the good old days. And this readiness to accept Spenser as at least a traditional classic is also apparent in a characteristic fling at the mob in the *Discoveries*.

There were never wanting those that dare prefer the worst poets.... Nay, if it were put to the question of the water-rimers works against Spenser's, I doubt not but they would find more suffrages; because the most favor common vices out of a prerogative the vulgar have to lose their judgments and like that which is nought.

It seems likely that Jonson, on the whole, was an admirer of Spenser, and that his animadversions are but those of a man who probably loved Spenser as he loved Shakespeare—"on this side idolatry."

Some Elizabethan traditions lived on with the work of Giles and Phineas Fletcher and their followers, who adored and plundered Spenser for allegorical figures, memorable lines, sometimes almost complete stanzas. Over all they embroidered the curious, stiff conceits that were rising high in favor. They were enthusiastic imitators of the Spenserian stanza. As Spenser had given new music to the eight-line stanza by the addition of a final alexandrine, so the Fletchers experimented by adding the long line to the rhyme-royal, the *ottava rima,* and many other current forms. The influence of the Fletchers was far greater than has been recorded in literary histories. They founded a distinct school of poetry which outlived the chilling influence of the Restoration and lasted for a hundred years. In Milton's day, most of the Cantabrigians, Crashaw, Joseph Beaumont, Thomas Robinson, and others, wrote more or less in their manner. In his boyhood Milton was enlisted in the School of the Fletchers and their influence is traceable even in his mature poems. These curious, half-diseased, half-divine poets were in one respect the truest Spenserians who ever lived. They did not distil the rarest essence of their master as did Milton and Keats and other great English poets. But they did more than merely loot *The Faërie Queene* for lines and stanzas. With the passing of the School of the Fletchers there passed the last ambitious, absurd attempts to rear the cumbersome, tottering framework of *The Faërie Queene* to the very stars. The eighteenth century poets, for the most part, imitated Spenser elegantly and superficially as they imitated all their masters. The romanticists, when they reached their period of full triumph, did not, in the same sense of the word, imitate their masters. They were inspired by them. But the Fletchers and their crew, besides plundering and botching lines, stanzas, episodes, and allegories, outlined gigantic schemes like that set forth in Spenser's letter to Raleigh, that superb manifesto of idealism, and turned Milton from his dreams of Arthur to write audaciously of God and Satan. With the School of the Fletchers such heaven-storming became a mode in England as it was already a mode on the continent. We cannot fairly but admire as well as laugh at the audacity with which the School of the Fletchers strove to rear Babels of poetry. And in this chaos Milton, whose devotion to Spenser we have already seen, saw light.

We may conclude our survey of the Age of Reason with a note on one of the earliest apostles of that neo-classicism which in England struggled with great difficulty through the ensuing Age of Literary Anarchy and gained supremacy at last only when Pope and Addison planted the standard on the heights.

The first important critical document of the neo-classicists was Sir William Davenant's preface to *Gondibert*. This has been inconsiderately damned by not a few, from Davenant's own day[3] to this, as crass and unsympathetic in its attitude toward Spenser. But to call Davenant unappreciative of Spenser is to read his preface without any sense of perspective. He depre-cated the older poet's choice of stanza and he shared in the generally increasing objections to the archaisms. Moreover, although the preface is emphatic in its identification of the ideal poet and the moralist, Davenant was not in sympathy with Spenser's method of inculcating virtue—"his allegorical Story . . . resembling, methinks, a continuance of extraordinary Dreams; such as excellent Poets, and Painters, by being over-studious, may have in the beginning of Feavers." But if we

---

[3] Aubrey writes: "Sir John Denham told me that A. BP. Usher, Lord Primate of Armagh was acquainted with ... [Spenser] by this token, when Sir W. Davenant's 'Gondibert' came forth, Sir John askt the Lord Primate if he had seen it? Said the Primate, 'Out upon him, with his vaunting preface, he speaks against my old friend, Edmund Spenser.'"

consider the general scheme of his essay we shall see that Davenant's estimate of Spenser only exemplifies a belief that criticism should be the noble art of praise with intelligent qualifications. He was about to propound the rules for an ideal epic and he began by naming those whom he considered the greatest writers of heroic poetry. He thus placed Spenser with Homer, Virgil, Lucan, Statius, and Tasso. He then pointed out the failings of each writer and Spenser hardly fared worse than any of the others. In this way Davenant gave Spenser implicitly the highest praise.

> *Spencer* may here stand as the last of this short File of Heroick Poets, —Men whose intellectuals were of so great a making (though some have thought them lyable to those few Censures we have mentioned) as perhaps they will in worthy memory outlast even Makers of Laws and Founders of Empires, and all but such as must therefore live equally with them because they have recorded their names; and consequently with their own hands led them to the Temple of Fame. And since we have dar'd to remember those exceptions which the Curious have against them, it will not be expected I should forget what is objected against *Spencer*, whose obsolete Language we are constrain'd to mention, though it be grown the most vulgar accusation that is laid to his charge.

Davenant's tone is obviously most apologetic. More than once he foisted his animadversions on "the Curious." He expressed a fear that his censures of the immortals would make Hobbes, to whom he addressed his preface, think him "malicious" in observing the faults which "the Curious" had found with revered writers. His detailed criticisms, restored to their context, become then of minor importance. There have been ardent admirers of Spenser, in every period, who could subscribe with little emendation to Davenant's complaints.

The Age of Reason, as I have already observed, verged rapidly and inevitably into an Age of Literary Anarchy when doubt, the essential comrade of reason, gained the upper hand.

III

Already we have had occasion to note the change from the Elizabethan Age of rapturous faith through an age of reason, of doubt, of unrest, to a positive literary anarchy which corresponded well with the great political upheavals which distressed England throughout the reign of the Stuarts. Elizabethan ideals were unified by their abounding faith. In spite of our disgust for the fulsome eulogies of Elizabeth, we must admit that, when the last shred of the courtier's mask is torn away, there glows a deep faith in the sovereign. And we have seen that a man like Spenser could glorify the queen with praise purified by the fire of a fierce and insistent criticism. But we have seen that the climax of the Elizabethan Age was a time of boyish panegyric, and that England's faith in her literature was so immense that sanely regulated literary criticism was practically impossible until the canker doubt had done deadly work. Then English poetry, which had moved in comparative harmony, gradually divided and subdivided itself into a hundred jarring sects. Hostile schools despised each other and doubted themselves. Often men became inconstant or inconsistent members of two warring cults. The neo-classical *credo*, which was to unify literature once more, gained ground slowly, and did not, as some have thought, triumph in the days of Waller, Denham, or Dryden. It struggled for bare existence till Pope and Addison became dictators.

The Age of Literary Anarchy had no well-defined beginning. Even such men as William Drummond of Hawthornden, Ben Jonson, and Edward Fairfax spread subtle seeds of sedition in their groping towards one of the new warring sects, neo-classicism. Drummond and Fairfax combined the Elizabethan love of sensuousness with a truly classical interest in form. The tastes of Fairfax descended to Waller, who was glad to acknowledge him as a model. Less obviously, Drummond was an influence because of his fondness for polishing the couplet (the form that the neo-classicists were to accept as supreme) and because his bookishness sent him directly back to the Latin poets again and again. His love of form shows itself in the fact that he experimented with more sonnet-schemes than any other poet in the language. In the abandon of the Elizabethan genius his almost over cultivated mind must have found some rough dissonances. Ben Jonson was a more definite classicist and his influence was immense. Of these three, Fairfax interests us most because, as the ardent student of Spenser and the acknowledged master of Waller, he linked Spenserian traditions with neo-classicism, the two currents of English literature that critics have long mistakenly regarded as antipathetic. In 1600 Fairfax published his translation of Tasso's epic, a version which, though in *ottava rima,* taught Waller how to fashion the smooth couplets that made him the model of all true believers in neo-classicism. Fairfax was an enthusiastic follower of Spenser and frequently departed from his original to draw nearer to *The Faërie Queene.* In emulating the highly wrought technique of Spenser and Tasso the translator doubtless found himself forced into that more conscious attention to finish which caught the eye of Edmund Waller who, in turn, gave unmistakable evidence of his first-hand acquaintance with Spenser. At all events, Waller and Dryden considered Fairfax to be one of their sacred authorities.

Along with these first classicists came decadent Elizabethans who had outlived the Elizabethan spirit of youth and in whom ruddy enthusiasm had become hectic disease, careless fancy metamorphosed into ingenious artifice, the sensuous extravagance of Petrarch laid aside for the stiffer conceits and the fever of Marini. Such a spirit laid prematurely a blighting finger on the large soul of Donne and spread even more insidiously through the religious ecstasy of Crashaw. By 1630 England's poetry was visibly disturbed by the struggles of these discordant forces.

From about 1650 to the end of the century the influence of Spenser was at its lowest ebb in the history of English poetry.

The cause of this lies precisely in that multiplicity of artistic theories that brought about the literary civil wars. When the Elizabethans thought that they tallied all antecedents they canonized Spenser in a thoroughly uncritical way. He was their morning star, their high priest of poetry. He was with Homer. The admiration of later writers was no less deep and sincere, but doubt had sharpened their critical insight. The influence of Spenser was hardly less great than that of any other writer. It was only that influences were legion. There were no great central convictions like those which inspired the Elizabethans, Augustans, and romanticists at their highest point of development. The wonder is that Spenser was received at all widely among so many antagonistic groups of writers.

The spirit of classicism had as yet but a thin voice in the literary affairs of the age. The heavy cloth of gold of the renaissance made a mantle which the poets were loath to relinquish. As late as 1679 the School of the Fletchers, for instance, was very much alive in Samuel Woodford's *Legend of Love* and its "Epoda" in Spenserian stanzas, accompanied by a critical preface of great interest to students of this period. Even in the eighteenth century, when neo-classicism held full sway, William Thompson registered his name as the last in this school with his *Hymn to May* (1757), a piece which closely followed Spenser's *Epithalamion,* avowed the influence of Phineas Fletcher's *Purple Island,* and is Elizabethan even in an age of trim parterres.

Literary anarchy became bewildering toward the close of the century, because English poetry, except for Dryden, had fallen largely among little men. The various warring creeds quarreled to the end. Marinism, which had found its first brilliant supporter in Crashaw, was upheld by men like John Norris of Bemerton in his *Miscellanies* (1678). Two very different schools warred against them: the boisterous satirists of the type of John Cleveland and Dr. Robert Wild, who battled with the decadent poets by using a rugged style which constantly broke down into reckless doggerel; Waller, Denham, and Sidney

Godolphin, who fought for neo-classicism. There was, besides
the School of the Fletchers, a great number of scattered, belated
Elizabethans. These men were often perfectly conscious of their
reactionary tendencies. Then there were some who wrote in-
consistently in different veins. Such a man was Sir Richard
Fanshawe, a good friend of the classicist Denham, but warm in
his sympathies for Elizabethans and Marinists. In 1676 a num-
ber of his miscellaneous poems appeared along with his trans-
lation of Guarini's *Il Pastor Fido*. ''A Canto of the Progress of
Learning,'' though in Spenserian stanzas, is far less florid than
some of his sonnets and lyrics and deals with a subject that his
friend Denham chose for one of his most formal and elaborate
poems in classical couplets. On the other hand the opening line,
''Tell me, O Muse, and tell me Spencer's Ghost,'' seems to indi-
cate that the master's poetry was not far from Fanshawe's
thoughts. Again he translated Virgil, the god of the Augustans,
in the Spenserian stanza, a form quite generally regarded, even
by its admirers in that day, as a dubious one for heroic poetry.
Charles Cotton continued at once the wholesome nature poetry
of Browne and Herrick, and wrote amorous lyrics in the vein of
Suckling and Lovelace, men who cared little for the quiet coun-
try, who preferred the rustle of the silk gowns of court ladies
to ''the wind among the reeds.'' Cowley's eccentric Pindaric
Odes fell into disrepute toward the close of the century. Yet
Thomas Flatman, one of the very few lyrists who wrote with high
seriousness at the end of the century, followed Cowley almost
exclusively. Flatman's two friends, Dr. Samuel Woodford, the
Spenserian, and Katherine Philips, ''the matchless Orinda,''
wrote often in the manner of Cowley. Yet Katherine Philips,
with her affected elegance and her importation of French ideals
from the Hotel Rambouillet, contributed definitely to the rise
of neo-classicism. Finally, Dryden, who was to give the death-
blow to Abraham Cowley, wrote one of his maturest poems,
''To Mrs. Anne Killegrew'' (1686) in the Pindaric and meta-
physical vein of the despised poet. Against the lyrics of the
court amorists we may pit the long line of religious lyrics from

Crashaw (himself as ardent a royalist as Lovelace or Suckling) to Vaughan. In the love-lyric, too, the approach of the dissolution of faith, of the Age of Anarchy, may be seen as early as in Habington's *Castara*, a somewhat uneasy, over-conscious attempt to fuse the erotic cavalier poetry with religion and Platonism, utterly unlike the spontaneous Platonism of the Elizabethans. Then complete cynicism broke in. At the close of the century Rochester, Sedley, Aphra Behn, and others were retailing the commonplaces of the amorists and striving to eke out their slender originality, to heal their shattered faith in the finer things of life with feverish sensuality, cynicism, and obscenity. Except for the slow and hotly contested rise of neo-classicism, this degradation of the court lyric is typical of the degradation of all English poetry. Neo-classicism promised at least a wholesome repression in style and a theory, if no more, of the moral responsibility of poetry in its highest moods. It promised a much-needed increase of intellectuality as opposed to unbridled fancy.

In turning to the heralds of Augustanism we must never forget that they were not outside the influence of Spenser and did not regard Spenser as necessarily opposed to their régime. We shall see how they came more and more to reconcile him with their ideals much as they reconciled Virgil. Sir John Denham classed Spenser and Jonson together as exponents of "Art" as opposed to the less-revered native woodnotes wild which were regarded with admiration well-tinged with qualifications

> Next (like Aurora), Spenser rose
> Whose purple blush the day foreshows;
> Old Mother Wit and Nature gave
> Shakespeare and Fletcher all they have,
> In Spenser and in Jonson, Art
> Of slower Nature got the start.

But it was Dryden who sanctified Spenser for the Augustans of the seventeenth and eighteenth centuries. With Dryden English criticism came to a brilliant climax and the Age of Literary Anarchy received complete and powerful expression. England

felt a growing interest in the well-marshalled French theories of
poetry but found them practically impossible to reconcile with
her sturdy native traditions and the restless spirit of the age.
When we learn to realize thoroughly how some writers took
refuge in an idolatrous worship of the classics, how others
clamored for the perpetuation of the Elizabethan manner, how
many caught up the extravagances of the English Marinists,
the attempt to goad jaded emotions with the highly spiced diet
of stiff conceits, and carried the hectic fancies of Cowley, Cra-
shaw, and their crew to excess beyond excess, how some gave up
hope of solution and sought false relief, like Butler, in cynicism
and rough mockery, how the exquisite idyllic vein of Andrew
Marvel could turn to vigorous but ugly satire, when we realize
that it was the day of a hundred schools, the Age of Literary
Anarchy, as it was the age of civil broils and political plots, then
we can understand Dryden with some human sympathy. In
Dryden's day uncertainty ran riot. His admirers and detrac-
tors have long puzzled over his vacillations in matters religious,
literary, and political. However servile he may have been, it
is difficult to deny that he was a man of strong if somewhat
fickle convictions that changed, not merely with the breeze of
public opinion, but with his own true moods. Some of his
inconsistencies are readily explainable by his enthusiasm for the
subject under immediate consideration. In his *Discourse on
Epick Poetry* (1697) he devoted some time to proving, in spite
of Aristotle, that heroic poetry is a greater form than tragedy,
but in his *Essay Of Dramatick Poesie* (1668), where all his
eloquence was being spent on the drama, he did not even pause
to support a confident parenthesis, "though tragedy may be
justly preferred to the other." In his *Preface* to *Sylvae; or The
Second Part of Poetical Miscellanies* (1685) he adjudges Spen-
ser's endeavor to imitate the rustic speech of Theocritus, by
an infusion of archaic and dialect words, unsuccessful.

Spenser has endeavoured it in his *Shepherd's Calendar;* but neither
will it succeed in English [any more than in the Latin tongue]; for which
reason I forbore to attempt it.

Yet in his *Dedication* of the *Pastorals* of Virgil (1696) he wrote:

But Spencer being master of our northern dialect, and skilled in Chaucer's English, has so exactly imitated the Dorick of Theocritus, that his love is a perfect image of that passion which God infused into both sexes, before it was corrupted with the knowledge of arts, and the ceremonies of what we call good manners.

Without pausing to consider any more of Dryden's many self-contradictions, we may turn to his comments on Spenser as disclosing matters most significant for our general conception of Dryden as a critic and our full appreciation of our poet. In his youth Dryden, like many young writers, was a victim of the poets of his own generation. His early servitude to the conceit-hunters is well known. He himself tells us in his *Dedication of The Spanish Friar* (1681) that he once thought "inimitable Spenser a mean poet, in comparison of Sylvester's *Dubartas.*" But he came to dub the idol of his callow days a writer of "abominable fustian."

In his maturity Dryden spoke enthusiastically and discerningly about Spenser. In *A Discourse Concerning the Original and Progress of Satire* (1693) he made his most elaborate criticism. In a long digression on heroic poetry, in which he asserted that no one equalled Homer and Virgil, he criticised Lucan, Statius, Ariosto, and Tasso; scorned utterly the French epics; but admitted that in England Spenser and Milton had the necessary genius and learning although both were open to many censures. Then follows the first elaborate criticism on record of Spenser's unity, a passage which I have already quoted in my discussion of the structure of *The Faërie Queene*. Dryden then goes on:

For the rest, his obsolete language, and ill choice of his stanza, are faults but of the second magnitude; for, notwithstanding the first, he is still intelligible, at least after a little practice; and for the last, he is the more to be admired, that, labouring under such a difficulty, his verses are so numerous, so various, and so harmonious, that only Virgil, whom he professedly imitated, has surpassed him among the Romans; and only Mr. Waller among the English.

It is important to note that Dryden's reasonable criticism of the unity of *The Faërie Queene* has become the conventional

comment to our very day. It is moreover worth special atten-
tion that Dryden places himself above the mere carping at
Spenser's diction. Indeed he did not always regard the archa-
isms as even "faults of the second magnitude." We have seen
that he first condemned but later praised the diction of *The
Shepheards Calender.* And in his discussion of Milton in this
same digression in the *Essay of Satire,* in a passage which I
have already quoted in my observations on *The Faërie Queene,*
he treats archaisms with a justice that is beyond reproach,
admitting their justification if they are "more sounding, or
more significant than those in practice," advising only moder-
ation and due attention to clarity.

Dryden's association of the names of Spenser and Virgil
here as master and pupil is only one of the many passages that
indicate that Spenser and the darling of the neo-classicists were
endeared to him as poetical comrades. In his *Dedication of the
Aeneis* (1697) he wrote: "I must acknowledge that Virgil in
Latin, and Spenser in English, have been my masters." Again:

> If the design be good, and the draught be true, the colouring is the
> first beauty that strikes the eye. Spenser and Milton are the nearest, in
> English, to Virgil and Horace in Latin; and I have endeavoured to form
> my style by imitating their masters.

This association of Virgil and Spenser is very significant because
it throws a clear light on an aspect of neo-classicism completely
misunderstood. The Augustans did not, as has been so con-
stantly averred, forget or despise Spenser. They found him, on
the whole, sufficiently reconcilable with their ideals and appre-
ciated sides of his poetry to which the romanticists, even to our
own day, have remained impervious or even hostile. Dryden
taught the Augustans to accept Virgil and Spenser as kindred
models. The cherished project of his own life was to write an
epic about Arthur, the hero of *The Faërie Queene,* or the Black
Prince, "wherein, after Virgil and Spenser, I would have taken
occasion to represent my living friends and patrons of noblest
families, and also shadowed the events of future ages, in the
succession of our imperial lines." But he was unfortunately

encouraged only with "fair words by King Charles II" and "my little salary ill paid."

The thorn which seems, however, to have pricked the sides of all who read Dryden, devoutly or sacrilegiously, is his apparently inordinate admiration for the faultless commonplaces of Waller and Denham with their rippling heroic couplets. In his *Epistle Dedicatory* of *The Rival Ladies* (1664) Dryden asserted of "rhyme" that "the excellence and dignity of it were never fully known till Mr. Waller taught it." In the *Defence of the Epilogue* to *The Conquest of Granada* (1672) he said: "Well-placing of words, for the sweetness of pronunciation, was not known till Mr. Waller introduced it." We turn to the *Essay Of Dramatick Poesie* and become belligerent when we read: "[The Elizabethans] can produce ... nothing so even sweet, and flowing, as Mr. Waller; nothing so majestic, so correct, as Sir John Denham." In the essay *Of Satire*, to be sure, this fetish-worship lends opportunity for gratifying praise of Spenser and a new interweaving of his name with Virgil's. For, having been advised by Sir George Mackenzie to imitate "the turns of Mr. Waller and Sir John Denham," it "first made me sensible to my own wants, and brought me afterwards to seek for the supply of them in other English authors." Not even "the darling of my youth, the famous Cowley," rewarded a search.

Then I consulted a greater genius (without offense to the *Manes* of that noble author) I mean Milton. But as he endeavours everywhere to express Homer, whose age had not arrived to that fineness, I found in him a true sublimity, lofty thoughts, which were clothed with admirable Grecisms, and ancient words, which he had been digging from the mines of Chaucer and Spenser, and which, with all their rusticity, had somewhat of venerable in them; but I found not there neither that for which I looked. At last I had recourse to his master, Spenser, the author of that immortal poem called the *Fairy Queen;* and there I met with that which I had been looking for so long in vain. Spenser had studied Virgil to as much advantage as Milton had done Homer; and among the rest of his excellencies, had copied that.

All this is truly mellifluous to the ear of the ardent Spenserian. But a famous passage in the Preface to the *Fables* (1700), the brilliant work of Dryden's full maturity, has been most unduly

exalted into prominence and cited as an example of that crass-
ness which is said to have tainted even the large mind of Dryden
in an age of literary narrowness. We expect only the choicest
wisdom in this preface. We gloat over the damnation of the
once revered Cowley. We breathe the fire of the noble eloquence
which exalts Chaucer. But, as Dryden's thought reverts to
metrics, our enthusiasm grows pale.

> Equality of numbers, in every verse which we call *heroic*, was either
> not known, or not always practised, in Chaucer's age.... We can only say
> that he lived in the infancy of our poetry, and that nothing is brought to
> perfection at the first. We must be children before we grow men. There
> was an Ennius, and in process of time a Lucilius, and a Lucretius, before
> Virgil and Horace; even after Chaucer there was a Spenser, a Harrington,
> a Fairfax, before Waller and Denham were in being; and our numbers were
> in their nonage till these last appeared.

These sentences have brought great reproach on the memory
of Dryden. It is surprising to see how widespread and uncom-
promising is the opinion that here Dryden, in his maturity,
capriciously expressed a senile preference for Waller and Den-
ham over Chaucer and Spenser. But it is to be observed that
most of Dryden's references to Denham and Waller have to do
with technique—and with the technique of the heroic couplet
solely. It is the "numbers" and "rhyme" (which readers of
the essay *Of Dramatick Poesie* will recognize as practically tech-
nical terms for the heroic couplet), which Dryden admired in
Waller and Denham. When Dryden wrote of the peers of the
ancients and considered poetry in all its aspects, he praised
Chaucer, Tasso, Spenser, Shakespeare, Jonson, Milton, and Cor-
neille in the highest terms. But Waller and Denham were not
mentioned. That he did not rate mere technique highest among
the qualifications of a poet is proved by a glance at his prefer-
ence for Chaucer over Ovid in the *Preface* to the *Fables*. From
his point of view Chaucer, in those days of imperfect knowledge
of Middle English, was an inferior metrist. The best he could
say of Chaucer's melody was that "there is the rude sweetness
of a Scotch tune in it, which is natural and pleasing though
not perfect." As a confirmed lover of Latin poetry he could

not but greatly prefer the artful cadences of Ovid's lines (though he was probably not blind to their saccharine qualities as compared with the stronger music of Virgil). Yet, in spite of Ovid's fancied metrical superiority, the Latin poet came off very badly in the comparison and was ranked definitely below Chaucer. In other words he placed Chaucer, whom he considered to live at a time when the English were "children," far above Ovid, a poet of the days of a great nation's mature culture and formal perfection. By the same token I do not hesitate to argue that while Dryden considered Waller and Denham to be distinguished as the perfectors of the popular heroic couplet of the day, he would not have dreamed a moment of placing them as high as Chaucer, Spenser, and Milton.

We have seen that whenever Dryden took a *genre,* a poet, or an ideal as the topic of an essay or a text for the exploitation of a pet theory he exalted the subject with a youthful enthusiasm for the interest of the hour and a fine indifference to what he had said before. When we consider the consistent and high praise in his many references to Spenser, it does not seem illogical to suppose that had he written an essay on his acknowledged master he would have glowed with an eloquence sublimated with his patriotic preference for English poets over the ancients and over the immaculate French rule-worshippers.[4] As it is, he has left some generalizations on Spenser that are in a spirit of admiration at once warm and rational. In the *Dedication of the Aeneis* he found that "the file of heroick poets is very short." There had been only one *Iliad* and one *Aeneid;* and Tasso was eminent, but far below.

After these three were entered, some Lord Chamberlain should be appointed, some critic of authority should be set before the door to keep out a crowd of little poets, who press for admission, and are not of quality.

Pulci, Bojardo, Ariosto, Le Moine, Scudery, Chapelain are huddled together with little discrimination and receive scant grace. But

---

[4] See the essay *Of Dramatick Poesie* for his preference of English and modern poetry.

Spenser has a better plea for his *Fairy Queen* had his action been finished, or had been one.   And Milton, if the Devil had not been his hero, instead of Adam.... After these, the rest of our English poets shall not be mentioned.   I have that honour for them which I ought to have; but if they are worthies, they are not to be ranked amongst the three whom I have named, and who are established in their reputation.

In the same essay we are told that "Spenser wanted only to have read the rules of Bossu; for no man was ever born with a greater genius, or had more knowledge to support it."   Today we fancy that we could prescribe something better than the fossilized Bossu.[5]   But like Dryden, we bow to Spenser's genius with a wish that he could have perfected a mould more vertebrate into which to pour the immense treasures of his mind though, if there is anything in my theory of his dream of a truly prophetic epic, we must add that something of his glorious audacity would perhaps have waned in any structure short of the superhuman.

Dryden, not content with placing Spenser as an epic poet in the severely chosen list that included only Milton, Tasso, Homer, and Virgil, exalted *The Shepheards Calender* to the highest rank among pastoral poems.   In his *Dedication* of his translation of the *Pastorals* of Virgil (1696), after having discussed the eclogues of Theocritus and Virgil, he added:

Our own nation has produced a third poet in this kind, not inferior to the two former. For the Shepherd's Calendar of Spencer is not to be matched in any modern language, not even by Tasso's Aminta, which infinitely transcends Guarini's Pastor-Fido, as having more of nature in it, and being almost wholly clear from the wretched affectation of learning. I will say nothing of the piscatory eclogues, because no modern Latin can bear criticism. It is no wonder that rolling down through so many barbarous ages, from the spring of Virgil, it bears along with it the filth and ordures of the Goths and Vandals. Neither will I mention Monsieur Fontenelle, the living glory of the French. It is enough for him to have excelled his master, Lucian, without attempting to compare our

---

[5] Luke Milbourne, a contentious parson, gained much notoriety, including a savage thrust from Pope (*Essay on Criticism*, ll. 462 sq.), for a book of acrid observations on Dryden's translation of Virgil. But Milbourne at least made just and grim sport of Dryden's prescription of Bossu for Spenser.

miserable age with that of Virgil or Theocritus. Let me only add, for his reputation,

> — si Pergama dextra
> Defendi possent, etiam hac defensa fuissent.

But Spencer being master of our northern dialect, and skilled in Chaucer's English, has so exactly imitated the Dorick of Theocritus, that his love is a perfect image of that passion which God infused into both sexes, before it was corrupted with the knowledge of arts, and the ceremonies of what we call good manners.

The obvious conclusions from these citations certainly add little but luster to Dryden's fame as a critic. Mr. Waller and Mr. Denham are given credit only for what they actually accomplished. To be sure, Dryden over-rated the heroic couplet, which from his point of view they perfected, as a measure. But it is absurd to suppose that he placed them, on these grounds, above the acknowledged masters of English poetry. As for Spenser, no man has praised him more nobly and more rationally than Dryden. We have little occasion to question the opinions of those who hold him to be the greatest English critic.

Many other critics and poets, even in this disconcerting Age of Literary Anarchy, wrote in praise of Spenser.[6] It is remarkable, in the midst of degeneration, in the midst of many conflicting influences and hostile ideals, to find Spenser admired and followed by poets in other respects so inimical to one another. His immortality did substantial service in preserving at this time the immortality of idealism. It would have been glory enough, indeed, to have inspired so largely Dryden alone. Meanwhile neo-classicism, so necessary to save English poetry at this crisis, was gaining slowly and painfully. And when the Augustans swarmed over their heights they did not forget Spenser; they found inspiration in him; they continued in Dryden's manner to place him near Virgil; and they reconciled one side of him (with perfect justification) with their own noble, if narrow ideals. It is not true that Spenser fell into disrepute, as so many historians have said; it is not true that it was necessary for the romanticists to "revive" him.

---

[6] Some of these are discussed and cited at length in my "Critics of Edmund Spenser," *Publications of the University of California* (1911).

IV

Much scholarship on eighteenth century literature has been a mad scramble in search of romanticism. Since Professor Phelps and Professor Beers traced its growth in the eighteenth century it has become so fashionable to detect signs of revolt, even among the most hard-shelled neo-classicists, that some brilliant critic of the future may gain distinction by turning the tables and by proving that a school of Pope actually existed. Of the many conceptions of the eighteenth century one of the most exaggerated is the notion that the influence of Spenser was one of the main forces that made for romanticism. It becomes necessary, then, to attempt, at this point, to describe romanticism.

For our purposes it is best to recall a number of the most commonly accepted types of romanticism, realizing how seldom they exist in combination, and that they are often unlike one another, occasionally even irreconcilable. The most distinctive feature of Coleridge's romanticism, in his greatest poems, is the passion for mystery, the power of suggestion, the devotion to things that *may* be real, although the poet seems rather glad also that they *may not* be real. In Wordsworth, romanticism lies in the intimate relating of man's soul and a benignant nature; it lies also in a serene introspection which plumbs the ego for depth beyond depth only to find there a more and more absorbing infinity that renders the poet momentarily forgetful of external nature. Romanticism revels in paradox. In the *Lyrical Ballads* Wordsworth was to make the ordinary seem extraordinary while Coleridge's assigned duty was to make the extraordinary seem ordinary. The romanticism of Byron is intense subjectivity in fierce play with forces outside, a spirit of individual revolt against many social institutions. In *Don Juan* it is his paradoxical task to conjure up scene after scene of idyllic purity only to break each one down with a cynical laugh. For romantic quest never ends on earth. Romantic irony must emancipate the poet from one dream and goad him on in search of a higher ideal in ceaseless, feverish unrest. Sometimes the romanticism of Keats, a luxurious heaping up of exquisite details, implies a protest against Byronic romanticism; it may be but the passion for things as they are; the delight of the bee in the flower brings no inevitable yearning for things as they should be. Often, however, Keats does yield to a mood of intense if vague longing as in his lovely protest against mutability in the "Ode to a Grecian Urn." Again, in a few lines in the "Ode to the Nightingale," in "La Belle Dame Sans Merci," in "The Eve of St. Mark," Keats is with Coleridge. In Shelley romanticism is, more broadly, the spirit of revolt; at its best, a peculiarly refined and intense spirit of aspiration and of intellectual adventure; in short a spirit of revolt that differs from Byron's in having a chariot-path more spacious, a goal more remote in fact but apparently more intimate, more radiant and clear. In Scott romanticism is a passion for the grandeur of the past which, however, by no means implies a dissatisfaction with the present; it is a play-world of Tories in their hours of leisure. We may conclude by noting two definitions. Professor William Lyon Phelps' "Subjectivity, Love of the Picturesque, and a Reactionary Spirit" must be accepted for some of the poets under consideration since (as I disagree with his inference concerning the influence of Spenser on the romanticists) I must accept a common ground on the basis of which I can disagree with him. His definition, though it reveals none of the deeper implications noted above, the pluralistic fever of romanticism, its love of irony, its love of paradox, its troubled hedonism, gives sufficient basis to refute his own conclusions. The famous phrase of Theodore Watts-Dunton's remains still suggestive—"The Renaissance of Wonder." This paragraph, while it does not absolutely define romanticism, because the term is too shifting to be rigidly conceptualized, describes it and is sufficiently inclusive in its list of qualities urged in defence of all newly discovered eighteenth century romanticists to justify its use as our talisman to discover romantic gold and to reject pinch-peck.[7]

It is certainly true that the great poets, if not all poets, are both romantic and classical. But one temper clearly predominates in all but a very few supreme personages. It will take a hardy investigator to find much romanticism in the first few decades of the eighteenth century. For my part, beginning as a romanticist-hunter, I gradually parted with my hopes. The amount of neo-classical survival even among the poets of the first third of the nineteenth century, is much more striking than the amount of significant romantic material even in the last half of the eighteenth. The classicism of Byron is much more remarkable than the romanticism of even Gray and Collins. The Neo-classical Despotism, once fully established, was profound and lasting. And we are at last learning through the distinguished criticism of Professor Irving Babbit a sense of the vigor of the great school of Boileau so long slandered since at least the days of Bishop Hurd.

In the search for neo-classical beginnings the desire to find signs of a new movement farther back than any investigator has hitherto indicated, we exaggerate the relations of Ben Jonson, Waller, Denham, even Dryden to this Neo-classical Despotism. I have already tried to make it clear that the latter part of the seventeenth century was not an Augustan Age, as the text-books would have it, but an Age of Literary Anarchy; that neo-classicism gained headway only with desperate slowness. The Neo-classical Despotism may be said (though exact dates are impossible) to have struggled into supremacy about 1709, the date of the appearance of the *Pastorals* of Pope and Ambrose Philips, of Prior's first poems, of the opening numbers of the *Tatler*, of the writing of Pope's dictatorial *Essay on Criticism*.

---

[7] I wish here to record a great indebtedness to Dr. Jacob Loewenberg of the Department of Philosophy of the University of California, who has greatly enriched Josiah Royce's profound interpretation of romanticism. Both set a humiliating example to literary men. For literary men are always mouthing the term and never know what they mean.

There is a most illuminating lesson in a study of the development, for better or worse, of Spenser-criticism in the hands of the classicists and romanticists. It shows the inability of any one age to appreciate all the merits of a supreme poet. Because of ephemeral obsessions men term one aspect bad which the next age will admire. The neo-classicist appreciated sides of Spenser to which the romanticists became stone-blind. The romanticists revealed in Spenser divers beauties that had been tarnished by the disregard of a century and certain beauties that had never before been discerned.

Two fallacious ideas about the neo-classical attitude toward Spenser are current: that he was unpopular even among many literary men, and that the Augustans approached him in a spirit of mockery. Professor Phelps, for instance, quotes some platitudes in Addison's boyish ''Epistle to Sacheverel'' to indicate how little Addison knew or cared about Spenser. But he does not take into consideration a long series of admiring references in Addison's mature work, including a prose allegory professedly in the manner of Spenser which Addison once aspired to develop in poetic form. Similarly Professor Phelps makes too much of the Spenserian burlesque, ''The Alley,'' which Pope and Gay wrote in a few moments of triviality. If we examine consistently all the vulgar parodies in eighteenth century poetry and made the same inferences, we are forced to conclude that the Augustans admired nobody, ancient or modern. In France, the fountain-head of neo-classicism, Virgil, when his divinity was at its height, was travestied by Scarron. We should remember also many parodies of Browning and Tennyson at times when these poets were widely revered by the general public and, most emphatically, by the parodists themselves. Eighteenth century adult England devoted occasional moments of recreation to parodies of their masters in that peculiarly pointless type of obscenity from which many boys now graduate during the grammar-school age.

The essential truth is that the neo-classicists had a genuine admiration for Spenser and that they appreciated a great aspect of his genius now misunderstood through the influence of literary epicures, from Leigh Hunt down to our "Art for Art's Sake" men who know not what they do. The Augustans appreciated Spenser's moral earnestness and his allegory. Nowadays we have a morbid fear of didacticism. We consider it all bad. The Augustans considered it all good. The golden mean is to know the difference between crude didacticism (almost any sermon, the *Essay on Man*), and artistic didacticism (the last lines of the "Ode to a Grecian Urn," the first lines of Tennyson's "Ulysses").

The Augustans also knew and often named many of Spenser's qualities which we admire today; his sweetness, his peculiar kind of naïve simplicity, his tenderness, his copious fancy.

They wrote so-called Spenserian "Imitations," not as a mere literary exercise, but because one of their fundamental ideals, based on a misinterpretation of Aristotle's phrase, was to imitate in a very literal and mechanical way which Aristotle never intended. By far the greater number of the eighteenth century and not a few of the notable nineteenth century imitations of Spenser were purely neo-classical. And the Augustans' imitations of Spenser are no more unlike the model than their Virgilian imitations are unlike their idol, Virgil. Occasional verses for king and patron, *vers de société*, satires, and moralizing poems were favorite forms in Augustan days and Spenserian inspiration was promptly poured into these moulds. In this manner of imitation they were followed even by Coleridge, Wordsworth, and Keats in a few shorter poems.

It is well to begin an account of the attitude of Augustan critics towards Spenser with an investigation of the ideas of the two dictators, Addison and Pope. In 1694 appeared Addison's "Epistle to Sacheverel," a very youthful account of the greatest English poets. It is simply a succession of boyish platitudes in decorous couplets. It echoes Sir William Temple's objection to the allegory of *The Faërie Queene* with all the gravity of an adolescent seer on a subject of which he is completely ignorant. But whatever he may have known or really thought about Spenser at first, Addison became, in his mature years, a deep admirer of *The Faërie Queene*. A comment in the *Spectator*, no. 62, where he made his famous classification of the kinds of "Wit," is extremely significant because it is at once thoroughly Augustan and in praise of Spenser. Whatever romantic tendencies Addison may have felt, he here admires Spenser because Spenser, if you please, is at one with all true believers. He is at one with Monsieur Boileau.

As true Wit consists in the Resemblance of Ideas, and false Wit in the Resemblance of Words, according to the foregoing Instances; there is another kind of Wit which consists partly in the Resemblance of Ideas, and partly in the resemblance of Words, which for Distinction Sake I shall call mixt Wit. This Kind of Wit is that which abounds in Cowley more than in any Author that ever wrote. Mr. Waller has likewise a great deal of it. Mr. Dryden is very sparing in it. Milton had a genius much above it. Spencer is in the same class with Milton. The Italians, even in their Epic Poetry, are full of it. Monsieur Boileau, who formed himself upon the Ancient Poets, has everywhere rejected it with Scorn.

For us the significant points are: the neo-classical mania for mechanical definition and classification, the surprising attack on the immortal Mr. Waller, the usual Augustan onslaught on the Italian poets, the fact that Spenser and Milton are classed with the authoritative Boileau and the venerable Ancients, even above Dryden. Plainly the Augustan readers were not to think meanly of Spenser here. It must be added, however, that Spenser, from another point of view, was once grouped by his urbane critic with the censured Italians. In the *Spectator*, no. 297, we read:

Milton has interwoven in the Texture of his Fable some particulars which do not seem to have Probability enough for an Epic Poem, particularly in the Actions which he ascribes to Sin and Death.... Such allegories rather savour of the Spirit of Spencer and Ariosto, than of Homer and Vergil.

But our critic seems to have recanted. For in a subsequent number, 419, Addison wrote of what Dryden called "the Fairy Way of Writing" in a tone that has been called romantic, and lauded these "allegories."

> There is another sort of imaginary Beings, that we sometimes meet with among the Poets, when the Author represents any Passion, Appetite, Virtue, or Vice, under a visible Shape, and makes it a Person or an actor in his Poem.... We find a whole Creation of the like shadowy Persons in Spencer, who had an admirable talent in Representations of this kind.

However "romantic" the general tenets of this paper may be considered, the comments on Spenser are but that praise of allegory which was becoming orthodox among the Augustans. We may assume that, at this later date, the revered Addison was crystallizing that neo-classical admiration for the allegory of *The Faërie Queene* which was of course perfectly native to the didactic temperament of the eighteenth century. A little later (*Spectator* no. 421) he asserts that "Allegories, when well chosen, are like so many Tracks of Light in a discourse, that makes everything about them clear and beautiful." Identifying "Fables" with allegory he writes approvingly: "Spencer's Fairy Queen is one continued Series of them from the Beginning to the end of that admirable Work." He regrets the slight cultivation of allegory and, in the *Guardian* for September 4, 1713, leaves us his most interesting tribute to Spenser.

> Though this kind of composition was practised by the finest authors among the ancients, our country-man, Spenser, is the last writer of note who has applied himself to it with success.... I was once thinking to have written a whole canto in the spirit of Spenser, and in order to do it, contrived a fable of imaginary persons and characters. I raised it on that common dispute between the comparative perfections and preëminence between the two sexes.
>
> Since I have not time to accomplish this work, I shall present my reader with the naked fable, reserving the embellishments of verse and poetry to another opportunity.

The "fable" is then transcribed.[8]   It is apparent that Spenser was not only favored by Addison, the critic, but was a definite force in the making of those graceful and attractive allegories which were widely imitated by the host of urbane essayists in the eighteenth century who took Addison as their model.

---

[8] Samuel Wesley's *Poems on Several Occasions* (ed. 2, 1763) contains a versification of "The Battle of the Sexes" in Prior-Spenserian stanzas.

Pope's admiration for Spenser is emphatically expressed in a charming Queen Anne sally to Hughes (1715). "Spenser," he wrote, "has ever been a favorite poet to me; he is like a mistress whose faults we see, but love her with them all." Pope's only elaborate comments are to be found in *A Discourse on Pastoral Poetry* which he prefixed to the 1717 edition of those youthful *Pastorals* where he avowedly imitated Spenser in general scheme and freely echoed him.[9] Although the preface owes something to Dryden it contains the fullest consideration of *The Shepheards Calender* that had yet appeared. Pope groups Spenser with Theocritus, Virgil, and Tasso; shakes his head dubiously over the satire, the diction, and the varied stanza-forms; but praises as "very beautiful" the device of the calendar without being at all blind to its inadequate working out. Finally, a eulogy (recorded by Spence in days when Pope discoursed in full maturity) will suffice alone to relegate all the implications which Professor Phelps and others have conjured out of Pope's vulgar Spenserian stanza, "The Alley" (the product of a trivial hour with Gay), to their deserved insignificance:

After my reading a Canto of Spenser two or three years ago to an old lady between seventy-eight and eighty, she said that I had been showing her a collection of pictures.[10] She said very right; and I know not how it is, but there is something in Spenser that pleases one as strongly in one's old age as it did in one's youth. I read the "Faerie Queene" when I was about twelve, with a vast deal of delight; and I think it gave me as much when I read it over about a year or two ago.

---

[9] Professor Phelps contents himself with quoting Dr. Johnson that Pope took Virgil for his pattern. I have gathered Pope's own avowal and other detailed evidence to the contrary in "The Critics of Edmund Spenser," pp. 152 sq., and "Spenser, Thomson, and Romanticism," pp. 54–55. Those who wish a glimpse of Spenser's very substantial influence on many other Augustan pastorals will find it also in "The Critics of Edmund Spenser."

[10] Perhaps no poet's name has been associated more persistently with pictures than Spenser's. We shall come presently to some charming passages in Leigh Hunt and Lowell which elaborate this point most alluringly —unfortunately with some very unjust inferences and suggestions. The most recent and by far the most discriminating of all treatments of this topic is Professor Jefferson B. Fletcher's "The Painter of the Poets," University of North Carolina *Studies in Philology*, XIV, 153 sq., April, 1917.

It becomes evident then that far from being cold, as has been more than once asserted, the two chiefs of the Augustans of the eighteenth century were not only warm admirers of Spenser but they made distinct contributions to the development of Spenserian criticism. It is worth emphasizing that they did this by no foreshadowing of doctrines that may by any means be called romantic. They weighed him in the neo-classical balance and found him wanting in very few respects.

Jolly, quixotic Dick Steele, too, had some gallant words for Spenser. It is easy to understand Sir Richard's admiration for Spenser's chivalric spirit. On November 19, 1712, he published a *Spectator* essay on Spenser. Professor Phelps, intent on proving the indifference to Spenser during the first decades of the eighteenth century, mentions the article under consideration but is inclined to question the sincerity of Steele's appreciation. But the paper certainly shows a knowledge of *The Faërie Queene*. Steele characteristically fixes on Britomart or Chastity for special admiration. He says justly that the "Legend of Friendship" is more diffuse. At least, then, he has been reading the third and fourth books of *The Faërie Queene,* a pastime that our ravens would have us believe quite out of date in our days of hurried and dyspeptic reading. He writes most sensibly and most refreshingly in praise of Spenser's use of archaisms.

His old Words are all true English and Numbers exquisite; and since of Words there is the Multa Renascentur, since they are all proper, such a Poem should not (any more than Milton's) subsist all of it of common Words.

Still, were this all, we might share Professor Phelps' doubt as to Steele's sincerity: "How far Steele was prompted to do all this by a real love of Spenser, or by the necessity of writing his sheet is hard to say." No doubt we might conjure up pictures of our beloved knight, somewhat muddled with port, tearing his hair at blear dawn over a *Spectator* article. A clouded but loyal and ecstatic memory of Addison on Milton and lo! our hero's pen wags madly about Spenser, upon whom he has nothing to say except what wells up from his good nature unsupported by knowledge. This would make a plausible and attractive picture. But there is more evidence besides the article quoted to make us believe that Steele's admiration for Spenser was full of his wonted sincerity and was founded on knowledge. In the *Guardian* for April 15, 1713, he again praised Spenser and asserted that Spenser and Ambrose Philips, in their pastorals, "have copied and improved the beauties of the Ancients." He followed Dryden in asserting that the English rustic language makes imitation of the Doric of Theocritus more possible than the language of the Latin poets. In the *Guardian* for April 17, 1713, in addition, he wrote a prose pastoral in which the great writers of eclogues were treated allegorically. Spenser is made the son of Virgil and the father of Philips and he is portrayed with warm eulogy. That Steele read Spenser *con amore* is further confirmed by a thoroughly representative article in the *Tatler* for July 6, 1710.

> I was this morning reading the tenth canto of the fourth book of Spenser, in which Sir Scudamour relates the progress of his courtship of Amoret under a very beautiful allegory, which is one of the most natural and unmixed of any in that most excellent author.

Steele appends a brief prose paraphrase "for the benefit of many English Lovers, who have, by frequent letters, desired me to lay down some rules for the conduct of their virtuous Amours." Spenser is quaintly and adroitly turned into a graceful eighteenth century essay. Surely we may conclude from all these tributes that Dick Steele, devoted if not always thoughtful lover of Prue, could hardly have resisted the fascination of Spenser's court of love.

Another one of the most urbane spirits of the day, Prior, paid liberal homage to Spenser. In 1706 he brought out *An Ode, Humbly Inscrib'd to the Queen. On the Glorious Success of Her Majesty's Arms.... Written in Imitation of Spencer's Style*. His preface is a capital example of the ease which the Augustan found in reconciling Spenser with Augustan ideals.

As to the Style, the Choice I made of following the *Ode* in *Latin*, determin'd Me in *English* to the Stanza; and herein it was impossible not to have a Mind to follow our great countryman *Spencer;* which I have done (as well at least as I could) in the Manner of my Expression, and the Turn of my Number: Having only added one Verse to his Stanza, which I thought made the Number more Harmonious; and avoided such of his Words, as I found too obsolete. I have, however, retain'd some few of them, to make the Colouring look more *Spencer's.* . . .

My Two Great Examples, *Horace* and *Spenser*, in many Things resemble each other: Both have a Height of Imagination, and a Majesty of Expression in describing the Sublime; and Both know how to temper those Talents, and sweeten the Description, so as to make it Lovely as well as Pompous: Both have equally That agreeable Manner of mixing Morality with their Story, and That *Curiosa Felicitas* in the Choice of their Diction, which every Writer aims at, and so few have reached: Both are particularly Fine in their Images, and Knowing in their Numbers.

Mr. Phelps quotes this passage as exhibiting "that confusion of ideals so often shown by the Augustans." He smiles at Prior's comparison of Spenser and Horace. But the comparison is really both suggestive and discerning. Here is an Augustan who appreciated the moralistic side of Spenser which we romanticists are too likely to neglect or despise. Just as Dryden, Addison, and others cherished Spenser by comparing him favorably with their idol Virgil, so Prior finds that Spenser had the happy faculty, in common with his own special master Horace, of combining the other qualities of poetry with a moral consciousness, an attitude marked by richness, ease, and grace that has been praised by all notable writers on poetics before our "art for art's sake" men degraded the function of poetry into something similar to that of choice confectionery. And certainly no finer application of *Curiosa Felicitas* has ever been made by poet or critic. Prior's distortion of the Spenserian stanza was indeed an example of Augustan limitation. Yet in this he was followed by an army of writers including poets as far apart in time and talents as Chatterton and Felicia Hemans. Typical Augustan "Occasional Verses" and didactic poems ran neatly into this mould. Yet the writers often knew their Spenser as well as their Prior.[11] Prior's scheme disregarded Spenser's subtle linking of quatrains and final couplet. Spenser's rhymes lead on and on in their caressing leisurely manner. Prior's scheme, ababcdcdeE, was doubtless pleasantly distinct to Augustan ears, suspicious of "linkéd sweetness long drawn out," ever craving the clean finish of the couplet-end. But in his preface to *Solomon*, Prior came to show a restless dissatisfaction with the couplet and he inserted a detailed eulogy of Spenser which Professor Phelps should not have neglected.

> In our Language *Spenser* has not contented himself with this submissive Manner of Imitation [i.e., the French and Italian manner of imitating the orthodox Classical epics]: He launches out into flowery Paths, which still seem to conduct him into one great Road. His *Fairy Queen* (had it been finished) must have ended in the Account, which every Knight was to give of his Adventures, and in the accumulated Praises of his Heroine *Gloriana*. The Whole would have been an *Heroic* Poem, but in another Cast and Figure, than any that had ever been written before. Yet it is observable, that every Hero (as far as We can judge by the Books still remaining) bears his distinguished Character, and represents some particular Virtue conducive to the whole Design.
>
> . . . .
>
> If striking out into *Blank Verse* as *Milton* did (and in this kind *Mr. Philipps*, had He lived, would have excelled) or running the Thought into *Alternate* and *Stanza*, which allows a greater Variety, and still preserves the Dignity of the Verse; as *Spenser* and *Fairfax* have done; if either of these, I say, be a proper Remedy for my Poetical Complaint, or if any others may be found, I dare not determine: I am only enquiring, in order to be better informed; without presuming to direct the Judgment of Others.

Nevertheless, with all his diffidence, Prior was outspoken in his objection to the couplet. He considered it "too confined," "too broken and weak for Epic," and that it tires both writer and reader. And all this is only too true in the case of poor Prior's *Solomon*, in which, though it was the ambition of his life, he did not dare to carry out his diffident suggestions of revolt.

---

11 See my "Spenser, Thomson, and Romanticism," *Publ. Mod. Lang. Assoc.*, 1911, pp. 56–59, for a detailed account of Prior's poetical indebtedness to Spenser and for a long list of Prior-Spenserians with evidence of their first-hand knowledge of Spenser.

We may now approach the Augustan attitude toward Spen-
ser through another medium, that of certain Spenser-scholars of
the period. John Hughes (1677–1720), whose discussion of the
structure of *The Faërie Queene* we have already examined, was
the greatest Spenser-scholar of the early eighteenth century and
his edition of Spenser (1715) must still be taken into account by
all special students. His methods were thoroughly Augustan.
He admired allegory and essayed an elaborate discussion of it
as Bossu and the other French makers of rules for the creation
of poetry had done for the epic. He formulates four rules by
which Spenser is found praiseworthy and "much more reason-
able" than Tasso. By virtue of the fourth rule—that allegory
"must be clear and intelligible"—Sir William Temple is found
wanting for declaring that Spenser's "moral lay too bare."
But, like the other Augustans, Hughes sees many other lovely
qualities in Spenser.

> The chief Merit of this Poem consists in that surprising Vein of fabu-
> lous Invention, which runs thro, and enriches it every where with Imagery
> and Descriptions more than we meet with in any other modern Poem. . . .
> His Abundance betrays him into Excess, and his Judgment is overborne
> by the Torrent of his Imagination."

As we have seen, Hughes followed Dryden in maintaining that
the "several Books appear rather like so many several Poems,
than one entire Fable," that the character of Arthur is not so
conceived as to weld the books firmly into unity. Hughes goes
on, however, most significantly, to argue that, though the whole
frame of *The Faërie Queene* would appear monstrous if it were
examined by the rules of epic poetry drawn from the practice
of Homer and Virgil, yet if examined by a consideration of the
qualities of "Gothick" art it proves itself less "majestick in the
whole," but "very surprising and agreeable in its parts."
From what may seem a timid but a somewhat romantic sally
Hughes promptly retreats to compare the *Orlando Furioso* with
The Faërie Queene in the most conventional manner of the neo-
classicists to the reproach of the former. Like a true Augustan

he insists that it is Spenser's moral allegory which exalts Ariosto's romantic trash into heroic poetry.

In the *Orlando Furioso* we every where meet with an exuberant Invention, join'd with great Liveliness and Facility of Description, yet debas'd by frequent Mixtures of the comick Genius, as well as many shocking Indecorums.... On the other hand, *Spenser's* Fable, though often wild, is, as I have observed, always emblematical: And this may very much excuse likewise that Air of Romance in which he has followed the *Italian* Author. The perpetual Stories of Knights, Giants, Castles, and Enchantments, and all that Train of Legendary Adventures, would appear very trifling, if *Spenser* had not found a way to turn them all into Allegory, or if a less masterly Hand had filled up his Draught. But it is surprising to observe how much the Strength of the Painting is superior to the Design.

Yet let those who think that this Augustanism is too crabbed to admit of real appreciation take note that Hughes, with unerring taste, praises delightedly almost all the most admired passages in *The Faërie Queene*. There are those who have thought that there was a tinge of romanticism in Hughes. Such critics would doubtless turn particularly to a sentence on allegory which seems to have a love of fantasy unusual for the age.

Allegory is indeed the *Fairy Land* of Poetry, peopled by Imagination; its Inhabitants are so many Apparitions; its Woods, Caves, wild Beasts, Rivers, Mountains and Palaces, are produc'd by a kind of magical Power, and are all visionary and typical; and it abounds in such Licenses as would be shocking and monstrous, if the Mind did not attend to the mystick Sense contain'd under them.

But if there is romantic eloquence here there is certainly most emphatic neo-classical reasoning. And there can remain no doubt that Augustan standards were sufficient for Hughes to establish Spenser as a great poet.

Joseph Spence, in a "Dissertation on the Defects of Spenser's Allegory" did something to supplement Hughes' attempt to close up this gap in French rule-mongering. Spenser, we are told, should not have mixed the "fables of Heathendom with the truths of Christianity." Boileau had damned this procedure. Spenser, too, was occasionally guilty of misrepresenting the allegories of the ancients. All this, to be sure, is mere neo-classical pedantry. But concerning "the Allegories of

[Spenser's] ... own invention" the censor wrote with neo-classical shrewdness. Though he considered the invention in *The Faërie Queen* to be "one of the richest and most beautiful that perhaps ever was," he protested quite justly that some of the allegories (e.g., the extravagant portrait of Discord who looks in two directions, whose tongue and heart are split) are overdone. Spence does not like the occasional indulgence in nauseous detail. Some of us approve of it but none of us can fairly scoff at an Augustan or romanticist for such a judgment. When the poet describes the Dragon's tail as three furlongs in length he very likely is, as Spence maintains, extravagant rather than great. Then comes the usual regret that Spenser followed Ariosto too closely and an orthodox lament at the need of rules for allegory:

> The reason of my reproducing these instances, is only to show what faults the greatest Allegorist may commit; whilst the manner of allegorizing is left upon so unfixed and irregular a footing as it was in his time, and is still among us.

And Spence goes on to apologize profusely for his strictures and closes roundly and loyally: "If ... [the faults noted] should prejudice a reader at all against so fine a writer; let him read almost any one of his entire Cantos, and it will reconcile him to him again." Professor Phelps and Professor Beers, in asserting that the Augustans looked with dull eyes on Spenser, write of the apologetic tone of his defenders. But here is a solid Augustan, a very Boswell to Pope, who apologizes to Augustans for presuming to take Spenser to task.

These more authoritative voices were swelled by many elaborate but equally laudatory utterances from men as diverse as professional literary critics to a religious reformer like John Wesley, who recommended to Methodists Spenser's *Faërie Queene* in the second year of a course in academic learning. But among the small men we need not here dwell. We may safely pass on the great dictator.[12]

---

[12] Once more I beg leave to refer readers who desire an accumulation of evidence to "The Critics of Edmund Spenser," pp. 150 sq., and "Spenser, Thomson, and Romanticism," pp. 60–61.

It is unfortunate that Samuel Johnson left us no rounded estimate of Spenser. His allusions to him are frequent but they are mainly incidental to a vigorous and wholesome crusade which Johnson was making against two hollow literary fashions: the insipid pastoral and the artificial "imitation." In his "Life of West" Doctor Johnson laid a heavy hand on "imitation."

His Imitations of Spenser are very successfully performed, both with respect to the metre, the language, and the fiction; and being engaged at once by the excellence of the sentiments, and the artifice of the copy, the mind has two amusements to-gether. But such compositions are not to be reckoned among the great achievements of intellect, because their effect is local and temporary, they appeal not to reason or passion, but to memory, and pre-suppose an accidental or artificial State of mind. An imitation of Spenser is nothing to a reader, however acute, by whom Spenser has never been perused. Works of this kind may deserve praise, as proofs of great industry, and great nicety of observation; but the highest praise, the praise of genius, they cannot claim. The noblest beauties of art are those of which the effect is co-extended with rational nature, or at least with the whole circle of polished life; what is less than this can be only pretty, the plaything of fashion and the amusement of a day.

It is absurd to see in this admirable piece of criticism, as some have, evidence that Johnson thought meanly of Spenser. The impressive fact is that the doctor had hit upon one of the greatest causes of the insignificance of eighteenth century poetry —a too restricted and academic interpretation of Aristotle's theory of imitation. The Augustan ideal of imitation has much to say to those who fondly think that they are disregarding all influence or precedent. They are at the other extreme from Joseph Hall, who, in the Age of Reason, thought that there was nothing new under the sun. All supreme poets have imitated quite as much as the Augustans, but they have imitated with a noble independence. Small poets profess to scorn imitation or, at the other extreme, imitate by academic and servile rote. Except for Thomson's *Castle of Indolence* and Shenstone's *School-Mistress*, which transcend the mere exercise in versification, the Spenserian imitation of the eighteenth century deserved the doctor's censure. And in the *Rambler* for May 14, 1751,

Johnson left clear evidence for the cautious and ranging reader that imitation, not Spenser, was his aversion by a well-directed attack on the ideal of imitation in general which strikes at the very roots of the matter.

> In the boundless regions of possibility, which fiction claims for her dominion, there are a thousand flowers unplucked, a thousand fountains unexhausted, combinations of imagery yet unobserved, and races of ideal inhabitants not hitherto. described.

Imitation, he thinks, is ruinous to the imagination. Surely there is no animus against Spenser here where the doctor censures even Virgil for being seduced into blemishes in his imitations of Homer because he was too eager to use all of Homer's material. The doctor then turns to the pestiferous Spenserian imitation.

> To imitate the fictions and sentiments of Spenser can incur no reproach, for allegory is perhaps one of the most pleasing vehicles of instruction. But I am far from extending the same respect to his diction or his stanza. His style was in his own time allowed to be vicious, so darkened with old words, peculiarities of phrase, and so remote from common use, that even Jonson boldly pronounces him to have written no language.

Of course Spenser's style was not "in his own time allowed to be vicious." Johnson doubtless knew only the criticisms of Sidney, Jonson, and Davenant; nothing of the references, like Fuller's, which warmly praised the diction and style of Spenser. Johnson is here purely neo-classical in praising the moral allegory and damning the stanza and diction. And in the Preface to his *Dictionary*, compiled at the same time he was at work on *The Rambler*, he half contradicts himself, like Ben Jonson on the identical subject, by naming Spenser's language as the standard for its time. Readers should, moreover, weigh with these citations an unequivocal sentence from "Milton" in the *Lives of the Poets:*

> Of ... [Milton] may be said what Jonson says of Spenser, that "he wrote no language," but has formed what Butler calls "a Babylonish Dialect," in itself harsh and barbarous, but made by exalted genius and extensive learning the vehicle of so much instruction and so much pleasure that, like other lovers, we find grace in its deformity.

In conclusion, we may note that Johnson's ability to appreciate a really good imitation of Spenser is established by his avowed admiration for Shenstone's *School-Mistress*.

Infuriated by the languid eclogues which teemed in his day, Johnson attacked the pastoral, another parasitic blight of Augustan poetry, in *The Rambler* for July 24, 1750. But his reference to Spenser was negligible, his strictures on Virgil most severe, and his general animadversions unexceptionable in the eyes of true criticism in any age. In his "Life of Ambrose Philips" he was willing to lend sanction to the high praise of Spenser's pastoral poetry in *The Guardian* by quoting it with no objections.

It is greatly to be regretted that Johnson never wrote elaborately on Spenser. His sane criticism, his clear-eyed kindliness would have ensured a memorable contribution. Reports concerning the omission of Spenser in *The Lives of the Poets* are conflicting. A "Life of Johnson" by Thomas Tyson in *The Gentleman's Magazine* for December, 1784, states that Johnson's "employers wanted him to undertake the life of Spenser. But he said Warton had left little or nothing for him to do." On the other hand, Hannah More in her *Anecdotes* relates:

> Johnson told me he had been with the king that morning, who enjoined him to add Spenser to his *Lives of the Poets*. I seconded the motion; he promised to think of it but said the booksellers had not included him in their list of poets.

Johnson's letters to Warton are full of a kindly interest in the forthcoming *Observations on The Faërie Queene*. He offers assistance. A critique on Spenser never came. But two passages in the Preface to his edition of Shakespeare (1765) imply a high general estimate of Spenser. Of Shakespeare's diction and versification he writes:

> To him we must ascribe the praise, unless Spenser may divide it with him, of having first discovered to how much smoothness and harmony the English language could be softened.

And à propos of *A Midsummer-Night's Dream* we read that "Fairies in his time were much in fashion; common tradition had made them familiar, and Spenser's poem had made them great."

Johnson's philippics against imitation were echoed by many who saw their justice from Robert Lloyd, wayward debauchee and light-hearted imitator of Mat Prior's Familiar Verse to the grave historian and implacably independent philosopher, David Hume.[13] But we must single out from among them only Oliver Goldsmith, Johnson's gentle admirer. Goldsmith followed Johnson in his admiration for Shenstone, but general opposition to Spenserian imitation. For Spenser himself, Goldsmith showed the warmest appreciation in an account of Church's edition of *The Faërie Queene* in Smollett's *Critical Review* (February, 1759). Thanks to Church: "We can now tread the regions of fancy without interruption, and expatiate on fairy wilds such as our great magician has been pleased to represent them." Unlike Johnson, Goldsmith shared the romanticists' distaste for allegory.

There is a pleasing tranquillity of mind which ever attends the reading of this ancient poet. We leave the ways of the present world, and all the ages of primeval innocence and happiness rise to our view.... The imagination of his reader leaves reason behind, pursues the tale without considering the allegory, and upon the whole, is charmed without instruction.

But there are plenty of fashionable Augustan dicta. "No poet," he states, "enlarges the imagination more than Spenser." He cites Cowley, Gray, Akenside, and others as examples. He warns poets to imitate "his beauties" not "his words," which are "justly fallen into disuse." He makes the usual complaint that Spenser followed Virgil too little and vicious medieval and Italian models too much. But the essay shows clearly how native were the lovely dreams of *The Faërie Queene* to Goldsmith's gentle, irresponsible spirit.

In the last few years the work of Professor Irving Babbit and Mr. Paul Elmer More has done much to turn the tables on

---

[13] See "The Critics of Edmund Spenser," pp. 156 sq.

romantic arrogance and to diagnose romantic maladies. At the same time we are gradually outgrowing the ill-considered contempt with which our romantic grandfathers estimated the Augustans. Let us now give over that somewhat supercilious or even false spirit of toleration with which we try to justify the Augustans in so far as they show symptoms, real or chimerical, of romanticism. Take them for what they were and what do we find? We find that they could accord a poet like Spenser warm appreciation from a purely neo-classical point of view and that interest in Spenser did not necessarily have anything whatever to do with romanticism. We find that the term "Spenserian Revival," which has long decked the chapters of many a text-book, is a misnomer. We find that the Augustans, like ourselves, occasionally said asinine things about Spenser, but that they had an appreciation of his high-seriousness much sounder than that which has gone current since the Triumph of Romanticism. Let us remember, at the close, that no man in any age ever said anything statelier about Spenser than the imperial Augustan, Gibbon:

The Nobility of the Spensers, has been enriched by the trophies of Marlborough; but I exhort them to consider the *Fairy Queen* as the most precious jewell of their coronet.

V

It was not that the influence of Spenser was a cause of the romantic revival but rather that (once romanticism had gained a foothold) Spenser was imitated in a romantic way which I want to emphasize. It was in no spirit of romantic revolt that an Augustan penned his mechanical "Imitation of Spenser" any more than it was when he imitated Virgil. But once the romantic seeds were sown there was infinite suggestion to be found in Spenser for an Apostle of Wonder.

The earliest exponents of what they vaguely termed Gothic or romantic were often not strong men with a new faith but decadents weary of the old. It was the passion of jaded, bookish minds for novelty in no exalted sense that made much of the romantic pose that later became romanticism. The tinsel trappings of a Walpole are not really romanticism according to our exalted ideas; nothing short of a Phoenix-birth out of such ashes could bring the Triumph of Romanticism. The eighteenth century men often connected romanticism with a comfortable melancholy and crocodile tears. Even in our own day Edgar Allen Poe has argued for the indispensability of a kind of luxurious melancholy in poetry. The jaded writers of the latter half of the eighteenth century cultivated graveyards, gloomy abbeys, thunderstorms, all comfortably conjured up in the warm and snug seclusion of the study. It was as artificial as Pope's pastorals.[14] And we must be cautious about linking this romantic prose too closely with the various types of romanticism represented by Wordsworth, Coleridge, Scott, Byron, Shelley, and Keats. With this warning we may turn to the men who are often named as the forerunners of romanticism.

Perhaps no men among the early romanticists have loomed larger in the eyes of recent critics than the brothers Joseph and Thomas Warton. And both must occupy a most important position in any attempt to estimate Spenser by the methods of collective criticism. Their passion for *The Faërie Queene* was doubtless first learned from their father, who wrote a very Augustan Spenserian imitation in the stanza adopted by William Whitehead and a group of the most frigid poets that could fill the pages of an elaborate history of eighteenth century poetry.[15] The good man's two sons, though ranked among the greatest students of Spenser, belong as Spenserian poets to the group of Whitehead. In the same group we find, for instance, Christopher Smart, who, before he went mad and composed his superb *Hymn to David*, composed in the vein of the laureate

---

[14] For a consideration of the heralds of romanticism among the Spenserians see ''Spenser, Thomson, and Romanticism,'' pp. 69–91, and ''The Critics of Edmund Spenser,'' pp. 160 sq.

[15] See ''Spenser, Thomson, and Romanticism,'' pp. 60 sq., for an account of this group and for evidence of their first-hand knowledge of Spenser.

Spenserian, Whitehead, his *Hymn to the Supreme Being on Recovery from a Dangerous Fit of Illness,* in a moment of dull sanity. In *The Pleasures of the Melancholy* Thomas Wharton alludes to Spenser in a somewhat romantic spirit.

> Such mystic visions send as Spenser saw
> When through bewildering Fancy's magic maze,
> To the fell house of Busyrane, he led
> Th' unshaken Britomart...

But his own imitations are so starched and remote from their model that were they our only evidence we should suspect that Warton had no first-hand knowledge of Spenser.

It is practically as critics only that the Wartons have achieved any permanence. Here they have been scarcely awarded the high position they should occupy. Yet to call Joseph Warton's *magnum opus,* the famous *Essay on the Genius and Writings of Pope* (1756), as Lowell calls it, "the earliest public official declaration of war against the reigning mode," is to tempt the reader into rather too exalted a notion of Warton's spirit of revolt. To be sure, there is much talk about things that are "romantic" and about things which have "a pleasing wildness." But the reverence for things "elegant" and "decorous" and the horror of "impropriety" are much more frequently expressed. However, in any of his moods Joseph Warton had an acute appreciation of Spenser. A propos of an attack on Pope's "Alley" he wrote a sustained panegyric on *The Faërie Queene.* Like the Augustans, he praised the allegorical "living figures whose attitudes and behaviour Spenser has minutely drawn with so much clearness and truth, that we behold them with our eyes, as plainly as we do on the cieling of the banquetting house." He quotes several examples, concluding with the description of Jealousy, and cries out with contagious enthusiasm:

> Here all is life and motion; here we behold the Poet or Maker; this is creation; it is here, might we cry out to Spenser, "it is here that you display to us, that you make us feel the sure effects of genuine poetry."

For those who have any temptation to suspect that the criticisms of Johnson and others on Spenserian imitations implied any hostility to Spenser, it may be well to note that Warton looked askance at the practice.

> It has been fashionable of late to imitate Spenser, but the likeness of most of those copies, hath consisted rather in using a few of his ancient expressions, than in catching his real manner. Some however have been executed with happiness, and with attention to that simplicity, that tenderness of sentiment, and those little touches of nature, that constitute Spenser's character.

It is to be observed that all this is only the usual Augustan criticism of Spenser and that these are some of the very points which have been culpably forgotten too often by romantic critics to our own day.

Warton's ranking of English poets, at the close of the *Essay,* is the most famous passage.

> Where then,...shall we with justice be authorized to place our admired Pope? Not, assuredly, in the same rank with *Spencer, Shakespeare, and Milton.*

The whole passage is a fine piece of criticism with perspective. It is not so much because those three great poets were exalted. That was unnecessary. They were praised by all. But the placing of Pope was the one great stroke. The age was close to a great man, in the same situation as certain sonneteers who sang, a few years ago, to "Shakespeare, Milton, Tennyson." It is not a limitation peculiar to people of the eighteenth century to overestimate their own poet. Warton's perspective would be striking in any age that lay at the foot of a mountainous personality like Pope. Warton, to be sure, seems to me to be an almost thoroughgoing Augustan. But the Augustans produced some great critics. It was perhaps romantic, but certainly not remarkably romantic, to write

> Where are the lays of artful Addison,
> Coldly correct to Shakspear's warblings wild.

In a word, Joseph Warton never passed very far beyond an occasional indulgence in a kind of romantic pose, sincere but superficial. When he was true to his best instincts he was solid Augustan.

Thomas Warton's temperament was larger, more mellow than that of his brother. It is not, however, merely because he was more of a romanticist. His attitudes towards romanticism and Spenser may be best interpreted through two lines of his verse:

> As oft, reclin'd on Cherwell's shelving shore,
> I trac'd romantick Spenser's moral page.

The word "romantick" here is in a precisely opposite situation to that of today. Then it was vague because it had little or no meaning. Now it is vague because it has a thousand meanings. It is significant, too, that Spenser was to Warton the pleasant "moral" Spenser of the Augustans. But Warton was rich-spirited enough to be the first English critic to apply the historical method with any skill. Centuries of literature swam into his learned ken. His *Observations on The Faërie Queene* still remains and will remain one of the most memorable books or essays ever written about Spenser. But Thomas Warton must not be considered as a very serious romantic revolter and therefore forced, as an ardent admirer of Spenser, to be apologetic in an unsympathetic age. His complaint that Spenser was "admired" but "neglected" is not to be taken as true in the sense of being a peculiar and widespread limitation of his age. We have examined a considerable body of evidence showing that Spenser was widely appreciated in the first half of the eighteenth century by those who were ordained then, as in all ages, to love him. Indeed any scholar of our own day might just as accurately refer to Spenser as "this admired but neglected poet." And we shall presently see, too, how much Warton owed to the really numerous Augustan admirers of the faërie poet.

The *Observations* begins with a brief review of romantic poetry, from Provençal to that of Ariosto and Tasso, in which we at once perceive, however inadequate the account from the point of view of modern investigators, the wide vision and the scholarly solidity of the man. He turns a calm brow from grovelling pedants and he is equally exalted above the slap-dash trifler in letters who is bound in by his own age. Warton insists that in order to appreciate a poet we must study the times in which he lived. But he remains too severely neo-classical when he finds that "Ariosto... rejecting truth for magic, and preferring the ridiculous excursions of Boyardo, to the propriety and uniformity of the Grecian and the Roman models"—wrote a very heterodox poem. Beni is scored for comparing Ariosto and Homer. Augustanism grows unendurably crass when the pedant Trissino is praised for having "taste and boldness enough to publish an epic poem written in professed imitation of the Iliad."

Tasso... took the ancients for his guides; but was still too sensible of the popular prejudice in favour of ideal beings, and romantic adventures, to neglect or omit them entirely.

.   .   .   .

Such was the prevailing taste, when Spenser projected the Faërie Queene.

All this—the regret that Spenser was misled by the romantic and damnable Ariosto—is Augustan criticism, pure and simple. Warton does not dream of praising Ariosto and approving Spenser's choice of models as we shall find the early romanticists doing. He only attempts an ample explanation by using the historical method.

The plan of *The Faërie Queene* is now examined and criticized just as Dryden, Hughes, and many more had analyzed it and found it wanting. Nay, Warton thinks Dryden is too mild in his condemnation of the unity of the poem. It is "inartificial," we are told, to introduce the hero of one book on a less dangerous exploit later: it sullies the hero's luster and does little for the unity. Warton follows Hughes with the suggestion that Spenser "might either have established *twelve Knights,*

without an *Arthur,* or an *Arthur* without *twelve Knights.''* It
is all neo-classical and all reasoning by *Barbara, Celarent, Darii,
Ferioque,* with the assumption that all premises are true.

But, once more under the influence of Hughes, Warton
abruptly strikes a blow for the defence.

> But it is absurd to think of judging Ariosto or Spenser by precepts
> which they did not attend to. We who live in the days of writing by rule,
> are apt to try every composition by those laws which we have been taught
> to think the whole criterion of excellence.

Spenser's poetry is ''the careless exuberance of a warm imag-
ination and a strong sensibility.'' He ''wrote rapidly from his
own feelings, which at the same time were naturally noble.''
''We scarcely regret the loss'' of ''that arrangement and
œconomy which epic severity requires'' in the face of Spenser's
appeal to ''feelings of the heart, rather than the cold approba-
tion of the head.'' ''In reading Spenser, if the critic is not
satisfied, yet the reader is transported.'' Here was a critic large
enough to appreciate Augustan sanity, yet able, at the same
time, to look beyond the rule if so required. Now, at last, we
stand truly on the brink of romanticism—yet on a greater eleva-
tion of judgment than either romanticism or classicism; for here
we have both.

Warton now leads us through a pleasant maze of facts and
speculations concerning Spenser's sources in the romances,
Greek legends, Ariosto, and Chaucer. Here, indeed, is a roman-
tic spirit of childlike wonder as, like Spenser himself, he pores
over the immense treasures of the past. He writes a charming
and unanswerable *apologia* for source-hunting.

> We feel a sort of malicious triumph in detecting the latent and obscure
> source, from which an original author has drawn some celebrated descrip-
> tion: yet this ... soon gives way to the rapture that naturally results from
> contemplating the chymical energy of true genius, which can produce so
> noble a transmutation.

With Spenser's stanza Warton is almost as unsympathetic
as were Jonson, Davenant, and the occasional Augustan who

happened to dislike it. He avers that its "constraint led our author into many absurdities": "to dilate ... with trifling and tedious circumlocutions," "to run into a ridiculous redundancy and repetition of words," and so forth. Warton was plainly blind to some of Spenser's most exquisite artifices. Yet he realizes certain advantages. The stanza, for instance, causes fullness of details. "Some images," he writes, "perhaps were produced by a multiplicity of rhymes." Dryden is quoted as saying that a rhyme often helped him to a thought. Spenser's extraordinary virtuosity is praised, but he is described as "laden with ... many shackles." Spenser's archaisms, which are naturally considered on the heels of the stanza, receive sensible and sympathetic treatment. But with an Augustan worship of decorous monotony, Warton could not see why Spenser did not place the caesura of his alexandrines invariably in the middle.

The tenth section, "Of Spenser's Allegorical Character," is of particular interest. Warton borrows Hughes's theory that allegory was a product of Spenser's age, of the pageants and spectacles which he considers more like Spenser's peculiar mode of allegorizing "than any other possible sources." Spenser's allegoristic method is compared with Ariosto's to the discredit of the latter (though Warton, like all Augustans, gives Ariosto credit for being a much more serious moralist than he really was). Warton follows Spence in condemning the intricate entanglings of allegory and realism as in the House of Alma. Warton, after Spence, like a good student of Boileau, attacks Spenser for mingling "divine mystery" with human allegory. He gives the same example as Spence: the Mount of Olives and Parnassus "impertinently linked together." But our critic decides that "allegorical poetry, through many gradations, at last received its ultimate consummation in the Fairy Queen." He concludes tamely by quoting what he calls (to his eternal discredit) "the just and pertinent sentiments" of Abbé du Bos:

It is impossible for a piece, whose subject is an allegorical action, to interest us very much.... Our heart requires truth even in fiction itself; and when it is presented with an allegorical fiction, it cannot determine itself, if I may be allowed the expression, to enter into the *sentiments* of those chimerical personages.

Warton, poring too long by a fatal minute over this stupid criticaster, was made as Midas when he heard Marsyas. He could not see in Spenser's allegory the magic that Thomas Gray saw with his poet's eye when he wrote in praise of *The Faërie Queene* and its

> Fierce war and faithful love,
> And truth severe, by fairy fiction drest.

He could not see that Spenser as he becomes allegorical almost always makes more direct and vivid transcripts from life than when he creates a Florimell in a spirit of irresponsible, unallegorical romance.

Thomas Warton has been described as apologetic in championing *The Faërie Queene*. On the contrary, he apologizes in the Postscript, like Spence, for having been "more diligent in remarking the faults than the beauties of Spenser." There was no need for a defence of *The Faërie Queene*. Warton was enabled to take many excellent ideas from Augustan critics of Spenser. He did not often fall into their absurdities. Rather, he united many of their soundest principles to the historical method and to something of the romantic spirit. It was this last, this spirit of childlike wonder, that led him to close his book with an enthusiastic and delightful quotation from *The Faërie Queene*.

> The waies, through which my weary steps I guyde,
> In this delightfull land of Faery,
> Are so exceeding spacious and wyde,
> And sprinckled with such sweet variety
> Of all that pleasant is to eare or eye,
> That I, nigh ravisht with rare thoughts delight,
> My tedious travell doe forget thereby;
> And when I gin to feele decay of might,
> It strength to me supplies, and chears my dulled spright.

It will be well for us, before we approach the radical romanticists, to examine James Thomson's great transitional poem with its Janus-vision of what was past and future for him. *The Castle of Indolence* is of absorbing interest to the most unimpassioned historical student of literature because of its extraordinary blend of Augustan and romantic elements and of equally absorbing interest to any catholic-minded lover of poetry because these elements combine remarkably to make a masterpiece. It appeared in 1748. Beginning years before as a mere piece of good-natured satire on his friends who had frequently accused him of indolence, it grew into a very serious and ambitious poem. There is an abundance of evidence, external and internal, of Spenser's first-hand influence. Indeed we are told by Shiels in his *Life of Thomson:* "he often said that if he had anything excellent in poetry, he owed it to the inspiration he first received from reading the 'Fairy Queen' in the very early part of his life." The descriptions of the land of Indolence, especially some of the opening stanzas, were certainly influenced by Spenser's description of the dwelling of Morpheus. From Merlin's magic "glassy globe," wherein Britomart first saw Artegall, derives Thomson's "Mirror of Vanity," a magic crystal globe, in which dreamers delighted to see:

> Still as you turned it, all things that do pass
> Upon this ant-hill earth; where constantly
> Of idly-busy men the restless fry
> Run bustling to and fro with foolish haste
> In search of pleasures vain, that from them fly,
> Of which, obtained the caitiffs dare not taste.

The Knight of Arts and Industry, who destroys the Castle of Indolence, the son of rough Selvaggio, who violated Dame Poverty, spending his youth running wild in the forest, is the lineal descendant of Spenser's Sir Satyrane, whose mother Thyamis was ravished by Therion, "a loose unruly swayne," and who was taught to roam the woods without fear. The Knight's companion, the bard, "in russet brown bedight," suggests the palmer who was Sir Guyon's mentor on a similar quest. The net in which the Knight entraps the wizard is like the net in which Guyon entangles the voluptuous, idle enchantress Acrasia. These and more materials from *The Faërie Queene* were skillfully used by Thomson.

I have said that the Augustans in imitating Spenser poured their inspiration into such favorite moulds as Occasional Verses for king and patron, *vers de société*, satires, and moralizing poems.[16] Satirical and moralizing poetry, of a most pronounced Augustan-Spenserian character, are much more prominent in *The Castle of Indolence* than the romantic elements. Of moralizing we have seen sufficient examples in the brief list of personages and situations borrowed from Spenser which I have just given. The spirit of gentle satire is one of the prime charms of *The Castle of Indolence* and should not be depreciated by those who go to Thomson only for romanticism. Thomson was a jolly good fellow. The spirit of burlesque appears in his earliest works. Even the ponderosity of his *Seasons* is occasionally lightened by a passage of merry Miltonism in the vein of *The Splendid Shilling*. The early edition of "Autumn" contained a description of a drinking-bout so uproarious that Lyttleton saw fit to strike it out in the reissue of 1750. Evidently only a genius was required to make Augustan-Spenserianism thoroughly delightful. There is fun worthy of Chaucer in *The Castle of Indolence*, in the waggish description, for instance, of Murdoch, Thomson's pastor-friend and biographer.

> Full oft by holy feet our ground was trod;
> Of clerks good plenty here you mote espy.
> A little, round, fat, oily man of God
> Was one I chiefly mark'd among the fry:
> He had a roguish twinkle in his eye,
> And shone all glittering with ungodly dew,
> If a tight damsel chaunced to trippen by;
> Which when observed, he shrunk into his mew,
> And straight would recollect his piety anew.

---

[16] The reader will find this classification worked out carefully in "Spenser, Thomson, and Romanticism," together with an analysis of some representative works under each head and copious lists of other poems.

Of the romanticism of *The Castle of Indolence,* a part comes from a Spenscrian love of sensuous detail, but a more striking part comes from a new and most significant spirit that takes no suggestion from *The Faërie Queene.* Full of Spenser's dreams and music he could write:

> A pleasing land of drowsyhed it was;
> Of dreams that wave before the half-shut eye;
> And of gay castles in the clouds that pass,
> Forever flushing round a summer sky:
> There eke the soft delights, that witchingly
> Instil a wanton sweetness through the breast,
> And the calm pleasures, always hovered nigh;
> But whate'er smacked of noyance, or unrest,
> Was far far off expelled from this delicious nest.

An oft-quoted stanza, on the other hand, will illustrate how far Thomson wandered into new mysterious regions.

> As when a shepherd of the Hebrid Isles,
> Placed far amid the melancholy main,
> (Whether it be lone fancy him beguiles,
> Or that aerial beings sometimes deign
> To stand embodied to our senses plain)
> Sees on the naked hill, or valley low,
> The whilst in ocean Phoebus dips his wain,
> A vast assembly moving to and fro;
> Then all at once in air dissolves the wondrous show.

However dim and shadowy Spenser's beings were he never questioned their reality. This question, "Is it reality or delusion?" this spirit of pampering a delighted doubt, was a new current in English romanticism. It could not exist in England until after the inflexible common sense of the Augustan Despotism had been weakened. Then, sceptical reason, combined with the luxurious dreams of Spenser which their creator, while he wrote, never disbelieved, produced the spirit of delighted doubt which Thomson cherished for a few brief and wistful moments. To find this spirit soaring unfettered England had to wait for the best work of Coleridge. It was a new note in English poetry.

Thomson's *Castle of Indolence*, then, is a typical Augustan "Imitation" of Spenser with a wonderful, exotic romantic tinge. Its neo-classical side is too often forgotten. Its satire and its moral allegory is of the very essence of Augustanism. And all this is good poetry despite the fact that the essence of Augustanism was to imitate self-consciously, superficially, mechanically. The second canto loses quality a little not because it is too Augustan but because it drops one of the Augustan-Spenserian elements—the enlivening sly satire. If we accept the common notion that *The Castle of Indolence* is a great poem we must respect Augustan-Spenserianism. On the other side the essence of romanticism is to imitate (though the romanticists are absurdly and morbidly afraid of the word) unconsciously or subtly and with proud independence. Much of the romantic side of Thomson and of many romantic Spenserians after him is in a spirit unknown to Spenser. For Thomson enriched English poetry with a new mood, one whose elusive light glimmers only in an occasional stanza—the spirit of delighted doubt.

With Richard Hurd (1720–1808) we come to the first important and uncompromising critic of the rebellious school who concerns us. His remarks of the "Plan and Conduct" of *The Faërie Queene* in his *Letters on Chivalry and Romance* open with a fine romantic swagger in which he flaunts his strong sympathy for Ariosto and the "Gothick" spirit. He decides to carry out Hughes' suggestion of weighing *The Faërie Queene* as a "Gothick" poem with more elaborateness and sympathy. But here he falters an instant and becomes a bit apologetic. "I have taken the fancy, with your leave, to try my hand on this curious subject." Here, after all, the apology of the Spenserian critics really begins. And it is not due to any unpopularity of Spenser but to the fact that they were advancing a somewhat new conception of him. We have seen that the neo-classicists apologized only when they were censuring Spenser. The romanticists apologized because they wished to link Spenser more closely to their own rebellious brotherhood. Hurd's analysis of the unity of *The Faërie Queene* we have already examined as

we approached the study of Spenser's epic. There was suf-
ficient unity, he thought, in the "relation" of the poem's "sev-
eral adventures to one common *original,* the appointment of the
Fairy Queen; and to one common *end,* the completion of the
Fairy Queen's injunctions." Prince Arthur was but an after-
thought, a sop to the classical Cerberus. It is interesting to
contrast Hurd and the Augustans at this point. The Augustans,
including Warton, lamented that Spenser was compelled by the
romantic prejudices of his time to follow the vicious example of
Ariosto. Hurd lamented that Spenser was compelled by the
prejudices of his time to allow classical ideals to play havoc
with his natural Gothic inclinations. We have seen in an
earlier chapter Hurd's novel approval and disapproval of the
structure of *The Fäerie Queene:* that Prince Arthur was
"essential," not "principal" in each book; that his admis-
sion was designed for special tastes, and that because this
admission justifies the "moral" not the "literal" story, "from
the union of the two designs there arises a perplexity, and con-
fusion, which is the proper and only considerable defect of this
extraordinary Poem." He is glad to leave his consideration of
the allegorical and the moral elements (towards which we shall
find him rather hostile) to launch forth in a breezy defence of
the Gothic method. Tasso is sneered at because "he thought fit
to *trim"* between Gothic and classical models. The French
scoffers at Ariosto are roundly scorned. (We must remember
that the Augustans had patted Tasso on the back and girded at
Ariosto.) And Hurd scores "our obsequious and over-modest
critics" for allowing themselves to be overriden by French
authority.

It grew into a sort of cant, with which Rymer, and the rest of that
school, filled their flimsy essays, and rambling prefaces.... A lucky word
in a verse, which sounds well and everybody gets by heart, goes further
than a volume of just criticism. In short, the exact, but cold Boileau
happened to say something of the *clinquant* of Tasso; and the magic of
this word, like the report of Astolfo's horn in Ariosto, overturned at once
the solid and well-built reputation of the *Italian* poetry.

Hurd closes with an utterance of even more enthusiastic romanticism that lifts him safely above the jaded connoisseurs of the Gothic in his time. He defends the "tales of Fairy" and the fantastic exploits of the unfettered imagination as the greatest material for epic poetry. Bad criticism, which had relegated such matters to children, is blamed as the result of the abuse of terms.

A poet, they say, must follow *nature;* and by nature we are to suppose can only be meant the known and experienced affairs in this world. Whereas the poet has a world of his own, where experience has less to do than consistent imagination.... Without *admiration* (which cannot be affected but by the marvellous of celestial intervention, I mean, the agency of superior natures really existing, or by the illusion of fancy taken to be so) no epic poem can be long-lived. I am not afraid to instance in the *Henriade* itself; which, notwithstanding the elegance of the composition, will in a short time be no more read than the *Gondibert* of Sir William Davenant, and for the same reason.

The "pomp of verse, the energy of description, and even the finest moral paintings" will not produce a great epic without the quality of "*admiration.*" By "admiration," I take it, Hurd means, in a slightly more restricted sense, what Theodore Watts-Dunton means when he characterizes romanticism as the spirit of "Wonder" which revolted against the Augustan "Acceptance."

Hurd's last words on Spenser explain what I have been frequently asserting—that the romanticists, though they discovered new beauties in Spenser, became blind to certain of the qualities of *The Faërie Queene* that had long been wisely cherished by Milton and by the Augustans. Because of the ridicule of chivalry and magic, Hurd thinks, Spenser was forced to give "an air of mystery to his subject" and to pretend "that his stories of knights and giants" were but the mantle "of an abundance of profound wisdom."

In short, to keep off the eyes of the prophane from prying too nearly into his subject, he threw about it the mist of allegory.

Fancy that had wantoned it so long in the world of fiction was now constrained, against her will, to ally herself with strict Truth if she would gain admittance into reasonable company.

What we have gotten by this revolution, you will say, is a great deal of good sense. What we have lost, is a world of fine fabling; the illusion of which is so grateful to the *charmed* Spirit, that, in spite of philosophy and fashion, *Fairy* Spenser still ranks highest among the Poets; I mean, with all those who are either come of that house, or have any kindness for it. Earth-born critics, my friend, may blaspheme:

> "But all the Gods are ravish'd with delight
> Of his celestial song, and music's wondrous might."

Hurd merits the highest praise for his spirited defense of the romantic side of Spenser. But, for all his eloquence, his depreciation of Spenser's allegory deserves reproach. Anyone who reads Spenser's contemporaries in Italy, France, and England can see that, despite the rapid growth of Augustan criticism on the continent, Fancy could easily wanton it at her own sweet will without feeling constrained to go masked in moral allegory. Spenser was not forced to constrain his copious visions within bounds, but the beautiful high-seriousness that always dwells with the greatest poets made him choose allegory uncommanded. Hurd and most succeeding romanticists have forgotten that there is much rich beauty in Spenser of which the moral allegory is "efficient cause," that many of the passages which they admire cannot be cherished consistently unless the allegory be accepted as artistic. Enthusiasm for the canto on Despair, to which the coldest reader of Spenser accords high praise, implies enthusiasm for the episode as allegory no matter what fine-spun theories the reader chooses to flaunt. The restraining power and architectonic value of Spenser's allegory, despite its incomplete working-out, will be apparent to any man who reads the *Poly-Olbion* of Drayton and the *Britannias Pastorals* of Browne, huge poems which had much of Spenser's heaped treasures of fancy and glimmering lore, but none of the deeper dreams of prophecy that impelled him to pour the riches into the vast, the too vast mould of the allegory and strive to erect a gorgeous, infinite-spired Utopia which would have shaped and perfected even the spacious court of Queen Elizabeth.

These opinions have brought us well into the camp of the

romanticists where fewer citations and explanations are neces-
sary for the reader of today. The Augustan attitude lingered
on for long with many critics; but most men followed in the
wake of Hurd. We are near enough our own time to conclude
this long survey of Spenserian criticism with a sketch of the
attitudes of four of the most delightful romantic admirers of
Spenser—Sir Walter Scott, William Hazlitt, Leigh Hunt, and
John Keats. From these men through Edward Dowden I may
pass to the conclusions that I would base on all these opinions
and on my own reading and rereading of Spenser.

In order thoroughly to appreciate Scott's attitude toward
Spenser we must glance at his poetry along with his prose. Like
many poets he has left evidence of his early delight in Spenser
to whose works he was introduced by Doctor Blacklock.

> Spenser I could have read forever. Too young to trouble myself about
> the allegory, I considered all the knights and ladies and dragons and
> giants in their outward and exoteric sense, and God only knows how
> delighted I was to find myself in such society.

And in the days of his maturity Scott's boyish appreciation
of Spenser remained essentially the same. For Scott was always
heartily a boy. Beyond a certain interest as a man of affairs
and an antiquarian in Spenser's political allegory,[17] he rather
abandoned himself, like all full-fledged romanticists, to the
delights of the rich succession of pictures stirred in Spenser
himself by most lofty purposes. Scott's romanticism, with its
love of antiquarianism, was not a strong spirit of rebellion, not
even a very strong spirit of wonder. Allowing for its immensely
superior vigor and its wholesome scorn of introspection, it has
something in common with the pretty trifling of Beattie. Scott's
romanticism involved little more than a change in what the
Augustans called "machinery." Take out your pagan divin-

---

[17] See his essay on Todd's edition of Spenser (*Edinburgh Review*,
1805): "But although everything belonging to the reign of the Virgin
Queen carries with it a secret charm to Englishmen, no commentator of
the Faëry Queen has taken the trouble to go very deep into those annals,
for the purpose of illustrating the secret, and as it were, esoteric allusions
of Spenser's poems.

ities; put in your knights. Add to this a change of landscape.
Describe a mountain or forest scene. Put in an indispensable
moon and a castle. This was the setting and the materials, not
for the sentimental reflections of a Beattie, but for the stirring
narrative and ring of the old ballad.

What Scott found in Spenser was the dim forest, the furtive
flash of armor as the sun stole through at intervals, silent
maidens who were to Scott mere vague flowers of medieval
landscape, and ever and anon a great castle upleaping unex-
pectedly in the silver, winding path. Even in the eager flow
of his narrative Scott delighted to pause and to contemplate
these lovely scenes. So he hit upon the happy device of using
Spenserian inspiration in a rather novel way. In almost all
his narrative poems he introduced Spenserian stanzas, generally
at the opening of his cantos, to linger over the setting before
the quick beat of the free tetrameters called to arms. He showed
a relic of Augustan-Spenserianism by occasionally employing
the stanza of *The Faërie Queene* for a moralistic prelude or
interlude, as the master himself did. Finally he strewed his
narrative with allusions to the beautiful pictures in *The Faërie
Queene*. In some of his later poems the intermediary influence
of Byron's *Childe Harold* appears to have tinged his introduc-
tory Spenserian stanzas. But, in general, the landscapes thus
gracefully limned and quietly water-colored are not disturbed
by the more personal, the stormier note of Byron. Almost any
of these stanzas taken at random will illustrate. The idyllic
scenes on the island in the second canto of *The Lady of the
Lake* are introduced by a charming setting.

> At morn the black-cock trims his jetty wing,
> 'Tis morning prompts the linnet's blithest lay,
> All Nature's children feel the matin spring
> Of life reviving, with reviving day;
> And while yon little bark glides down the bay,
> Wafting the stranger on his way again,
> Morn's genial influence roused a minstrel gray,
> And sweetly o'er the lake was heard thy strain,
> Mix'd with thy sounding harp, O white-hair'd Allan-Bane.

The Spenserian allusions with which the Ariosto of the North, ever haunted by visions of *The Faërie Queene,* strewed richly his poems may be exemplified by a passage from *Marmion* which conjures up scenes with the delight of a child rocking himself into ecstasy by a fire-place and recalling his store of fairy-tales.

> Not she, the Championess of old,
> In Spenser's magic tale enroll'd,
> She for the charméd spear renown'd,
> Which forced each knight to kiss the ground,—
> Not she more chang'd, when, placed at rest,
> What time she was Malbecco's guest,
> She gave to flow her maiden vest;
> When from the corslet's grasp relieved,
> Free to the sight her bosom heaved;
> Sweet was her blue eye's honest smile,
> Erst hidden by the aventayle;
> And down her shoulders graceful roll'd,
> Her locks profuse, of paly gold,
> They who whilom, in midnight fight,
> Had marvell'd at her matchless might,
> No less her maiden charms approved,
> But looking liked, and liking loved.
> The sight could jealous pangs beguile,
> And charm Malbecco's cares a while;
> And he, the wandering Squire of Dames,
> Forgot his Columbella's claims,
> And passion, erst unknown, could gain
> The breast of blunt Sir Satyrane;
> Nor durst light Paridel advance,
> Bold as he was, a looser glance.
> She charm'd at once, and tamed the heart,
> Incomparable Britomart!

Thus, too, *The Vision of Don Roderick* closes with Spenser's favorite method of saying adieu.

> But all too long, through seas unknown and dark,
> (With Spenser's parable I close my tale,)
> By shoal and rocks hath steer'd my venturous bark,
> And landward now I drive before the gale .
> And now the blue and distant shore I hail,

> And nearer now I see the port expand,
> And now I gladly furl my weary sail,
> And, as the prow light touches on the strand,
> I strike my red-cross flag and bind my skiff to land.

Scott was always a hearty, delighted boy and this lovable trait is no better illustrated than in his Spenser-worship.

The beautiful things in Spenser were ever straying in some convenient corner of Hazlitt's mind. Hazlitt shares with Byron in *Don Juan* the supreme honors in English literature for the mastery of the fine art of quoting. So adroitly does Hazlitt slip a fine phrase or verse from a beloved writer into the rich texture of his own prose that he becomes a second creator, as great as the first, and we gain the double delight of the rich originality of two master-spirits. This is one of the most effective and difficult of stylistic accomplishments. Hazlitt quoted Spenser à propos of things in general, often very quaintly. Spenser does not desert him even as he goes with keen eagerness to a prize-fight. "We felt as much disconcerted," he writes in one place with recondite knowledge, "by the uncalled for phrensy of this theatrical Amazon, as the Squire of Dames in Spenser did, when he was carried off by the giantess Orgygia." Coleridge's *Lay Sermon* reminded him of "a gentle husher Vanitie by name."

Hazlitt certainly penned some of the most piquant comments on Spenser ever written. "The essence of Spenser's poetry," he tells us, "was a continuous, endless flow of indescribable beauties like the galaxy or milky way." He says penetrating things about the vexed question of Spenser's passion.

> But he has been unjustly charged with a want of passion and strength. He has both in an immense degree. He has not indeed the pathos of immediate action or suffering, which is more properly the dramatic; but he has all the pathos of sentiment and romance—all that belongs to distant objects of terror, and uncertain, imaginary distress.

After all the endless talk about Ariosto and Spenser, Hazlitt makes the best comparison ever written.

If Ariosto transports us into regions of romance, Spenser's poetry is all fairy-land. In Ariosto we walk upon the ground, in a company, gay, fantastic, and adventurous enough. In Spenser, we wander in another world, among ideal beings. The poet takes us and lays us in the lap of a lovelier nature, by the sound of softer streams, among greener hills and fairer valleys. He paints nature, not as we find it, but as we expected to find it, and fulfills the delightful promise of our youth.

Hazlitt is quaintly non-committal on the problem of Spenser's allegory.

But some people will say that all this may be very fine, but that they cannot understand it on account of the allegory. They are afraid of the allegory, as if they thought it would bite them: they look at it as a child looks at a painted dragon, and think it will strangle them in its shining folds. This is very idle. If they do not meddle with the allegory, the allegory will not meddle with them. Without minding it at all, the whole is as plain as pike-staff.

Hazlitt was a literary epicure, the product of the romantic attitude toward Spenser, who has done incalculable good for the master and yet has encouraged men to take *The Faërie Queene* as an intellectual anesthetic. If we tempered our Hazlitt and all the romanticists with Milton, Dryden, and Addison for an antidote, then we should get much nearer the perfect conception of Spenser. But I must leave the reader with a relish of Hazlitt rather than of my polemics.

In reading the Faery Queene, you see a little withered old man by a wood-side opening a wicket, a giant, and a dwarf lagging far behind, a damsel in a boat upon an enchanted lake, wood-nymphs, and satyrs; and all of a sudden you are transported into a lofty palace, with tapers burning, amidst knights and ladies, with dance and revelry, and song, ''and mask, and antique pageantry.''

From boyhood to the days of his sunny maturity, when he poured out his graceful garrulous essays, Spenser haunted Leigh Hunt like a passion. He tells us, in his *Autobiography,* that he secured an odd volume of Spenser at Christ's Hospital and completed about a hundred stanzas called *The Fairy King* which ''was to be in emulation of Spenser.'' From that time Spenser was his favorite among all poets. In 1801 he published his *Juvenilia, or a Collection of Poems, Written between the*

Ages of Twelve and Sixteen. The most ambitious effort is
"The Palace of Pleasure; An Allegorical Poem in Two Cantos.
Written in Imitation of Spenser." His hedonistic *Story of
Rimini* (1816), so important in the history of nineteenth century
romanticism, shows the influence of Spenser, the sensuous
builder of the Bower of Bliss, both for better and for worse.
In his uneven but luxuriant book, *Imagination and Fancy*
(1844), we find the keynote of Leigh Hunt's attitude toward
Spenser. When the charming and garrulous old critic says that
Spenser's "versification is perpetual honey," he says something
precious, and half true, but very dangerous to full appreciation.
He compares scene after scene of concentrated loveliness with
some appropriate picture (Raphael, Titian, Poussin, Salvator
Rosa, a doubtful band of comrades) which hangs in the great
galleries of Europe. No book could be more sage and seductive
to teach both youth and crabbed age to adore Spenser. Yet I
must be ungracious enough to charge Hunt with a good deal
of responsibility for the conception current today of Spenser as
a pictorial poet and nothing more. When he says that "Spen-
ser is the farthest removed from the ordinary cares and haunts
of the world of all the poets that ever wrote, except perhaps
Ovid," he is positively libelous both in his general statement
and in his comparison of "our sage and serious" poet with the
delightful old Roman voluptuary. Spenser's pictures have been
admired until we have come to slur over or grudge him all
credit as a writer of narrative and as a philosophic poet. This
is absurdly extreme. And had Hunt himself appreciated more
unreservedly some of Spenser's larger qualities, his own verse
would doubtless have been less saccharine and spineless. But
it seems almost sacrilegious to quarrel with this affable old
literary epicure. To be sure he is ready to concede, among three
"objections against this divine poet," first of all that "he
wrote a good deal of allegory"—and this in the same category
with the admission that he "has a great many superfluous
words." He will allure us into a bower of bliss by assuring us
that Spenser's "allegory itself is but one part allegory and

nine parts enjoyment." As if there was not the enjoyment that is godlike in his allegory *qua* allegory! Leigh Hunt can quote with approval Coleridge's assertion that Spenser "has placed you in a dream, a charmed sleep: and you neither wish nor have the power to enquire, where you are, or how you got there." It is this sort of siren-song that leads even a grave poet like William Vaughn Moody to write to a friend, in a mood which we must relish but also suspect with all Spenser's own puritanism: "I stick a good round straw into a cask of Spenser or Hardy, and suck myself to sleep—to dream of orchards and 'golden-towered Romance with serene lute.'" To be sure we should be a sorry lot of fools if we were incapable of such splendid triviality. Spenser himself would invite it. But we should not consider that we were really and strenuously reading Spenser. Rather we should feel aware of merely dallying with the alluring pages of some vellum-bound volume of *The Faërie Queene*, lying in a meadow and catching but the half of the poet's secret, filled with a drowsy joy till our half-closed lids would fall, allowing the page to remain revealed only through the haze of our own fantastic embroiderings and through the iridescent blur of the sunlight stealing through our fallen eye-lashes. To be sure this is not reading Spenser. But this attitude of Hunt's is compounded of inseparable venial sin and sovereign virtue. And how well he can wave his wizard's wand over the querulous! What of Spenser's superfluousness? cry the querulous. "His forced rhymes, and his sentences written to fill up," responds Hunt, "which in a less poet would be intolerable, are accompanied with such endless grace and dreaming pleasure, fit to

> ˙ Make heaven drowsy with the harmony,

that although it is to be no more expected of anybody to read him through at once, than to wander days and nights in a forest, thinking of nothing else, yet any true lover of poetry, when he comes to know him, would as soon quarrel with repose on the summer grass." Those of us who marvel over the faint but happy sunshine of Leigh Hunt's old age may perhaps find the quaint and curious recipe for his elixir of life in this short apostrophe to Spenser.

> Around us are the woods; in our distant ear is the sea; the glimmering forms that we behold are those of nymphs and deities; or a hermit makes the loneliness more lonely; or we hear a horn blow, and the ground trembling with the coming of a giant; and our boyhood is again existing, full of belief, though its hair be turning grey; because thou, a man, hast written its books, and proved the surpassing riches of its wisdom.

It is well to glance, by way of climax, at Keats, one of the truest Spenserians who ever lived, though even Keats missed some of Spenser's loftiest qualities and could not draw from him his highest pleasures. Cowden Clark's pleasant story of how he awakened the poetic impulse of Keats by reading Spenser's *Epithalamion* is too familiar for quotation. But though Spenser was Keats' first chosen master we find also the intermediary influence of such Spenserians as the late Augustans, Leigh Hunt (a somewhat effeminate mentor), and the garrulous William Browne. Everybody remembers that Keats' first known poem is an "Imitation of Spenser" (c. 1813), quite Augustan, despite his early love for Spenser himself. Like any enthusiastic youngster he found the works of inferior Spenserians like the fabled "lost books" of *The Faërie Queene* and knew not the gay tin-foil beaten thin from the deep-hued red gold. In his maturity he seemed at times almost a perfect reincarnation of Spenser. Yet at the close of his life he could write "Spenserian Stanzas on Charles Armitage Browne" in the vein of good-humored personal satire much cultivated in the eighteenth century and given consummate expression in Thomson's *Castle of Indolence*. Like any Augustan-Spenserian, he gave his own turn to the episode of Artegall and the giant in a "Spenserian Stanza" of political allegory romantic in its politics but Augustan in its artistic method. To Keats, with his eyes dilated by the French Revolution and by many new political visions, the giant's spirit of revolt seemed crude; but (and Keats was right) it seemed far more worthy than Artegall's inflexible conserv-

atism. Yet in mere style, as far as we may abstract it from
content, the stanza might have been attributed to Samuel
Croxall, a Spenserian of the first decade of the eighteenth cen-
tury who wrote new cantos for *The Faërie Queene* as satires of
contemporary political events. Here Spenser is confuted in an
· Augustan-Spenserian, superficial, and mechanical imitation. A
political satire which confutes Spenser and preaches democracy
—truly an astounding combination of influences!

> In after-time, a sage of mickle lore
> Yclep'd Typographus, the Giant took,
> And did refit his limbs as heretofore,   ·
> And made him read in many a learned book;
> And into many a lively legend look;
> Thereby in goodly themes so training him,
> That all his brutishness he quite forsook,
> When meeting Artegall and Talus grim,
> The one he struck stone-blind, the other's eyes wox dim.

The Cap and Bells or The Jealousies is Keats' most complex
piece of Spenserianism. This unfinished attempt to write a
popular humorous fairy-tale in Spenserian stanzas was done
towards the close of his life in the very grip of Giant Despair.
Keats worked with real enthusiasm; but it was a pathetic
attempt to play the motley with a cracked heart. Eighteenth
century Spenserianism and Byronic satire jostle along side by
side with the spirit of *The Faërie Queene*. There are some good
stanzas in the poem, especially some gay-colored city pictures.

> The morn is full of holiday; loud bells
> With rival clamours ring from every spire;
> Cunningly-station'd music dies and swells
> In echoing places; when the winds respire,
> Light flags stream out like gauzy tongues of fire;
> A metropolitan murmur, lifeful, warm,
> Comes from the northern suburbs; rich attire
> Freckles with red and gold the moving swarm;
> While here and there clear trumpets blow a keen alarm.
>
> .   .   .   .
>
> Onward we floated o'er the panting streets,
> That seem'd throughout with upheld faces paved;
> Look where we will, our bird's-eye vision meets
> Legions of holiday; bright standards waved,

> And fluttering ensigns emulously craved
> One minute's glance; a busy thunderous roar,
> From square to square, among the buildings rav'd,
> As when the sea, at flow, gluts up once more
> The craggy hollowness of a wild reefed shore.

The child Keats is alert again for the moment. The ghost of Spenser walks in modern London town and, with a touch of his wand, transforms its sooty grandeur into a glimmering Thule domed with golden dreams. But the poem is from the flotsam and jetsam of Keats' mind.

Eighteenth century Spenserianism is not a part of the great poetry of Keats. And all that remains of the Huntean worship of Spenser as a divine confectionery is only beautiful in the mature works. Porphyro, heaping the candied apples, quinces, and manna and dates from Fez in golden dishes, regardless of lurking foes, while his Madeline slept an azure-lidded sleep; the delight in "blanched linen, smooth and lavender'd," hushed carpets that should never have been put into real castles—these are relics of the deliciousness of Hunt—but most bewitching poetry. "The Eve of Saint Agnes" has more of the spirit of Spenser than any poem since *The Faërie Queene*. Yet the microscope reveals little or no tangible imitation. We have here the essence of romanticism—to follow subtly and deeply where the neo-classicists followed superficially and mechanically—not so much to imitate in their sense as to emulate. For once, at least, the critic who deals with the most valuable method of studying literary influences in that most arid manner which is bringing his school so unfortunately into disrepute must be silent unless he has sense enough to say that Keats divined the essence of Spenser and recreated him. One could write the poem as easily as to label its magic. There is more than Spenser in "The Eve of Saint Agnes." But that is not my present concern. Let me quote two stanzas which I should describe as sheer Spenser if they were not also sheer Keats who, for the moment, is the bard of *The Faërie Queene* in a new incarnation.

A casement high and triple-arch'd there was,
All garlanded with carven imag'ries
Of fruits, and flowres, and bunches of knot-grass,
And diamonded with panes of quaint device,
Innumerable of stains and splendid dyes,
As are the tiger-moth's deep-damask'd wings;
And in the midst, 'mong thousand heraldries,
And twilight saints, and dim emblazonings,
A shielded scutcheon blush'd with blood of queens and kings.

Full on the casement shone the wintry moon,
And threw warm gules on Madeline's fair breast,
As down she knelt for heaven's grace and boon;
Rose-bloom fell on her hands, together prest,
And on her silver cross soft amethyst,
And on her hair a glory, like a saint:
She seem'd a splendid angel, newly drest,
Save wings, for heaven:—Porphyro grew faint:
She knelt, so pure a thing, so free from mortal taint.

A catalogue of later opinions is unnecessary. Much that has distinction in later-day criticism of Spenser has been found strewn through the pages of the earlier chapters of this book. Endless, alas, are the pale comments of writers of text books who have bolted *The Faërie Queene* in preparation for their task with all the terrifying velocity with which the ghastly dyspeptic Americans in *Martin Chuzzlewit* devoured their dinner —"in huge wedges." A few words about Spenser's worship of beauty, a fling at his structure, a raising of eyebrows over the allegory, and all the necessary paragraphs in any proper history of English literature are complete. Such is the baneful influence of literary epicures like Hurd, Scott, Leigh Hunt, and other brilliant writers whose utterances culminate in Lowell's glowing and memorable but dangerous essay on Spenser, which, with all its masterly appreciation of one side of the poet's genius, has had a warping influence on many and on some even a blighting influence. For the offspring of the literary epicures are bound to be the literary dyspeptics. In the conclusion of the first chapter I quoted two of what I did not hesitate to call the brilliant Luciferean utterances of Lowell.

And since I have in later chapters scattered many of the truer splendors of that great essay with many a word of praise and deep gratitude, perhaps I may be pardoned if I cite a few more passages from this master-critic to emphasize the eloquence and plausibility with which he has stamped his sophistries about Spenser upon us like a curiously fascinating signet.

Hazlitt bids us not mind the allegory, and says that it won't bite us nor meddle with us if we do not meddle with it. But how if it bore us, which after all is the fatal question? The truth is that it is too often forced upon us against our will, as people were formerly driven to church till they began to look on a day of rest as a penal institution, and to transfer to the Scriptures that suspicion of defective inspiration which was awakened in them by the preaching.

Once we admit with Lowell that "the true use" of Spenser is "as a gallery of pictures which we visit as the mood takes us, and where we spend an hour or two at a time, long enough to sweeten our perceptions, not so long as to cloy them"—once we admit this then we are vexed at the very things for which Spenser burned out his large and generous life. A picture gallery, to dally in only! No wonder we should grow restive. Like Hurd, Lowell makes the mistake of thinking Spenser was forced into an artificial double-scheme, a poem plus a moralistic or allegorical veneer.

The problem for Spenser was a double one: how to commend poetry at all to a generation which thought it effeminate trifling, and how he, Master Edmund Spenser, of imagination all compact, could commend *his* poetry to Master John Bull, the most practical of mankind in his habitual mood, but at that moment in a passion of religious anxiety about his soul. *Omne tulit punctum qui miscuit utile dulci* was not only an irrefragable axiom because a Latin poet had said it, but it exactly met the case in point. He would convince the scorners that poetry might be seriously useful, and show Master Bull his new way of making fine words butter parsnips, in a rhymed moral primer. Allegory, as then practised, was imagination adapted for beginners, in words of one syllable and illustrated with cuts, and would thus serve both his ethical and pictorial purpose. Such a primer, or a first instalment of it, he proceeded to put forth; but he so bordered it with bright-colored fancies, he so often filled whole pages and crowded the text hard in others with the gay frolics of his pencil, that, as in the Grimani missal, the holy function of the book is forgotten in the ecstacy of its adornment. Worse than all, does not the brush linger more lovingly along the rosy contours of his sirens than on the modest wimples of the Wise Virgins?

It is perfectly and manifestly absurd to suggest that Spenser's art lingers more lovingly over Immodest Mirth, Phædria, let us say, than over Charity, that the sentimental and lascivious Malecasta is more fondly made alluring than Britomart standing over her in her virgin smock with her blazing falchion upraised. But let us not pause to quibble over matters of detail. Spenser's lingering over his sirens is highly moral. People have long loved Acrasia in her Bower of Bliss without daring to admit it unless, like some perverse later-day artists, they have tried to convince people that they were immoral or, if they were more timid, took refuge in reticence or in an attack on Spenser's moralistic passages. People have not realized that Acrasia portrays a vice that is but a virtue in excess and must, by all the demand of truth, be represented as lovely and be accepted with delight at first unreserved, then followed, before excess comes, by the same recoil that tells us of Guyon's stern justice. It is amazing to find Lowell following Hurd in declaring some allegorical veneer necessary to an age whose wilful and indulgent poetry he knew so well. Did he think that Sir Philip Sidney was insincere in that immortal prose in which he declared poetry more practical in its nature than either history or philosophy? Surely he had read Shakespeare's unblushing and unallegorized *Venus and Adonis*. Lowell, unfortunately, lived in a generation when immortal British utilitarianism had just overreached itself in that stolid march begun by Bentham and continued by the two Mills. Lowell succumbed to that transcendentalism which was imported by Coleridge, Carlyle, T. H. Greene, and the Cairds for an antidote, a transcendentalism which was and is exotic, reactionary.

But I may best confront Lowell once more, as I did at the beginning, with what I believe to be the greatest essay on Spenser ever written, "Spenser, the Poet and Teacher," by Edward

Dowden, whose recent death leaves the position of England's
most magisterial and most poetic critic of our day to be filled.
This age is still too much devoted to the doctrine of Art for Art's
sake (though many have professed to have abjured it) to be in
harmony with the ideals of Spenser or Milton.   Poets who are
ineffectually concerned with pale, anemic Isoldes gazing sadly
into the solitary West cannot understand the full beauty of
figures like Una, who symbolizes Truth.   They admire only the
colors, not the exquisite lines of the picture.   Had they Spenser's
richer view, their poetry would not so often confuse the white-
ness of beauty with the preternatural whiteness of leprosy.
They are for all the world like the exclusive and selfish people
in Boccaccio who assembled in rural sequestration to divert each
other with stories while their comrades in the city groaned with
the plague and stretched out imploring hands for help.   If you
make poetry the gilded plaything of an exclusive and esoteric
cult, you are doing as did Boccaccio's fine lords and ladies.   You
will have none of the humanity of the Man of Law and the
Prioress, you will have none of the lofty imagination of the
Knight and the Squire.   On the other hand, the *literary* "real-
ists" in poetry who are rapidly and happily annihilating the
précieux are themselves open to the serious charges of mere
propagandism, of slipshod workmanship, of a certain bright
hardness, of a certain predisposition towards pathological sit-
uations and characters, of a failure to be sufficiently defiant
of things as they are.   And even the *philosophical* realists are,
as Royce justly notes in *The World and the Individual,* com-
mitted to a stiff conservatism because of their over emphasis of
"external relations."   Spenser studied Plato and Aristotle and
knew Sidney, the poet and statesman, dreamer and doer.   There-
fore he had a profounder understanding of the function of
poetry than our romanticists or our realists.

But I must hasten on to plunder the "great and gracious"
utterances of Edward Dowden before I attempt to marshal my
own conclusions.   In a paragraph on Spenser's "October,"
Dowden reacts against that pathetic and everlasting prating

on mere form, which is one of the ways in which those who indulge an attitude like Lowell's toward Spenser, in which their close kinsmen, the Art for Art's sake men, and their more distant relatives who emphasize an imperialistic, intellectualistic philosophy for philosophy's sake, become entangled in their own unconscious *reductio ad absurdum* of their own ideals. Dowden unmasks this by contrasting it with Spenser's ideal of poetry.

In what way does Spenser conceive of poetry? We know how in periods which were not creative, periods which are not breathed upon by divine ideas, which are not driven by the urge of strong emotions, poetry comes to be looked on as primarily an art, or even as an accomplishment, and it is treated as if its function were to decorate life much as the artistic upholsterer decorates our houses. At such a time great regard is had to the workmanship of verse exclusive of the burden and inspiration of the song, and elegant little specimens of mosaic or of enamelling are turned out of the workshops of skilled artists; until the thing descends into a trade. In the creative periods there is not less devotion to form and workmanship; but the devotion is of a less self-conscious kind, because generative powers work in the poet with a rapturous blindness of love, and he thinks of himself less as a master of technique (though he is also this) than as a man possessed by some influence out of and beyond himself, some dominant energy of Nature or of God, to which it is his part to submit, which he cannot lay claim to as if it were an attainment of skill, and which he dare not call his own. At such times poetry aims at something more than to decorate life; it is spoken of as if it possessed some imperial authority, a power to bind and to loose, to sway man's total nature, to calm, to regulate and restrain, and also to free, to arouse, to dilate the spirit—power not to titillate a particular sense, but to discipline the will and mould a character. In such a tone of high assumption Spenser speaks of poetry.

We may safely remember that this passage was written at a time when poetry was much more in the hands of the puny and tired offspring of the giant Victorians and of certain querulous revolutionists who talked too much about *fin de siècle* and symbolism, elements which were to blend in a most naughty and intoxicating witch's brew. These men despised words like "content," and "ethical" and estimated poems by the beauty of single lines. Edward Dowden would not deny that our present age is highly creative. Of that we may be sure. But the small fry who stung him to make his scornful contrast are still with us as poets; and their kindred critics of Edmund Spenser, the last generation of the literary epicures, are legion especially in universities where their languid admissions and thin crackling sarcasms are unendurable.

There is a passage in this great essay on "Spenser, the Poet and Teacher," a passage so complete in its summing up of the qualities of Spenser and of all the greatest poets, that it should silence such dry locust-shrilling and freshen such intellectual sultriness as with a breeze from mountain snows.

> How, then, should we read the "Faery Queen"? Is it poetry? Or is it philosophy? Are we merely to gaze on with wide-eyed expectancy as at a marvellous pageant or procession, in which knights and ladies, Saracens and wizards, anticks and wild men, pass before our eyes? or are these visible shows only a rind or shell, which we must break or strip away in order to get at that hidden wisdom which feeds the spirit? Neither of these things are we to do. The mere visible shows of Spenser's poem are indeed goodly enough to beguile a summer's day in some old wood, and to hold us from morning to evening in a waking dream. The ethical teaching of Spenser extracted from his poetry is worthy a careful study. Raphael drew his fainting Virgin Mother as a skeleton in his preparatory study, and the student of Raphael may well consider the anatomy of the figure, because whatever an artist has put into his work, that a critic may try to take out of it. So the moral philosophy of Spenser even apart from his poetry may rightly form a subject of study. But the special virtue of the "Faery Queen" will be found only by one who receives it neither as pageantry nor as philosophy, but in the way in which Spenser meant that it should be received—as a living creature of the imagination, a spirit incarnate, "one altogether," "of a reasonable soul and human flesh subsisting."

After the morbid fear of Puritanism which fails to remember that there were and are many kinds of Puritanism and which, in all its rampant indiscrimination, is nowadays often crassly considered the essence of true catholicity, and after the many contrasts of Bunyan and Spenser (Macaulay's and Lowell's and Yeats' and scores of others) which invariably patronize Spenser, it is most refreshing to read Dowden's opinion.

> Spenser's conception of life was Puritan in its seriousness; yet we think with wonder of the wide space that lies between the "Faery Queen"

and our other great allegory, the "Pilgrim's Progress." To escape the City of Destruction and to reach the Celestial City is Christian's one concern; and all his recompense for the countless trials of the way lies upon the other side of the river of death. His consuming thought is this: "What must I do to be saved?" Spenser is spiritual but he is also mundane; he thinks of the uses of the noble human creatures to this world in which we move. His general end in the poem is "to fashion a gentleman or noble person in virtuous and gentle discipline." "A grand self-culture," I have elsewhere said, is that about which Spenser is concerned; not, as with Bunyan, the escape of the soul to heaven; not the attainment of supernatural grace through a point of mystical contact, like the vision which was granted to the virgin knight, Galahad, in the mediaeval allegory. Self-culture, the formation of a complete character for the uses of earth, and afterwards, if need be, for the uses of heaven,—this was subject sufficient for the twenty-four books designed to form the epic of the age of Elizabeth. And the means of that self-culture are of an active kind—namely, warfare,—warfare, not for its own sake, but for the generous accomplishment of unselfish ends." Bunyan, with whom the visionary power was often involuntary, who could live for a day and a night in some metaphor that had attacked his imagination, transcribed into allegory his own wonderful experience of terrors and of comfort. Spenser is more impersonal: he can refashion Aristotle in a dream. But behind him lies all the sentiment of Christian chivalry, and around him all the life of Elizabethan England; and from these diverse elements arises a rich and manifold creation, which, if it lacks the personal, spiritual passion of Bunyan's allegory, compensates by its moral breadth, its noble sanity, its conciliation of what is earthly with what is divine.

These quotations we may crown with Edward Dowden's own ardent and opulent conclusion, one of those many passages which, as I have before suggested, are a triumphant refutation of any insinuation that such an arbiter's devotion to ethical elements makes him purblind to what some people jealously refrigerate in some special retreat, closely guarded from the contamination of rigorous thought and labeled "Esthetic."

"A better teacher than Scotus or Aquinas." Yet we are told by the Dean of St. Paul's, that in giving himself credit for a direct purpose to instruct, Spenser "only conformed to the curiously utilitarian spirit which pervaded the literature of the time." It is the heresy of modern art that only useless things should be made beautiful. We want beauty only in playthings. In elder days the armour of a knight was as beautiful as sunlight, or as flowers. "In unaffected, unconscious, artistic excellence of invention," says one of our chief living painters, "approaching more nearly to the strange beauty of nature, especially in vegetation, mediaeval armour perhaps surpasses any other effort of human ingenuity.'' What if Spenser wrought armour for the soul, and because it was precious and of finest temper, made it fair to look upon? That which gleams as bright as the waters of a sunlit lake is perhaps a breastplate to protect the heart; that which appears pliant as the blades of summer grass may prove at our need to be a sword of steel.

. . . .

Most lovers of Spenser, whether of the long procession of singers whom he has taught his opulence in every century or of the great brotherhood he has made poets in the less conspicuous walks of daily life, can, with but few minor alterations, write their first confessions in the quaint words of the poet Cowley.

> But, how this Love came to be produc'd in me so early, is a hard Question: I believe, I can tell the particular little Chance that filled my head first with such Chimes of Verse, as have never since left ringing there: For I remember when I began to read, and take some Pleasure in it, there was wont to lye in my Mother's Parlour (I know not by what accident, for she her self never in her Life read any Book but of Devotion) but there was wont to lye *Spenser's* Works. This I happen'd to fall upon, and was infinitely delighted with the Stories of the Knights, and Giants, and Monsters, and brave Houses, which I found every where there though my Understanding had little to do with all this) and by degrees with the Tinkling of the Rhyme and Dance of the Numbers, so that I think I had read him all over before I was twelve Years old, and was thus made a Poet as irremediably as a Child is made an Eunuch.

Mr. John Mackinnon Robertson, in his *Essays towards a Critical Method* has suggested that all literary arbiters give some account of themselves that in their revelations the judicious reader may learn to be wary of their heresies. Mr. Robertson is himself a very distinguished logician but he is refreshingly free from that ''complex,'' apparently largely traceable today to the influence of the post-Kantian idealists, which is so jealous of the absolute sovereignty of reason and so convinced of its existential supremacy that it insists vaguely but vehemently on a sharp dualism between the so-called ''logical'' and the so-called ''historical.'' In America, for instance, the more orthodox disciples of Royce are never tired of girding at James' remark that ''the history of philosophy is to a great extent that of a certain clash of human temperaments'' with the contemptuous question: "What is temperament?" In so far as they care to protest against that vague, dangerous, and sentimental use of the word by which many so-called "artistic" people try to justify their irresponsibilities and superstitions, one may be in entire sympathy with them. But in so far as they ignore the perfectly clear descriptions of temperament which are developing under the investigations of modern psychologists like Mr. Alexander F. Shand they are imitating the proverbial ostrich. But one has only to read, for instance, *The Spirit of Modern Philosophy* or to attend the lectures of any good Roycian to see what odd contradictions between theory and practice entangle these dialecticians. The same problem has caused trouble in literary criticism where we have, on the one hand, Sainte-Beuve with his insistence on the complete relevancy of biographical considerations for his keen analysis of the thought of his author-subjects and, on the other, Tennyson's sentimental horror that future generations would misjudge his poetry because of too great a knowledge of his life and because of an illogical insistence that his life had any significantly permanent connection with his writings. By an ironical consequence, comprehensible enough to those who agree with Sainte-Beuve and William James, some very serious misunderstandings of Tennyson's poetry in our own day have been recently traced to our imperfect knowledge of his life. And if the critic must needs insist upon the revelancy of his poet's "temperament" surely the general reader, as Mr. Robertson suggests, may rightly demand some pertinent confessions from the critic himself. Without going into a discursive autobiographical sketch, then, I feel that I must needs emulate Cowley and write for a moment "Of Myself" in order that the reader may link with more discrimination the foregoing history of opinions about Spenser with the final ingathering of my own conclusions.

It is particularly important that the reader should know that I am widely accused by my friends of a passion for "whitewashing the poets." The reader may form his own conclusions. But I feel that I may fairly claim at times not to be whitewash-

ing the poets but scraping away the drab stucco with which
many have smeared the fair edifices of the master-spirits. There
is no libel of the poets worse than the pseudo-judicious attitude
of some academicians and the eulogy or vituperation of some
poets.

I am also accused of romantic egoism and impressionism.
That may be just. I am impressed with its plausibility by the
very fact that in theory I am often very inimical to romanticism.
Whatever is good in my enthusiasm for Spenser is born of
the ministrations of my mother and father, to whom I have
dedicated this book and who have given me, above all other
teachers, the knowledge of Spenser which has impelled me to
devote many years to his praise. My father, who, being dead,
lives with me more intimately present than ever, taught me from
childhood a strange familiarity with the paths of Faërie Land.
I do not think that he ever read a line of Spenser. But he was
a "verray parfit gentil knight" who never lost a sweet dignity
in the midst of defeat and who moved slightly bewildered
through the mart, much like Sir Guyon in the halls of Mammon,
with a steady courage and a sober cheer. It was my mother
who, like Cowley's, first put *The Faërie Queene* in my way.
Indeed she nursed me with epic fable long before I could read.
And one of my earliest memories is of lying luxuriously in bed
while she read to me from prose paraphrases of Bojardo and
Ariosto and I floated away at times on the hippogriff to the
castle of the enchanter or again rose fiercely clutching my little
wooden sword at the tales of "turneys... and inchantments
drear" to hack and hew at my pillow metamorphosed of a sud-
den into the turban of a Saracen. From the paraphrases I passed
soon to the complete romances and poems and I remember my
annual rereading of the Rose translation of the *Orlando Furioso*
and of Sir Thomas Malory. I was thirsty for full information.
So my mother, with a wise disregard of the usual parental law,
let me wander without shamefastness in unexpurgated editions.
Spenser himself came, I do not remember exactly when, as a
glorious climax. But it is not so much my mother's reading

of epic poetry as her life of sacrifice and toil at my father's side that made Spenser real to me. For in her courageous entrance into the workaday world, in order that I might go to college and university, I came to understand the reality of Spenser's Una passing through untold hardships to rescue her Red Cross Knight.

In home and in university I have spent some years in studying Spenser's masters and fellows, in writing dissertations on his followers and critics. But far more important, to my mind, has been my long companionship with the poet himself; and on my many rereadings and meditations and on the luminous presences of my mother and father I would base mainly this following encomium.

The difference between Spenser and the earlier English singers of his century is the difference between a coracle making its way along a river sinuous, silver, and palely luminous and an argosy "with portly sail" riding under meridian gold suddenly swinging before us on the open sea. This sudden splendor comes even in *The Shepheards Calender*. And just as Spenser's mellow autumnal splendor illumines certain portions of his boyish poem, so his perennial April boyishness bourgeons waywardly even in the exquisite fragment of his last years, for all its "elfin gravity." For, from the days he sat as poor Colin Clout on a little hill and broke the pretty pipes with which he played to Rosalind to the days when he swept to a condor-height, Spenser, never for long world-weary, appears again and again as boyish as any undergraduate propped up against a dormitory wall eagerly pulling out his notebook in the heydey of aspiration to impale a happy thought.

In *The Shepheards Calender* Spenser's most negligible mood is that of the lover, the mood which almost all its critics have emphasized at length, but a mood which is a little whining, a little morbid, and conventional if rich in its floriation. In the best and happiest moments of this early poem he appears like a delighted child lost out among strange meadows. He is suggesting in vigorous fables caught from his reading of Chaucer a new vein for the pastoral, a vein fantastic but also richly national and tinged with a saving salt of humor that might, if it had been sufficiently followed and elaborated, have saved the artificial form in later song. The roundelay of Willye and Perigot is the most refreshing example. It is the new life of the pastoral, the gaiety of Chaucer, the fairy grace of Clement Marot, the buoyancy of Theocritus; but above all, in its delightfully perilous nearness to rigmarole, it is the artless simplicity of simple folk long lost in bucolic poetry, now divined strangely enough by an aristocratic poet. And in this first ambitious poem, as in his last, beauty and goodness move together quietly consentient. Spenser never believed either in the pedantic heresy that virtue is its own reward or in art for art's sake. In *The Shepheards Calender* we find that noble combination of splendid eulogy purified by audacious criticism which was always the special excellence of the Don Quixote of English poets. When will his critics learn that he never wore the smirking vizard of the courtier? For along with the song to Elisa in "Aprill" and the thrilling hope for the union of Leicester and Elizabeth that rings out in the trumpet-tones of "October" we have his Parthian but mortal attacks on church and court and queen.

A list of Spenser's audacities, gathered from many a passing comment in this book, may well leave the scoffer dumbfounded. Let us remember the young and obscure poet of *The Shepheards Calender* already raising his voice against his queen's attempt to curb Puritan preaching and "prophesying." Let us remember with this his ironical portrait in "Mother Hubbers Tale" of the ignorant and corrupt type of priest whom Elizabeth would have moulded. To be sure *The Shepheards Calender* appeared anonymously and "Mother Hubberds Tale" was "called in." But we have seen good evidence that "Mother Hubberds Tale" created a lasting stir in its short first flight, whether in manuscript or in print. And it is certain that the authorship of *The Shepheards Calender* was easy for the curious to discover. Moreover it was almost madness to satirize, as in

"Mother Hubberds Tale," the rumored French marriage when the bold words of Stubbes were answered with a brutal and felonious punishment. It was most quixotic to stir up the old contempt for the French suitor in the delineation of Bragga-dochio in the second book of *The Faërie Queene* even though accompanied with the matchless tribute to Elizabeth as Bel-phoebe. Here indeed was true patriotism in a poet most absurdly called unpatriotic—the only worthy patriotism, that which both blames and exalts. It was most audacious to write as a complement to the satire on the French marriage a daring exhortation to the queen and Leicester in "October" and to catch up the prophecy of "October" in the great allegory of *The Faërie Queene*. It was not advisable for a young poet with his spurs yet to win to allow his spirit of religious reform to reach such a furious climax in "September." It was perhaps wrong-headed, it was certainly reckless to devote one stern and lofty book of *The Faërie Queene* to a defence of Lord Grey and to a defiance of his foes. It was very indiscreet and loyal to praise Harvey, an old friend, in the days when Nashe and other redoubtable university wits were launching brilliant satire at the quasi-dictator with the rapidity of a machine-gun spout-ing mud and jewels.[18] It was undiplomatic and true-hearted to eulogize Raleigh in *Colin Clouts Come Home Again* when he was in most doubtful standing with the queen. It was tactless and most faithful to remember in the *Prothalamion*, written perhaps at Essex House and mindful of the glory of the Spanish exploit of Essex, that here once dwelt Leicester now dead but, even dead, a rival to a man as generous and as jealous as the younger lord whom Fortune had brought into possession of Leicester's demesne. It was somewhat undiscerning and dan-gerous but courageous to wage unceasing war on Lord Burghley not, be it remembered, because of petty personal grievances, but

---

[18] But I ought to refer here to Dr. Grosart's "Memorial-Introduction" to Harvey's *Works*, Huth Library, I, p. xlvi, 1884, for a point of view concerning the relations of Spenser and Harvey in this particular connec-tion that would, if it could be established, knock out this bit of evidence of Spenser's chronic audacity.

because Burghley was a Philistine with all the virtues and vices of the tribe. Truly here was the Don Quixote of English poets, like the Don Quixote of Cervantes both unpractical and practical, ready to tilt at a windmill, efficient and grimly precise in planning a detailed program of militarism against Irish insurgents, a dreamer of boundless dreams and a tireless doer of grim deeds in behalf of the splendid and terribly fallacious doctrine of imperialism. Those who today romanticize about "Pan-Americanism" or the "open door in China," with a blend of economic greed, practical plans for military defence, and vague chivalric dreams, should understand Spenser's vision. They may justly admire it. But they should contemplate the tragedies in Ireland, still teeming even three hundred years after Spenser's death, before they swear allegiance to the policies in which he believed.

But it is more pertinent here to revert to our admiration for Spenser's loyalty, so discriminating, so intrepid. Most sustainedly audacious was the scheme of *The Faërie Queene,* an epic which, for all its imperfections, was a complete expression of the Phaeton-like genius of the English renaissance. It was a scheme which has been taxed enough with its defects. For Spenser planned a new form of epic, an epic which with its "darke conceit" was to dictate the future to a great sovereign and a brilliant lord and a country that was leaping to a rivalry with the world-powers of centuries. I have noted three present-day views of the epic: that of the purist who would deny the diadem-title to such works as the *Orlando Furioso, The Faërie Queene,* and even *Paradise Lost;* that of Baudelaire, Jules Laforge, of Croce and his disciples who deny the reality of *genre* altogether; and that of the pseudo-evolutionists like Brunetière, who say that the epic has become merged in the novel or, at least, that it is a form that will never glorify the literature of modernity. The mistakes of purists in past centuries should have made them a sterile race. When we remember that Vida was shocked at Homer's introduction of Thersites, when we remember that the Augustan rule-mongers forbade the epic the right to deal with Scriptural subjects, when we are mindful of their insistence on episodes and "machines," on the proper descent of a wax-figure Venus on a wire, an Iris, or a Mars to harangue, let us say, a Columbus, we should be careful in making too many indestructible rules for orthodox epic. We should be wary lest the writer of a new epic is not convicting us of being blind fools in not seeing that while he has kept all that is necessary for the integrity of epic he has made new and infinite possibilities. And if the rule-mongers had been less extreme perhaps the revolt of Croce and his school would have been less extreme. Perhaps they would have seen that the classification of *genres*, if made by minds ready to admit of rich variation, might be after all most luminous, might be indeed quite as real as the classification of works according to nations, and as suggestive and as organic for comparative purposes as the grouping together of certain works by one author: the *Venus and Adonis* and the *Henry the Fifth* of Shakespeare, for example. Similarly, he who would declare the epic a dead *genre* would be less hardy perhaps if he were confronted with a conception of epic more elastic, more liberal. So it proves that if we begin to interpret *The Faërie Queene* as an epic of the future made by a poet with a superb arrogation of omniscience we realize that the scheme—however great the failure—was progressive in what it set out to do. All the essential qualities of epic are here. Do you deny reality? You cannot in any intelligible sense, when you consider it a fervid epic of prophecy which would necessitate allegory. Do you deny it martial action? Here you are more plausible. But there are in *The Faërie Queene* many martial passages most vivid. And Spenser was learning what all moderns are learning—that simple action in itself is not great material. We must consider the significance of the deed as well as the doing. Romances, with their fantasy, rather than ballads were his materials. And romances, by their very indulgence in the fantastic, taught him a certain contempt for the mere action which the ballad naïvely worships. Spenser saw dimly what Milton clearly discerned when the later poet found an epic hero in .Ada^m and heroic action in his fall and self-conquest after condemnation.

> Since first this subject for heroic song
> Pleas'd me, long choosing and beginning late
> Not sedulous by nature to indite
> Wars, hitherto the only argument
> Heroic deemed, chief maistrie to dissect
> With long and tedious havoc fabled knights
> In battles feigned (the better fortitude
> Of patience and heroic martyrdom
> Unsung).

To be sure Milton was inconsistent and his inconsistencies led him at times into ridiculous errors, as for instance in some passages that described the battle between the angels and the devils. But now in the midst of these very wars which thunder about us in our own days, even after our deepest hopes of peace, a quiet voice which whispered momentarily to these two old poets murmurs quite clearly and continuously to us. Some day the advancing proletarian will write his epic. It will be heroic; it will be about struggle; but it will not be about war. The first rude studies for that epic may be found already in the syndicalism so rhapsodically defended by Sorel. But in Sorel it is still tainted with naïve theories and artificially grafted onto the dogmatic intuitionalism of Bergson which is essentially a philosophy for a conservative leisure-class quite as much as are transcendentalism and most neo-realism. A briefer but sounder insight towards that epic of the future may be found in Mr. Bertrand Russell's *Why Men Fight.*

The first book of *The Faërie Queene* is nearly perfect in its fulfilment of the requirements for an epic of the future. I have dwelt particularly on its expressions of a hyperbolical hope that England (the Red Cross Knight) if it will but avoid the Falsehood and misrule of a Mary Queen of Scots (Duessa)[19]

---

[19] We should remember that though the first three books of *The Faërie Queene* were not published till three years after the execution of Queen Mary, the letters of Harvey and Spenser show that Spenser was at work upon his epic at least seven years before her death.

and the overweening worldly power of the Catholic Church (Orgoglio)[20] and Anglican corruption (the House of Pride), lest it fall into the toils of Despair—England may, with the help of Leicester and with the simple teachings of true Holiness, grow strong to slay the Dragon (Evil) and recover Eden, that is to say, restore the Golden Age, become Utopia.

The second book is not quite so sure and we may attribute this slightly more abstract, slightly paler attitude partly to the febrile influence of Tasso. But, thanks to the better side of the influence of the vivacious Ariosto, it is full of spirited and delightfully grotesque actions. And it is firm in the general outlines of its structure. Arthur is still splendid as the super-hero. Guyon keeps always in sight of his ultimate quest through which he passes triumphant. And Spenser is not to be thought of as being a devil's advocate, under the thin guise of preaching, for the most delightful of the seven deadly sins. In this very book he sets the Golden Mean (Medina) above Perissa (Wantonness) and the Puritan Elissa (Prurience). Why is it that Lowell smiles over Spenser's preaching and broadly hints approval of what he considers his most sweetly sinful aberrations? For what reason does Spenser's voluptuousness seem wholesome by contrast with Tasso's half-delighted, half-troubled luxuriousness? Why does Spenser show no tinge of regret? Why is his recoil so hearty, so simple, and final? The words that describe Acrasia might be transcribed in an epithalamium. This is because Spenser realized that sensuousness becomes a vice only when it runs into excess. Some vices, hypocrisy for instance, are absolutely antipodal to virtue. The sensuality that ruins is nothing but a virtue grown to excess and therefore a vice long holding the glow of its old loveliness, but doomed

---

[20] I must remind the reader in passing of my contentions earlier in this book that Spenser's opposition to Catholicism was political, that his avowed fondness for rich and beautiful service and his avowed contempt for the bareness advocated by the extreme Puritan would allow room for a qualified appreciation, at least, of Catholic ritual, that his patriotic fear of Rome as a world-power was plausible enough to be understandable .to any modern partisan and should arouse quite as much admiration as anger in any truly catholic Catholic, Protestant, or Free-thinker since it was an attitude noble, if narrow.

in time to become unhealthy since it tends in excess to inconstancy and idleness and, at last, especially in conjunction with pettier vices like gluttony, moulds the beast like the hog Gryll. Guyon may pause over its fascinations with a delight that is, while not ignorant or naïve, quite innocent. He is Temperance and too strenuous to need prohibition. When Spenser comes, in a later book, to give us a picture of Lust, his whimsically dilated fancy conjures up a giant purple-nosed and elephant-eared, a cannibal who violates and then devours. For while sensuousness can be tender and devoted, lust has no care for the loveliness that feeds its rapacity. It masters and consumes at the same moment.

As I said in Chapter I, the word teacher seems perforce so bound up with pedant and preacher in the crudest sense that it has been difficult (since the days when Childe Harold, Alastor, and Endymion wandered about the earth to minister deliciously and exclusively to their own immortal souls) to conceive of teaching as anything but impertinent prose. Hence comes the charge against Spenser's allegory, urged for centuries only by an occasional isolated and quickly submerged voice, but now rising from a host of poets and academicians like a locust-parody of a song on a sultry midsummer day in a dry, thin crescendo. After one has renounced the allegory it is very easy to renew the charge of tediousness. For a while we wander in the Faërie realms intoxicated by pictorial luxuriance, by sensuous music, like Andrew Marvel in his garden.

> What wondrous life is this I lead!
> Ripe apples drop about my head;
> The luscious clusters of the vine
> Upon my mouth do crush their wine;
> The nectarine, and curious peach,
> Into my hands themselves do reach;
> Stumbling on melons, as I pass,
> Insnared with flowres, I fall on grass.

We talk absurdly of Spenser's serenity as omnipresent and we mean by serenity that irresponsible mood of the literary epicure

which Spenser, for all his luxuriousness, would have despised.
We talk of Spenser's lovely unreality. So in our warped appre-
ciation we soon grow heavy-eyed and call *The Faërie Queene*
tedious. Yet what if we find that, despite the critics, Spenser
is not serene except in rare moods but, in fierce contrast, eager
with eulogy, denunciation, prophecy? What if we find that,
despite the generalities of the text books, he is real at his highest
moments and (strange paradox!) real just in proportion as he
is allegorical? Nobody has ventured such an assertion before;
yet it is just as clear and obvious as sunlight. Turn to Book
Three, where two of his most famous women, Florimell and
Britomart, share largely the foreground. Florimell the fair—
who has absolutely no allegorical meaning whatsoever except
in one of the briefest moments when, in Book Five, she stands
beside Florimell the false—is the palest of all the ladies of
Spenser's bower. She is but a shadow beside Britomart, who
is Spenser's most vividly conceived woman, a character espe-
cially loved by the poet himself, so real that we hear her noblest
and most trivial words and are shown explicitly her most stately
and most trivial gestures, yet nothing if not allegorical; for she
is Chastity, who humbles the lewd and sentimental Malecasta,
who thwarts the lustful purposes of Busirane, who slays the
virago Radigund. The appearance of Florimell, on the one
hand, I have noted as the almost invariable signal for the rend-
ing of the structure of *The Faërie Queene*. The adventures of
Britomart take form in some of the strongest and most lasting
arches of the great crumbling edifice. The characters of Spen-
ser, when firmly drawn, have at once allegorical meaning and
reality precisely because they are drawn from models right out
of contemporary life: court ladies and knights and fierce Irish
kerns, mobs of London and of Cork, kings of Spain and France,
a queen, and an empress.

Romance purified by the firmly sinewed Spenserian allegory
becomes reality. But much of Book Three is irresponsible and
discursive romance unalloyed. This was not due merely to the
difficulties of the heaven-storming structure. But Leicester

·died; corruption persisted; Burghley seemed blind to the vast dreams of the impetuous imperialists. Disillusion came. And so the story of Florimell's remote sorrows and meaningless adventures lured the poet far afield to seek solace for his fading hopes of making of England a Utopia. Both general structure and character delineation are most real where allegory is the fullest and most fervid. But the poet could not hold to the real without becoming sordid and bitter. And this is precisely what he becomes when he is not purely romantic. In lieu of the more splendid sins, the worthy foes of heroes, instead of Lucifera and Acrasia, we find Sclaunder and Ate, Strife. Cynicism, so unnatural to Spenser, creeps in with the Squire of Dames. Petty knights like Paridell and Blandamour and Turpine throng and jangle. And as Professor Grierson says: "The later cantos of *The Faerie Queene* reflect vividly the unchaste loves and troubled friendships of Elizabeth's Court." All the defects that shatter Book Four are foreshadowed in the third book. It is absurd to speak only of Spenser's ambrosial serenity. Even his own sorcery could not change the cup of hemlock that he found forced into his hands. We must get rid of Wordsworth's fallacious conception of "mild Spenser" easily cheering himself with the "glow-worm lamp" of the *Amoretti* when called from Faërie Land to "dark ways," first by remembering that ardent Spenser's Faërie Land was located in these same "dark ways" of Ireland and England, that his exaltation saw about to spring up along them the spacious avenues and opulent palaces of Utopia with fronts and portals more gorgeous than the most lavish imagination of Moorish architecture and domes ' more gay-colored than Saracen ever dreamed and spires more audacious than Goth ever dared; it behooves us, in the second place, to remember and feel deeply the sorrow that shook the poet when he saw those dreams, more real than the most magnificent personal ambitions, fade for all his protest, into a gray squalor like the huddled dwellings of London.

So it came about, I believe, that while he was sojourning for a space in England he allowed Ponsonby to collect his *Com-*

plaints. These were not the splenetic outbursts of a peevish courtier disappointed over some denial of feline hopes. The most querulous and uncritical complaint, "The Teares of the Muses," was a very boyish poem, with definite marks of early composition, thrust in with poems more grandly somber. "The Ruines of Time," though poor in execution, was noble in theme, in its sorrowing over the crumbling of a great family, and united with the "Visions of the Worlds Vanitie" and the translations from Marot and Du Bellay as an expression of one of the principal moods of the book, a mood which, latent or dominant, was always dwelling with Spenser, the sorrowful recognition of the passing of earthly beauty and grandeur. A second mood, with a tinge of bitterness in "Virgils Gnat," faintly gay and deeply melancholy in "Muiopotmos," came through a sense of the futility of his own idealism as far as his immediate hopes of being followed as a seer were concerned. The poet of *The Faërie Queene* grows quaintly bitter as the poet conceives of himself as a gnat; he smiles at himself in the rôle of Clarion, a butterfly. Here the bitterness modulates into an evasive gaiety, a short lived Alice-in-Wonderland mood. But even here he turns from his joy in Clarion's evanescent "delight in liberty" to meditate on that Titaness who appears in his boyish paraphrases for Van der Noot and in his last lines—Mutabilitie. The third mood of the *Complaints* is to be found in the vitriolic satire of "Mother Hubberds Tale," a haughty and spirited arraignment of court and church and queen. To Spenser the far-seeing policies of Burghley were hidden in fox-like craft and cold hesitancy marking the crawling Philistine and, perhaps, the arch-traitor. So the poet paused in his moment of doubt over the temporal veracity of his epic of prophecy to collect and publish a volume not of personal complaints in our modern sense but of defiances. With these we may group the elegies with their gentler sorrow and, as a climax completing a full circle of moods always characteristic of Spenser, we may recall *Colin Clouts Come Home Again* with its chivalric loyalty to Raleigh, its hymn to Elizabeth coupled with a fierce attack on court corruption, and for a close its "celestial rage of love" which brings him near that calm which ultimately came to him when he could contemplate with healthy self-control the power of Mutabilitie in the confluence of things.

And for the brief interval of his love-making the poet finds further solace from his sorrow over change and corruption. The waves erasing his lady's name written fondly on the strand serve but to inspire him with a belief in her sweet earthly immortality through his songs. The *Amoretti* must take high rank among sonnet-sequences by virtue of its unique and real-istic contour of moods: the mood of patient chivalry, the mood of querulous protest, the sustained exultation in love victorious, the queer bitter quirk at the end leaving the lovers with a most plausible caprice and an abruptness most plausible because so different from an artistic and symmetrical close triumphant or tragic—leaving the lovers separated by meddlesome gossipers. Then a silence, except for a handful of incongruous Anacreontics and then—the *Epithalamion,* in which abandon and chastity find their perfect union in harmonies which inspired Donne in the only poem in which he turned from his own fiery and fantastic ways to imitate Spenser with the bold refrain of his *Epithalam-ion made at Lincoln's Inn,* "Today put on perfection, and a woman's name." As we read the *Amoretti* it is as though we had been listening in a grave cathedral to quaint, delightful, and inappropriate chamber-music in many moods and caprices on antiquated citoles and viols and shawms, a music now plain-tive, now jocund. Then, when the *Epithalamion* sounds, one would think that a young god had stolen up into the loft to the organ and, pulling out stops never heard or dreamed of on earth before, had flooded and convulsed a thousand pipes of spacious girth with a celestial and riotous song.

We now return with the poet to his master-work and we pass with him through the depths as we read the last three books of *The Faërie Queene.* We must put aside the warped conceptions of gentle Spenser, Spenser the querulous, Spenser the flattering opportunist, Spenser at heart the hedonist, on the ·

surface an allegorist. We must consider not only the serenity, the utopianism, the court-worship, the sensuousness of our poet, but also his ferocity, independence, critical acumen, moral consciousness. We must not confuse Spenser's loyalty with that of a Horace or a Racine. We may remember, without falling into the superstitions of pseudo-anthropologists like Gobineau, Chamberlain, Ludovici, Madison Grant, that Anglo-Saxon bards before had interpreted their loyalty to their patrons with a fine blend of hero-worship and a sense of equality such as that which we find in *The Wanderer*. We may think of these things and remain properly contemptuous of the patron system as a bulwark of art, properly aware of the fact that cautious ethnology finds no uniquely divine traits in the Anglo-Saxon, Teutonic, or any other ''race.'' I cite Anglo-Saxon bards not to establish any mythical continuity of tradition or to flaunt a bigoted race-superstition in the fact of figures as lofty as those of Horace and Racine, but merely to point a psychological comparison as well as a contrast of certain individuals irrespective of their nations.

From now on the qualities noted as signs of the tottering structure in the third book of *The Faëric Queene* grow ever more and more serious. The moral allegory becomes capricious and bitter. The political allegory deals no longer with prophecy, but with the successes in the past of Leicester, or with the disgrace of Lord Grey, matters of inexorable history. The fourth book is invertebrate. Its alleged heroes appear only in episodes. The ending is but a beautiful digression hastily rounded off with a conclusion of the scattered and irrelevant adventures of Florimell and the son of Cymodoce. The book purports to deal with Friendship, but the dominant figure of the book is the hideous antitype, Ate, Strife, a personage drawn with the lurid extravagance of a hand that trembles with rage.

Book Five is sternly unified, mainly by its mood of proud and implacable scorn. It is an avowed ''treatise'' with a fierce repression of all the warmly colored pageants which have flowed through the earlier books. It is a bold defense of the dead, disgraced commander whose friendship, even in memory, could bring the poet little but reproach; like an iron gauntlet hurled in the teeth of the court. We must not resent its narrow hero-worship of a man at once noble and yet so revolting as to seem almost lycanthropic. For Spenser's hero-worship, like Carlyle's, is always a shade nearer an enlightened anarchy than a neo-feudalism in spite of its protestations in such passages as the debate with the giant. One can imagine both Spenser and Carlyle less reactionary if they could have lived to see the dawn of syndicalism and ready, like true aristocrats, intellectuals, champions of work, to unite with the proletariat against the ancient foe of both aristocrat and laborer, the double-tongued bourgeoisie who arose with the capitalistic Florentines of the thirteenth century.

Book Six is serene at times on the surface. But the hero, Sir Calidore, disappears on his quest for a long space, only to reëmerge as a shepherd renouncing that sterner life which is at once public service and self-perfection. The most exquisite passages, the meditations of old Meliboe and the love of Pastorella, are only a renaissance version of the philosophy of the ivory tower. Arthur, super-hero, appears but only in futile combat with the grotesque Jack-in-the-box, Disdain, and in behalf of the silly Mirabell. At the end of the book comes the cry of anguish and the last completed portion of the epic closes abruptly.

In these last three books the great poem becomes like a huge and confused armorial emblazonry wrought by some stricken yet still half-divine titan-smith on a shield so vast that time wears dim his earliest images before he has worked into relief his latest imaginings. We have seen the perfect structure of Book One. We may remember the exultant promise in Canto Eleven of a battle with paynim to be recounted in the twelfth book, doubtless a visioning of the result of the union of Elizabeth and Leicester and the consequent birth of an imperialism in which England would silence the haughtiest powers of Europe. We are not likely to forget the prelude to Book Two, which tells us explicitly that Faërie Land is real, because it is England. We remember how sustainedly the great quest of Guyon (though paler in prophetic significance) remains before us. Then in Book Three come the first lapses and a close brilliant but detached. And the last books are a most sorrowful and confusing contrast to the earlier. Book Four opens with an uneasy attack on the Philistines, the bourgeoisie of the court, the modern diplomats, with a probable reference to Burghley in particular. It scatters into episodes and ends with a beautiful but inconsequential pageant and plighting of troth. Book Five opens with an account of the goddess Astræa, Justice, and her disgust with the present world. It turns from future and present to defend the deeds of a dead friend. And, although it celebrates these with a fanatical fervor, it must needs tell of a guerdon most ironical and distressing, the onslaught of the hags Envy and Detraction and of the Blatant Beast, Slander. Book Six is siren-voiced with the poetry of defeat and, even after it recovers itself momentarily to tell of Sir Calidore's capture of the Blatant Beast, it suddenly veers into a mood the most bitter of all as Spenser cries out in distress over the escape of Slander, his ravages, and the futility of ever seeking to master him again. So closes the last completed book of the epic that set out not to glorify history but to make it; it closes with a poet's hate of hate, with a poet's horror of Malebolgian vices.

Disillusion, if it is touched ever so lightly with insincerity, is likely to breed cynicism. But disillusion like Spenser's proves the most wholesome preparation in the universe for faith. Whatever our philosophy, we may believe with Royce that the way to a constructive vision of really great scope is through despair and sweeping scepticism.

And therefore it is that, in the first moment of his new insight, the pessimism comes to him. "This warfare cannot be ended," he despairingly says. But has he uttered the final word? For he has not yet added the reflection that we are here insisting upon. Let him say: "Then I too have an end, far-off and unattainable though it seems, and so my will is not aimless."

So Royce wrote in his earliest volume of philosophy, *The Religious Aspect of Philosophy*. And in one of his last books, *The Sources of Religious Insight*, he reaffirmed his emphasis on the "reflexive turn" with great beauty.

Cynics and rebels, ancient sages and men who are in our foremost rank of time, can agree, and have agreed, in maintaining that there is some goal of life, conceivable, or at least capable of being, however dimly, appreciated—some goal that, if accessible, would fulfil and surpass our lesser desires, or would save us from our bondage to lesser ills, while this goal is something that we naturally miss, or that we are in great danger of missing—so that, whatever else we need, we need to be saved from this pervasive and overmastering danger of failure.

> "Oh, love, could thou and I with fate conspire
> To grasp this sorry scheme of things entire,
>   Would we not shatter it to bits and then
> Remould it nearer to the heart's desire?"

Thus Fitzgerald's Omar expresses, in rebellious speech, the need of salvation. "What is your greatest hour?"—so begins Nietzsche's Zarathustra in his opening address to the people. And he replies: "It is the hour of your great contempt"—the hour, so he goes on to explain, when you despise all the conventional values and trivial maxims of a morality and a religion that have become for you merely traditional, conventional, respectable, but infinitely petty. Now, if you observe that St. Paul's epistle to the Romans, despite its utterly different religious ideas, begins with an analogous condemnation of the social world as it was, or as it always naturally is, you may learn to appreciate the universal forms in which the need for salvation comes to men's consciousness, however various their creed.

Just so Spenser's disillusion proves for him the most wholesome preparation in the universe for faith. It teaches that one can never fraternize with Faith without equal friendship for Faith's comrade, Doubt. There are those who will find the word "natural" less vague and negligible than Royce seems to find it. With Professor F. J. E. Woodbridge we should remember Mr. George Santayana's sentence that with Aristotle "everything ideal has a natural basis and everything natural an ideal development." We will feel in Spenser's swan-songs some anti-naturalistic confessions of defeat. "Idealists" (in the technical philosophic sense) in all ages are certainly too ready to look

superciliously at immediate issues of the sort which lent glorious
fervor to Spenser's youthful days. Idealists may go even to
such extremes as does Mr. George Santayana (assuredly an
"idealist," for all the sentence quoted above and for all his
attacks on what he calls the Calvanism of his transcendental
friends) who is so jealous for the utter ideality of his ethical
and esthetic ideals that he would glorify them by putting all
persons as well as things under a materialistic category and
would consider even that subtle "existence" which puzzles his
colleagues a dull word with a rather plebeian connotation. For
some idealists nothing exists except "values." For Mr. San-
tayana "values" are so precious that they must not be tainted
even with the most rarified conception of "existence." The
professional idealist hates a professional mystic, like the Spenser
of the swan-songs, but does not succeed in freeing himself from
the charge of mysticism. It makes little difference whether you
say, with the philosophic "idealists," that values, purely rational
in a perfect system, are the only "existence" or whether, with
Mr. Santayana, you imply constantly that values are so pure
that they alone are uncontaminated by existential qualities.
In either case you will build yourself an ivory tower, air-tight,
life-tight. Spenser was too inconsistent to do this. We may
not praise him for his inconsistency. But we may be glad that,
despite his tendency towards "idealism" in his last years, his
final gospel was only partly a gospel of defeat; that it blundered
into a gospel of self-conquest with a renewed enthusiasm for
human living.

Out and out mystics, like the Spenser of the last two *Hymnes*,
will tell you that they apprehend the unity of things, the
harmony above mutability, intuitively. If you ask them what
they mean by intuition, they are unable to answer. To them
articulate thought is dangerous, befogging, carnal. Mystics are
certainly subject to what Mr. Owen Wister calls an "optimistic
squint." They would solve the tough pluralisms which per-
sistently bewilder us in life by a premature pantheism. They
insist on absolute solutions and so condemn themselves to

annihilation or parasitism. But the *Prothalamion* is proof that Spenser had not become hopelessly other-worldly.

With the *Hymnes* and the fragmentary cantos on Mutabilitie he turns in adoration to an orient light which, on the whole, is more impressive for its revelation of self-conquest than of defeat and renunciation. There are not wanting signs in these poems that Spenser could distinguish between that peace which is but a base swoon and that peace which is the inner quiet that often comes to heal one who has definitely consecrated himself to a life of toilsome questing towards ends which slip ever on ahead like the splendid threshold of the horizon. It is strange that no one of Spenser's many readers throughout the centuries has grasped or emphasized the most dramatic process of his development, the change from exultant prophecy to the *de profundis* and the final reconquest which, if too mystical for our sterner moments, is yet courageous and most impressive, an ineffable Prospero-mood. There is a love-interlude, the *Prothalamion,* in which the poet with a delicate kind of cajolery smiles his sympathy for two pairs of lovers, brushing aside swiftly some visitations of personal sorrow, and turning from a digression in his winningly tactless and pertinacious mood of loyalty to Leicester even after death to glorify young Essex. It is the work of a poet who has already seen death with calm regard, who has visions of immortality, but who pauses a moment, smilingly, to place coronals of young flowers on the brows of youth. It shows that Spenser did not renounce life for all the mysticism of his *Hymnes* and last cantos. His talk of eternity was no anodyne for himself in defeat. It was not other-worldliness but a super-worldliness. That doctrine of other-worldliness, so fiercely repudiated by the modern opponents of mysticism, Spenser never utters in person but puts it into the mouths of fiends and voluptuaries. Despair nearly persuades the Red Cross Knight with his eloquence over "eternal rest." But Heavenly Contemplation dumbfounds Saint George with a vision of celestial glories only to send him back to earth. The song which Phædria, Immodest Mirth, sings to Guyon is in the seductive music of a quietism in which professional mystic and voluptuary find common grounds of preference. But Spenser's own vision of eternity involved the endless active ascent towards Heavenly Beauty, Sapience. I have described it as the projection of the life of aspiration on earth into eternity. Perfection is the goal, but perfection is never to be reached. Yet the arcana of the universe may be seen and comprehended after death by the still restless wanderer. In Book Seven, those last cantos on a subject which perplexed Spenser unceasingly from the days of his *juvenilia* to the swan-songs, Mutabilitie and Jove appear sometimes naïvely and intimately human, their divine symbols like naught but tiny stars spangled over their robes; and sometimes they appear remote, drawn with colossal curves. Spenser was carrying by anticipation out of what he deemed the temporal into what he deemed the eternal a doctrine which is clear enough and practical enough among great men, an attitude which sees no incompatibility between egoism and altruism, because it realizes that in order to attain the richest happiness and the truest power you must improve your community, while in order to improve your community in a permanent way you must hurry always towards an unattainable self-perfection. Spenser phrases the paradox in an abstract and in a rather superficial way. But he speaks courageously and with infinite tenderness. Undefeated, in no wise fundamentally disenamored of his most noble earthly ideals, but seeing what seemed to him their larger fulfilment in the universe, like one who had entered an immortal state before he had crossed the portals of death, he stood up in a mood not of adulation undesired by God, but rather like a reverent comrade of God.

. . . .

This was Spenser's heritage from the Platonists. To the Greeks, as John Dewey puts it: "Change as change is mere flux and lapse; it insults intelligence. Genuinely to know is to grasp a permanent·end that realizes itself through changes, holding them thereby within the metes and bounds of fixed truth." To many of us today it all seems too easily hopeful in appearance and in fact fatal to that less high-sounding salvation which we feel it man's privilege to seek. I agree with John Dewey that with Galileo and Descartes there arose an attitude which, when Darwin enriched it by his organization of the biological sciences, was to play havoc with the Greek and Scholastic teleology. I find this attitude to be the great emancipator of science and far more emancipating to real religion than many timorous ecclesiasts have believed. But while our philosophy cannot be entirely like Spenser's, our lives still find perennial inspiration in his life and poetry.

Lightning Source UK Ltd.
Milton Keynes UK
UKHW020750081118
331957UK00010B/1257/P